Gender and the Path to Awakening

Gender and the Path to Awakening

Hidden Histories of Nuns in Modern Thai Buddhism

Martin Seeger

Silkworm Books

The author has rewritten content from the following, with the permission of the publishers:

Seeger, Martin. "'Against the Stream': The Thai Female Buddhist Saint Mae Chi Kaew Sianglam (1901–1991)." *South East Asia Research* 18, no. 3 (September 2010): 555–95. © 2010 SAGE Journals. Used with permission of SAGE Publications.

Seeger, Martin. "The Changing Roles of Thai Buddhist Women: Obscuring Identities and Increasing Charisma." *Religion Compass* 3, no. 5 (2009): 806–22. © 2009 John Wiley & Sons. Used with permission.

Seeger, Martin. "The Inspiring Life Story of a Twentieth-Century Thai Buddhist Woman: Khunying Yai Damrongthammasan (1882–1944)." Afterword to *Lives of Early Buddhist Nuns: Biographies as History*, by Alice Collett, 231–45. New Delhi: Oxford University Press, 2016. © 2016 Oxford University Press. Used with permission.

Seeger, Martin. "Orality, Memory, and Spiritual Practice: Outstanding Female Thai Buddhists in the Early 20th Century." *Journal of the Oxford Centre for Buddhist Studies* 7 (2014): 153–90. © 2014 Martin Seeger.

Seeger, Martin. "Reversal of Female Power, Transcendentality, and Gender in Thai Buddhism: The Thai Buddhist female saint Khun Mae Bunruean Tongbuntoem (1895–1964)." *Modern Asian Studies* 47, no. 5. (2013): 1488–1519. © 2013 Cambridge University Press. Used with permission.

Seeger, Martin. Review of *Meditation in Modern Buddhism: Renunciation and Change in Thai Monastic Life*, by Joanna Cook. *South East Asia Research* 20, no. 1 (March 2012): 151–56. © 2012 SAGE Journals. Used with permission of SAGE Publications.

ISBN: 978-616-215-147-7

First edition published in 2018 by
Silkworm Books
P.O. Box 296, Phra Singh Post Office, Chiang Mai 50205
info@silkwormbooks.com
http://www.silkwormbooks.com.

Cover photo by Martin Seeger
All photos by author unless otherwise credited

Typeset in Garamond Premier Pro 11.5 pt. by Silk Type

Printed and bound in Thailand by O. S. Printing House, Bangkok

5 4 3 2 1

For Adcharawan, Atipa, and Chayagorn

Contents

List of Illustrations ix
Acknowledgments xi
Notes on Romanization, Translations, and Language Conventions xv

Introduction 1
Chapter 1 The Female in Thai Buddhism 17
Chapter 2 Biography and Hagiography: Female Practitioners in Modern Thai Buddhism 47
Khunying Damrongthammasan Yai Wisetsiri (1882–1944) 62
Mae Bunruean Tongbuntoem (1895–1964) 70
Mae Chi Kaew Sianglam (1901–91) 83
Mae Chi Nari Karun (1876/77–1999) 92
Mae Chi Phimpha Wongsa-udom (1912–2010) 97
Mae Chi Soda Sosut (1920–2009) 101
Chapter 3 Female Sainthood in Modern Thai Buddhism 107
Chapter 4 Material Expressions of Female Sainthood 139
Chapter 5 The Importance of Orality and Memory in Spiritual Practice 181
Chapter 6 Experiencing Gender 215
Conclusion 247

Abbreviations for Pali texts 253
Notes 255
Glossary 293
References 299
Index 329

Illustrations

Map of Thailand ... xviii

Figure 1. Hagiography of Mae Bunruean Tongbuntoem together with a medallion amulet ... 6
Figure 2. Cover page of cremation volume of Khunying Damrongthammasan (Yai Wisetsiri) ... 11
Figure 3. Statue of Mae Chi Wuek in Ban Chiwuek ... 14
Figure 4. The ordination hall of Wat Thammikaram ... 64
Figure 5. Picture of Khunying Yai as *mae chi* ... 66
Figure 6. First editions of Khunying Yai's texts ... 68
Figure 7. Mae Bunruean shrine in Wat Awutwikasitaram ... 73
Figure 8. Cremation volume of Mae Chi Phimpha Wongsa-udom ... 99
Figure 9. *Stūpa* built for Mae Chi Soda Sosut ... 104
Figure 10. *Matichon* front page showing devotees after the cremation of Luang Ta Mahabua, and a picture of the metal coffin ... 145
Figure 11. Amaradevo Bhikkhu's book *Phra that: Marvelous things of Buddhism* ... 148
Figure 12. Mae Chi Kaew medallion amulet ... 155
Figure 13. Mae Chi Kaew *stūpa* in Wat Pa Kaew Chumphon ... 160
Figure 14. Mae Chi Kaew *stūpa* in Ban Huai Sai ... 160
Figure 15. Phra That Phanom *stūpa* in Nakhon Phanom Province 164
Figure 16. Statue of Mae Bunruean next to those of the Buddha and Jīvaka-Komārabhacca in Wat Awutwikasitaram ... 169
Figure 17. Khun Mae Bunruean Tongbuntoem Museum in Wat Samphanthawong ... 170
Figure 18. Phra Phuttho Noi amulets ... 171

Figure 19. Amulet magazine with a picture of a Phra Phuttho Noi amulet on its front page ... 172
Figure 20. Medallion amulet with the effigy of Mae Bunruean ... 173
Figure 21. Small statues of Mae Bunruean ... 173
Figure 22. Small statue of Mae Bunruean ... 173
Figure 23. Amulet of Mae Chi Nari Karun ... 175
Figure 24. Locket amulet with the effigy of Mae Chi Nari Karun 175
Figure 25. Miniature glass *stūpa*s with the relics of Luang Pu Man, Mae Chi Kang, and other practitioners of the Thai forest tradition ... 178
Figure 26. Khunying Yai as a laywoman ... 186
Figure 27. Statue of Somdet Phra Buddhaghosacariya (Jaroen Ñāṇavaro) in Wat Khao Bang Sai ... 192

Acknowledgments

Over the course of the last ten years I interviewed numerous Thai Buddhists in order to learn more about female practitioners whose life stories and religious impact and significance had not been given the scholarly attention they certainly deserve. Given the high number of interviewees and conversation partners during the research period, it is inevitable that the following list of names is far from complete; I would like to apologize to those I have failed to mention. To all the people I spoke with, however, I want to extend my deepest gratitude for their willingness to share their ideas, experiences, and views. I was able to learn so much.

First of all, I would like to thank Somdet Phra Buddhaghosacariya (P. A. Payutto) who often gave me so much of his precious time answering my questions about Theravada Buddhism, nuns in early Buddhism, and Thai *mae chi*s. Following our conversations I was able to develop many ideas that helped me to pursue the research this book is based on. I wish to thank the following persons for their time, support, and the valuable ideas they have shared: Phra Sumedho, Phra Jayasāro, Phra Paisal Visalo, Phra Prasitsarasophon (Mantabhāṇī, Wat Phra Sri Mahathat), Khruba Jaeo Sianglam (Dhammadharo, Wat Pa Wiwekwatthanaram), Phra Inthawai Santussako (Wat Pa Na Kham Noi), Phra Ratchasutthimoli (Katobhāso, Wat Thammikaram), Phra Rajapariyattimuni (Thiab Siriñāṇo, Wat Phra Chetuphon), Phra Srivinayaphon (Sairung Indāvudho, Wat Awutwikasitaram), Phra Sophonvachirabhorn (Sawai Jotiko, Wat Arun Ratchawararam), Phra Khru Wisanpanyakhun (Bunmi Sumaṅgalo), Phra Khru Winaithonphuwanat (Kittinātho, Wat Khao Bang Sai), Phra Dutsadee Methangkuro, Phra Pramote (Pāmojjo), Phra V. Vajiramedhi, Phra Charles (Nirodho, Wat Umong), Luang Pho Kamjon (Varapañño), Bhikkhu Sīlaratano, Luang Pho Khanong (Dhammadhīro), Amaradevo

Bhikkhu, Bhikṣuṇī Nirāmisā, Dhammanandā Bhikkhunī, Mae Chi Bunmi Wetchasan, Mae Chi Kritsana Raksachom (Wat Mahathat), Mae Chi Suni Saensasom, Mae Chi Khrueawan (Wat Hin Mak Peng), Sikkhamata Paniya (Santi Asok), Mae Chi Arun Phet-urai (Thai Mae Chi Institute), Mae Chi Suphaphan Na Bangchang (also known as Mae Chi Vimuttiyā), Mae Chee Sansanee Sthirasuta, Ajan Jitsai Phadungrat (Thammamata Project), the *mae chi*s of Wat Samphanthawong and Wat Klai Kangwon (Wat Saraphatdi), Mae Chi Nathathai Chattinawat (Wat Pak Nam), Prasop Wisetsiri, Kingkaew Atthakorn, Wibha Kongkanandana, Anake Nawigamune, Sulak Sivaraksa, Dhanapon Somwang (Sripatum University), Phayap Khamphan, Somnuek Jasen, Toi-ting (Phanphimon Khotchasut), Boy Thaphrajan, Nat Faenphanthae, Benja Rungruangsilp (Chulalongkorn University Libraries), Kittisak Rungrueangwatthanachai (Buddhadasa Indapanno Archives), Phakdiphuri, Peter Skilling, Trasvin Jittidecharak, Louis Gabaude, and Samon Thophaengjan.

Special thanks to Naris Charaschanyawong who often provided me with ideas and texts, some of which were difficult to find. He also participated in many of the interviews I conducted with monks, *mae chi*s, and laypeople during the research period. I would also like to thank the following persons for their comments on drafts of the manuscripts of this book or portions of it: Ven. Gavesako Bhikkhu, Donald Swearer, Justin McDaniel, Mudagamuwe Maithrimurthi, Catherine Newell, Victor King, Adcharawan Seeger, Michael Parnwell, Joanna Cook, Naris Charaschanyawong, Frances Weightman, Mark Williams, Caroline Rose, Alice Collett, and Guillaume Rozenberg. In particular, I would like to thank Bhikkhu Anālayo who has given me so much of his precious time to read and provide numerous valuable and detailed comments on drafts of the manuscript at various stages.

Joel Akins of Silkworm Books has done a great job during the editorial process and thanks to his detailed comments and patience, I was able to improve the accessibility of my text significantly.

I would like to thank my wife Adcharawan for patiently discussing with me many of my translations from Thai into English, during numerous intensive night sessions.

The research this book is based on has been supported financially by the British Academy, the School of Languages, Cultures and Societies of the University of Leeds, and the Research Committee of the Association of Southeast Asian Studies in the United Kingdom (ASEASUK) funded by the British Academy; I am very grateful for their generous support. I wish to thank the National Research Council of Thailand for giving me permission to conduct fieldwork in Thailand.

Notes on Romanization, Translations, and Language Conventions

Many Pali and Sanskrit terms have been incorporated into the Thai language. As a consequence of this process, their spelling and pronunciation often significantly deviate from their original Pali/Sanskrit form. In this book, I employ the Pali terminology instead of the Thai form of these terms when my sources or I undoubtedly refer to Pali canonical terms or concepts, even in cases when the sources use these technical terms in the Thai form or pronunciation. Thus, I use, for example, the Pali words *dukkha*, *bodhisatta*, and *nibbāna* instead of the romanized Thai words *thuk*, *phothisat*, and *nipphan*, respectively. When the original Pali/Sanskrit word has developed a new meaning in the Thai language that differs significantly from its original meaning in Pali, I maintain the Thai form. I should mention though that often a clear differentiation is rather difficult here. I hope that this approach will facilitate access to those readers who are familiar with Pali terms.

For Thai names and terms I used the romanization guide of the Royal Institute of Thailand. There is one significant exception though: unlike the Royal Institute of Thailand guide, I romanize the initial Thai letter จ not as *ch* but as *j*.

Even though I have tried to be as consistent as possible with the romanizing of Thai words, it is inevitable that there are some inconsistencies. This is due to the large amount of different sources I used and the different preferences of romanizing a Thai name into Roman scripts. When I refer to a Thai person or their title, I use what I believe is the most commonly known spelling of their names. Thus, I write, for example, Somdet Phra Buddhaghosacariya and Nidhi Eoseewong, and not Somdet Phra Phutthakhosajan and Nithi Iaosiwong, respectively. When I refer to a Thai layperson in the endnotes and bibliography, I follow the Thai norm of referring to the first name first, followed by the family name.

Over the course of his monastic career, a monk may successively have a number of different ecclesiastical titles, while his ordination name (*chaya*) will normally not change. Monks with an ecclesiastical title are very often referred to by their title and not their ordination name, which may or may not be added in parentheses after their current title, with or without their first name. Take, for example, Somdet Phra Buddhaghosacariya (Jaroen Ñāṇavaro). Here, "Somdet Phra Buddhaghosacariya" is the title conferred by the Thai king, while "Ñāṇavaro" is the name this monk received at his ordination. "Jaroen," however, is the monk's personal name. As a result of the complexity of this system, an individual monk may be known by several different names and his works published under sometimes many different names. When I refer to a monk's ordination name, which is always in Pali, I use the Pali spelling rather than a romanized form of the Thai. Apart from the bibliography, I will refer to a specific monk with the name he is most widely referred to in the literature or among his disciples, not taking into account the different titles he may have had over the course of his monastic career. Doing so would significantly complicate my referring to individual monks. When writing or talking about a monk, Thai people may put the following terms in front of the monk's name in order to express respect: Luang Pu or Luang Ta (both meaning "Venerable Grandfather"), Luang Pho ("Venerable Father"), Ajan ("Teacher") or Khruba ("Teacher"—used commonly in the North and Northeast of Thailand), or Phra Ajan ("Venerable Teacher").

For the Pali texts I use in this book, I availed myself of the Chaṭṭha Saṅgāyana Tipitaka Version 4.0 (CST4) and BUDSIR 7 for Windows CD-ROM version by Mahidol University. For my references to Pali texts I normally refer to the editions published by the Pali Text Society.

If not otherwise stated the translations from Thai and Pali are mine. Here I should explain that the cited interviews were conducted in Thai and subsequently translated into English. To show the reader at a glance whether a cited source is in Thai, I cite Thai texts by their year of publication according to the Thai Buddhist calendar dating system (*phutthasakkarat*) and not the Christian calendar. To convert from the *phutthasakkarat* system to CE one needs to subtract 543; for example, the Thai Buddhist year 2540 is 1997 CE. However, until 1940, the *phutthasakkarat* system began the new year in the month of April. This means that for dates from January to the end of March prior to 1941, one needs to subtract 542 to derive the year in CE from the year given in the *phutthasakkarat* system. When I was unable to ascertain a specific month for an event or publication before 1941, I subtracted 543 when I wanted to give the year in CE.

Map of Thailand

Introduction

In front of the evening assembly of local villagers, the [great meditation master] Luang Pu Thet Desaraṅsī asked me, "How is your meditation going, nun?" At that moment, I was contemplating the five aggregates of existence [*khandha*], and only felt anxiety and confusion; I perceived everything as *dukkha* [unsatisfactory]. Thus, I answered, "I cannot see anything else apart from *dukkha*." The master replied to this, "What is it that is to be seen when one has become ordained? It is to see *dukkha*! This is all what ordination is about!" . . .

Many years later, when he had become a high-ranking [and famous] monk, he repeatedly tried to persuade me to accompany him [to another province]. I said to him, "You, Master, are now a high-ranking monk.[1] As for me, I am too lazy to constantly receive people from privileged classes. . . . This is not what I want. I prefer to spend my time in the forest and lead a simple life like ordinary people do. This is what makes me satisfied." Thereupon, he said, "I think like you. I too have always wanted to live in the seclusion of the forest. The Truth [*dhamma*] and the practice [*ubai*] are not confined to men and ordained people. Women and laypeople can equally profit from them."

From the autobiography of Mae Chi Phimpha Wongsa-udom[2]

At the beginning of my research for this book in 2007, I had thought that this project would not take very long, as there seemed to be only a rather small number of female practitioners Thai Buddhists have regarded as somehow outstanding or worthy of high respect or deep faith.[3] In particular, Thai Buddhist women revered due to the belief that they have achieved Buddhist sainthood seemed to be extremely rare. In contrast to this, there is a large number of living and deceased male monastics who have been widely revered as saints, as is obvious throughout the country; posters in shops and private houses, amulets, books, videos, and the like venerating male Thai saints are ubiquitous. Based on my reading a decade ago of Thai and Western historical and contemporary sources on Thai Buddhist women, I assumed an extreme rarity of female sainthood in modern Thai Buddhism. (I will discuss this dearth in academic writing in more detail in chapter 1.) Apart from the names of a rather small number of living revered Thai female Buddhist practitioners and teachers, I was then aware of an even smaller number of deceased women who had been highly revered as saints due to their exemplary Buddhist practice and comportment. In particular, at the beginning of my research I sometimes came across the names of Mae Bunruean Tongbuntoem and Mae Chi Kaew Sianglam. But I was repeatedly told that these two women were quite extraordinary and exceptional, and there were probably no other Thai women who excelled in areas of Thai Buddhist practice comparable to these two women, that is in the development of supernatural powers and supramundane states of mind (i.e., the achievement of one of the four levels of awakening). In addition, I had come across the names of Upāsikā Ki Nanayon (Ko. Khao Suan Luang, 1901–78) and Ajan Naeb Mahaniranon (1898–1983). These two women have been revered for their pedagogical skills and inspiring spiritual practice—some texts also describe them as having attained supramundane states of mind, but rather inconspicuously compared to texts about Mae Bunruean and Mae Chi Kaew. Thus, I was initially only able to find a small number of Thai texts on these four women's lives, teaching, and veneration; the number of texts in English was even smaller, and some of these practitioners had not even been mentioned in English literature at the time I started this research in 2007. I was aware of no academic sources in Western languages, and hardly any in Thai on Mae Bunruean and Mae Chi Kaew; in Thai academic work, one could only find some short references to Mae Bunruean, but I had not found anything substantial on Mae Chi Kaew.[4] I did find some short English texts on Upāsikā Ki Nanayon and Ajan Naeb though. But once I pursued serious research on Thai Buddhist women I quickly understood that there are many more women, deceased and alive, who have been highly revered for their spiritual practice and attainments as well as their inspiring teachings. I came across stories, names, and anecdotes that formed most interesting biographies of many other female practitioners who are believed to have led inspiring religious lives, achieved supramundane states of mind, or been local religious leaders. It was clear by then that academia had seriously neglected this field.

Studying Female Renunciants in Modern Thai Buddhism

Along with Jeffrey Samuels, I believe that "any understanding of Buddhist monastic culture and temple building must begin with specific, in-depth descriptions of human experiences and human subjectivity."[5] Thus, this book is primarily based on my long-term textual and ethnographic study of three remarkable female Buddhist practitioners of modern Thai Buddhism: Khunying Damrongthammasan (Yai Wisetsiri, 1882–1944), Mae Bunruean Tongbuntoem (1895–1964), and Mae Chi Kaew Sianglam (1901–91). Even though my research was centered around these three women, biographies of and other texts by or about a significant number of other female practitioners, in particular Mae Chi Nari Karun (1876/1877–1999), Mae Chi Phimpha Wongsa-udom (1912–2010), and Mae Chi Soda Sosut (1920–2009) were vital in reaching an understanding of female Thai Buddhist practitioners. The lifetimes of the women investigated in this study cover a period of nearly 140 years (late nineteenth century to the present day), and they lived during different but continuous and overlapping time periods.

Through an examination of their different social backgrounds, upbringing, and historical and geographical contexts, I provide a comparative analysis of these women's spiritual life and work. In this way much can be learned about the complexities of female renunciation and gender relations in modern Thai Buddhism. In this regard, I want to challenge the generalized and oversimplified descriptions of female practice and gender relations and hierarchies that one can often find in discussions on gender in Thai Buddhism. Therefore, this book gives a historical account of female renunciation. I also discuss trends and changes over the last 140 years that can be demonstrated in these women's biographies. However, this book should be understood more as an investigation of pertinent themes and issues that emerged in my study of their biographies, texts, and veneration than a straightforward history or series of biographies. I am deeply concerned with how these women perceived themselves and their spiritual practice. The aim is to understand their religious experiences and modes of expression—how they described and reflected on their spiritual aspirations, paths, and achievements, as well as the obstacles on their path. Furthermore, I seek to understand how their admirers and other Thai Buddhists have perceived and interpreted their lives, teachings, and achievements. A particular focus in this respect is on a number of contested points in relation to female sainthood in modern times. It is of course not easy—sometimes even impossible—to keep the self-perceptions of the female practitioners apart from the perceptions of them by others, in particular in cases where I did not have the opportunity to interview these women directly but had to rely on hagiographical texts or other sources. Even when autobiographical texts are available, the identification and investigation of self-perceptions pose a number of specific challenges to the researcher due a variety of reasons (to be explored in chapter 2).

All six of the female practitioners I investigate in some depth have already passed away. Two of them died during the research period; I was able to visit them before they died and revisited their monastic residences after their death in order to study the buildings, texts, and devotional practices that have emerged since their death. This means that in these two cases I was able to observe how the hagiographical process unfolded.

A major reason why I have chosen to focus on deceased female renunciants is that the events surrounding their deaths, funerals, and other postmortem episodes are often important elements in their hagiographical narratives and the development of devotional practices. The reasons as to how and why this is the case will be discussed later in detail. While the focus is on deceased Buddhist women, I will also take into account data from biographies of living female practitioners and the interviews I conducted with them. Some of the women I interviewed were reluctant to talk about themselves but preferred to instruct me on Buddhist teachings and practice. For them, understanding and implementing the Buddha's teaching is of much more importance than spending time talking about oneself or other individuals. This is a rather typical attitude and often made my research challenging. I will discuss this reluctance to speak or write about oneself further in chapter 2.

In addition to the investigation of texts written about these women, in particular hagiographical texts, I also make use of the findings of my ethnographic research at sites of veneration. I examine the ways in which these women have been venerated, with a particular emphasis on the veneration of their relics, if existent and accessible. My numerous interviews with devotees of the women in my study have helped me to identify the biographical themes that are regarded as most characteristic of a specific revered figure. Often the renunciants' biographies contain numerous stories about their religious experiences, often of a supernatural kind, but in many cases there is a limited number of stories that have become part of a central theme, narrative, or characteristic story of a particular renunciant. Why and how have certain motifs and themes become more accentuated, widely known and circulated, retold, and promoted than others and thus become representative of the whole biography of the revered figure, while other stories or biographical elements have been neglected or even forgotten? This research question was not only very helpful when trying to understand the particularities in the biographies and veneration of specific revered figures, but it is also fruitful in my discussion of more general issues and concerns in modern Thai Buddhism. In the case of Mae Bunruean for example, her biographies contain numerous unusually advanced skills and powers and interesting events, but only a number of her supernatural and curative skills (for example, she is said to have made a young mango tree blossom overnight, and she purportedly had the ability to endow amulets with powerful protective energy) are widely known and celebrated while her impressive homiletic skills remain almost unknown. Her sermon texts are rather difficult to find, while books and articles on her supernatural powers and amulets can be easily found; one of these books has even been sold at 7-Eleven shops throughout the country, often together with a medallion amulet showing Mae Bunruean's effigy. Some devotees even told me that they want to get a copy of Mae Bunruean's book not because they want to study its content but because they believe that the physical book with her texts contains supernatural powers. One of Mae Bunruean's hagiographers writes, "Khun Mae [Bunruean] has used her

FIGURE 1. Hagiography of Mae Bunruean Tongbuntoem together with a medallion amulet with her effigy

mind powers [*athitthan jit*] to make the book sacred. It should be stored on a high level. It can protect the house and avert dangers."[6]

Another important aspect of my approach is the comparison of biographical and devotional elements with pertinent ideas and practices described in the sacred texts of Theravada Buddhism—primarily the Pali canon and Pali commentarial texts (*aṭṭhakathā*). Here I of course do not intend to impose an ahistorical and textualized form of Buddhism on actual practice and belief; but, as I will demonstrate in this book, even though there are numerous religious practices and ideas that do not seem to be directly related to concepts in the Pali canon and commentaries, there is an astonishingly high number of notable similarities in terms of practice and concepts, and an abundance of references to Pali canonical or postcanonical teachings, concepts, and paradigms. In fact, I was often impressed by the frequency and precision with which the women of my study and their biographers referred to and then interpreted, adopted, and implemented Pali canonical teachings and regulations on monastic discipline (*vinaya*). One of my main objectives here is to examine the ways in which these women had access to and tried to internalize a plethora of Pali canonical and postcanonical narratives and concepts that shaped, informed, and enriched their spiritual life.

However, I want to point out that, given the high number of parallels and similarities to Pali sources that one can find in the biographies and veneration of the women of my study, this book does not attempt to provide an exhaustive comparison between early Buddhism and modern Thai stories and devotional practices. Rather, I will make and reflect on some comparisons in order to demonstrate what kinds of comparisons can be made. A comprehensive study with all references to and more reflections on the similarities between ancient Pali texts and modern Thai hagiographies would be a different book.

While my study relies to a large extent on vernacular and Pali Buddhist texts, I need to emphasize that this does not mean that I want to pursue a reductionist interpretation of women's role in Thai society by trying to explain gender or gender roles entirely through a Buddhist (doctrinal) lens, even within the "Buddhist realm." As has repeatedly been stated, even though Buddhism has had a pervasive influence on Thai society, Thai social organization and practices have also been shaped by other sociocultural or religious phenomena, such as nationalism, the monarchy, and indigenous religious beliefs; at the same time, political and economic aspects also play a significant role here.[7] All these aspects and phenomena have had a significant influence on and may sometimes have reinforced each other, being complexly intertwined and constantly evolving. Nonetheless, I will try to show that a focused investigation of these women's lives and their veneration that considers canonical and postcanonical ideas and practices is an insightful exercise, as it allows us to better understand their and their admirers' modes of expression, concerns, and objectives. The reason for my focus on Buddhist texts is simple; as has already been pointed out, for these women, their biographers, and their devotees, ideas from Pali literature are often perceived as normative and formative for their religious practice and teaching. This observation also applies to critics who challenge specific religious ideas and practices in the veneration of, or texts by or about, these women.

The textual research and study of the other sources, together with an ethnographic examination of Thai Buddhist beliefs and devotional practices, also show that a number of beliefs and practices in the veneration of Thai saints cannot be found in authoritative Pali texts but are important for understanding the particularities of female saints in modern Thai Buddhism. Here I will look, for example, at beliefs regarding Buddhist amulets that were consecrated by female practitioners, contain parts of their relics, or carry their effigy. This approach allows us to gain a better appreciation of the roles of female practitioners in modern Thai Buddhism, which is relatively often investigated through the lenses of a preoccupation with male practitioners. In this respect, Joanna Cook mentions in 2009 "an under-appreciated aspect of Buddhist women's practice: that of the accomplished and charismatic teacher." Here, she also observes that "the hagiography of males who have attained this position [of the accomplished and charismatic teacher] is a long-standing academic and anthropological concern."[8]

My purpose is not to reconstruct the lives of the women of my study "as they were" but to describe and analyze the ways in which their lives have been depicted, constructed, and understood in relation to issues of gender. I use hagiographical and other biographical accounts of them together with texts they have authored as a focal point to unravel and examine Thai beliefs in connection with female sainthood and female Buddhist practice in modern Thai Buddhism. Thus my objective is not to attempt to identify "historical truth" but rather to undertake a hagiographical analysis, focusing on gendered particularities and other relevant issues.

Sources

My study differs from others on Thai female Buddhist practitioners (see chapter 1) in that I not only base my arguments on ethnography and interviews but also, to a significant extent, analyze written sources, especially biographical and homiletic texts. Many of my textual sources have not yet been translated, and many are also extremely rare. In particular, cremation volumes, "a literature unique to Thailand,"[9] have been a valuable source for my research. For more than a hundred years, these books have been published and distributed for free on the occasion of funerals in order to generate religious merit. They often constitute invaluable sources for biographical, historical, cultural, and religious data. Their circulation figures vary significantly, depending on the circumstances of their publication, financial resources, and the social importance of the deceased person. However, as expressed in the words of Grant Olson, this kind of literature is "scattered and ephemeral. . . . One fellow researcher in the field asked, 'How would I have gotten this book had I not been in just the right place at the right time?'"[10]

The cremation volume for Khunying Damrongthammasan (often referred to as Khunying Yai; henceforth I will follow this practice), which was published in 1946 some two years after her death, and its recent accidental discovery, well exemplify not only the importance these books have had for my research but also their ephemerality. Despite Khunying Yai's high social position (she belonged to the nobility), there is a deplorable scarcity of sources on her life, in particular her Buddhist practice and the way she acquired the enormous and detailed knowledge of Buddhist canonical teachings she must have had to be able to compose her numerous Buddhist texts. There were only a small number of fragmentary biographical accounts, some of which contain incomplete or conflicting data. The picture of her (fig. 26, p. 186) in the ordination hall of the southern monastery Wat Thammikaram, which she and her husband started to build in the 1920s, carries the wrong years of her birth and death. My co-researcher on this project, Naris Charaschanyawong, and I expected that there was a cremation volume for Khunying Yai, given her high social status, so we asked all our key informants, sometimes even repeatedly, whether such a book existed. Over four years of research we were consistently told that there had been no time to produce one, as Khunying Yai had died during the turmoil of World War II. Also, none of the many Thai libraries in which we went looking for the cremation volume seemed to have a copy.[11] Not even Khunying Yai's closest living family members were aware of the existence of a cremation volume for her. After a while, for Naris and me it simply became a fact that no cremation volume was produced for Khunying Yai. However, when doing research in the monastery of Wat Khao Bang Sai in Chon Buri in August 2015, looking through thousands of old and dusty books, we by accident came across a copy of her cremation volume. This little book, which showed signs of serious deterioration, as insects were eating through it, contains a hitherto unknown picture of her (fig. 5, p. 66) together with one of her texts whose authorship was falsely ascribed to Luang Pu Man Bhūridatto (1871–1949). This esteemed monk was the founder of the Thai forest tradition and was believed by many to have been a fully awakened one (arahant). The foreword was by Somdet Phra Buddhaghosacariya (Jaroen Ñāṇavaro, 1872–1951), Khunying Yai's teacher and one of the most famous and important monks of his time. The cremation volume contains valuable biographical information on Khunying Yai not found elsewhere. It allowed us to reconcile several seemingly conflicting biographical sources, confirmed her authorship of the texts falsely attributed to Luang Pu Man (for more on this, see chapter 2), and provided insights into both her remarkable knowledge of Buddhist doctrine and her literary work.

The textual materials of my study are quite diverse. Thus, I have made use not only of autobiographical and biographical texts but also of amulet magazines, Buddhist magazines on the supernatural, and sermon texts by or about the women of my study (often available as MP3 files or online publications), as well as comments on Buddhist blogs and amulet websites. However, in order to investigate these women's lives and their religious impact as comprehensively as possible, in addition to analyzing textual materials I have also studied videos and other visual materials available online. Thus, photographs, paintings, and architecture are

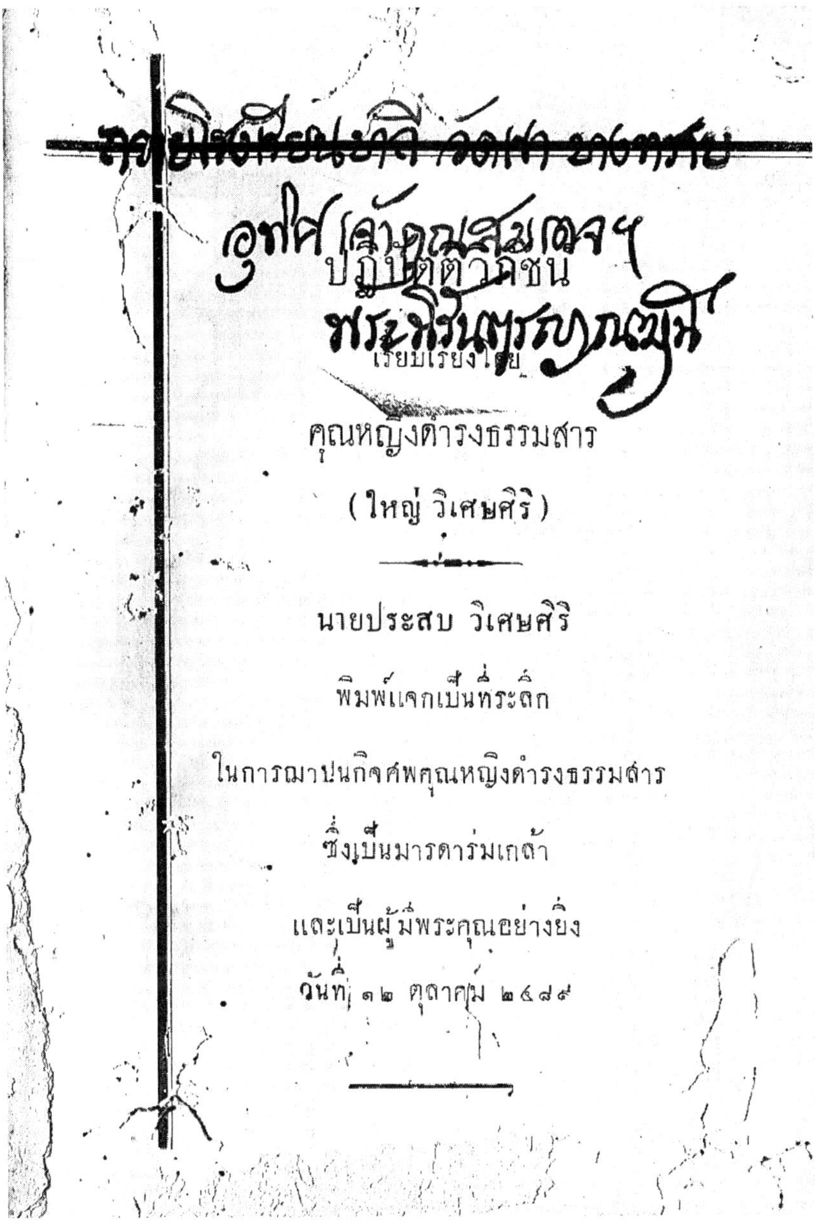

FIGURE 2. Cover page of cremation volume of Khunying Damrongthammasan (Yai Wisetsiri), published in 1946, some two years after her death

important sources for my study. Needless to say, given the increasing ease with which they can be produced and accessed nowadays, films are often a much more effective means of disseminating a biography than a book or other printed text. Similar things can be said about texts produced and engaged with online. These textual and visual materials are often analyzed in relation to the findings of my ethnographic research.

I would argue that more often than not, Thai Buddhists learn about saints and outstanding practitioners through listening to oral accounts, watching films, or visiting sites of veneration rather than reading books. This is despite the fact that often books containing the biographies of a Buddhist saint are produced in high number. As the famous intellectual monk Phra Paisal Visalo put it in my interview with him about the aforementioned texts authored by Khunying Yai,

> For a long time people believed they were written by Venerable Luang Pu Man, whom Thai people revere and eulogize. I sometimes wonder whether most people who acquire a copy of these texts read it or not. But there is an inherent belief that simply by printing this book one gains great merit. The people sponsoring the publication may not have read the texts themselves![12]

In my research I often had to rely on the memory and oral accounts of monastics and laypeople, often because of the aformentioned amazing scarcity of written sources. Only rather recently have printed biographies of a small number of female Thai Buddhist practitioners and teachers been printed and disseminated on a large scale. For this reason it was often difficult, if not impossible, to find (reliable) sources on the lives and teachings of female practitioners, in particular those who had lived and died in the first half of the twentieth century or before. Particularly in the case of the two renunciant sisters whose traces can be found in the small northeastern village Ban Chiwuek, the vicissitude and frangibility of oral tradition have become clear. Long before I actually went there in 2012, I had heard about the remote Ban Chiwuek and its main monastery Wat Chiwuek. The reason I was in high hopes of finding the biography of an interesting female practitioner was that both the monastery and the village itself were carrying the name of a female practitioner who was so highly revered locally that villagers decided to erect a statue of this *mae chi* (*mae chi*s are women who shave their hair, keep either the eight or ten Buddhist precepts, and wear white robes) in the local temple. This seemed to be quite unusual to me, as I was aware of only a handful of other similar monuments in Thailand. What I found in addition to the obviously only rather recently erected statue of Mae Chi Wuek, however, was only one written source in the form of a small stone tablet with meager biographical data underneath the monument. On this tablet, one can read,

> It has been orally transmitted that more than a hundred years ago, there were two ordained [*nak buat*] sisters who were ordained as *chi*s wearing white robes and practicing observances [*bamphen phrot*]. They arrived from Ubon Ratchathani Province. The older *mae chi*'s name was Wan, while her younger sister was called Wuek. Both were practicing ascetic practice [*dhutaṅga*] and practices of austerity. They were heading toward the central part of Thailand, but when they entered the area of Phimai District in Nakhon Ratchasima Province, Mae Chi Wan settled down in this district in order to persevere there with her religious practices. As for Mae Chi Wuek, she traveled further to Nonsung District, which nowadays is the Kham Sakaesaeng District. She settled down and persevered in her religious practices in what is nowadays the village Ban Chiwuek. From that time onward the people thus have called this village Ban Chiwuek, and the monastery also obtained the name Wat Chiwuek after the name of Mae Chi Wuek. Nowadays, some material artifacts give evidence, such as a stone altar [*thaen sila*] and a stone Buddha image that has served as the main image of a monastic building [*phra prathan sila*]. However, much has now been destroyed. But one can still take them for assumptions [about the village history?].

Additional interviews with local villagers did not reveal any more information on Mae Chi Wuek's life and practice. What I did learn though was that following inquiries from current residents about the village's past some twelve years ago, the villagers of Ban Chiwuek decided

FIGURE 3. Statue of Mae Chi Wuek in Ban Chiwuek, with stone tablet underneath the statue

to raise money in order to erect a statue of Mae Chi Wuek and another of her older sister Mae Chi Wan, each of which cost 50,000 baht, together with the stone tablet. The reason for this was to prevent further loss of the village's history. In my interviews with locals I learned that the scant information on the stone tablet derived from a villager who died at the age of eighty around the year 1980. At that point, so I was told, he was the only person with a memory of Mae Chi Wuek; he himself had only heard about the two *mae chi* sisters but had never actually met them. In the local monastery there is no *mae chi* community, and as far as people can remember there has never been a permanent *mae chi* community in this area. Mae Chi Wuek and Mae Chi Wan are not the only women for whom little information remains. In fact, I believe that much data on the lives or even the existence of a high number of locally highly revered female practitioners have irretrievably been lost due to an unwillingness to record their biographies, a lack of interest in their biographies, or reliance on oral tradition rather than writing.

By delving into histories such as these I seek to locate my research in the Thai religious landscape by discussing the religious roles of women in modern Thai Buddhism. I do not intend to provide a comprehensive overview in this regard as this would be a formidable, if not impossible, task. It needs to be noted that within Thailand there are numerous regional differences and idiosyncrasies with regard to the understanding of the religious roles of women. These understandings have been evolving in complex ways, are influenced by numerous contestations and ideas from abroad, and are accompanied or prompted by institutional changes. I thus describe a complex semantic field that is in flux and often locally idiosyncratic. This will become clear in the first chapter, in which I establish some of the major themes that are to be investigated in more depth in later chapters. Doing so will allow me to discuss the complex ambiguities of, and some of the more recent changes in, the roles of women in modern Thai Buddhism. The chapter will also give an overview of a number of the relevant contexts in which the women of my study are to be examined. In the necessarily fragmentary overview of the perceptions of the female in Thai Buddhism in this chapter, I will also refer to and review the previous scholarship on women in Thai Buddhism that is relevant for my own arguments.

Chapter 1

The Female in Thai Buddhism

Sometime in the early twentieth century, Luang Pu Man met his mother, Jan Kaenkaew, again after he had been away for a long time. He told her about his many journeys on foot through the forest, and his spiritual development. He also gave her instruction on Buddhist practice and asked her to pursue her own spiritual practice "on the path to liberation from suffering." Thereupon, Jan developed strong faith. She took leave from her children and grandchildren and became a *mae chi*, receiving ordination from the great meditation master Luang Pu Sao. Despite her old age, she pursued intensive austere practices, such as

> wandering through the wilderness of the forest just like the monks do and eating only one meal a day for the rest of her life. She possessed an unrelenting determination.

She received a lot of training, which allowed

> the arising of clear knowledge and the termination of all doubts. She addressed her son with the following inspired utterance [*udāna*]: "I have overcome my doubts. I will not be reborn again!" Thus, one can assume that Luang Pu Man was extremely satisfied with this, and he said to her, "Now, I have entirely fulfilled my obligation to you, my mother. This was the last duty [to you] that I had to fulfill." Afterward Luang Pu Man told some monks, "My mother has attained the third level of awakening."
>
> One of the major hagiographies of Luang Pu Man[1]

Whenever my mother changed her clothes, I would have to abandon my task immediately, no matter what I did in that

> moment; I would hurry to get her clothes so that I could wash them. My mother would frequently say to me, "You do not need to wash my clothes." I would then say, "As I cannot become ordained as a monk, I do not know how I could fulfill my obligations to you. I would like to wash your clothes for you. Even though it is a small thing, it is better than nothing."
>
> Autobiography of Mae Chi Prathum Choti-Anan[2]

Gender Imbalances in Thai Buddhism

It has repeatedly been observed that women play a significant role in Thai Buddhism through their daily support of monks by preparing and giving food to them in the morning. Many more women than men seem to support the monastic community in ways crucial for the sustaining of male Buddhist monasticism in Thailand. When looking at the Thai monastic community itself, however, there quite obviously exist significant gender imbalances as well. While according to official statistics Thailand may have more than 250,000 Theravada monks (*bhikkhu*) and more than 50,000 male novices (*sāmaṇera*) over the course of one calendar year, there are no officially recognized nuns (*bhikkhunī*) or female novices (*sāmaṇerī*) of the Theravada ordination lineage.[3] Thai women who wish to become ordained can do so by either becoming a *mae chi*[4] or seeking novice or higher ordination abroad. While there are probably no more than 20,000 *mae chi*s in Thailand, only a relatively small number of women have the necessary means and determination to become ordained outside Thailand.[5] In 2015 the number of Theravada *bhikkhunī*s in Thailand was probably around a hundred.[6] Thus, even though the percentage of ordained Thai men has been in decline,[7] when compared with the percentage of ordained Thai women there are still many more men in robes than women.

According to the Pali canonical texts, however, during the time of the Buddha there were many women who left lay life and became *bhikkhunī* in order to pursue their practice toward ultimate liberation (*nibbāna*). Many of these women were highly praised by the Buddha, while receiving enormous respect from the Buddhist lay community. We can read in the

Pali texts that the Buddha established the *bhikkhunī* order after he had founded the male monastic order. In the Theravada tradition, a *bhikkhu* has to follow 227 monastic rules, while a *bhikkhunī* has 311 rules to follow. Despite the many examples from canonical literature of fully ordained and awakened women, anthropologists have observed that in contemporary Thai Buddhism, the ordination of women is normally not encouraged.[8] The traditional gender expectation of Thai women to always take care of their families, especially their aging and ailing parents, is still widespread. In this regard, Monica Lindberg Falk writes that "the ideal Thai woman is a dutiful daughter who is expected to marry and become a caring wife and a self-sacrificing mother. . . . Men's ordination is highly prized, whereas women who leave the lay life deviate from Thai cultural values."[9] However, more recent research I have pursued together with Mae Chi Kritsana Raksachom shows that these attitudes seem to be changing or at least are not uniform across the country. Thus, *mae chi*s we have interviewed report that they receive similar respect from laypeople to that accorded monks. Even monks, so it was reported to us, would acknowledge *mae chi*s as ordained ones (*nak buat*). In some communities, the role of and respect given to *mae chi*s were described to us as increasingly closer to those of monks.[10]

This points to the complexities, dynamics, and local differences in attitudes, practices, and concepts of gender relations in present Thai society, and scholars have advanced a range of quite divergent arguments in seeking to explore and explain such complexities, and particularly the role and influence of Buddhism in their development and perpetuation.[11] Discussions have explored the question of whether the status of women and men is "relatively equal" (although different) or whether women are more or less attached to "the world" than men. Swearer notes that "students of Thai Buddhism debate whether or not Buddhism constrains the development of women, devalues them as persons, or is silent when violence is waged against them.[12]

Be that as it may, in addition to and often apparently as a consequence of the absence of an officially acknowledged *bhikkhunī* order, there are a number of other obvious indications of the male domination of Thai Buddhism. For instance, according to the Thai academic Kulavir Prapapornpipat, who describes herself as a "Buddhist feminist," the following statement of an abbot of a famous monastery in the north of Bangkok articulates a gender bias that one may come across in Thai Buddhism, whether implicit or explicitly stated:

> Women are the gender with little merit; they cannot be ordained and are not able to attain awakening. For these reasons, they have to create a lot of merit . . . and make a vow so that they can be reborn male in their next life. Then they will be able to become ordained and achieve awakening and be free from suffering [*dukkha*].

Kulavir Prapapornpipat notes, however, that "these kinds of teachings" seem to be disappearing from Thai Buddhism.[13] At the same time, Penny Van Esterik, writing in 2000, comments that "the idea of rebirth as a woman as a result of misdeeds in past lives is widespread in Thailand."[14]

In addition to this there still exist "unsaid prejudices" in connection with belief in the polluting powers of women.[15] In a number of temples, in particular in northern Thailand, there are signs informing women that they are forbidden to enter specific areas within the temple; they are for example not allowed to go near *cetiya*s (bell-shaped shrines or *stūpa*s)[16] in which powerful Buddha relics are believed to have been enshrined; women are also sometimes barred from getting close to specific wells. Here, the belief is that menstrual blood could magically pollute or interfere with the wholesome powers of relics or holy water. Also, Thai women were taught that they are not allowed to enter the ordination hall (*uposathāgāra*) during their menstrual period.[17]

Moreover, in temple mural paintings women are often depicted as obstacles for and seducers of men who pursue the path to *nibbāna* (the soteriological goal in Theravada Buddhism). A mural in the famous southern monastery Suan Mokkh, for example, depicts a bare-breasted woman with a giant snake tail trying to infatuate a man. This mural has the title *Lust, the enemy of peace* (*Rakha sattru haeng santi*). Furthermore, in Thai there is a saying that "women are the enemy of the saffron robes" (*phuying pen sattru khong pha lueang*). Based on a Pali canonical narrative, murals such as the scene showing Māra's (the Buddhist "evil one") three daughters dancing in front of the meditating Buddha can be found in many of the country's over 40,000 monasteries.[18] Māra's daughters here personify lust, desire, and aversion and try to tempt the Buddha.[19] In her interesting investigation of Pali literature, Alice Collett recently argued, however, that in the ancient Indian context and in relation to the evidence of the Pali canon itself, "it is not women's bodies per se that are being conceived as the problem, but rather the adorned and ornamented body (which could be either male or female)."[20] At the same time, it should be mentioned here that the Pali canon also contains a story in which Māra, taking the form of a young man, tries to seduce the nun Khemā.[21] This story, however, is not widely known in current Thai Buddhism.

In the Pali canon, the most authoritative scriptures of Thai Theravada Buddhism, women are said to be "the stain of the holy life."[22] There are other passages in the Pali canon where women are depicted in an unfavorable light. For instance, in the *Paṭhamakaṇhasappa-sutta* and *Dutiyakaṇhasappa-sutta*,[23] women are compared with a "black snake"; here women are said to be, among other things, "impure," "ill smelling," "dangerous," and "double-tongued." This passage also says that women "bear ill will," and "have terrible poison."[24] Elsewhere in the Pali canon it is said that "being a woman is suffering."[25]

It must also be mentioned in this context that, as already indicated above, the Pali canonical texts also incorporate numerous passages where women are depicted in a favorable light, and many specific outstanding women, both lay and monastics, are highly praised and reported to have achieved high levels of spiritual attainment and superhuman powers.[26] Buddhist studies scholars have tried to explain this multivocality—the often seemingly conflicting canonical views on women—by a multitude of theories in connection with the history of the emergence of the Pali canonical texts.[27] The German scholar monk Anālayo Bhikkhu, for example, has argued that Pali canonical "passages voicing attitudes of negativity towards women appear to be [later additions] . . . or at least require contextualization."[28] It seems that the textual multivocality on the topic of women will always be a problematic question in Buddhist studies (for more on this, see below).

Be that is as it may, religious symbolism in Thai Buddhism is quite obviously dominated by symbols representing revered males, and Thai Buddhist hagiography seems to have been mainly concerned with the lives of male practitioners. The observer of Thai Buddhism not only comes across innumerable Buddha images but also the ubiquitous amulets of deceased and living Thai saints, seemingly all male. However, as I will show in this book there are amulets that have been produced by or depict images of female Thai Buddhist practitioners; but these are normally extremely difficult to find, as the production of amulets and statues showing female practitioners has happened on a much smaller scale and is a rather recent phenomenon.[29]

At the same time it must be said that many of the Buddha images seem (at least from a Western perspective) to be genderless—particularly those of the Sukhothai era (13th–15th century)—but nevertheless depict a male: Buddha Gotama. Colored posters in all sizes depict the most famous accomplished practitioners of Thai Buddhism, such as the highly and widely revered Somdet Phra Phutthajan To Phrommarangsi (1788–1872); the spiritual father of the Dhammakāya movements Luang Pho Sot of Wat Pak Nam (1884–1959); the southern monk Luang Pu Thuat (16th–17th century);[30] or the saints of the Thai forest tradition, starting with Luang Pu Man Bhūridatto (1871–1949) and Luang Pu Sao Kantasīlo (1859–1941), can be found in restaurants, libraries, private houses, offices, and so on. Mostly, these posters are displayed higher than the head of the viewers if technically possible, and often near a shrine. All these monks, who are widely believed to be saints, are male. Even in taxis and many private cars all over the country, often the passenger can admire pictures, amulets, and small statues of these male saints attached to the console or hanging from the rearview mirror. The practice of endowing amulets with auspicious magical powers has been described as an exclusively male domain, while women, as already mentioned, have rather been believed to be the source of magically polluting powers due to their menstrual blood.[31] Recently a number of large images and image collections of charismatic monks have been erected in Thailand—again, all depicting male saints in Thai Buddhism, such as the huge image of Luang Pu Thuat in Prachuap Khiri Khan Province showing him in meditation posture; the monumental eighteen-meter-high image of Somdet Phra Phutthajan To Phrommarangsi, also located in the Prachuap Khiri Khan Province; and the 101-meter-high *stūpa* being built by Luang Pu Sri Mahāvīro in Roi Et Province, in which visitors can find a collection of statues of the most important figures of the Thai forest tradition, all monastic and male.[32] In addition, numerous *stūpa*s and museums have been built for saints of the forest tradition to venerate them and to depict their lives and spiritual achievements as paradigms for the Buddhist community.[33]

Nevertheless, despite the ubiquity of religious symbols, films, and books expressing veneration for the male accomplished practitioners, we may also find symbols and places of veneration of accomplished female practitioners, albeit to a smaller degree and only sporadically. Here, as examples, I should mention the murals in the famous *vihāra* (shrine hall) with the reclining Buddha of the old and prestigious Bangkok royal monastery Wat Phra Chetuphon (more widely known as Wat Pho) that depict thirteen accomplished and "foremost" (*etadagga*) *bhikkhunī*s and ten foremost female lay followers (*upāsikā*) of the time of the Buddha.

The Phra Mahathat Napphaphonphumsiri *stūpa*, which was built by the Royal Thai Airforce on the highest mountain of Thailand, Doi Inthanon, to commemorate the sixtieth birthday of Queen Sirikit in 1992, also depicts in tile mosaics a number of outstanding nuns and lay followers from the time of the Buddha. Furthermore, Wat Thepthidaram in the middle of Bangkok, which was built by Rama III (r. 1824–51) to honor his daughter Wilas, houses fifty-two *bhikkhunī* statues in a number of different postures. On pillars of the ordination hall of the monastery Wat Pathum in another part of Bangkok, one can admire beautiful paintings of *bhikkhunī*s and female lay followers from the time of the Buddha.

Furthermore, I should also mention the veneration of the hugely popular Chinese Mahayana female Bodhisattva Jao Mae Kuan Im (Guan Yin): "Worshipped at altars in private houses or businesses and through spirit-medium cults, she is among the most popular deities and draws a large number of mediums around the country, predominantly women of Sino-Thai origin."[34] Also, in the North of Thailand, a statue of Queen Cāmadevī (7th/8th century)—the legendary first ruler of the Mon kingdom of Haripuñjaya—located in the middle of the town Lamphun is highly revered and even believed to possess miraculous powers: "Day and night dozens of devotees—Lamphūn citizenry, visitors, and tourists—present offerings of flowers, candles, and incense and respectfully kneel before Cāmadevī's heroic, standing image much as devotees venerate the image of the Buddha."[35]

Further to the east of the country, a statue of the heroine Thao Suranari in the city center of Khorat is also highly venerated. Northeastern Thais hold this woman in high regard because Thao Suranari is believed to have been crucial in quelling a rebellion during the time of Rama III.[36] Another example of esteemed women is the many pictures of Princess Suphankanlaya, the older sister of the heroic Ayutthaya king Naresuan (r. 1590–1605), which are part of a devotional cult that recently emerged around her and can be found all over the country.[37]

It is noticeable, however, that all these symbols represent accomplished female practitioners of two kinds. They are either depictions of women who apparently lived during the time of the historical Buddha or a Buddhist period before or beyond Thai history, or they represent Thai heroines who are not widely venerated for spiritual accomplishments but rather for their achievements in the secular realm. This clearly points to the contrast between women being revered for their spiritual achievements during the time of the Buddha and women in the modern Thai context, who are widely venerated apparently mainly because of their nonspiritual accomplishments.

What *seems* to be widely absent, though, are images and symbols of accomplished female practitioners of Thai Buddhism. The same observation seems to apply to Thai bookstores too; one is able to find quite easily numerous books on male Thai Buddhist teachers, meditation masters, and saints, as they are often displayed in shop windows or promoted as bestsellers. Books on female practitioners, in particular on those who are believed to have attained arahantship (that is, full awakening), are often conspicuously missing. One may find books by or about the two enormously popular *mae chi*s Mae Chi Sansanee Sthirasuta (leader of the Sathira-Dhammasathan) and Mae Chi Thotsaphon in many bookstores. The former is highly respected for her social engagement and her pedagogical skills; the latter is believed to be able to "look into former lives."[38] However, neither is widely revered as a saint (*ariya-puggala*, see chapter 3).

Thai bookstores offer books with titles like *Arahants . . . exist indeed: Siam is not devoid of arahants* (*Phra arahan . . . mi jing: Sayam prathet mai wang jak phra arahan*).[39] In this 544-page book, the lives of fifteen male monks, all still alive when the book was published, are described.

Another very popular book, which has gone through at least ten printings since its first publication, is *The moment of attainment: Arahants do really exist* (*Winathi banlu tham: Phra arahan mi jing*).[40] This book, which has also been extended to several volumes, gives accounts of numerous male monks who have lived in the twentieth century and are believed to have attained arahantship, the highest stage of Buddhist sainthood.

Numerous VCD documentaries on the lives of Buddhist saints (*ariyasong*) are easily available and can be found in big supermarkets or monasteries. However, even though I have been collecting these VCDs for more than ten years now, so far I have not come across even one VCD that contains the biography of a female Thai Buddhist saint.

In fact, there is now at least one documentary film on Mae Bunruean Tongbuntoem. This film was broadcast on Thai TV and is now also available on YouTube.[41] As of August 2017, this film was viewed on YouTube by an impressive number of nearly 77,000 viewers. There is also a hagiographical documentary film on the life of Khun Mae Jandi Lohitdi (1930–2013). This film was watched on YouTube by over 111,000 viewers as of August 2017.[42] Here it should be noted that Khun Mae Jandi's biography and spiritual practice have been gaining increased attention due to the fact that she was the younger sister of Luang Ta Mahabua (Ñāṇasampanno; 1913–2011), one of Thai Buddhism's most influential monks, who is widely revered as an arahant. The making of documentaries on female practitioners who are believed to have achieved spiritual attainments is a rather recent phenomenon though, and there are still many more documentaries of a similar nature on male practitioners. There are, for example, numerous films on YouTube about Luang Pu Man and other forest saints, many of which have been watched by hundreds of thousands.

However, these apparent absences and imbalances by no means imply that contemporary female Buddhist saints do not exist in Thailand. Indeed, one of the major objectives of this book is to show that they most definitely do and did exist but have until quite recently been overlooked by both Thai and Western scholarship on Thai Buddhism (for more on this oversight see below). This seeming lack might partly be explained by the fact that the number of (known) female saints, when compared to their male counterparts, seems to be extremely low at present. In this respect, Lindberg Falk comments more generally that "nuns do not have many ascetic role models and are often inspired instead by famous Thai monks."[43] Furthermore, as I will demonstrate in this book, the translocal veneration of female saints in Thailand is a rather recent phenomenon.[44]

*Mae chi*s and *Bhikkhunī*s

The socioreligious situation of Thai *mae chi*s has been discussed in the context of attempts to revive the Theravada nun (*bhikkhunī*) order, with one of the most recent being undertaken by the Thai Buddhist studies scholar Chatsumarn Kabilsingh, who herself was ordained as a *bhikkhunī* in Sri Lanka in 2003. Her ordination as a female novice in 2001 had already led to still-ongoing, sometimes fervent, debates about the possibility of reviving the Theravada *bhikkhunī* order.

The Thai Saṅgha Supreme Council (Mahatherasamakhom), the governing body of the Thai monkhood, has repeatedly made clear that the revival of the Theravada female order, which is believed to have vanished in the eleventh century, is considered impossible due to technical reasons; they argue that due to the absence of *bhikkhunī*s who could perform their part of the ordination procedure, ordination as a Theravada *bhikkhunī* is no longer possible. Probably the most authoritative expression of this stance is a monastic regulation first promulgated by Supreme Patriarch Krommaluang Chinawornsiriwat in the late 1920s that forbids (*ham*) Thai monks (and novices) to ordain women as novices or nuns (*bhikkhunī*). He argued that a valid ordination procedure for a female novice (*sāmaṇerī*), as prescribed by Pali canonical law, has to be performed with the help of a (Theravada) *bhikkhunī*; however, "the *bhikkhunī* [order of the Theravada] has ceased to exist [as their] lineage ended [*khat chuea sai*] a long time ago."[45]

The debates on the possibility of the revival of Theravada nuns have been triggered by a variety of arguments by scholars who believe that a Theravada *bhikkhunī* order can and should be established in Thailand. It has been argued, for example, that the present Thai *saṅgha* authorities are perpetuating an androcentrism that was introduced to Indian Buddhism by later tradition but that is alien to original Buddhism. Another argument that has been put forward in these debates is that establishing a *bhikkhunī-saṅgha* would help to countervail a number of inequalities that exist between genders in Thai society. Others have argued that allowing ordination for women in Theravada would be in conformity with human rights and Thai constitutional law.[46]

A number of Theravada scholars have pointed out, however, that the question of female ordination is not a human rights issue but rather a question of consistently following the monastic regulations believed to have been established by the historical Buddha. Or in the words of Ṭhānissaro Bhikkhu, "The Buddha provided no mechanism for [the *bhikkhunī-saṅgha*] revival. (The same holds true for the Bhikkhu Sangha, or monks' order. If it ever dies out, there is no way it can be revived.)"[47] In contrast to this, other scholars have argued that the authoritative Pali canonical texts would allow the legitimate ordination of Theravada *bhikkhunī*s.[48]

Since these arguments and counterarguments have been repeatedly and extensively described and discussed in recent scholarship,[49] I will not review them at length here. What is important to point out is that in the course of these debates it has been suggested that Thai *mae chi*s, whose presence in Thai society can be attested to for at least three hundred years,[50] may potentially be a satisfactory alternative to the missing *bhikkhunī* order.[51] Several Thai scholars, however, are rather skeptical about this suggestion, and "many view [the *mae chi* institution] as a poor substitute for the *bhikkhuni* ideal."[52] It has been argued that *mae chi*s' identity is rather blurred and that in many aspects *mae chi*s are clearly disadvantaged when compared to Thai monks.[53] Generally, so it is argued, they do not receive the same amount of respect and support that Thai monks automatically do as a result of their ordination and wearing the saffron robes. Also, *mae chi*s have often been described as having a low religious and social standing compared to that of monks. In 2000 the Thai scholar Tavivat Puntarigvivat wrote that *mae chi*s "have a social status that is even lower than that of ordinary women."[54] Muecke reports in 2004 that there were views of *mae chi*s "as parasites on society, of no benefit and superfluous because monks and novices already meet society's religious needs."[55] Even their ordained status is not universally acknowledged.[56] In this connection, the Thai scholar of Buddhist studies Somparn Promta maintained that "if we [in Thai society] would [fully] acknowledge the ordained status of *mae chi*s, the demands for space for the *bhikkhunī-saṅgha* would not exist or would at least not be as intense as they [currently] are."[57] The Thai professor of philosophy Suwanna Satha-anand argued, "I suspect that it might be possible that [the reason] some support *mae chi*s is the attempt to inhibit discussion [about the revival] of *bhikkhunī*s."[58]

During the last two decades or so, both Thai and Western academia have been paying increasing attention to the changing socioreligious role of Thai Buddhist women, in particular but not only those of *mae chi*s. Lindberg Falk, for example, has observed an increasing number of nunneries in Thailand in recent decades. This has empowered *mae chi*s, as they can govern themselves independently from monks and they "have become visible in the local communities, and their interaction with the lay people has often come to resemble the relationship between the monks and the laity."[59] During her fieldwork in the late 1990's, Lindberg Falk noticed that the roles of monks and *mae chi*s were becoming more similar in a number of ways; for instance, *mae chi*s underwent an ordination procedure that was designed based on canonical standards; they officiated in ceremonies and went for alms (*piṇḍapāta*).[60]

In addition to this, as access to education has been very much dependent on the individual background and the temple or nunnery with which the *mae chi* is affiliated, efforts have been made to provide *mae chi*s with the possibility of a more systematic education. Thus, the educational possibilities for *mae chi*s have significantly improved during the last twenty years as three centers of secondary or tertiary education for *mae chi*s have been established. The two Thai Buddhist universities now offer the same programmes for *mae chi*s that they do for monks.[61] In addition to this, Steven Collins and Justin McDaniel have observed a large and increasing number of *mae chi* Pali scholars who are highly respected.[62] The conclusion of their research on this topic is that in current Thai Buddhism women play a prominent role in monastic education. Today, at the same time, it seems that "*mae chis* are gaining increasing support from the laity."[63]

With regard to the improving situation of *mae chi*s, the Thai monk-intellectual Phra Paisal Visalo identifies three factors for this change: first, more educated women wanting to become ordained as *mae chi*s;

second, the concerted and systematic effort of *mae chi*s themselves (see below); and third, "support of middle-class laywomen who day by day have a better opinion of *mae chi*s."[64] These changes should, of course, not disguise the fact that "many *mae chiis* still live under difficult circumstances [yet that] today nuns have better chances of acquiring education and they have stipulated rules and regulation [*sic*] that provide a basis for their practice and for recognition as worthy religious persons by the laity and by monks."[65]

At the same time, a number of Thai scholars have argued that the nonexistence of a Theravada *bhikkhunī* order does not necessarily mean that women are denied opportunities for Buddhist practice similar to those available to Thai men. Some would go even further and say that potentially the *mae chi* institution offers better opportunities than the *bhikkhunī* order, since *bhikkhunī*s would necessarily have to be institutionally subordinated under the male *saṅgha* (as required by the normative canonical monastic regulations) and would consequently not be able to enjoy the flexibility and many liberties the *mae chi*s possess or could develop.[66]

Based on their reading of the relevant Pali canonical texts, a number of traditionalist[67] Thai scholars and thinkers regard the introduction of Theravada *bhikkhunī*s as impossible due to technical reasons, as mentioned above. However, they do not perceive this as an intractable situation for women who want to pursue Buddhist practice or education. Despite their consistent insistence on the perpetuation of Theravada's traditional conservatism in this respect, they regard Thai Theravada as being quite flexible, and have proposed a variety of alternative avenues of practice for Thai Buddhist women. For traditionalists, the establishment of a new institution or the improvement of the situation of Thai *mae chi*s is not necessarily seen as a poor substitute for the *bhikkhunī* order, but rather it is promoted as a chance for women to use the creative potential of the tradition to circumvent difficulties that the existence of a Theravada *bhikkhunī* would necessarily entail.[68] In this way the creation of new institutions or the amelioration of already existing institutions would allow for a greater flexibility. Furthermore, the latter approach would make "it easier to win acceptance from the more conservative sector of Thai society."[69]

In this vein, the introduction of a "*bhikkhunī* [order] in a new form" or the establishment of an alternative institution that takes the Sri Lankan *dasasilmātā* as a model has been suggested.[70] Alternative names for Thai Buddhist women who keep at least the eight precepts have also been suggested, like *bhāvikā* (one who trains herself), *nekhammikā* (female renunciant)[71] or *sammānārī*, a compound consisting of "correct/proper" (*sammā*) and "woman" (*nārī*), which, when pronounced in Thai, has a phonetic resemblance to *sāmaṇerī*.[72]

One of Thailand's most influential Buddhist thinkers of the twentieth century, Buddhadāsa Bhikkhu (1906–93), also seems to have had a rather conservative approach in this matter.[73] Despite his rather critical textual approach and "creative hermeneutics,"[74] Buddhadāsa did not pursue the restoration of the *bhikkhunī* order but left as a legacy the concept of the "*dhamma* mother" (*thammamata*). His disciples developed this concept into an institution with a clearly defined identity based on the eight precepts, a strict admission process, and a comprehensive curriculum for the study of Buddhist teaching. Its objective is to offer women an alternative institution for the study and practice of Buddhism with the aim of attaining *nibbāna*.[75]

Another alternative institution has been created by the controversial Santi Asok community. Despite having separated himself from the official Thai Theravada order, and despite his untraditional and contentious teachings (for example, on vegetarianism and the concurrence of arahant and *bodhisatta* status), the outspoken and radical Thai Buddhist thinker and Santi Asok leader Samana Phothirak seems not to be challenging traditional interpretations of the respective *vinaya* texts in connection with *bhikkhunī* ordination. His group Santi Asok has designated a category of professional female ascetics known as the *sikkhamat* (who wear brownish robes and shave their heads) to which women can only be admitted gradually in a long and complex preparation period.[76] Admission is not guaranteed, though, as the permissible number of *sikkhamat*s is strictly regulated in a one-to-four ratio with the number of male Santi Asok renunciants (*samana*).[77] Sunai Setbunsang explains that this is to reflect the concern expressed in the *vinayapiṭaka* that an integration of women into the Buddhist *saṅgha* "might" negatively affect the longevity of Buddhism.[78] *Sikkhamat*s were originally called *chi krak* (brownish-wearing Buddhist female celibate), but afterwards the names *mae nen* (novice-mother), or *sikkhamat*, were chosen, as the association with *mae chi*s was perceived as unfit. The reason for the choice of these appellations was to make them more easily distinguished from the traditional *mae chi*s and to communicate clearly their status as "really" ordained women with a stricter code of discipline than that of *mae chi*s.[79]

While also suggesting the possibility of new alternative institutions, the scholar-monk Phra Payutto, who is highly revered for his expertise on the Pali canon, has argued that "provided it is well organized, the ordination of women as *mae chi*s may have equal results [as the *bhikkhunī* order]."[80] Phra Payutto has also repeatedly and emphatically argued for the amelioration of the disadvantaged position of *mae chi*s.[81]

Although at the moment it is not clear how it will happen, given the increasing support both from intellectuals and Buddhist laity it seems only a matter of time before a Theravada *bhikkhunī* order will take root in Thailand. It will probably take longer in Thailand than in Sri Lanka as there is still a wide range of difficulties that have to be overcome.[82]

It seems that despite a growing number of people who want Thai *bhikkhunī*s, there is still significant resistance or indifference in Thai society to the ordination of *bhikkhunī*s.[83] In addition, research has suggested that even many *mae chi*s seem not to want to be ordained as a *bhikkhunī*, saying that it is too difficult to keep the 311 rules of the *bhikkhunīpāṭimokkha*, referring to the nonexistence of an acknowledged *bhikkhunī* order, or maintaining that the current situation is sufficient for the practice and spiritual realization of the *dhamma*; some even say that demanding a *bhikkhunī* order would be an expression of *kilesa* (mental defilements) and attachment, which would be inappropriate for *mae chi*s.[84]

In our interview in 2007, the famous Thai monk Phra V. Vajiramedhi argued that "in the next decade the space [available to] *mae chi*s in Thai society will increase faster than that of *bhikkhunī*s," as *mae chi*s are already established to some extent. At the same time, *bhikkhunī*s are only in a very early formative stage.[85] Even the ordination of Thai women into Buddhist traditions other than Theravada is still not easy, as brownish-robe-wearing "ordained women" are quite a new thing in Thai society and there is still "not enough collective consciousness" for this novelty.[86] Santi Asok's brownish-wearing *sikkhamat*s are only acknowledged by insiders or even sometimes regarded as followers of other non-Theravada Buddhist schools.[87] Female monastics, be it *bhikkhunī*s or *mae chi*s, might not be (consistently) recognized by the state as ordained ones, but it seems to be only a matter of time before they will have accumulated enough institutional charisma to allow them to gain respect and support from the Thai people in a similar vein to the male *saṅgha*. There are reports that influential Thai monks are actively supporting female novices or *bhikkhunī*s, particularly in the North of Thailand.[88]

Obscuring Identities of *Mae Chi*s

Thai *mae chi*s are characterized by their practice of keeping the eight or ten precepts, their white robes, and their shaven head and eyebrows. In Thai society *mae chi*s can be seen occupying a great variety of roles, such as social workers, mediums, meditation masters, teachers of Pali and Abhidhamma studies, recluses, and temple servants. They might live in a monastery together with monks, in a nunnery, temporarily in the forest, or in private houses.[89] The motivation to become a *mae chi* varies quite considerably. While some want to fulfil a vow (*kae bon*), others hope to solve their personal problems; others, meanwhile, become *mae chi*s in the hope of gaining better access to education, while others want to escape economic hardship or wish to help society or Buddhism. Still others want to pursue the realization of *nibbāna*.[90]

According to the most authoritative Thai dictionaries in this respect (*Dictionary of the Royal Institute*, Phra Payutto's *Dictionary of Buddhism (Lexicon edition)*, and the new *Matichon Dictionary*), *mae chi*s are unanimously defined as ordained persons (*nak buat*).[91] In 1937 the Supreme Court of Thailand also ruled that "according to the law [*kotmai*] the word 'to become ordained [*buat*]' . . . includes the meaning of ordination as a *mae chi*. This is because in old laws there is nowhere a reference to *bhikkhunī*s or to *sāmaṇerī*s, but there are many references to *mae chis*."[92] This position by Thai legal bodies was underscored more recently too. In 2013, referring to the *Dictionary of the Royal Institute*, the Thai Office of the Council of State declared that *mae chi*s are ordained ones (*nak buat*) and thus, according to the Thai constitution, do not have the right to vote, like other ordained ones, such as monks and novices.[93] Also, as So. Chanasongkhram points out in the *Manual for Thai mae chis* by the Thai Mae Chi Institute, the Pali-language request for ordination for *mae chi*s, which is to be recited as a national standard, includes the following Pali phrase: *Pabbajjaṃ maṃ bhante saṅgho dhāretu* (May the venerable *saṅgha* regard me as one gone forth). So. Chanasongkhram points out that the Pali word *pabbajjaṃ* here carries the meaning of "ordained" (*buat*). This is in line with the manual's translation of the Pali phrase into Thai as "May the venerable *saṅgha* regard me as an ordained one [*nak buat*] in the Buddha's teachings [*dhammavinaya*]."[94]

But despite this and their rather long existence in Thai society (at least over three hundred years), Thai government institutions have by no means been unanimous on the definition of a *mae chi*. For instance, while the Ministry of Transport and Communications perceives them as being not ordained, the Ministry of Interior treats them as being ordained; the former Department of Religious Affairs also did not regard *mae chi*s as ordained.[95] As a consequence and manifestation of this blurredness or obscurity of identity, there are a number of areas where *mae chi*s are clearly disadvantaged; while *mae chi*s, as just mentioned, are not allowed to vote (like monks), they do not automatically receive reduced fees for travel (unlike monks) or free welfare benefits, such as free medical treatment (unlike monks), and they have to endure other legal inequalities.[96] Here it must be noted, though, that in this context I describe a structural problem. Depending on the individual fare collector, official, or doctor, *mae chi*s might still be treated similarly to monks in many of these areas since—as shown in this book—many Thais do have high respect for *mae chi*s and regard them as ordained.

Another manifestation of the state's reluctance to acknowledge *mae chi*s is that on their ID card there is no provision made for the title "Mae Chi." *Mae chi*s are simply called "Miss" or "Mrs."[97] In addition to this ambiguity caused by the contradictory stance of Thai government bodies, there also exists an ambiguity in the Thai language. In connection with the word *mae chi*, Thai people and even Thai academics[98] do not have a standardized use of classifiers; while some use the classifier for monks (*rup*), others use the classifier for ordinary people (*khon*). The same nonuniform usage can also be observed with regard to the use of special vocabulary often reserved for monks, such as the verb "to eat" (*chan*); often for *mae chi*s, Thai people use *than ahan* or *than khao*, which are more formal phrases for laypeople. In short, some Thais use the ecclesiastical vocabulary for *mae chi*s at least to some extent, while others do not.[99] Also, in Thai one can come across the phrase *buat pen upāsika* which, when translated literally, means "to become ordained as a female layperson."[100] Thus, it has been argued that *mae chi*s are "situated in-between the worldly and the otherworldly."[101] Further linguistic inconsistencies as a consequence of the blurred definition of what a *mae chi* is can be observed in scholarly discourse in the English language. In Western scholarship the ambiguous status of ordination has also become visible. While a number of scholars use the words "ordained" and "ordination" with regard to *mae chi*s,[102] others don't. As an example of the latter, Rita Gross writes "large numbers of women continue to wear the white robes of the non-ordained *maechi*, living a quasi-monastic life without ordination"; *mae chi*s have also been called "quasi-nuns" and even "lay nuns"; Ruth-Inge Heinze argued that "the *mae chi* in Thai monasteries cannot . . . be called 'nuns.' They are lay women who took the ten precepts."[103]

Also, in terms of the possibility of spiritual practice, this very much depends on the individual temple in which the *mae chi* is living. Whereas in some temples *mae chi*s are well-supported in their practice, in others they have to spend a large proportion of time performing manual tasks like cleaning and cooking for the monks in order to receive as recompense free food and accommodation.[104] There are even reports that due to lack of material support *mae chi*s have had to abandon their *mae chi* status in order to work for money so that they could be reordained once they had enough savings. Due to budget limitations, organizations that materially support *mae chi*s, such as the Thai Mae Chi Institute, founded in 1969, or various foundations that have been set up in monasteries, can usually help only in extreme cases, such as sickness or death.[105]

Despite the structurally disadvantaged, inferior position and commonly rather low status of *mae chi*s compared to that of monks, an apparently growing number of *mae chi*s, such as Mae Chi Sansanee Sthirasuta, Mae Chi Thotsaphon Bunthewaphithak, and Mae Chi Chandra Khonnokyoong, have achieved a notably high standing and in some cases gained a huge number of influential devotees and disciples. Many of these *mae chi*s—but by no means all—are former members of the Thai middle-class, while their followers and supporters are also in many cases middle-class.

The debates regarding the revival of the Theravada *bhikkhunī* ordination lineage, the observed similarities of roles between monks and *mae chi*s, and the female practitioners I am discussing in this book indicate a demarginalization and significant redefinition of the religious roles of women. In the following chapters, I will show that an increasing number of widely acknowledged Thai women excel as *dhamma* teachers, are revered as Buddhist saints, or are highly esteemed for their social engagement or knowledge of Buddhist teaching. This does not, of course, mean that formerly there were fewer outstanding female Buddhist practitioners in Thailand.[106] But, facilitated and expressed by the print media, internet, other digital devices, and material culture like icons and architecture, these contemporary Buddhist women have been recognized to a much broader extent and have a much higher number of followers. Local veneration of female saints has become translocal, which is particularly clear in the case of Mae Chi Kaew, as will be shown in subsequent chapters.

Nonetheless, can the existing Thai *mae chi* institution have the potential to be a satisfying and sufficient substitute for *bhikkhunī*? Many people, including Thai scholars, doubt that it can factually or potentially be a real alternative to the missing *bhikkhunī* order.[107] So far, there are only individual *mae chi*s or practicing Thai women who, based on their religious or social accomplishments, have developed a certain amount of charisma either through their practice or through their specific personal background and social standing. Neither the *mae chi* institution as a whole nor any other similar institution has been able to build up what I call here a "charisma of office" or "institutional charisma" that would equal that of the monks.[108] The saffron or brownish robes of Thai monks have become a powerful cultural symbol in Thailand to which sometimes even magical properties are attributed. Based on their ordination, monks are automatically placed at the social peak of Thai society and even the members of the Thai royal family will show their respect to a monk, irrespective of the monk's former social status. The material support given to monks is analogous; the Thai sociologist Apinya Feungfusakul recounts that Thai people may make donations to the wearers of robes even when they assume that a specific "monk" has actually committed a *pārājika*—that is, has technically and irredeemably lost his monkhood status. She also explains that "sometimes, when a monk asks for a donation, some people may not want to give anything but feel uncomfortable [about the situation and may decide] that it is better to make a donation [anyway] . . . not wanting to cause any harm to the saffron robes."[109]

The ordination act is vital in endowing Thai men with this institutional charisma that derives from the belief in an unbroken ordination lineage that is assumed to have been initiated by the Buddha himself.[110] In this respect, the white robes of the *mae chi*s have an inferior cultural and spiritual importance as they are not regarded as powerful signifiers of an unbroken lineage reaching back to the Buddha. Theravadins believe that the intactness of their tradition has been achieved by their rigid conservation and regular reviewing of original form and meaning by means of rehearsals (*saṅgīti*) and their biweekly recitation of the *pāṭimokkha*. This recitation of the *pāṭimokkha* is the "unified, collective expression of purity that acknowledges, legitimates, and perpetuates the *bhikkhusaṅgha* as the authentic bearer of the spiritual path that was articulated by the Buddha."[111] It also underscores the importance that this tradition attributes to the *vinaya*, the code of monastic discipline, in its working against semantic erosion: "The *vinaya* is the duration of the Buddha's teaching. When the *vinaya* is existent, it means that the teaching is existent."[112] A change of this traditional practice and stance might entail loss of authenticity. Faithfulness to it, though, is not only regarded as the only means to connect to the historical Buddha as the ultimate and sole source of authority but also as the only way to make original Buddhist practice and teaching available to future generations.

At the same time, the brown or saffron robes are also a pragmatically communicative means of indicating that its wearer is practicing at least the ten precepts, which, most importantly in this context, includes the nonacceptance of money. The white *mae chi* robes, however, do not convey this meaning, as the general view in Thai society is that *mae chi*s practice the eight precepts "only" and are therefore able to handle money. This was one reason why one Thai *sāmaṇerī* who received her lower ordination (*pabbajjā*) in Sri Lanka decided to become a female novice (*sāmaṇerī*) after having been a *mae chi* for twenty years. She explains that for women who want to practice the ten precepts and are not renowned in Thai society, this can be problematic as it might cause "unwholesome thoughts" (*akusalacitta*) in the laypeople, who might suspect *mae chi*s who do not handle money of being beggars.[113] She also argues that laypeople might suspect that *mae chi*s only pretend to have no money or might even think that *mae chi*s are greedy (*khi lop*). In addition, she pointed out that white-robed *mae chi*s might not feel confident enough (*mai kla tham*) to seek alms as some regard this activity as not being sanctioned by the Pali canon.[114]

Nidhi Eoseewong shares the opinion that *mae chi*s cannot be a substitute for *bhikkhunī*s as Thai society in general, he argues, does not regard them as ordained ones (*nak buat*) due to the fact that they do not represent the ritual mediator between the profane and the sacred (*sing saksit*) in the same way that monks do.[115] Also, Muecke has argued that despite *mae chi*s' vow of celibacy, "social constructions of their role are grounded in sexuality." She also notes that there are "prevalent notions that *maechii* threatened monks' celibacy."[116]

In addition to their often-unacknowledged position as "truly" ordained, we see that the identity of *mae chi*s is quite diffuse and nationally inconsistent,[117] as there is no canonical source of clearly defined identity *mae chi*s could refer to as their standard. Thai scholars' attempts to identify a canonical paradigm for Thai *mae chi*s have so far not been able to raise the prestige of *mae chi*s nationwide on an institutional level.[118] In contrast to monks, *mae chi*s do not have a given identity but have had to face the challenge of creating one.

For this reason and to raise their esteem in Thai society, several approaches have been adopted; a *mae chi* college supported by the Thai supreme patriarch (*saṅgha-rāja*) and a member of the royal family has been established with the aim of providing higher education rooted in traditional *dhamma* studies and to be a national center of information and networking for all nunneries.[119] Also, the Thai Mae Chi Institute has produced a handbook for *mae chi*s regulating behavior, dress, and the performance of ordination with the aim of establishing a uniform practice for all *mae chi*s. Furthermore, the Thai Mae Chi Institute requires *mae chi*s to have a special *mae chi* ID card.[120]

Another initiative to raise the esteem of *mae chis* is the *mae chi* college's attempts to propagate the linguistic invention *mae chi saṅgha*, a hybrid of Thai and Pali, as a strategy to corroborate their status as "real ordained ones [*nak buat*] and to emphasize [their] *saṅgha*-like communality. This is a linguistic means that aims to make the (male) *saṅgha* regard the *mae chis* as an [equal] fellow *dhamma*-farer [*sahadhammika*]."[121]

A major problem for the creation of a nationwide standardized identity is that the Thai Mae Chi Institute receives only limited support from monasteries and nunneries, and not all *mae chis* are registered with it (only about one third are). Thus, the Thai Mae Chi Institute has not yet been able to serve as a comprehensive institution that could enforce nationwide unity and consistent standards of practice and behavior.[122]

The blurredness and variety of *mae chi* identity are a double-edged sword. While *mae chis* face the challenge of enhancing their esteem and creating a clear identity that is suitable for their spiritual practice, they possess more potential in developing individual, specific modern identities and have more freedom and flexibility as they do not have as many monastic rules to follow as monks.[123] This point is vital for some *mae chis* who do not want to take the precept of not touching money as this would be rather impracticable given their involvement in social work (*sangkhom songkhro*).[124]

Mae chis are not able to create and enforce a nationwide standardized practice as monks can do by referring to the canonical *vinaya* and the Thai Saṅgha Act. This is also a reason why for *mae chis* it is difficult to purify their ranks, for example by exclusion of *mae chis* with "inappropriate," image-damaging behavior, or to consolidate or demonstrate a clear standard of practice by which laypeople could measure right and appropriate practice and behavior.

In the case of the famous and controversial Mae Chi Thotsaphon Bunthewaphithak,[125] the freedom and flexibility that *mae chis* have in contrast to monks also becomes apparent. Mae Chi Thotsaphon is believed to possess supernatural powers, which enables her to attract a huge number of followers, including Thai celebrities. Her followers believe that she is able to look into the former lives of other people to help them to "correct their [negative] *kamma*" from their previous lives. As the monks are constricted by their monastic training rules that forbid such practice, she uses the freedom of not being confined by these specific monastic rules to use her supernatural powers to help people. Mae Chi Thotsaphon explains,

> There still are monks and those who have attained levels of awakening [*ariyasong*] with an intensive and successful practice. These practitioners possess many more skills than I do. But monks are not allowed to boast with their skills, nor are they allowed to talk about them, as this may be regarded as claiming to have extraordinary spiritual achievements [which is problematic with regard to their monastic discipline]. *Mae chi*s are not monks, however. *Mae chi*s adhere to fewer training rules than monks, who have 227 rules to follow. I therefore want to use this opportunity to help people with faith in Buddhism and want to correct their individual *kamma* that they have caused. My practice here may be regarded as a mouthpiece [*pak siang*] for the monks."[126]

Relevant Previous Scholarship

The recent attempts to introduce Theravada nuns (*bhikkhunī*) into Thailand have received broad attention by Buddhist studies scholars, anthropologists, and activists and triggered numerous lively debates on the religious role of women in Thai Buddhism generally, on the national and international level.[127] While much earlier scholarship seems to have largely focused on the hardships and inequalities women have to cope with in Thai Buddhism, more recently scholars have been describing more positive experiences of Thai Buddhist women. In 1990 Allan Bessey complained that "scholars have often acknowledged the low status of monastic women and their secondary supportive role in Thai Buddhism, however with few exceptions has there been any in-depth analysis of their status and role."[128] Here he also argues that this is despite the fact that "some women are performing a role that is akin to that of the monk and that this should be recognised."

The situation has changed in the interim, as Western scholarship has produced a number of important works on the roles and more positive perspectives and experiences of female practitioners in present-day Thai Buddhism; Bessey himself argued in the same and very interesting article (albeit often unfortunately overlooked by scholarship) that *mae chis*' "role is becoming less peripheral," giving examples of some female meditation teachers.[129] During her fieldwork in the late 1990s Lindberg Falk observed that the roles of monks and *mae chi*s have become more similar in a number of ways,[130] while Collins and McDaniel more recently noticed that there is a large and increasing number of *mae chi* Pali scholars who are highly respected. As McDaniel observes, "in the modern period women play a prominent role in monastic education."[131]

At the outset of this discussion, it is important to point out that there is of course also a substantial amount of Thai-language work on *mae chi*s and female practitioners available. This book has benefited enormously from these sources (see especially the notes of the previous three sections of this chapter).[132] It is regretful that (too) often Thai and Western scholarship on *mae chi*s (and Thai and Theravada Buddhism more generally) have ignored each other, despite the fact that both sides have produced a significant number of valuable studies.

Those interested in the contemporary socioreligious role and religious experience of Thai Buddhist women generally and of *mae chi*s more specifically have also had recourse to four interesting book-length publications in English over the the last seventeen years. Even though these books are all, to a large extent, based on participant observation, they approach Thai *mae chi*s from rather different angles, thereby complementing one another in many respects.

The first is Sid Brown's *The Journey of One Buddhist Nun: Even Against the Wind*, published in 2001. It gives a fascinating, insightful, and detailed account of the life of one Thai *mae chi* (with the pseudonym Wābī), while paying significant attention to this *mae chi*'s experiences in her meditation practice. Considerable attention is also paid to the history and work of the aforementioned Thai Mae Chi Institute, established in 1969. By connecting Pali texts with experiences in contemporary Thai Buddhism, Brown, who lived for over a year among *mae chi*s, shows not only how these texts are understood by Thai Buddhist practitioners but also how they can be used to understand Thai Buddhist practice, life and aspiration. The focus on one particular life story and its many contexts (scriptural, sociological, institutional) offers a broad range of valuable insights into Thai religious life and beyond, or as Brown put it, "the reader is welcomed into Wābī's life and learns along the way about Thailand, gender in Thailand, Buddhism, meditation, māechī, and monasticism."[133]

Second is Faith Adiele's *Meeting Faith: The Forest Journals of a Black Buddhist Nun*, first published in 2004. In her early twenties, Adiele, an African-American, decided to research the lives of Thai Buddhist women by temporarily becoming a *mae chi* herself and residing in a forest monastery in northern Thailand. The accounts of her ordination, experience with meditation, and monastic life complement her personal analysis to teach readers much about the author's own spiritual journey and reflections on identity, race, gender, and culture. In this way, it differs from other studies about the lives of particular *mae chi*s or the role of *mae chi*s in general in contemporary Thai Buddhism.

Next, Monica Lindberg Falk's *Making Fields of Merit: Buddhist Female Ascetics and Gendered Orders in Thailand*, published in 2007, is based on her doctoral thesis of 2002. As part of her fieldwork, Lindberg Falk lived for more than a year in a *mae chi* residence (*samnak chi*), which the *mae chi*s themselves were in charge of (in contrast to many Thai monastic communities, in which *mae chi*s live together with—although spatially separated from—monks and are often placed under their direction). She also gathered data from visits to *mae chi* communities in other regions of Thailand. In seeking an understanding of *mae chi*s' religious life and experience, Lindberg Falk investigates, among other things, *mae chi* ordination, beliefs in the alleged polluting powers of menstrual blood, motivations for becoming a *mae chi*, *mae chi*s' access to education, their monastic roles and routines, the *bhikkhunī* ordination debate in Thailand, and *mae chi*s' attempts to gain legal recognition. In this way, Lindberg Falk is able to provide a fairly comprehensive and ethnographically solid study of the religious life of Thai *mae chi*s, while succeeding in challenging many misconceptions and simplifications about Thai *mae chi*s' life and their religious aspirations and practice.

Finally, Joanna Cook's *Meditation in Modern Buddhism: Renunciation and Change in Thai Monastic Life* is also to a large extent about the life and religious experience of *mae chi*s in contemporary Thai Buddhism (even though this is not clear from its title), focusing on one particular monastic community. In addition to the analysis of female monasticism, Cook offers a myriad of valuable insights into various other aspects of contemporary Thai Buddhist practice not immediately related to gender and into the role and status of *mae chi*s. In fact, even though the book is relatively short, the reader is presented with a huge range of different approaches to and perspectives on the monastic life and meditative experience of Buddhist monastic practitioners more generally and *mae chi*s in particular. The highly original analyses are based on data gained from long-term participant observation; Cook was ordained as a *mae chi* in a northern Thai monastery that is very much devoted to the practice of *vipassanā* (mindfulness) meditation. Cook examines *mae chi*s' own perspectives and experiences in relation to the gendered hierarchy in which they are embedded and seen (and see themselves) as inferior to monks. She observes and discusses a "stark contrast" between *mae chi*s' perception of "their monastic duties and the institutional organization of Buddhist monasticism"[134] and the way they are widely depicted in rather negative terms (for more on this see chapter 6). In contrast to and thereby complementing Lindberg Falk's study, Cook bases her investigation on fieldwork conducted in a monastery in which *mae chi*s live together with male monastics—not independently in a nunnery. This allows Cook to discuss the difference of views on gendered hierarchy between how *mae chi*s understand their roles and actions and how they are understood in academic literature.

These four major contributions on Thai *mae chi*s are very enriching to our understanding of female monasticism and practice in current Thai Buddhism.[135] However, when looking at both Western and Thai scholarship investigating aspects of modern Thai Buddhism, including the studies referred to above, it appears that individual female practitioners who are highly revered or even believed to be "noble ones" (*ariya*; i.e., those who have attained levels of awakening) have hardly been discussed or even mentioned at all.[136] This applies in particular to Thai Buddhist women whose monastic or teaching career took place before the 1960s.

However, one can find a brief academic discussion of Ajan Naeb Mahaniranon (1898–1983), one of the first widely respected female Thai Buddhist teachers, in an article by John Van Esterik first published in 1982. Ajan Naeb was "thought by many of her followers to be well on the way to nirvana. They believe she is a *sotapanna* [a "stream-enterer," i.e., one who has achieved the first level of awakening; see next chapter]."[137] Also, in 1995 the American scholar monk Ṭhānissaro Bhikkhu provided a short account of the life and spiritual practice of Upāsika Ki Nanayon (1901–78), also known as Ko. Khao Suan Luang, who "was arguably the foremost woman Dhamma teacher in twentieth-century Thailand."[138] In line with Bessey's observation referred to above, Ṭhānissaro Bhikkhu argued that even though

> much has been written recently on the role of women in Buddhism, . . . for all of Upasika Kee's accomplishments in her own personal Dhamma practice and in providing opportunities for other women to practice as well, socio-historical books on Thai women in Buddhism make no mention of her name or of the community she founded.[139]

It must be noted that even though this has changed since then to some extent, there is still no book-length study of Upāsikā Ki Nanayon or Ajan Naeb in English despite their enormous importance for modern Thai Buddhism. In order to help remedy this situation to some extent at least, and even though they are not at the center of my investigation, I will repeatedly refer to Thai texts about and by Ajan Naeb and Upāsikā Ki Nanayon to substantiate my major arguments.

Thus, despite the fact there are some academic sources on individual Thai female practitioners, we must state that when scholarly works examine the life of highly venerated Thai monastics, these are mostly male individuals,[140] or as Cook puts it, "the hagiography of males who have attained this position [of the accomplished and charismatic teacher] is a long-standing academic and anthropological concern."[141]

While there is a conspicuous lack of more comprehensive in-depth studies of locally and nationally influential female Buddhist practitioners and teachers in Thailand and the attendant symbolic representation,[142] in addition to the work referred to above there are some influential studies in the fields of Thai and Buddhist studies that have mentioned, albeit often only briefly, *mae chis* in connection with the spiritual accomplishments of men.

In his influential book on Thai Buddhism *The Buddhist Saints of the Forest and the Cult of Amulets*, Stanley Jeyarajah Tambiah briefly mentions practicing *mae chis* but does not discuss their religious experience or how they are perceived in their local communities. His work focuses on hagiographies and veneration of male saints. He reports that "in forest hermitages [*mae chi*s] were considered a burden to the meditation masters."[143] While this statement may be valid to some extent in some monasteries, it certainly generalizes and oversimplifies the relationships monks (of the forest tradition) and *mae chi*s have had and may have. In fact, as I will show in this book, there are numerous cases where *mae chi*s received special attention from the great masters of the forest tradition and were themselves meditation masters.

Similarly to Tambiah in this respect, James Taylor's major work on renunciants of the Thai forest tradition does not discuss female practitioners in any depth but contains only a one page-long section on them, in addition to some brief mentions elsewhere in the book. Taylor writes that

> the *mae chii*, or perhaps *chii phraam*, control the cooking and domestic chores, particularly important at forest *samnak* far from the nearest village. . . . Resident *mae chii* come under the control of the teacher, but in fact have very little contact except at times of calendrical Buddhist festivities or *dhamma* talks on the weekly holy days.[144]

But in fact, the prominence of some female renunciants among the monks of the Thai forest tradition has been noted. In her frequently quoted 1997 book *Forest Recollections: Wandering Monks in Twentieth-Century Thailand*, Kamala Tiyavanich provides impressive accounts of the religious experiences and life stories of a number of well-known male renunciants but does not discuss female Buddhist practitioners in any depth. She only briefly discusses some renunciant women who are mentioned in the accounts of male practitioners. She devotes a rather small section of some six pages, entitled "Women as Spiritual Equals," to this topic. She argues that

> in regional traditions there were prominent women renunciates but their identities and teachings do not appear in official records because they were devoted to meditation rather than scholastic training. Nevertheless, some of these women ascetics remained in the memory of elderly people and monks. There is plenty of evidence that teachers of regional Buddhist traditions held female ascetics in high esteem.[145]

Kamala also states that the monks of the forest tradition "met many laywomen and mae chis . . . who surpassed monks in their meditation," and in "many local traditions, female renunciates were respected by monks as well as local laypeople, and they attracted many personal followers."[146]

In this book, I intend to corroborate these statements by Kamala and thus in some ways complement her work by focusing on the biographies and veneration of some of these highly revered female practitioners of the forest tradition. I will also show that while Kamala is right to some extent about the availability of sources on the biographies and spiritual practice of these female practitioners, the situation is not as dire as she seems to suggest. Even though written sources on female practitioners may not be found as easily as those of male practitioners, over the course of my research I was able to locate numerous biographical texts by or on these women. Kamala is of course right in her statement that we may often find (only short) references to these women's lives in the biographies of the male practitioners.

Since the publication of Kamala's book in 1997 there have been some major developments in relation to more widespread veneration of Thai Buddhist women and the production of biographical texts on them. This applies particularly, as I will discuss in later chapters, to the textual production on the life and spiritual practice of one of the most famous female practitioners of the Thai forest tradition, Mae Chi Kaew Sianglam, a direct disciple of Luang Pu Man; here we have seen numerous publications in Thai over the course of the last twenty years or so, and then also a book-length biography in English, written by the Western monk Ajan Dick Sīlaratano and published in 2009.[147]

It seems fair to say that existing Thai and Western scholarship reflects the gendered imbalances within Thai Buddhism at large that I have discussed in this chapter. The life, spiritual practice, texts, veneration, and symbolic depictions of outstanding female Buddhist practitioners and teachers have received relatively little attention in scholarship.

However, it must also be noted that we have seen an increasing number of publications in Western languages over the course of the last fifteen years or so on individual female practitioners and monastic communities. This is a welcome development in the study of Thai Buddhism, where scholars have often tended to focus on the religious roles, experience, activities, achievements, and institutions of male Buddhists. As a result of previous scholarship, readers have gained only a partial, often rather one-sided or even distorted, picture of Thai Buddhism as the agency of Thai Buddhist women and their complex relationships to monks have not been sufficiently taken into account and examined in depth.

With this book I want to demonstrate that more scrutiny of outstanding female practitioners will help to gain a clearer and more comprehensive understanding of the complex and multifarious roles of women in modern Thai Buddhism. To sum up, I would like to quote Collins and McDaniel:

> The idea of a *mae chi*'s life as "beautiful," with meticulous and inspiring pedagogy, sophisticated learning and meditative expertise as goals and values *per se*, with intrinsic virtue as well as instrumental value in reducing suffering and leading to nirvana, has not been emphasized enough in the existing literature, which tends too often to concentrate on the issue of *bhikkhunī* ordination, and more generally to focus on *mae chis*' hardships (which are often many), and on discrimination in the Thai ecclesia."[148]

Chapter 2

Biography and Hagiography: Female Practitioners in Modern Thai Buddhism

> Every time [the elderly *mae chi*] Khun Yai came, she received useful meditation instruction from Luang Pu Man. On these occasions, monks and novices would secretly approach the pavilion where Khun Yai was talking with Luang Pu Man in order to listen to her questions about meditation and his answers. . . . Most of her questions arose from her own direct experiences in meditation and concerned [different] matters such as the internal experiencing of the [Four] Noble Truths or the external encounters with deities [*devas*] and *brahmas*. . . . Luang Pu Man praised this elderly *mae chi*, telling the monks, "She achieved a high level of insight into the *dhamma*—this is rejoiceful. Among us monks, there are many who may not be able to achieve her level of knowledge."
>
> From one of the major hagiographies of Luang Pu Man[1]

Hagiographical texts of male charismatic Thai Buddhists are extremely popular in current Thai Buddhism. This is apparent through the ubiquity of these texts throughout the country, often given away for free at monasteries or sold in bookstores, and the obviously high costs with which some of these books have been produced. In line with my observations in the previous chapter about gender imbalances in Thai Buddhism, hagiographical texts about female Thai Buddhist practitioners are generally rare, though there are some notable exceptions.

Yet despite the fact that much of my research material was difficult to obtain or acquired by chance, it is clear that there do exist numerous life story texts by or about Thai female practitioners. The more I have looked for life stories of female Buddhist practitioners in modern Thai Buddhism over the course of my research, the more I have come across autobiographical and biographical texts. Often, however, these accounts are orally transmitted; those that are printed often have low circulation figures and may be distributed only locally or within small communities. I regard these texts as treasures, as they allow us to gain valuable insights into female perspectives on renunciation, spiritual practice, and gender relations. I have accumulated a significant number of these texts, and due to the vastness of this material it will take me many years to investigate these texts comprehensively. In this book I will focus on a small number of female practitioners whose life and practice I regard as significant, representative, or insightful for the purposes of my study.

In this chapter I present and discuss at some length the biographies of Khunying Damrongthammasan (Yai Wisetsiri), Mae Bunruean Tongbuntoem, and Mae Chi Kaew Sianglam. In addition, I will also provide shorter summaries of the life stories of Mae Chi Nari Karun, Mae Chi Phimpha Wongsa-udom, and Mae Chi Soda Sosut, as their hagiographies contain some interesting elements and perspectives that help to further and strengthen my analysis and arguments. Each biography is preceded by a discussion of the sources I have used.

Like Mae Chi Kaew, the three latter *mae chi*s were students of famous meditation masters of the Thai forest tradition. Khunying Yai and Mae Bunruean, however, were students of famous monk teachers who spent most of their monastic life in the urban context of Bangkok. The majority of the six female Buddhist practitioners investigated in some depth in this book have spent a significant amount of their lives as *mae chi*s and died as *mae chi*s. The only exception here is Mae Bunruean Tongbuntoem, who was ordained as a *mae chi* twice but then decided to disrobe both times.[2] Nonetheless, I argue that even though she practiced and lived in the middle of Bangkok, much of the time outside a monastery, her life should be described as that of a renunciant; toward the end of her life she even increasingly followed precepts similar to those of a monastic.

Throughout my presentation of these women's biographies, I frequently refer to Pali canonical and postcanonical literature to demonstrate how Pali literature has functioned as a blueprint for how these women or their hagiographers express and reflect on personal spiritual experiences and insights. The hagiographies and other relevant texts may also use Pali language and concepts in order to legitimize or reject these women's spiritual experiences and achievements. This does not mean, however, that all experiences and spiritual insights are related to or are attested in the authoritative Pali scriptures. It may even be stated forthrightly in the hagiography that the spiritual experiences and insights of the successful practitioner of meditation cannot be found in the sacred scriptures. This stance is nicely expressed in one the major hagiographies of Luang Pu Man: "The *dhamma* that is not written down in the Pali canon can be compared to the amount of water in the great ocean, while the *dhamma* that appears in the Pali canon is comparable to the amount of water in a small jar."[3] In fact, from the viewpoint of traditional Theravada Buddhism, a number of hagiographical elements and ideas may be regarded as problematic or even in contradiction with the teachings found in Theravada's authoritative scriptures. A good example of this is the motif that the successful practitioner of meditation is able to meet the Buddha or other fully awakened beings who lived during the time of the Buddha.[4]

However, before I provide summaries of these six women's hagiographies, some general observations about biographical and autobiographical writing and hagiographical literature in Thai Buddhism are due.

Biography and Hagiography in Modern Thai Buddhism

The earliest Buddhist texts available do not contain a continuous life story of the Buddha but rather focus on his teachings and the development of his monastic community. As Frank Reynolds and Charles Hallisey have argued, "Episodic fragments, preserved in the Pali and Chinese versions of the early Buddhist literature are embedded in sermons attributed to the Buddha himself and illustrate points of practice or doctrine."[5] There is evidence that various traditions after 200 BCE produced continuous biographies of the Buddha, using "scattered accounts" of earlier texts and "floating oral traditions."[6] It needs to be noted here though that there are differing opinions among Buddhist studies scholars as to when a continuous biography of the Buddha was first composed.[7] In contrast to the lack of such a biography of the Buddha in the earliest Buddhist texts, there is an abundance of hagiographical literature in modern Thai

Buddhism, not only about saints of early Buddhism but also about revered Thai individuals of the nineteenth and twentieth centuries with a particular focus on those who are believed to have been exceptionally successful in their spiritual practice. This reflects the enormous popularity of charismatic Buddhist individuals in current Thai society.

Significant hagiographical writings on Thai monks have, according to Charles Keyes, emerged only since the beginning of the twentieth century, "that is, after a radical change had occurred in Thai literature, stimulated by Western influences and especially by the introduction of printing." He adds, however, that even though "a written biographical tradition was late in developing in Thailand, oral biographies of monks and other individuals have long existed."[8] According to McDaniel, there are hagiographies as old as the origins of the printing of Thai cremation volumes in the late nineteenth century.[9]

Be that as it may, in the early twentieth century there was a strong increase in the number of written life accounts of monks. The arguably most influential and well-known of all hagiographies of highly revered Thai monastics is the biography of Luang Pu Man, authored by Luang Ta Mahabua and published in book form in 1971. This biography, declared by Tambiah to be a "masterpiece,"[10] contains numerous passages on the supernatural and supramundane experiences of Luang Pu Man, while incorporating typical Buddhist patterns of life-story telling.

Since then, numerous biographical texts on Luang Pu Man and many of his disciples have been published.[11] While many of these books have been commercially very successful, hagiographical texts are often given away for free and made available online in various formats. Many hagiographical publications contain biographies of more than one monk. Typical titles read *The moment of attainment: Arahants do really exist*, *Sixty-eight noble members of the saṅgha [*ariyasong*]*, and *The final rebirth of a noble member of the saṅgha [*ariyasong*] with miraculous powers*. Often, these books contain not only biographical but also sermon texts.

The cremation volume of Luang Ta Mahabua is one of the most impressive examples of modern Thai Buddhist hagiographies. Printed several months after his funeral in 2011, it contains 928 pages of high-quality paper with detailed accounts of his life and that of his fellow practitioners and students, numerous photos, sermon texts, diagrams, maps, and sketches. It weighs nearly five kilograms. The staggering number of copies printed was 135,000. Inside the book, it says in red, "Only to be distributed as a free gift of *dhamma*. This book is not for sale."[12]

Although the sacred biographies of monks of the Thai forest tradition have been particularly popular in Thailand, there are of course also seemingly countless biographical texts of monks who do not belong to the Thai forest tradition. The number of copies produced often varies significantly depending on the fame of the master, the number of followers, availability of funding, and other factors. Some of these monks may be known and revered on a local level only, while others are venerated on a national level. It must be noted here, however, that a high circulation figure of hagiographical and homiletic texts does not necessarily imply that large numbers of Thai Buddhists read these texts.[13] What seems often more important is to generate merit through contributing to the printing costs of these texts so that they can then be given away as a gift of *dhamma* (*dhammadāna*). More recently, a new genre of Thai Buddhist hagiographical literature has emerged and apparently become quite popular in Thailand: cartoon books of the Buddha, fully awakened or other noble disciples who lived during the time of the Buddha, or contemporary revered monks.[14] The 2011 cartoon book on Luang Ta Mahabua, for example, contains sketches of major episodes of his spiritual journey from "the beginning of his life to the day he died and entered *nibbāna*."[15] It also contains photographs of his funeral and relics. Included in the book is a free VCD with a biographical documentary on Luang Ta Mahabua entitled *The noble [*ariya*] monastic of Wat Pa Ban Tat: The noble one of [our] land*. I should also mention here the hagiographies of highly revered monks of modern Thai Buddhism spread on other media, such as documentary films on VCD and increasingly on YouTube.

Autobiography: Unwillingness or Reluctance to Talk or Write about Oneself

Among the earliest texts of Indian Buddhism are a number of autobiographical narratives about a practitioner's life and practice. In addition to a relatively small number of autobiographical statements attributed to the Buddha, the famous canonical texts *Theragāthā* (*Verses of the elder monks*) and *Therīgāthā* (*Verses of the elder nuns*) "*may* contain autobiographical material"[16] and are thus rather exceptional. It should be mentioned here that the verses on the whole are about the *dhamma* and contain to a lesser degree biographical information.

In an impressive textual analysis, Kathryn Blackstone convincingly concluded "that, in all likelihood, the *Therīgāthā* was composed by women, does represent a female perspective on the life of renunciation, and was probably designed as a model of liberation specifically for women."[17] Also, the late canonical books *Therāpadāna* and *Therī-apadāna*, probably dating from the post-Asokan period, contain to a large extent the life stories of numerous male and female fully awakened disciples of the Buddha. Life stories recounted in both these works appear to be autobiographical, as most are narrated in the first person.[18]

Cook has observed that "in Buddhism broadly, hagiographic narratives have focused almost exclusively upon men."[19] While this is certainly true, it is interesting to note that given the enormous interest people have in their lives, autobiographical material of both male and female Buddhist practitioners is still relatively rare. This can partly be explained by the fact that Buddhist monks are prohibited by their monastic code (*vinaya*) from talking to laypeople about their personal spiritual accomplishments. In connection with this, the concern of Buddhist practitioners is normally to spread Buddhist teachings rather than to talk about one's own personal spiritual experiences or insights[20] (even though there are also a number of notable exceptions to this; see next chapter). Thus, at first the famous Thai scholar-monk Phra Payutto (1939–), for example, was reluctant when a researcher approached him with the desire to record his biography. Grant Olson—the eventual author of the biography—notes, "As we continued to keep in contact about this project, he eventually acquiesced and said that it could be done in the hopes that it might be 'of Dhammic value to the people.'"[21] Luang Pu Thet, one of Luang Pu Man's most famous direct disciples, explained his initial reluctance to the publication of his autobiography:

> In truth, I first wrote this *Autobiography* only for myself, to show my appreciation of a life wearing the saffron robe. There was no

> thought of publication because I would have felt rather ashamed at the idea, for an autobiography is self-promoting. Even when people asked to have it printed for me, I still wasn't happy with the idea. . . . I realized that if I didn't agree it would get written after I was dead anyway."[22]

Yet it appears that since the first half of the twentieth century an increasing number of autobiographies by monks, in particular those belonging or close to the forest tradition, have been produced. Thus, in addition to Luang Pu Thet's text we also have autobiographical texts authored by other famous monks, such as Chaokhun Guṇūpamācariya (Siricando, Jan, 1857–1932), Luang Pu Li (Dhammadharo, 1907–61), and Luang Pho Wiriyang (Sirindharo, 1921–). Many of these autobiographies have been very popular. The autobiography of Luang Pu La (Khemapatto, 1912–96), for example, had twelve printings within seven years with a circulation figure of altogether 130,000 copies.[23]

Biographies and Autobiographies of Female Practitioners

It appears that biographical literature on accomplished female Thai Buddhist practitioners emerged significantly later than that on male monastics. As far as I can ascertain, the first Thai woman widely revered for her spiritual practice and achievements for whom we have substantial written biographical accounts is Mae Bunruean. For her funeral in 1964 a voluminous cremation book of nearly four hundred pages, with a circulation figure of four thousand copies, was published. However, as I will discuss in more detail below, the hagiographical process in her case started no later than 1946, when short texts about her spiritual practice, supernatural powers, and healing skills were published in two different publications.[24] Mae Bunruean's cremation volume of 1964 contains numerous texts about and by her in addition to photos of her. The care with which the volume was prepared, its sheer size, and the fact that it was prepared within only fifty days (the time between her death and cremation) together with its textual content reveal the enormous respect her students and devotees must have had for her. Her cremation volume was also republished at least once. Copies of the original edition are nowadays sought after but extremely difficult to find; this is reflected by the fact that on online auctions copies of her cremation volume may be valued at up to 17,000 baht (approx. 500 US dollars).[25]

Mae Bunruean was also the first female practitioner about whom the popular monthly magazine *Lokthip* (*Divine world*), devoted to meditation monks and in existence since 1982, published a biography (see below and chapter 3).[26] In 1983, the well-known Thai historian Sathuean Suphasophon published an interesting hagiographical account of Mae Bunruean in *Transworldly powers: Magazine of Buddhist practice*; he describes her as "maybe unrivaled among all those known for their marvelous supernatural powers in the current epoch in Thailand, no matter whether ordained or lay. . . . Her excellent spiritual practice allowed her mind to achieve the level of full awakening [arahant]."[27] It cannot be excluded that there have been older biographies of Buddhist female practitioners, but it seems that Mae Bunruean's hagiographies belong to the first widely circulated substantial biographical texts of a highly and widely revered Thai female practitioner. They may very well be the first of their kind, ascribing a wide range of supernatural powers and often, but importantly not always (see below and chapter 3), supramundane achievements to a Thai woman.

In recent decades we have seen an increasing number of biographies about and homiletic texts by female practitioners. However, biographical texts about female practitioners before 1950 are often fragmentary, most of them written by disciples or admirers, having first been remembered and transmitted orally, as was the case in ancient India. The hagiographies of Mae Bunruean emerging in the 1960s and more recently those of Mae Chi Kaew are certainly exceptional not only with regard to the explicitness with which sainthood is ascribed to Thai women but also in terms of their length, number of printings, high publication costs, figures of circulation, and comprehensiveness.

There are also a number of autobiographical texts by female practitioners in Thai Buddhism that are of significant length, but this is the exception—most if not all of them being rather recent;[28] only seldom and in exceptional cases do we have homiletic or autobiographical texts of *mae chi*s or other female practitioners produced prior to 1950.[29] Similar to the male monastics' concern that an autobiography may be perceived as "self-promoting," female practitioners seem to have been rather unwilling to write about themselves. For them autobiography may have been perceived as even more problematic than for male monastics.

Mae Chi Phimpha Wongsa-udom (1912–2010), for example, only reluctantly agreed to write down an account of her life when she was "ordered" (*sang*) to do so by her teacher Luang Pu Thet:

> I was worried that people will not understand or not believe my words and that this may lead to criticism in various forms, which then may cause damage. Thus, I was holding this back for a long time. [But] when I thought about . . . the indescribable, overwhelming goodness Luang Pu Thet [showed to me over many years] . . . I hurried to compile all those stories I was able to remember.[30]

She also first wavered when it was suggested that her instructions on spiritual practice should be printed as a book and distributed. She was concerned that people might think she was trying to become famous. Only after she was reassured that her teaching may be of value for future generations of Buddhist practitioners due to the insight it offers did she agree to have a high-ranking monk make the decision whether her text should be made available to the wider public.[31]

This is in line with comments made by the monk Luang Pho Khanong Dhammadhīro, the owner and former longtime editor of the popular magazine *Lokthip*. Since 1982, *Lokthip* has published on a monthly or bimonthly basis in more than five hundred issues biographies and other stories of meditation monks and, to a lesser degree, of *mae chi*s. Consumed by a largely urban readership and also distributed to Thais living abroad, the magazine initially had a monthly circulation of 40,000–50,000. But in the 1990s scandals about a number of famous charismatic monks, such as Phra Yantra Amaro, greatly unsettled a large number of Thai Buddhists,[32] and the number of copies produced each month dropped significantly. At the time of my interview with Luang Pho Khanong in 2012, it was 10,000.

Luang Pho Khanong argued that even though there are numerous "skilled" (*keng keng*) *mae chi* practitioners, they would normally not talk about their own experiences or lives. They would first need to receive permission to do so from a senior monk of the community in which they live:

> When [*mae chi*s] live in a monastery with monks, they are required to follow the regulations of that community. Even monks who have a teacher would not want to be seen as indicating that they are more famous or eminent than their teacher. In the case of *mae chi*s, this would be deemed even more inappropriate. The only exception is when a senior monk agrees with and gives support to the [making of a biography of his students].[33]

Thus, another reason for *mae chi*s' unwillingness to publish autobiographical texts may also be their embeddedness in gendered hierarchies in addition to the respect they have for their teacher.[34] Here it is interesting to note that the two 1946 publications with texts about Mae Bunruean came into existence in the first place through the initiative of Mae Bunruean's teacher, the high-ranking monk Phra Maharatchamangkhalajan (Thet, Niddesako), abbot of Wat Samphanthawong (see below). Also, even though Mae Bunruean was still alive, people asked Phra Maharatchamangkhalajan for permission to publish the accounts on Mae Bunruean.[35]

Up until the date of my interview in 2012 with Luang Pho Khanong, in its entire history of thirty years with more than five hundred issues altogether, *Lokthip* had never had a female practitioner on its front cover. A photo of a monk whose biography is presented in the issue would normally appear on the cover. Luang Pho Khanong explained, "If we put a *mae chi* on the front cover, the copies of that issue would not sell well." Life stories of *mae chi*s have been only rarely published in *Lokthip*. Thus, based on their experience with readers' feedback and reception, for *Lokthip* stories about *mae chi*s are supplementary (*rueang rong*) whereas those of monks are central and of main importance (*ek*).[36]

The absence of a *bhikkhunī* order in Thailand's history must also be referred to when explaining the lack of a stronger interest in the life stories of female renunciants. Due to their practice of a high number of Buddhist precepts and representation of the "holy life" (*brahmacariya*), the life of a *bhikkhu* or a *bhikkhunī* is regarded as exemplary and to be emulated.[37]

The lives of *mae chis* and laypeople are of much less importance in this respect.

Another typical example for *mae chis*' (and monks') reluctance to talk about themselves is Mae Chi Kaew's reply to a writer who in 1984 asked to interview her with the intention of producing a biography. Mae Chi Kaew said, "I have become ordained—I do not have a history, I do not have a past. There is nothing at all that would [be worth] mentioning."[38] After her death in 1991, however, numerous texts on her life and spiritual practice were printed and widely disseminated (see below). A 2007 biography was reprinted six times within two years; it attributes Mae Chi Kaew's reluctance to have a biography made to her "humbleness" (*thom ton*). She "hid herself away in order to practice meditation."[39] I will discuss the reasons for the postmortem proliferation of hagiographical literature in the case of Mae Chi Kaew in chapter 4.

Similarly, even though highly revered by her admirers and believed to have been been well-advanced in her spiritual practice, there are hardly any sources on the interesting life of Mae Chi Prachumphon Jaksurak (1911–83). Mae Chi Prachumphon spent most of her spiritual life in cemeteries and in solitude, pursuing intensive meditation practice and regularly meditating by contemplating corpses. We have a written, albeit very short, dialogical account on her life in the first place only because the famous meditation master Luang Pho Jaran Ṭhitadhammo of Wat Amphawan (Singburi Province), prompted by some laypeople, interviewed Mae Chi Prachumphon shortly before her death for some two hours and this interview was recorded, transcribed, and then printed as a small book.[40] Without the coming together of these factors and the involvement of a high-ranking monk, it is unlikely that a written account with first-person elements would have come into existence. Surely, much information on her remarkable religious life and experiences would have been lost forever.

As for Khunying Yai, despite her elevated social position, the profound admiration many people had for her, her unusually advanced scholarship and brilliant literary output, and, in connection with this latter point, her significant impact on Thai Buddhism, no one had written any detailed biography on her until my co-researcher and I did so only recently. In her case, we had to reconstruct her biography from oral accounts and a limited number of very short written references.[41] It is clear that she was not interested in promoting herself; after all she did not even mention herself as the author of her major texts but preferred to publish them anonymously (see below). The initial passage in one of her many profound texts, a dialogue between two anonymous individuals, nicely reflects, I believe, the lack of interest in autobiographical or biographical activities that she and other Thai Buddhist practitioners, male and female, have harbored:

> *Tho.*: "I have not seen you for a long time. Are you doing well [*pen suk* (Pali *sukha*) *sabai di rue*]?"
> *To.*: "When expressed in conventional ways [*sammati*], I am fine. But the five *khandhas* [aggregates] are *dukkha* [suffering]. Thus, if I answer that I am fine [*suk*; Pali *sukha*] that would be in conflict with reality."
> *Tho.*: "I ask in line with the conventions of the world, in the way people are used to having conversations with each other, when they have not met each other for a long time. When you give me an answer like this, I do not get an understanding of whether you are doing well or not."
> *To.*: "*Sukhā vedanā* [pleasant feelings] are *saṅkhāra* [constructions], *dukkha vedanā* [unpleasant feelings] are *saṅkhāra* too. Thus, they both are *dukkha* [unsatisfactory]. I cannot see any kind of *saṅkhāra* that is permanent or *sukha*. I can only see *saṅkhāras* that are impermanent and *dukkha*. You and I are [Buddhist] practitioners and have been at the monastery for a long time. For this reason, we should converse in a way that is in line with reality."
> *Tho.*: "You do not like talking about worldly things at all, even one single word. Thus, in the following I will ask you only with regard to the right practice [*sammāpaṭipatti*]."
> *To.*: "Questions about the right practice I will be happy to give answers to; as for worldly things, we should get weary of them at long last [*sia thi*]."[42]

According to this thinking, the world is and is to be seen as void of any permanent self, as it entirely consists of fickle processes. Thus, talking about oneself is something to be avoided as it may not be useful or may even be detrimental to one's spiritual practice. Small talk or talking about one's life is perceived as trivial and shallow when compared to a discussion of the Buddha's teaching.

In fact, as Khunying Yai makes clear in her texts, there is an urgency to transform one's perception in order to realize that persons are ultimately fleeting processes rather than stable entities. For this task no time should be wasted, as Khunying Yai argues, referring to the canonical *Dhammapada* verse (182), "Hard is it to be born a man; hard is the life of mortals. Hard is it to gain the opportunity of hearing the Sublime Truth, and hard to encounter is the arising of the Buddhas."[43] In the above dialogical passage, as is typical, Khunying Yai has the person more knowledgeable in Buddhist doctrine refuse to answer questions about personal well-being but reply in Buddhist doctrinal terminology, unapologetically and immediately redirecting the conversation to a discussion of Buddhist doctrine.[44] However, here it should be noted that the Buddhist doctrine and belief in the nonexistence of a permanent self (*anattā*) may not necessarily rule out autobiographical activities for a Buddhist practitioner, as Janet Gyatso showed in her study of the influential eighteenth-century Tibetan master Jigme Lingpa. In fact, Gyatso argues that "in Tibet it was precisely the introduction of the ideology of 'no-self' that marked the dawn of self-written stories of the self."[45]

Some other general observations about the texts by and about female Thai Buddhist practitioners are due before I summarize the lives of the major women in my study. Many of the texts I have consulted are poorly edited and do not contain any notes or clues as to their exact origin or context. While many *mae chis* were reluctant to write down or be interviewed about their personal history, as shown by the examples above, it must also be noted that many of the *mae chis* of earlier generations simply were not able to write at all. Mae Chi Phimpha for example, having never attended school, learned how to write when she was about sixty years old and only then wrote down an account of her life.[46]

Also, the texts authored by these women were often revised by others, as in the case of Mae Chi Phimpha, or a number of other people may somehow have been involved in the writing or compiling of the texts. Thus it is often difficult, if not impossible, to isolate the original "female voice" and to ascertain whether specific information came directly from the female renunciant herself or from other sources.

In Thai language more generally and with the biographical material I was working on, the distinction between biography (*chiwaprawat*) and autobiography (*attachiwaprawat*) is often unclear and blurred. The biography of Mae Chi Wanjai Chukon (1934–), a famous meditation master and student of the founder of the modern Thai Dhammakāya meditation movement Luang Pho Sot Candasaro, is a good example of this. Her life account of 2006 is identified as autobiography. It consists, however, of passages quite obviously written by her students (*sityanusit*) and probably more or less direct quotations from herself, sometimes indicated by quotations marks. Often, it is not clear what was written or said by the subject of the biography, what was added, and to what extent the autobiographical text may have been edited by someone else.[47] Also, in the Thai narrative style it is not unusual for the narrator to use specific third-person nouns, such as "teacher/master" (*ajan*) or "mother" (*mae*), when referring to himself or herself.

What also needs to be mentioned is that biographies of revered practitioners serve, in the words of Tambiah, "a moral, didactic purpose—the story of a saint was told not for its own sake but to edify and chasten the reader and listener."[48] Or in the words of Sulak Sivaraksa, "in the Buddhist view the biography is to remind those who read it or hear about it that they must meditate on suffering, change and impermanence, and that all things are essenceless."[49] In this way, the biographies investigated in this book possess interesting similarities with early Indian Buddhist texts in their underlying themes. This can be shown through a comparison with the Pali canonical collection *Apadāna*. This collection consists, to a large part, of autobiographies attributed to direct male and female disciples of the Buddha. Sally Mellick Cutler explains that the "*Apadāna* can . . . be placed within the genre of didactic or homiletic literature in which stories are used to illustrate and interpret doctrinal points, particularly for the edification of pious lay people."[50]

Bhikkhu Sīlaratano, the author of the English hagiography of Mae Chi Kaew Sianglam, writes,

> I have also resorted to my imagination to fill out the picture of her life and her practice, adding graphic details to fashion a vibrant and clear mental image of the woman and her extraordinary achievements. This is not a work of scholarship so much as a narrative biography that is intended to provide a source of inspiration to those who are devoted to Buddhist practice. With that purpose in mind, it is hoped that this book will be viewed mainly as an invitation to contemplate the depths and subtleties of mind that are experienced on the Buddha's path to total liberation.[51]

Thus, the objective of producing a hagiography here is to inspire, motivate, and exemplify Buddhist values and ideals rather than to provide an exact and comprehensive historical account.[52] The biographical author may add personal interpretation or imagination, often in a way that makes it impossible to differentiate between "original" account, direct quotation, and further elaboration and interpretation.

As the obfuscation between factual account of experience and pedagogical objectives is of minor or even no concern to the hagiographer or to the religious reader, correct chronological sequencing of events is often irrelevant, while anecdotes from previous lifetimes may be embedded in the biography in order to show the validity of the workings of the law of *kamma*, exemplify specific Buddhist teachings, and explain current realities.[53] The didactic and exemplary aspects of these biographies also become visible by the fact that these texts are interspersed, often seemingly randomly, with rather long extracts of Buddhist teachings.

My approach to and understanding of the hagiographical material of my study can best be expressed by the words of Paul Williams: "The hagiography as a whole is to be read as an ideological document, reflecting the religious interests of the community which put the hagiography together."[54] Consequently, in the following I will not only provide straightforward summaries of biographical accounts but also highlight and discuss issues that these women's biographers, devotees, or the women themselves have regarded as meaningful or expressions of larger issues. It is not uncommon that the different biographical texts of my study contain or consist of, sometimes to a large extent, identical texts or textual passages. This is particularly true when key events in the life of the female practitioners are described or the words of an authoritative figure are referred to. A specific text version may have become accepted as the most authoritative source for later publications; later sources may extensively quote word-for-word from this earlier source without necessarily indicating this, while also adding new textual materials. My retelling of the female practitioners' life stories in this chapter is often based on a vast amount of different textual sources (in addition to my interviews). Nonetheless, when I quote from such biographical texts directly I cite only one example, based on what I regard as the most influential or authoritative source. In subsequent chapters I will then turn to a more focused investigation of specific pertinent issues that emerge from these women's biographies and veneration.

Khunying Damrongthammasan Yai Wisetsiri (1882–1944)

Summary of Sources

As already mentioned, despite her extraordinarily interesting biography, her brilliant contributions to Thai Buddhist literature, her donation of historically significant Buddhist edifices, and her closeness to a number of the most well-known and influential Buddhist monks of her time, there is hardly any surviving historical evidence on Khunying Damrongthammasan's life. (Khunying is an honorific title; she is often more informally called Khunying Yai and in the following I will also use this designation.)

One possible reason for this may be found in the fact that she died in the turmoil of World War II. Another—possibly much more important—reason, however, seems to be that she appears to have been a humble person who did not want her life and religious work to become well known (see previous section). The lack of sources has made the study of her life rather difficult. For this reason, some biographical details that will be presented in this section are, at the moment at least, often not entirely clear and sometimes even based on inconsistent evidence. A substantial amount of data derives from interviews with people who either met Khunying Yai or possess relevant knowledge based on what they learned from people who had been close to her.[55] Some important biographical details stem from documents of a case in 1937 at the Supreme Court of Thailand. The following life account together with the discussion of her religious impact makes clear as to why a study of her life has been long overdue and is important for a better and more complete understanding of Thai Buddhist intellectual history, Buddhist literature, and gender in Thai Buddhism.

Family Background and Life before Renunciation

Khunying Yai was born in 1882[56] as the only daughter of the nobles Phraya Kasetraksa (Chuang), minister of agriculture, and Khunying Kasetraksa. She married the senior official Phraya Damrongthammasan (Sang Wisetsiri, 1867–1940), a famous judge who also belonged to the nobility. Their only child, a boy, died at a very young age. However, Khunying Yai took care of and developed a close relationship with Prasop Wisetsiri, her husband's son by another wife. Prasop became her adopted child (*luk buntham*). Khunying Yai lived in a very privileged social stratum, and it has been reported that she was close to the royal family of King Rama VI (r. 1910–25). Her family must have been very rich, owning much property in central Bangkok. In Bangkok's Chinatown Khunying Yai and her husband owned the tallest building of its kind in Thailand at that time, a seven-story building that still stands. Their wealth allowed them to donate plots of land to a number of important temples. Her adopted son, Prasop Wisetsiri, has childhood memories of Khunying Yai collecting the rent from the many properties she owned. Throughout her life Khunying Yai suffered from pain that was probably related to an extreme form of diabetes. She must have concealed her physical suffering well, as only people close to her were aware of her pain.

It has been orally transmitted that Khunying Yai once had a dream about a distinctive location with unique features near the sea. A friend helped her identify this place in the southern province of Prachuap Khiri Khan. The location she dreamed about was the prominent Khao Chong Krachok hill with a height of 245 meters, located right next to the Gulf of Thailand, offering a marvelous view of the seascape and coastline. In 1922, together with her husband, Khunying Yai donated a plot of land next to the hill for the construction of a monastic setting that was to become the famous royal monastery Wat Thammikaram. One year later, King Rama VI himself went there to observe the construction work on the monastery, and he also made donations to it. Nowadays, albeit in a new setting not far from the original one, Wat Thammikaram has become the largest and most important Dhammayuttika-nikāya monastery in the whole province of Prachuap Khiri Khan.[57]

FIGURE 4. The ordination hall of Wat Thammikaram, which Khunying Yai and her husband started to build in the 1920s

Buddhist Education and Practice

From the writings of Phra Thepsumethi (Yuak Cattamalo, 1914–2002), the revered and well-known abbot of the Ratchaburi temple Wat Sattanatpariwat, we know that Khunying Yai "from a very young age had a love for the study of Buddhist teaching." When she was no more than ten years old, she became a student of the famous meditation teacher Somdet Phra Wanarat (Thap, Buddhasiri, 1806–91), the abbot of the famous Bangkok temple Wat Somanat Wihan.

Later in life she became a student of the influential and high-ranking monk Somdet Phra Buddhaghosacariya (Jaroen Ñāṇavaro), abbot of Wat Thepsirin, also one of Bangkok's major temples. In the foreword to her cremation volume printed in 1946, some two years after her death,

Somdet Phra Buddhaghosacariya writes about his former student being able to memorize a huge number of central Pali canonical texts, such as the long *Mahāsatipaṭṭhāna-sutta* of more than thirty pages, both in Pali and Thai.

Phra Thepsumethi confirms this when he reports that Khunying Yai had a "profound and detailed" understanding of Buddhist doctrine and an unusual ability for remembering Buddhist texts. According to him, she was able to memorize the entire content of the famous Pali canonical book *Dhammapada*, which consists of 423 verses. However, Phra Thepsumethi not only praises Khunying Yai's scholarly skills (*pariyatti*) but also emphasizes her outstanding achievements as a practitioner of meditation. He reports that as a result of her advanced meditation, Khunying Yai was not only able to recollect her own former lives but also perceived the kammic consequences of other people's actions.

He also seems to have believed that Khunying Yai may have achieved supramundane states of mind. This is in line with oral accounts; it was believed that Khunying Yai had attained one of the four stages of awakening (i.e., that she was an *ariya-puggala*). In 1933 she was ordained as a *mae chi* by her teacher Somdet Phra Buddhaghosacariya at the Bangkok temple Wat Thepsirin. She remained in the white robes of a *mae chi* until her death in 1944.

After her ordination she spent most of her time at Wat Thammikaram, rigorously practicing meditation. She lived, however, not inside the monastery but next to it in a monastic dwelling (*kuṭī*) she had built. She entered the monastery every day in order to practice meditation and recite Buddhist texts in the ordination hall there.

An interesting and important element in her biography is her close long-term relationship with another female Buddhist practitioner, Khunnai Thang Kotchasut (1858–1944). Upāsika Ki Nanayon (Ko. Khao Suan Luang), one of the best-known female Thai Buddhist practitioners and meditation teachers, is reported to have stated that Khunnai Thang "practiced *dhamma* on a high level." Khunnai Thang's biography contains many similarities to that of Khunying Yai. In this way, Khunnai Thang "left her household life and built a hut in front of the Ratchaburi monastery Wat Sattanatpariwat." She spent the last thirty years of her life there, and her cremation volume tells us that she "studied and practiced Buddhism

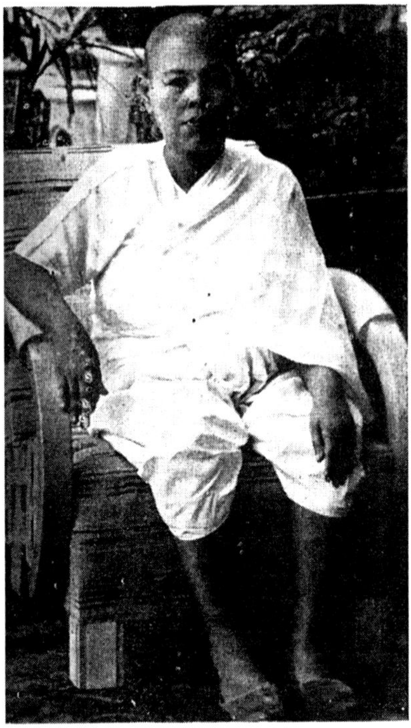

ชาตะ ๒๔๒๕ มรณะ ๒๔๘๗

FIGURE 5. Picture of Khunying Yai as *mae chi*, published in her cremation volume

rigorously [*yang khreng khrat*]. . . . It looked as if she was increasingly practicing Buddhism with increasing age. . . . In order to intensify her study of Buddhism, she increasingly was in contact with monks advanced in Buddhist practice, taking their practice as her guidance." She is also reported to have been a supporter of a large number of monks.[58]

There are numerous parallels in the biographies of Khunying Yai and Khunnai Thang: both have been acknowledged for their Buddhist practice and knowledge of Buddhist doctrine; both spent the final part of their lives in a monastic environment by having dwelling places constructed just outside a monastery; both studied Buddhism under the guidance of highly respected monks; and both have been described as extremely humble. Khunying Yai often met Khunnai Thang in her monastic dwelling in order to engage in conversation about Buddhism.

Both studied Buddhism with a small number of local Ratchaburi women who shared their deep interest in the study of Buddhism. This group of women met, probably regularly, in the evening in order to recite and discuss Buddhist texts and practice meditation. According to the biographical data available, like Khunnai Thang, Khunying Yai intensified her Buddhist practice toward the end of her life; it has been reported that she pursued solitary practice, mostly in the ordination hall of Wat Thammikaram, for whole days and nights.

Anonymous Authorship

As far as we know, during this final period of her life Khunying Yai did not produce any texts or give any public teachings. During the 1930s, however, she authored some remarkable texts; five of these have a dialogical format while others are poems in the traditional Thai verse meter *khlong si suphap*. Probably the first of her texts was published in relation to a 1931 writing competition on eight questions on the Buddhist teaching.[59] Laypeople and possibly also monks were asked to submit short essays on these questions. Prince Wiwitwanpricha, a son of King Rama IV and himself an author of texts on Buddhism, was asked to act as a judge in this competition. He decided that Khunying Yai gave the best answers to the questions on the level of *ek-u*. The expression *ek-u* probably derives from the Pali words *eka* (one) and *uttama* (highest, best) and may be translated as "most excellent one." Her short essays were published as a book with a number of other submissions to the competition

During the next ten years she published many texts on Buddhist doctrine, most of which are in a dialogical form while some are poems. The five dialogical texts she published between 1932 and 1934 now belong to the most well-known and widely disseminated texts of modern Thai Buddhism. They consist of profound dialogues on a variety of Buddhist teachings, repeatedly discussing various aspects of the "right practice" toward awakening, the various levels of awakening, and the ten *saṃyojana*s (fetters that bind human beings to rebirth). An unusual feature of these texts is that they contain numerous and precise references to Pali canonical scriptures, reflecting an enormously comprehensive and keen knowledge of Pali texts.

FIGURE 6. First editions of Khunying Yai's texts, which were published anonymously

However, what is interesting about these five texts is that it was decided to publish them anonymously. We do not know why Khunying Yai decided to do so and whether the decision to publish her texts anonymously was her own. We can only speculate about it; in fact, there may of course be not one single but a variety of reasons for this decision. As I have argued elsewhere, Khunying Yai "may have thought that people of her time considered it inappropriate for a woman to discuss Buddhist doctrine on such a profound level. After all, this work is, as far as we know, one of, or may be even, the first of its kind ever 'authored' by a Thai woman."[60] Another possible explanation may be that the conversations described in these texts had actually taken place in this or a similar form or at least prompted her ideas for these texts (which is indeed the impression the reader has when reading them), and Khunying Yai may have decided to keep these texts anonymous for this very reason. If true, the conversations on which the texts may be based may have taken place among the group of women who met at Wat Sattanatpariwat in order to discuss Buddhist teaching and practice. We may never know the real reason(s) for the absence of the author's name in the first publications.

Be that as it may, the decision to publish most of her texts anonymously has had some momentous implications for the history of the texts themselves. After their original publication in the 1930s these five texts have been republished in numerous different editions without people being aware of who authored the texts. Over the years they have become widely celebrated masterpieces of Thai Buddhist scholarship, and it was stated that "when considering the knowledge of and views on the *dhamma* expressed in these texts, it is likely that this is the writing of someone with a comprehensive and profound knowledge of Buddhist teaching [*pariyatti*] and practice [*paṭipatti*]."[61] Elsewhere, it was argued that "in order to be able to expound the Buddha's teaching so purely, the author [of these texts] must not only have had deep spiritual experiences in Buddhist practice but also possess literary skills with a clear and concise style in discussing the Buddha's teaching."[62]

The fact that these texts have been published several times over several decades without any author mentioned, together with the profound knowledge of Buddhist teaching they demonstrate, must have contributed to the authorship of these texts being attributed to Luang Pu Man, despite the fact that Luang Pu Man never claimed to have written them.[63] At the moment, it is not entirely clear how and when exactly the wrong attribution of authorship happened, but it must have occurred for the first time some forty years ago. Since then, however, numerous editions, sometimes with high circulation figures, mention Luang Pu Man as author of Khunying Yai's texts. Recently, together with my co-researcher Naris Charaschanyawong, I have been able to conclusively demonstrate that Khunying Yai is the real author of these texts.[64] With their profundity and the comprehensive Buddhist knowledge they demonstrate, it seems that these texts may be the first of their kind ever authored by a Thai woman.[65]

Death

After her dhammic compatriot Khunnai Thang passed away in 1944, Khunying Yai traveled to Ratchaburi to participate in the funeral. There, shortly after the funeral and probably in relation or as a consequence of her severe diabetes, she must have felt unwell. Oep Na Bangchang, one of the most famous physicians in Ratchaburi of his time, examined her health and concluded, "You will have a long life." To this Khunying Yai replied, "You do not need to comfort me," as if knowing that her death was imminent. At about eight o'clock that night, she asked a monk (or possibly several monks) to recite specific Buddhist texts for her and engage in a discussion about Buddhist doctrine with her. After this conversation, Khunying Yai said, "I am going now. I will relinquish my life right here." She prostrated herself three times in front of the monk(s), collapsed, and, to the disbelief of those present, died immediately.

Because this happened during World War II, her corpse was kept at Wat Sattanatpariwat until the end of the war, when it then was taken to Wat Thammikaram. There a simple cremation attended by 100–200 people was held on the beach in front of the ordination hall that she and her husband had built and in which she spent numerous days practicing meditation and reciting Buddhist texts. Senior monks from Bangkok and Ratchaburi attended the funeral. Her remains were taken to the Bangkok monastery Wat Thepsirin in 1946 for a second funeral rite but were eventually put into the base underneath the main Buddha image in the ordination hall of Wat Thammikaram. Only by squeezing into the narrow gap between the wall of the ordination hall and the base of the main Buddha image will visitors be able to see the plate with her name on it, which covers the compartment that contains her remains.

Mae Bunruean Tongbuntoem (1895–1964)

Summary of Sources

In contrast to the sparse availability of written sources on the life of Khunying Yai, there exists a huge amount of hagiographical texts on Mae Bunruean. For the following biographical account of her life (which is not always necessarily in chronological order) I have consulted most, if not all, of the major hagiographical accounts[66] about and the available sermon texts and letters by Mae Bunruean, as well as the posters displayed at various places in the Bangkok monastery Wat Awutwikasitaram during the research period.

In addition to this, I have made use of the numerous interviews I have conducted with monks, *mae chis*, professional amulet collectors (*sian phra*), and people who "possess faith" (*mi sattha*) in Mae Bunruean.[67] My account of her life is further informed by my own participant observation of devotional practices undertaken with belief in the sacredness of Mae

Bunruean, and my observations during visits to various sites of her veneration.[68]

These interviews and group interviews (up to five people) with Thai men and women who have faith in Mae Bunruean often occurred in circumstances that made them unsystematic and spontaneous. However, this method proved to be very productive as it allowed me to gather numerous ideas and anecdotes about Mae Bunruean or personal encounters with her (including postmortem encounters). In this way I was able to collect valuable additional hagiographical data that do not exist in printed form but have been transmitted orally among the faith community and a number of professional amulet collectors (most of whom also have strong faith in Mae Bunruean). Thus, I was able to explore why and how people revere Mae Bunruean.

In particular, the oral accounts show, as I demonstrate below, that Mae Bunruean's biography does not end with her death but goes far beyond the "end" of typical biographical texts. The interviews and participant observation also allowed me to gain a better understanding of how Mae Bunruean's hagiographies have been interpreted and which hagiographical elements have had the most significant impact on her followers' faith and religious practices. Thus, the following selection of the accounts on her life and hagiographical elements is based not only on an analysis of the hagiographical texts themselves but also to a large extent on how her followers ascribe importance to or interpret specific hagiographical accounts or characteristics of Mae Bunruean's sainthood and personality. For these reasons, the interviews and observations, even though not always explicitly mentioned and referred to, have been extremely revealing and provided valuable contextualization for my research.[69] Also, a substantial amount of material used derives from amulet magazines and online sources such as blogs, YouTube videos, and amulet websites.

Mae Bunruean's major biography was first published for her funeral in 1964, and it seems that many, if not all, of the biographies published later are based on this hagiography. When compared to other major hagiographical texts of modern Thai Theravada, this one is distinctive in that it was written not by one but by more than a hundred authors. What seems to be the main biography, a text comprising some twenty-seven pages, is embedded in some one hundred shorter texts of altogether more than 120 pages. In addition, sermon and written texts about Mae Bunruean by high-ranking monks have also been included. There are also a number of sermon and other texts authored by Mae Bunruean herself.

The main biographical text seems to be in line with biographical conventions by largely following the chronology of Mae Bunruean's life and work and being quite systematic in the way these are presented and discussed. The short texts are all written by different authors, who give brief accounts of individual encounters with Mae Bunruean or their experiences with her supernatural powers; these do not follow any apparent chronological order.

The size of these texts varies significantly; while some are no longer than eight lines, others cover several pages. Many of these texts end with the notation that it was written in order to testify to the supernatural occurrences that the author observed when with Mae Bunruean, a typical concluding sentence being, "Thus, I have written down [this account] as evidence so that I and others can worship [Khun Mae Bunruean]."[70] In this way, many of these short texts appear to be case studies of miraculous healings of a wide range of illnesses, in many cases, seemingly incurable.

Others give short accounts of other miraculous happenings. Thus some of them report that in an unusually short period of time Mae Bunruean was able to cover long distances on foot that a "normal" person could not have managed.[71] Several of these accounts also mention that despite walking unprotected in the rain Mae Bunruean did not become wet. Similarly, several people observed that mud would not defile her shoes in weather conditions where this would normally be the case. A number of these stories give details and circumstances of accidents during which the author's life was saved or serious physical injuries prevented thanks to the wearing of an amulet endowed with protective power by Mae Bunruean.

The beginning of this hagiographical process probably has to be sought in the initiative of the highly respected and high-ranking monk Phra Maharatchamangkhalajan (Thet, Niddesako, 1886–1967) of Wat Samphanthawong, whom Mae Bunruean regarded as her meditation teacher. It has been reported that when he became aware of an increasing number of rumors about Mae Bunruean's supernatural abilities, he asked people to write down their experiences and submit their accounts to him.

This seems to have happened in 1946.[72] These "accounts by witnesses of [her] spiritual practice" and miraculous abilities to heal were published twice in different formats in that year. Phra Maharatchamangkhalajan eventually organized a committee consisting of "knowledgeable monks and laypeople" to investigate these reports, ascertaining the "righteousness" (*khunnatham*) of these miracles and authenticating them. The conclusion of this investigation was that, according to authoritative Pali scriptures of Theravada Buddhism, these supernatural abilities "may" be possible for someone with advanced meditative achievements (*jhāna*).[73]

The hagiographical accounts of Mae Bunruean do not end, however, with her death in 1964. This is why, when I was interviewing her devotees, very often the interviewee talked about her as if she were still present and able to influence other people's lives through her supernatural powers. Some devotees even reported to me that Mae Bunruean appeared as an apparition or mental image (*nimit*) to her devotees. Others told me about miraculous healings that took place thanks to the beneficial power of Mae Bunruean, retained by objects she had consecrated.[74] Even after her death, in "chanting [their] wishes" (*suat kham athitthan*) her disciples ask her to "keep helping to protect us from any danger and from any illness, and be your children's impetus to be always successful in a righteous way."[75] The statues of her in the shrine devoted to her in Wat Awutwikasitaram are treated not merely as a reminder of Mae Bunruean but as if she is present. They are addressed by devotees as "Khun Mae [Bunruean]" and partly covered with gold leaves that devotees attach to them. Also, through

FIGURE 7. Mae Bunruean shrine in Wat Awutwikasitaram

these statues healing powers are invoked, and devotees make donations to and prostrate themselves in front of them. Touching them, so it is believed, may transfer beneficial energies. This of course reminds us of scholarly debates on the complex problem of the presence or absence of the Buddha in relics and images of him (see also chapter 4).[76]

Family Background

Mae Bunruean Tongbuntoem was born in the Bangkok district of Min Buri on March 10, 1895, into a poor family. Her father worked as a fruit gardener and was married three times. Mae Bunruean was the second child of his first marriage. The biographies tell us that she grew up in a loving and giving family. At the age of fifteen she developed a strong interest in traditional Thai massage. Her grandfather, himself a renowned masseur, gave her a massage manual and instructed her in Thai massage.

While still young, she received teachings in Buddhist doctrine from the famous meditation monk Luang Ta Phring, abbot of the monastery Wat Bangpakok, who was also her uncle. The biographies report that because of her meetings with Luang Ta Phring she developed a deep confidence in Buddhism and became inspired to pursue Buddhist practice.

When she was of "an appropriate age,"[77] Mae Bunruean married Police Corporal Joi Tongbuntoem, who was based in a police station near the renowned Bangkok monastery Wat Samphanthawong. Their marriage is described as "smooth" (*riap roi / rap ruen*), and it has been reported that Mae Bunruean's husband tried to please his wife. Since they did not have any children of their own they adopted a girl. Mae Bunruean was a skilled tailor and traditional midwife (*mo tamyae*). She also treated people by massaging them without charge.

Buddhist Practice

Mae Bunruean led a religious life that was characterized by living virtuously, keeping the Buddhist precepts, chanting religious texts, making offerings to the local temple, and studying the Buddha's teaching (*dhamma*). Nevertheless, the biographies describe her as rather "tough," "resolute," and "speaking with a loud voice." It is reported that she even used physical force to convey the meaning of Buddhist teachings, such as by slapping (*top*) or kicking the backside (*te kon*) of a disciple (*luk sit*).

This was perceived as a Zen method of teaching that was to help others to gain "sudden" (*chap phlan*) understanding.[78]

When still married, she took up the practice of meditation. Inspired by the *dhamma* teaching that she listened to in the nearby monastery Wat Samphanthawong, she eventually became a *mae chi* in 1927 in that very same monastery. It is reported that during her first time as an "ordained *mae chi*" (*buat pen chi*), she achieved excellent results as a consequence of her determined meditation practice; not only did she develop the four *jhāna*s (mental states of meditative absorption), but also taking these highly concentrative states of mind as a "ladder" she was able to attain (the six) *abhiññā*s ("super-knowledge": supernatural powers, divine ear, ability to read another's mind, recollection of former lives, divine eye, and knowledge of the ending of mental intoxicants[79]). The available biographies are unanimous in agreeing that she achieved the four *jhāna*s, but some are less specific when referring to her achievements with regard to the *abhiññā*s; in some life accounts it is only mentioned that she achieved "*abhiññā*." Here it is not further specified as to which and how many she is believed to have attained. This vagueness of some biographies is quite significant, as the achievement of the sixth *abhiññā* is tantamount to the attainment of arahantship, which according to traditional Theravada teaching a layperson can reach but then must either pass away or become ordained on that very same day. I will discuss this interesting point in detail in the next chapter.

It is not entirely clear how long she stayed in the robes of a *mae chi* probably for only a few months. Anyway, it has been reported that after she disrobed, she agreed with her husband that she should practice the eight Buddhist precepts (*sin paet*), which include abstaining from unchaste conduct (i.e., from sexual activity). In 1936 her husband lost his life in a fire at the age of forty-two. She never remarried. At one point she was reordained as a *mae chi* temporarily.

Mae Bunruean's Supernatural Powers and Popularity

It is reported that the first of many—and arguably one of her most famous—supernatural occurrences is reported to have happened in 1927, when she returned from Wat Samphanthawong to her home. The account here is reminiscent of the Buddha's own biography:

> During that night, she could not sleep. Her husband and adopted child, both asleep, were gnashing their teeth and snoring. She felt dhammically agitated [*dhamma-saṃveja*] and weary [*buea*]. Therefore, she made a vow [*tangsat athitthan*; literally to establish (oneself in) truth and make a vow] to enter the pavilion [of Wat Samphanthawong]. When she ended her vowing, [she realized that] she had arrived inside the pavilion in accordance with her vow. She was not able to explain how she was able to leave her room and enter the pavilion.[80]

The way the hagiographical accounts describe her leaving her family during that night is interesting: looking at her sleeping family she perceived the weariness of life ("gnashing teeth"). This "watershed moment"[81] is a recurring theme in Thai Buddhist literature and Thai temple murals; not only the Buddha himself but also some of his male disciples are believed to have left their family during the night after being dhammically agitated (*saṃvega*) when they look at their wife or harem and become weary or disgusted.[82] The story goes that when asked by skeptical friends to perform the miracle (*patihan*) again, she demonstrated her supernatural ability by once more miraculously appearing inside the locked pavilion for witnesses so that they could verify this.

The hagiographies describe numerous further miracles that Mae Bunruean was able to perform, and explain that this ability was due to the enormous mental powers that she possessed as a result of her high spiritual attainments. Thanks to these powers and spiritual accomplishments she was also able to miraculously endow objects, like stones, mangoes, oranges, water, and peppercorns, with positive, protective, and curative energies. Once charged with beneficial energy, these objects are reported to have been used by Mae Bunruean's devotees to heal ailments, such as cancer, tuberculosis, kidney disease, and so forth.

Mae Bunruean very quickly became famous thanks to her effective healing. The hagiographies recount that she was able to heal people whom doctors could not help. Thus, we can read that she used her "divine ear" (*hu thip*) and "divine eye" (*ta thip*) to diagnose accurately patients' illnesses. Mae Bunruean not only gave massages as a means of curing people but also used the power of her vows (*athitthan*) and objects she charged with positive energy.

In particular, her enormous power of asseveration (*athitthan*), which she and her followers used to relieve people from hardship and prevent misfortune, figures prominently in many hagiographical accounts and has arguably become the most important characteristic of her sainthood. Mae Bunruean's hagiographies report that with her enormous powers she was able to affect inanimate things—for example by endowing objects with energies, making the rain stop, or making illnesses disappear. People believe that her extremely pure, highly developed practice and intent allowed her to use the power of her words as an "act of truth" (*sacca-kiriyā*) to make these things happen miraculously.

This is reminiscent of the extremely well-known Buddhist story of the former ruthless killer, Aṅgulimāla, who became a fully awakened one (arahant) after being converted by the Buddha. The Pali canon reports that Aṅgulimāla relieved a pregnant woman from her childbirth pains by invoking the truth, "Sister, since I was born with the noble birth [*ariyāya jātiyā jāto*], I do not recall that I have ever intentionally deprived a living being of life. By this truth, may you be well and may your infant be well."[83] This utterance became the popular *Aṅgulimāla-Paritta* (protective mantra) which is often chanted by Thai Buddhist monks and is believed, along with some other canonical texts, to possess healing or protective powers.[84] It is also reported that her supernatural powers allowed Mae Bunruean to perceive the spirit of a dead person waiting for rebirth.

One of her most famous miracles took place in 1951 when, according to her hagiographical texts, she used the power of her wishing (*athitthan*) to cause a young mango tree, which had been planted only thirteen months before, to blossom overnight in a season in which these trees normally do not do so (*phit wela ruedukan*). Here, she made the following vow: "If Buddhism will prosper in the future, let this mango tree blossom [*ok cho*]."[85] Some of her hagiographies tell us that numerous witnesses observed this miracle and are able to certify that it really happened.

Mae Bunruean's mango-tree miracle bears similarities with a lesser-known miracle performed by the Buddha when he was challenged by heretics (*titthiyā*). This story is told in the birth story number 483 and the commentary text of the *Dhammapada*. Here the Buddha miraculously had a mango tree instantaneously grow from a mango seed.[86]

Mae Bunruean was not only revered because of the healing and supernatural powers and insights that people believe she had. In addition, the hagiographies emphasize her homiletic skills, which were based on a deep and thorough understanding of Buddhist doctrine. People flocked to her *dhamma* talks, many of which were later printed in books. Her biographies also recount that Mae Bunruean imbued amulets and Buddha statues with positive energies and was involved in supporting Buddhist temples through fundraising.

The number of her followers constantly increased, and she eventually established the religious group Samakkhiwisutthi, which met regularly between 1949 and 1955 in a house her followers built for her so that they could practice meditation and chant Pali texts with her, ask for cures, or listen to her Buddhist teachings. It is reported that numerous people "became interested in Buddhism and abandoned wrong and wrongful behavior"[87] because of their encounters with Mae Bunruean.

She also repeatedly traveled to numerous provinces in all of the major parts of Thailand in order to cure sick people. An indication of her widespread popularity during her lifetime is that when she visited the distant town of Udon Thani in 1953 she was welcomed by a large crowd of people at the railway station.[88] She never accepted any money as payment for her treatments, and she helped people regardless of their social status. Thus her many followers not only came from all over Thailand but also included people from all social strata, including descendants of the royal family, soldiers, policemen, officials, and merchants. There were even monks who regarded themselves as admirers or followers (*luk sit*) of Mae Bunruean.

Even though Mae Bunruean shaved her head in order to indicate her religious practice based on Buddhist precepts (*sīla*), in contrast to Thai *mae chi*s she wore light green and grey, yellowish, or brownish clothes. It is reported that Mae Bunruean did not decide to become a permanent *mae chi*, because she thought that she would then have to follow the rules of the Saṅgha Supreme Council. This, however, "would make it difficult for her to use her supernatural powers to help people."[89]

Her biographies indicate that with increasing age the way she led her life became more and more similar to that of the monks, as regulated by their monastic code (*vinaya*). In this way, toward the end of her life she decided, for example, neither to touch men older than seven years of age nor to ask for any consumer goods.

Mae Bunruean's Kammically Inscribed Body

As expressed in the words of the forest monk and famous meditation master Luang Pu Thet, "a basic tenet of the Buddha's teachings is that the mind and body work together, but that the body lies under the control of the mind."[90] In line with this idea, a frequent theme in Thai hagiographical literature concerns the anomalies in the saint's body as markers of spiritual purity or consequences of past *kamma*.[91] Another recurring hagiographical element related to this theme is the physical inviolability resulting from advanced mind powers.

In Mae Bunruean's hagiographies these themes form a major element as well. As I will discuss in more depth in chapter 4, in the eyes of her devotees Mae Bunruean's advanced spiritual achievements and her supernatural powers have become objectified not only in the Phra Phuttho amulets that she produced but also postmortem in her crystallized relics. However, even during her lifetime her spiritual superiority had become manifest to her devotees in her body. These kinds of physical manifestations depicted in Mae Bunruean's hagiographies can be related to similar occurrences described in the Pali literature.

The body of the Buddha famously bore the "thirty-two marks of a great man" (*dvattiṃsamahāpurisalakkhaṇāni*), which the Buddha had acquired as "the effect of countless lifetimes of virtuous deeds" and which made visible the Buddha's extraordinariness.[92] In the *Lakkhaṇa-sutta* it is explained that due to the Buddha's practice in former lifetimes, neither dust nor dirt would stick to his body in his present lifetime.[93] Having just achieved the first level of awakening, the skin color of one of the Buddha's foremost monks, Sāriputta, is described as "pure" and "bright."[94] There are many more examples in the Pali canon showing that spiritual attainment can become manifest in the saint's body. As mentioned above, the hagiographical tropes of Mae Bunruean's bodily purity frequently occur in her biographies; Mae Bunruean's body is defiled neither by rain nor by mud. In addition to this, her skin is described as impenetrable when a dog tried to bite her; whereas all other victims of this dog were left with bleeding wounds, only Mae Bunruean's skin was not damaged at all.[95] For the hagiographical element of invulnerability of the body as a consequence and manifestation of advanced spiritual attainment, there are also precedents in the Pali literature. According to Pali commentary texts, the laywoman Uttarā, for example, remained unhurt when the prostitute Sirimā threw a pot of boiling oil onto her head. The oil felt "like cold water" to Uttarā as a result of her virtue.[96]

Interestingly, however, in the eyes of her devotees, Mae Bunruean's body not only became a physical manifestation of her superior morality but also at the same time objectified and made visible her ambivalent *kamma* from previous lives. Her hagiographies tell us that due to her significantly advanced meditative achievements Mae Bunruean was able to recollect former lives. Thus, Mae Bunruean told her disciples that in one rebirth, some thousand years previously, she had been reborn as a daughter of a king of Chiang Mai (*phra jao Chiang Mai*). At the age of ten she participated in a ceremony during which the golden spire of a *cetiya* (bell-shaped Buddha shrine) was cast. While the material was melting she secretly added one of her golden ankle bracelets to the melting pot as a meritorious act. As a consequence of this, her nursemaid was punished as she was deemed responsible for the loss of the bracelet. Since the princess remained silent (*choei sia*) during this, as a kammic consequence Mae Bunruean had been reborn into a poor family in her present life.

The goodness (*anisong*) of her donating the bracelet, however, so the story goes, caused the appearance of marks on the sole of her left foot that resembled a *cetiya* and a flag. Only at the age of sixty did Mae Bunruean reveal these auspicious marks to her disciples. Printings of these marks on her foot were later reproduced on posters and postcards, which devotees display in their houses in order to prevent evil energies from entering the house. In this way, while not only believed to be magically efficacious, pictures of her kammically inscribed body also remind her followers of basic principles of the Buddhist kammic law, according to which no intentional action, however fleeting, is without its consequences.

Again there exist precedents in Pali literature for this episode. Khujjuttarā, one of Buddha's foremost female lay followers, made fun of a hunchbacked *pacceka-buddha*—one who achieved full awakening by himself but does not teach the *dhamma*—in one of her former lifetimes and was reborn disabled with a hunchback herself. This theme of physical manifestations as a consequence of a pure mind or *kamma* from previous lifetimes is not only recurrent in Pali literature but unsurprisingly is also frequently found in hagiographical literature of male saints in modern Thai Buddhism.

In this way, for her devotees Mae Bunruean's body has not only become the source of supernatural, apotropaic powers but also a homiletic device that demonstrates and authenticates the universal validity of Buddhist teaching.

Death and Funeral

Starting in 1963, Mae Bunruean's health began to deteriorate, and in the following year she suffered from kidney problems, anemia, and high blood pressure. Against the will of her followers, she refused to see a doctor or seek medical treatment in a hospital. For nine months her illness confined her to bed. Again against the will of her disciples, she declined to use on herself the supernatural powers she had used so often to help others, explaining, "If I would use [my ability to make supernatural] vows [*athitthan*] in order to help myself, it would mean I want to be alive, want to be happy, want to meet new things in the world [*phi phop*]. This all [however] would be [an expression] of mental defilements [*kilesa*]. I cannot do this."[97] These words were interpreted as a manifestation of her fully awakened status.

By the beginning of September 1964, her health had deteriorated significantly. She hardly ate anything and had great difficulty talking, as her throat filled with sticky phlegm. Many weeks before, Mae Bunruean had ordered her disciples to stop the big clocks in her house shortly after eleven in the morning. At 11:20 a.m. on September 7, 1964, she "entirely peacefully" and "without any sign of worries" passed away at exactly "the time she ordered the big clocks to be stopped, as if she had known the time of her death."[98] Knowing the time of one's death in advance is also a recurring theme in Buddhist literature. Famously, as the *Mahāparinibbāna-sutta* recounts, the Buddha knew that he would pass away in three months' time. Similarly, this trope can often be found in hagiographical texts about Thai monks; Luang Pu Man, for example, is reported to have accurately predicted some thirteen years before his death how long his life would last.[99]

Hearing the news of Mae Bunruean's death has been described as a hugely traumatic experience for her many disciples, who had utmost devotion and love for their leader, whom they not only regarded as a teacher and healer but also as a mother figure (*khun mae*). The way her hagiographies describe her equanimity when faced with imminent death, and her refusal to prolong her life by using her supernatural powers, demonstrated to her devotees that she had completely given up any attachment to life and had no fear of dying. This reminds us of fully awakened saints described in the Pali canon, such as the Buddha himself or Upasena, who, when bitten by a poisonous snake, shows that he "has abandoned all clinging to life and for whom death is nothing to be afraid of . . . but is just the end of [the cycle of rebirth]."[100]

Mae Bunruean's funeral ceremonies were attended by a number of high-ranking monks, such as Somdet Phra Buddhaghosacariya (Wat, Vāsano) of Wat Rajabophit and Phra Ratchayandilok, who gave sermons in front of the coffin, praising Mae Bunruean's Buddhist practice. On this occasion Somdet Phra Buddhaghosacariya (Wat), who ten years later became the supreme patriarch of the Thai *saṅgha*, said that Mae Bunruean "had enormous mind powers [*kamlang jitjai khemkhaeng*] due to her marvelous [*na atsajan*] Buddhist practice." Her meditation teacher Phra Maharatchamangkhalajan (Thet, Niddesako), himself a high-ranking monk, wrote an obituary for her in which he abundantly praised her exceptional understanding and teaching of Buddhist doctrine.

Her body was cremated in the Bangkok monastery Wat That Thong on October 25 of the same year. It has been reported that during her cremation her remains turned into relics, which in Thai Buddhism is regarded as an extremely rare event, particularly for a woman.[101] Immediately after her funeral the relics were distributed in small, flat cases (*talap*) inscribed with "*nibbāna* element" (*that nipphan*). The transformation, during which parts of the dead body turn into crystallized objects, is believed to happen in cases of people who are believed to have achieved full awakening (see chapter 4). Right up to the present day her followers have come together every Sunday to commemorate the goodness and life of Mae Bunruean at Wat Awutwikasitaram.[102]

Mae Chi Kaew Sianglam (1901–91)

Summary of Sources

The biographical details of the life of Mae Chi Kaew presented in the following section derive from a variety of sources, most notably from an increasing number of printed hagiographies and also from sermons and talks by the famous and extraordinarily influential forest monk Luang Ta Mahabua Ñāṇasampanno, who played a significant role in the life of Mae Chi Kaew.[103]

Information on the life of Mae Chi Kaew is also taken from the bilingual tables (English and Thai) that are attached to the walls in the museum on the ground floor of her *stūpa* in Ban Huai Sai. I have also relied upon the MP3 CD-ROMs of talks in the Thai and Phu Thai languages by Phra Ajan Inthawai Santussako (who had a long and close relationship with Mae Chi Kaew and has been centrally involved in various projects to spread and promote her reputation).

My own interviews with a number of key informants have also been an important source. I interviewed *mae chi*s who had lived with or been inspired by Mae Chi Kaew, monks who had known her particularly well or were involved in the publication of her biographies or the construction of her *stūpa* in Ban Huai Sai, and laypeople whose understanding of Thai Buddhism has been influenced by Mae Chi Kaew's life story.[104] In addition, I visited various places that are important in Mae Chi Kaew's life story or have become places of veneration for her—notably Ban Huai Sai, where she lived and where various memorials to her have been erected. During these visits I studied the religious symbolism that has developed as an expression of her veneration.

Family Background and Early Childhood

Mae Chi Kaew Sianglam was born on November 8, 1901, in the village Ban Huai Sai, Amphoe Khamcha-i, in the northeastern Thai province of Mukdahan.[105] She was the youngest of six children and was given the name Tapai. When Tapai was four years old her mother died, and several years later her father, a local magistrate, remarried. In common with people in her village, Tapai belonged to the Phu Thai ethnic group.[106] It is reported that the first of the many supernatural occurrences in her life took place when she was only one year old and she had a vision (*nimit*) of a divine horse that visited her in order to persuade her to accompany it to a heavenly city. The hagiographies also tell us that when she was between five and six years old she was able to recollect past lives and therefore became renowned for her ability to enter highly concentrative states of mind (*jhāna*) from a very early age.

It is reported that in another vision—one of the most famous of her many mental images—she recalled a former life during which she was reborn as a chicken with many chicks, two of which were later reborn as humans in her current lifetime and became famous monks of the Thai forest tradition. The story goes that as a chicken mother, she had to face extreme hardship in the constant search for food not only for herself but also for her many chicks. Once, while listening to the sound of the *dhamma* (here meaning the Buddha's teaching) during a sermon, however, her mind became joyful. This incident allowed her to make a resolution (*athitthan*) to escape the realm of animals (*tiracchāna*) and to be reborn as a human being.

In the influential *Visuddhimagga*, one of the most representative and authoritative texts of the Theravada tradition and authored by the fifth-century Theravada scholar Buddhaghosa, we can find a similar story; while the Buddha was teaching the people of Campā, a frog listened and was killed by a cowherd who inadvertently put a stick through the frog's head. The frog was instantantly reborn in the Buddhist heaven of Tāvatiṃsa. The reason for this favorable rebirth was, so we can read in the *Visuddhimagga*, "none other than his perception of a (special) quality in the Buddha's voice."[107] Similar stories about bats, a deer, a fish, and a snake can be found in later postcanonical Theravada scriptures as well.[108]

Tapai's father, concerned that others might regard her as insane (*sia sati*), warned her not to mention her supernatural experiences. Later in life, Mae Chi Kaew recounted that as a girl she could go to the monastery only in the company of her parents, and that she had to sit as far as possible away from monks. In contrast to this, however, as Barend Jan

Terwiel notes, boys are "not kept away from monks. On the contrary, parents often like to present their small sons to a monk when they meet and note with approval how their children are touched and blessed."[109]

Encountering the Great Master

In 1917, the village of Khamcha-i was visited by the two foremost meditation masters of the Thai forest tradition, Luang Pu Sao Kantasīlo and Luang Pu Man Bhūridatto, together with some seventy of their disciples (*luk sit*), many of whom later became famous and influential meditation masters (such as Luang Pu Dun Atalo, Luang Pu Lui Candasāro, Luang Pu Khao Anālayo, and Luang Pu Thet Desaraṅsī).[110] Tapai's encounter with Luang Pu Sao and Luang Pu Man is described as the catalyst that led to her strong interest in Buddhist teaching and practice. Her faith in Luang Pu Man must have been quite profound from the very beginning, as Tapai donated a plot of land to him shortly after their first encounter.

Her hagiographies tell us that one night, following Luang Pu Man's instruction on meditation and having developed deep concentration, Tapai had another vision, in which she watched her own body getting older and deteriorating until eventually she died. Her corpse was then consumed by maggots, and only her skeleton remained. While convinced of her own death during this vision, she worried that she would not be able to donate food to Luang Pu Man the next morning. The vision continued, however: after villagers had taken her corpse to the cemetery, Luang Pu Man arrived and touched parts of her body with a stick. Whichever body part was touched by the stick rotted away until only her heart remained. Luang Pu Man picked up her heart, saying that it was indestructible. After regaining consciousness the next morning, Tapai was disappointed as she believed she had had a dream instead of having practiced proper meditation. After having reported to Luang Pu Man the content of her "dream," however, she was told by him that this was not a dream but a vision; instead of failing in meditation, she had actually made extraordinary progress in her meditation practice. During the rainy season of that year, Luang Pu Man paid special attention to Tapai's meditational progress and visions. When asked why Tapai was able to achieve such rapid progress in meditation, Luang Pu Man explained, "This young girl practiced meditation in many former lives, which is the reason why the principle of the impermanence of all conditioned things [*aniccā vata saṅkhārā*] had so deeply and completely been ingrained in her mind."[111]

When Luang Pu Man and the cohort of his disciples were about to leave Ban Huai Sai in order to pursue *dhutaṅga* practices (austere practices)[112] elsewhere, he addressed Tapai. On what followed, there are at least two different accounts, which might not necessarily be seen as contradictory. One account has it that Luang Pu Man said to Tapai, "If you were a boy, I would have ordained you as a novice so that you could have come with me. But since you are a girl, accompanying me would be difficult with regard to the *dhammavinaya* [the teaching (*dhamma*) and monastic regulations (*vinaya*) of the Buddha]. . . . Stop practicing meditation!" Luang Pu Man, so some accounts explain, wanted her first to "use up" her *kamma* as a layperson before eventually meeting a suitable teacher in the future, when she would be able to continue with her meditation practice. According to another account, however, before leaving Ban Huai Sai, Luang Pu Man asked Tapai whether she wanted to join him as an ordained one (*buat*). Tapai's older sibling did not give her permission to become ordained, arguing that if Tapai were not able to remain ordained, it would be difficult for her to find a husband once she returned to lay life.[113] Luang Pu Man then prophesied that she would be a layperson for another twenty years before eventually becoming ordained. He then forbade her to continue with her meditation practice, as her mind was too "venturesome" (*lot phon*) and without Luang Pu Man's instructions and guidance she might go insane (*pen ba sia sati dai*).[114]

Prolonged Life as a Householder

As there was no local school Tapai did not learn how to write, although she was able to acquire reading skills. In all the available life accounts, Tapai is consistently described as having been humble, frugal, hardworking, and highly perseverant. She possessed many traditional skills, such as basket-making and weaving. She was knowledgeable with regard to local herbs and planted mulberry for raising silkworms. At the age of seventeen, following the wish of her parents, Tapai married Bunma Sianglam despite having no interest in married life. She did not become pregnant, but in the tenth year of their marriage they adopted a daughter, whom they named Kaew (the villagers then began to call Tapai "Mae Kaew" which translates as "mother of Kaew").

Bunma forbade his wife to practice meditation at the local temple and only permitted her to participate in Buddhist chanting (*suat mon*) and to donate alms food for the monks in the morning. At the age of thirty-four, once her adopted daughter was able to take care of herself, Tapai asked Bunma for permission to be ordained (*buat*). Two years later, after repeated requests and the supportive mediation of a widely respected uncle, her husband eventually allowed her to become ordained as a *mae chi* on the condition that after one rainy season (*vassa*) she would return to lay life.

In 1937, Mae Kaew at the age of thirty-six was ordained as a *mae chi* at the local temple. After twenty years of refraining from meditation practice, she was now able to devote her energy to prolonged sessions of walking and sitting meditation. Though ordained, she occasionally went to her former home to undertake household chores. At the end of the rainy season Mae Chi Kaew did not want to disrobe as she saw that her husband was, despite their earlier mutual agreement, flirting with women, gambling, and consuming opium. Unwilling to return to lay status, on the first day after the *vassa* she pretended to have disrobed by wearing dark clothes on top of her white robes and returning to her house to carry out household chores while still keeping the eight precepts. When she tried to go back to the monastery, her husband asked her to eat with him, which she could not do without breaking the precept of not consuming solid food after noon. When her husband tried to grab her arm, she ran away. Her "very angry" husband who had known she wanted to return to the monastery followed her with the intention of bringing her back to the house.[115] While she was trying to escape, Mae Chi Kaew's outer clothes slipped off. Two elder brothers of Mae Chi Kaew came to help by holding the husband back so that she could finally reach the monastery. After this incident, Mae Chi Kaew decided never to disrobe and to terminate her relationship with Bunma.

Life as a Renunciant

Mae Chi Kaew spent the years between 1938 and 1945 on a mountain some thirty kilometers away from Ban Huai Sai, practicing meditation intensively in a physically demanding environment that tested her resolution. During this time, the hagiographies tell us, she had numerous supernatural experiences, such as teaching the *dhamma* to *nāga*s (mythical snakes), encountering ghosts (*phi*), and conversing with the spirits of dead animals.

In 1945, Mae Chi Kaew returned to Ban Huai Sai and built an independent nunnery there. There were no more than eight *mae chi*s residing in the nunnery. Apart from being materially underresourced, a major obstacle for this small *mae chi* community headed by Mae Chi Kaew was the absence of a teacher. Mae Chi Kaew had to seek out disciples of Luang Pu Man, and in the process stayed for a two-year period with the renowned meditation teachers Luang Pu Fan Ācāro and Luang Pu Kongma Cirapuñño. Visiting Ajan Man himself entailed much hardship, as the *mae chi*s had to face a difficult journey of up to twelve days in order to receive meditation instruction from the master. Also, it seems that her visits to Luang Pu Man were perceived by his lay followers as disruptive.

All the life accounts stress the close relationship between Mae Chi Kaew and Luang Pu Man. It is reported that when Luang Pu Man became seriously ill he visited her in vision, flying through the sky and hovering in the air in order to let her know that his death (*nipphan*) was imminent. Even during the night he passed away in 1949,[116] Luang Pu Man flew to Mae Chi Kaew to tell her that she missed the opportunity to see him alive again, despite his previous visits during which he had invited her to do so. Prior to the radio announcement of the great teacher's death she had already burst into tears.

In 1950 one of the major disciples of Luang Pu Man, Luang Ta Mahabua arrived in Ban Huai Sai. Luang Ta Mahabua, who is widely believed to have achieved arahantship in 1950, realized that Mae Chi Kaew was too captivated by her meditative abilities and therefore unable to make further substantial progress toward *nibbāna*. Luang Ta Mahabua recounts,

> [I told Mae Chi Kaew] to by no means go outside [in her meditation]. I had to take these measures so that she would develop knowledge about the inside. These things [being able to have visions, perceive ghosts, and visit heavens and hells] are knowledge about the outside and not the inside. It is not

> understanding mental defilements [*kilesa*]. She had to study the inside in order to be able to get rid of her mental defilements. But she did not comply. She argued with *me*, her teacher [*ajan*]. When this happened, I chased her away saying, 'Go. . . . Go away . . . There are no philosophers here.' Crying, she departed"[117]

This harsh method of instruction eventually succeeded, however. Mae Chi Kaew was able to overcome her "stubbornness" and understood that her supernatural abilities were not really conducive to her spiritual progress. Following Luang Ta Mahabua's instructions, Mae Chi Kaew changed her meditation technique, by now observing the inner aspects of her mind and body without letting herself be distracted by the kinds of visions she had experienced before.

Horrific Deconstructions of the Body

The kinds of horrific deconstructions of her body that Mae Chi Kaew was repeatedly experiencing during her meditational exercises are particularly remarkable and often accentuated in the hagiographies. In addition to the above mentioned vision in which she experienced the decay and decomposing of her own body, the various life accounts contain further mental images in which Mae Chi Kaew sees her body decaying or even "methodically chop[ped] . . . to pieces. Slashing repeatedly with the sharp knife, [Luang Ta Mahabua] dismembered her whole body; cutting it into smaller and smaller fragments. . . . [He] dissected each part further until nothing remained of her body except a disjointed heap of flesh, bones and sinews."[118]

In her meditation practice Mae Chi Kaew dissected the various bodily organs and parts of her own body, and she thereby "understood that the entire body was disgusting and repulsive."[119] These hagiographical elements are both in language and content reminiscent of life accounts of female saints of early Buddhism (and certainly deserve a more thorough comparative investigation); the former courtesans Ambapālī and "Abhaya's mother" (Padumavātī) objectified their own bodies to study their decay and foulness (*asubha*). They received their meditation instructions from members of the male *saṅgha*. Vimalā, another former courtesan, received an "anatomy lesson" from one of the Buddha's foremost disciples when

Mahāmoggallāna, whom she had tried to seduce, said to her, "Oh you skeletal hut of bone plastered over with flesh and tendons."[120]

Attainment of Awakening

Her hagiographies tell us that not long after having started to practice under the guidance of the great master Luang Ta Mahabua, at dawn on November 1, 1952, while resting from practicing walking meditation (*doen jongkrom*) Mae Chi Kaew was able to attain full awakening (*banlu tham khan sungsut*):

> She felt tired from having done walking meditation for the whole night and therefore sat down on a bamboo platform under a phayom tree to get some rest. While reclining in order to lie down and thinking, "I will rest for a moment and then boil rice," she perceived a rumbling noise as if lightning were hitting the platform on which she was resting. At the same time, there was a noise saying, "The rebirths have come to an end!" Her tears were flowing copiously in joy.[121]

After this event, Mae Chi Kaew followed Luang Ta Mahabua to various provinces in Thailand, took care of his mother, and helped him build his famous monastery, Wat Pa Ban Tat in Udon Thani Province. In 1967 Mae Chi Kaew returned to Ban Huai Sai and spent most of the last twenty-four years of her life in her nunnery. Between 1973 and 1977, in the company of other *mae chi*s and villagers from Ban Huai Sai, she paid numerous visits to famous meditation masters in Thailand's Northeast in order to exchange knowledge. These travels also allowed her to build up a network of practicing *mae chi*s of the forest tradition.

Throughout her ordained life, Mae Chi Kaew pursued Theravada's so-called "austere practices" (*dhutaṅga*), such as eating only once a day and wearing robes made of cloth used to cover dead bodies. Such *dhutaṅga* practices are the "hallmark of the wandering forest monk."[122] She also consistently practiced the eight *sīla*s and the ten *kusala-kammapatha* (wholesome courses of action).[123]

Death and Funeral

In 1977, Mae Chi Kaew was diagnosed with tuberculosis, diabetes, and lung cancer. Despite her severe medical problems, she continued her disciplined meditation practice and strict adherence to monastic rules for the next fourteen years. Dr. Phensi Makaranon, who was her personal physician for the last fourteen years of her life, recounted,

> All those who had the opportunity to know and experience the real Mae Chi Kaew [*ong jing*], were deeply overwhelmed and impressed by her enormous humbleness and gentleness and how she always deeply appreciated the goodness [*bunkhun*] other people had done for her. She even held every medicine tablet [respectfully] above her head before taking it.[124]

Before Mae Chi Kaew's death, Luang Ta Mahabua visited her for the last time and instructed those who took care of her not to try to prolong her life artificially: "Let this old women go in a natural way. . . . She has been in this world not for herself. Don't interfere."[125] Mae Chi Kaew's last words before her death (*pacchimā vācā*) are reported to have been,

> Do not doubt in [the value] of [Buddhist] practice and do not be careless with it. Having practiced only a little is already a gain, for it is a reality to be understood by the individuals themselves. Be your own refuge. Reflect on yourself—who is being born, getting older, suffering, and dying. *Rūpa* [form] and *nāma* [name/mind], life does not belong to us. Do not defile yourself with *dukkha* [suffering]."[126]

According to the biographical accounts, Mae Chi Kaew passed away peacefully on June 18, 1991. The cremation, which was held in her nunnery five days after her passing, was attended by some two hundred monks, many *mae chi*s, and hundreds of laypeople. Luang Ta Mahabua ordered the omission of the usual funeral chanting (*suat matika bangsakun*),[127] explaining, "[Mae Chi Kaew] has done enough for herself."

In the Thai Buddhist religious system, it is believed that the chanting of these Abhidhamma texts generates merit (*bun*, Pali *puñña*) for the deceased. Luang Ta Mahabua's prohibition thus seems to imply that the generation of merit would not be required for Mae Chi Kaew as he was convinced that Mae Chi Kaew had already been fully awakened and therefore would not be reborn anymore; the intended recipient of the well-intentioned transfer of merit no longer existed but was utterly "extinguished" (*nibbāna*).

When Mae Chi Kaew's body had completely burned, a heavy rain started and doused the funeral pyre even though there had been a clear sky for the whole morning.[128] It is reported that some two to three years after her cremation parts of her remains crystallized (see chapter 4). In April 2006 a group of disciples of Mae Chi Kaew with the support of the well-known northeastern monk Phra Ajan Inthawai Santussako (abbot of Wat Pa Na Kham Noi) was able to complete a *cetiya/stūpa* some twenty-four meters high next to Mae Chi Kaew's nunnery (see fig. 15 in chapter 4).

The then Thai *saṅgha* supreme patriarch Somdet Phra Ñāṇasaṁvara named it Cetiya in Commemoration of the Triple Gem. The biographical accounts emphasize that this *cetiya* was built to commemorate the "victory" of "the fully awakened female follower of Buddha." On May 21, 2006, the *cetiya* was officially opened in a ceremony in which Luang Ta Mahabua enshrined parts of the crystallized remains of Mae Chi Kaew. On Sunday of the last week in March each year, her devotees hold a ceremony to recollect Mae Chi Kaew's work and achievements.

Mae Chi Nari Karun (1876/77–1999)

Summary of Sources

Mae Chi Nari Karun is not (yet) famous on a national level but is known and revered only among a rather small number of devotees and practitioners. There is a limited number of sources on her life. No cremation volume was produced for her well-attended funeral on August 12, 1999. However, in order to celebrate her life and spiritual achievements and motivate others "to take her spiritual practice as an example,"[129] the construction of a small museum is planned for the village of Ban Nongyang near the northeastern city Sakon Nakhon, where she spent the last years of her life. It is hoped that the publication of a small "pocket book" that contains her hagiography will help motivate people to make monetary donations toward the museum's construction costs of approximately one million Thai baht (roughly 30,000 US dollars).

For the following life account I have depended on the two short hagiographies published in *Lokthip* in 1984 and 2015, respectively. The hagiographies are clearly to a large extent based on an interview that her first biographer conducted with her.[130] In addition, I have interviewed Samorn Thophaengjan, who looked after Mae Chi Nari during the final seventeen years of her life, and Phakdiphuri (pen name), one of Mae Chi Nari's main hagiographers.[131] There were handwritten notes of Mae Chi Nari Karun, but unfortunately these were eaten by termites at some point and are now irretrievably lost. A biography of Mae Chi Nari was made while she was still alive but probably distributed in very small number; copies were given to her students, but despite sustained efforts I have not been able to find a copy.

Life of Mae Chi Nari Karun

The available sources tell us that Mae Chi Nari was born the second of three children in a village in Sakon Nakhon Province in either 1876 or 1877. She belonged to the same ethnic group as Mae Chi Kaew, the Phu Thai. Her father was a cattle dealer and village headman. Thus, it can be assumed that she must have spent her childhood in a relatively wealthy family. Her parents married her to Khun Wandi, with whom she had six children: four girls and two boys.

One day her local community was visited by Luang Pu Man, who went for alms there. No one in her community wanted to give alms to him though, as, so one of her biographers explains, the local community adhered to the worship of ancestor spirits (*phi banphaburut*). They were not yet familiar with the Buddhist practices of merit-making and alms donation. Only Mae Chi Nari decided to give alms to Luang Pu Man, and having done so got involved in probably only a short conversation with the venerable monk.

After this event, at the age of forty, she suddenly and without any apparent reason developed the strong wish to become ordained. Her biographers do not mention any hardship that she had to endure that might have been the catalyst for this decision. Quite the opposite—her family life is described as harmonious, full of mutual love, and without any problems.[132] Nevertheless, the wish to become a renunciant became so strong that she "felt that if I did not become ordained I would certainly have to die."[133]

The biographers also do not state an explicit connection between her encounter with Luang Pu Man and her decision to become a Buddhist renunciant—a very unusual decision in her local community, in particular for a woman. The way her hagiographers present this episode though allows the reader to assume that her encounter with Luang Pu Man may have been the catalyst for her decision.

It is reported that while having the strong wish to renounce lay life, she experienced an astonishing (*mahatsajan*) mental image (*nimit*): while eating one of her favorite dishes, she saw her food together with the dish turn into crystal (*klai pen kaeo pai mot*). When she looked at herself, her body together with the clothes and shoes also turned into clear crystal. She then perceived a spotless, white crystal disc hovering over her and landing on a crystal tray in front of her. She also saw two Buddha images hovering over her and settling on her shoulders: a black Buddha statue on her right shoulder and a golden one on her left. At the same time, she felt as if she were levitating upward and then saw a monastery. She was overwhelmed with indescribable (*sut ja phannana*) joy.

The way the story has been told is that this vision lasted for seven days, on the final day of which she saw the Buddha himself visiting her home. No one else was able to perceive these phenomena, even though she maintained that she neither was asleep nor had her eyes closed. Her children claimed that she had gone insane.

Prompted by these phenomena, she wanted to renounce lay life immediately and told her husband that she would look "for three new wives for him to replace her."[134] Her husband, though not accepting this offer, nevertheless allowed her to go forth. He agreed to her renunciation because he possessed faith (*sattha*) and actually rejoiced at her decision. Luang Pu Man provided the articles necessary for her ordination and instructed three of his main disciples to perform the ordination ceremony for her. Her ordination caused great excitement in her and many neighboring villages as the ordination of a woman was something hitherto unseen in these communities. The ordination was attended by many people, and some 700 baht was donated during this occasion. This was a considerable amount of money at that time and reflects the admiration people had for the renunciation of Mae Chi Nari.

It is not entirely clear as to when her ordination took place, but she must have been around forty years old. However, despite being ordained, it "was still necessary for her to continue living in her house for a while in order to take care of her youngest child, who was only two years old."[135] When visiting Luang Pu Man to consult him about questions relating to her visions, she took her whole family with her. She first practiced meditation at home but then moved into a monastery after having received a letter from Luang Pu Man in which he asked her to do so. She then spent three rainy seasons at the forest monastery of Wat Pa Ban Nong Phue, where Luang Pu Man was also residing. Afterward she moved to the famous monastery Wat Sutthawat in Sakon Nakhon. There she lived continuously for at least four decades.[136]

It is reported that Mae Chi Nari was able to remember her former lifetimes. Thus, she was able to recollect that she was reborn not only in many different countries as a human being with different professions, such as king, soldier, and farmer, but also as animals. Being able to perceive this process of being born and passing away, and the suffering intrinsically connected to this constant becoming, made her weary (*buea nai*) of constant rebirth. Interestingly, it is reported that in her former lives she had been reborn as a male only, and only in her current lifetime had she been born as a woman. The reason given for this is that "in a former life time she wanted to know how women feel when having a child and how strong the pain is when giving birth. This mere curiosity [*phiang khae songsai yak ru*] caused her to be reborn as a woman."[137] In her hagiographies we can read that Mae Chi Nari was also able to remember how she had been the blood relative of a number of famous monks of the Thai forest tradition. Similarly to what we can read in Mae Chi Kaew's hagiographies, it is reported that in former rebirths Mae Chi Nari had associations with famous monks; for example, she had been the younger brother of Luang Pu Man and a parent of Luang Pu Lui Candasāro.

The biographers tell us that in 1974 the king and queen of Thailand visited Wat Sutthawat in order to pay homage to the relics of Luang Pu Man in the monastery's museum. The queen had a new cottage built for Mae Chi Nari as the old one was worn down. Princess Sirindhorn is reported to have given her new robes, as she saw that the ones Mae Chi Nari wore were black from their long usage.

Mae Chi Nari told one of her biographers that a large number of people came to visit in order to listen to her teachings. There was a constant flow of people from Bangkok and many places in northern Thailand. Sometimes groups of up to fifty people on tour buses came from various parts of Thailand to see her and listen to her teachings. It is reported that Mae Chi Nari taught not only humans but also deities who came to ask her questions about Buddhist teaching. One of her hagiographers tells us that at least two people achieved supramundane states of mind because they had followed her instructions. Her biographies are replete with accounts about supernatural occurrences. Thus, it is related that in meditation she met not only canonical arahants such as Ānanda, Mahāmoggallāna, and Udāyī but also the Buddha himself.[138] After his death in 1949, Luang Pu Man frequently visited Mae Chi Nari in visions.

Mae Chi Nari's daily routine was characterized by simplicity and strict religious practice. Only once a day, at nine in the morning, did she consume solid food. Sometimes when she was pursuing intensive meditation practice she did not even consume any food at all for up to fifteen days. At the age of 106, when she started to be unable to look after herself, she moved to the property of a Thai woman whom she had formerly looked after while young and whom she loved like her own daughter.

Luang Pu Lui, a famous direct disciple of Luang Pu Man, provided 20,000 Thai baht per month for her livelihood. The adopted daughter took care of Mae Chi Nari until her death on July 1, 1999, at the age of 123. Her funeral was held in a local temple fifty days later on August 19, 1999. Presumably in order to celebrate her enormous age, exactly 123 monks were invited to participate in the ceremony, but nearly four hundred monks attended; among them were famous and high-ranking monks. In addition to this, there were more than one hundred *mae chi*s and laypeople in the tens of thousands. The ceremony was presided over by three well-known senior monks from northeastern Thailand.

After the cremation of her remains, many people asked for relics of her bones. It has been reported that "after the cremation, her remains turned into clear white relics [*phra that*], confirming her status as fully awakened one [arahant]."[139] Now her devotees are raising money to build a museum in order to display her relics together with the inner garment robe that she received directly from Luang Pu Man and other utensils, such as her bedding and the wheelchair that she received from Luang Pu Lui. The museum, which has a rather modest budget of one million baht, is to provide a place for the veneration (*sakkara bucha*) of Mae Chi Nari and to celebrate her life as a model for other women to follow.

Mae Chi Phimpha Wongsa-udom (1912–2010)

Summary of Sources

The following life account is to a large extent based on Mae Chi Phimpha's autobiography, interviews with monastics close to her, a sermon given at her cremation,[140] and a number of informal interviews with devotees. I visited Mae Chi Phimpha in July 2008, two years before her death. However, she was too weak for a formal interview. Her autobiography provides numerous insights into Mae Chi Phimpha's spiritual journey, fears, and doubts in a personal and honest way. What is conspicuous in her biography, at least when compared with those of other *mae chi*s and saints of the forest tradition, is the scarcity of references to supernatural occurrences and supramundane attainments. While there are some short accounts of supernatural events in her autobiography, the majority of the text gives a rather continuous account of her monastic career together with personal thoughts and Buddhist teachings. Her major teacher, Luang Pu Thet Desaraṅsī, who himself was believed to possess supernatural abilities and to have achieved full sainthood, is said to have not supported the demonstration of supernatural powers as he did not want people to become infatuated with or attached to these abilities. He also did not, at least in public, speak about supramundane attainments he and a number of his students are believed to have achieved.[141]

Life of Mae Chi Phimpha Wongsa-udom

Mae Chi Phimpha was born the youngest of three daughters in the northeastern province of Nong Khai in 1912. From an early age she was interested in Buddhist practice. In her autobiography she remembers that in her youth she worked hard, pursuing several jobs, such as rice planting and clearing the forest. She did not have the opportunity to attend school and only learned how to write when she was probably sixty years old.

When she was about seventeen years old a number of well-situated men wanted to marry her. She declined all of them, as she was determined to find a husband who was "kindhearted." At the age of twenty she decided to marry Khim Wongsa-udom. The marriage went smoothly. Every holy day (*wan phra*) they went together to a temple in order to pursue Buddhist practice there. Already before her ordination as a *mae chi* she had become an instructor of Buddhist teaching. She was suffering from bad health and fainted frequently. At the age of thirty-one she gave birth to a son. Both Mae Chi Phimpha and her husband Khim loved their child very much. But overstrained from living with a newborn, Khim started to lose his temper and use rude language, something he had never done before in their relationship of more than ten years. Their relationship started to sour. Mae Chi Phimpha thought, "Our child is the reason why we become disunited [*taek samakkhi*]. Can our child take us to heaven and *nibbāna*?"[142] Her child died before reaching the age of five months. The death of her newborn showed her quite plainly the suffering of being a layperson (*thuk khong khwam pen yu khong kharawat*). She wanted to be ordained, so she gave her husband permission to marry a new wife. Being very much in love with his wife, he cried and told her, "In this life I will never want to have another love!" She thereupon tried to persuade her husband that they should both be ordained. After her relentless repeated attempts to persuade him, her husband finally but only reluctantly agreed.

Realizing that as renunciants they could not stay in the same place, they intended to be ordained at different places. Mae Chi Phimpha describes her thoughts while on her way to her ordination: "I feared that my husband would change his mind and abandon the idea of becoming ordained. But if he did not become ordained how could I become ordained? I am his possession [*rao pen sit khong khao*]. If he said I had to disrobe, I would have to comply. These were my only thoughts."

When she was thirty-three years old, they were both finally ordained, having donated their house to a temple and given away all other belongings to relatives. Mae Chi Phimpha received her ordination from

Luang Pu Mahathongsuk, abbot of the famous northeastern monastery Wat Sutthawat and a direct disciple of Luang Pu Man. Their decision to renounce lay life brought support and encouragement from many people. Once ordained, they went their separate ways.

She received frequent instruction from a monk and practiced meditation in a cemetery. She says, "There were no thoughts at all about the past or about the future. My mind was fully focused on the dead. My ear was solely listening to the voices of the dead. My eyes were perceiving only the dead."[143] In her second year as a renunciant she went to Laos to pursue Buddhist practice. Mae Chi Phimpha had to encounter many obstacles during her ordained life. In her autobiography she describes her

FIGURE 8. The 2010 cremation volume of Mae Chi Phimpha Wongsa-udom, in which her autobiography was republished

fears when feeling unprotected in a monastery without monks, strong concerns and doubts about whether she would be suitable for the life of a renunciant, desperation, and her failures in spiritual development.

Her autobiographical account often reads more like a homiletic text than an account of her life; it contains instructions for meditation techniques that seem to be based on personal experience and on sermons from other teachers she listened to rather than the interpretation of canonical texts.

Even though not particularly accentuated, her autobiographical account contains a number of elements similar to those described in the hagiographies of forest monks: for example, encountering wild animals, such as tigers and snakes, while practicing meditation in the forest, encountering ghosts of the forest (*phi kongkoi*), and gaining the ability to understand the language of animals as a consequence of successful meditation practice.[144] Through her meditation practice she learned how to defeat her fears and develop mental fortitude.

Mae Chi Phimpha changed her monastic residence many times, moving several times from and to the Laotian side of the Mekong River. Shortly after Laos became a communist republic in 1975, she moved back to the Thai side again and stayed at Luang Pu Thet's famous Thai forest monastery Wat Hinmakpeng for the rest of her life. In her life account she tells her readers that Luang Pu Thet looked after her very well, providing her with clothes, food, and, when necessary, health care. Luang Pu Thet was full of praise for Mae Chi Phimpha, referring to her as "a woman with a lion heart who practiced meditation and sacrificed her life without any regret. . . . All *mae chi*s should take her as a model."[145]

Funeral

Mae Chi Phimpha died at the age of ninety-eight on April 15, 2010. Her cremation was held in Wat Hinmakpeng, not far from her monastic cell, on May 9, 2010. The funeral pyre, a concrete construction, had been especially built for her and was beautifully and splendidly decorated with numerous flowers and plants. Some three hundred monks and two hundred *mae chi*s together with approximately one thousand laypeople attended her funeral.

It has been reported that at the very moment her body was moved to the cremation place, the sky suddenly closed up despite the extreme heat on that day. The procession following the car that transported her coffin was extremely long. The famous and highly revered northeastern monk Phra Ajan Inthawai Santussako gave a sermon during the funeral ceremonies. In this sermon he repeatedly praised Mae Chi Phimpha as an outstanding practitioner, saying, for example, that

> Mae Chi Pimpha was an honorable *mae chi* . . . with a virtuous mind. . . . Even though I am not able to confirm this for sure, in my heart I strongly believe that [Mae Chi Phimpha] has reached one of the four levels of sainthood [*phra ariya*]. Let's wait to see what her bones will tell us once we have cremated her bones [*atthithat*] and body. Then we will see, because her bones will be the evidence."[146]

Not long after her death devotees had the idea of building a *stūpa* for enshrining her relics.[147] So far these plans have not materialized. Her remains have been put in a number of small transparent reliquaries in the form of *stūpa*s. On various internet forums it has been reported that parts of her bodily remains turned into crystalline relics (*phra that*; see chapter 4); some claim that this had already happened in the early morning of the day after her cremation. Even though she and her teacher Luang Pu Thet never made any claims, at least in public, that she had achieved supramundane states of mind, shortly after her death it was publicly maintained that Mae Chi Phimpha is a Buddhist saint (*ariya*).[148]

Mae Chi Soda Sosut (1920–2009)

Summary of Sources

The following account is based on a memorial book printed for the occasion of the merit-making ceremony one hundred days after the passing away of Mae Chi Soda. This small book contains not only hagiographical texts but also a number of her teachings that were first orally transmitted by her students. In addition, it comprises of a number of handwritten notes by Mae Chi Soda. I visited Mae Chi Soda in her remote and difficult-to-find monastic residence in July 2008, a few months before her death. She did not agree with the writing of a biography of her while alive, as she wanted to avoid becoming famous. Three years after her death I visited the monastic residence again and interviewed her ordained son, Phra Udom Ciradhammo, who is also her hagiographer.[149]

Life of Mae Chi Soda Sosut

Like Mae Chi Kaew and Mae Chi Nari, Mae Chi Soda ethnically belonged to the Phu Thai. She was born on December 11, 1920. She only had one younger brother and grew up in Sakon Nakhon Province. Mae Chi Soda completed the fourth grade of primary school. She became a trader and married Li Khenya, with whom she had twelve children. Ten of her children died at a young age.

Every holy day (*wan phra*) she closed her shop in order to practice meditation at a temple. Even though she had a good social status due to her good income, she had the wish to follow the example of her parents, who both had become renunciants. In 1975, once her youngest son had completed his education and she felt sure that he had become independent, she told him that she wanted to pursue her desire to be ordained. When noticing her determination her whole family supported her decision to become a renunciant.

In January 1976, she was ordained as a *mae chi* by the famous forest-tradition monk Luang Pu Juan Kulajeṭṭho (1920–80) in his monastery Wat Phuthok, in Bueng Kan Province in northeastern Thailand. This monastery is one of the most famous monasteries in Thailand because of not only the fame of its abbot, Luang Pu Juan, but also the remarkable giant sandstone outcrop on which Luang Pu Juan built the monastery.[150]

From the very beginning of her renunciant life, Mae Chi Soda pursued a strict and determined practice, often meditating for long, continuous periods. Her biography makes clear that Mae Chi Soda received broad support for her spiritual practice, which does not seem to have been restricted in any way; when her son had become a monk in the very same monastery, he brought to his mother food that he had received during his daily alms round. Mae Chi Soda was allowed to practice meditation in total isolation from the monastic community and was able to consult the great meditation master Luang Pu Juan on an almost daily basis in order to discuss her progress in her meditation practice. Once, so her biographer tells us, Luang Pu Juan instructed her, "Mae Chi, I forbid you from hovering with your astral body above [the monastery] Phuthok, as placing oneself higher than the heads of monks and novices is a demeritorious deed [*pāpa*]."[151]

There is another interesting episode in her biography: While staying at Wat Phuthok, one day Luang Pu Juan asked her to leave the monastery (no reason is given as to why), and a fortune teller (*mo du*) foretold that if she did not leave Wat Phuthok she would die within the next seven days. Nevertheless, Mae Chi Soda decided to stay and continue with her usual practice. Luang Pu Juan then asked her, "Mae Chi, tell me, didn't I chase you away? Why are you still here?" To which Mae Chi Soda replied, "Luang Pu Juan did not chase me away, but what he has been chasing away are my mental defilements [*kilesa*]." To this, Luang Pu said, "She is a diamond of the first water [*phet nam nueng*] of Wat Phutok, indeed. She truly already is number one!"

After having spent four rainy seasons in robes, she visited her home and practiced meditation together with a local monk, who built a cottage for her so that she could practice meditation in solitude. It is reported that in 1984, while sitting in meditation for four hours, she had a mental image (*nimit*) in the form of a voice from inside her mind. This voice asked, "Do you need liberation [*tongkan lutphon mai*]?" The story goes that, upon answering in the affirmative, she was told that the way to liberation was extremely hard, and she would have to practice the following until the end of her life: to refrain from eating rice and any food made from meat, milk, fish, or fish sauce; to refrain from taking medicine when sick; and to refrain from asking for food she liked. Without hesitation Mae Chi Soda accepted this code of practice.

Over the course of her monasic life, her fame must have increased significantly, as a growing number of people, both local and from far away, visited her in order to pay respect to her and discuss Buddhist teaching with her. On some days she had so many visitors that she felt exhausted. In order to protect her time for meditation, visiting hours had to be established.

Some seven years after the death of her meditation master Luang Pu Juan in 1980, laypeople built her a monastic residence in the province of Sakon Nakhon on a remote plot of land that belonged to her son. Her biography tells us that by radiating loving-kindness to others (*phae metta*), Mae Chi Soda was able to relieve pain and positively influence the course of an illness.

Mae Chi Soda passed away peacefully at ten o'clock on the night of February 1, 2009. The cremation of her body took place only four days later. The funeral was attended by more than 400 monks, some 120 *mae chis*, and more than 10,000 laypeople, including people from Bangkok

FIGURE 9. *Stūpa* built for Mae Chi Soda Sosut in the Thippayasathanwisutthimak Dhamma Practice Residence, Ban Dongmothong, Sakon Nakhon Province

and even abroad. Her hagiography tells us that "her bones turned into beautiful relics [*phra that*], thus without any doubt showing Mae Chi Soda's purity."[152]

Her relics, together with a fiberglass, life-sized statue of her, are now at display in a *stūpa* that one of her devotees had already erected for her during her lifetime. Some of her relics were enshrined on the second floor of the *stūpa*, in the base of a Buddha statue. Visitors can, however, also admire her crystalline relics, kept in small glass *stūpa*s in the main room of the *stūpa*'s first floor. Visitors may even hold the half-bone, half-crystal relics in their hands in order to study them more closely. Her devotees expressed the strong respect they have had for her:

> Mae Chi Soda completely penetrated the Buddhist teachings and therefore had no attachments [any longer]. She no longer clung to the five *khandha*s, which is the fuel for rebirth. Her determined practice is a beautiful example, and she fought long to overcome various obstacles on the noble path [*ariya-magga*] until she reached the termination of the cycle of rebirth, of becoming, aging, becoming sick, experiencing pain, and finally of dying.[153]

Chapter 3

Female Sainthood in Modern Thai Buddhism

What makes a saint a saint in modern Thai Buddhism? This is a question for which there is no straightforward answer. Unlike in the Catholic Church, in Thai Buddhism there is no clear, formal process or act by which a saint is declared and recognized as a saint. During the time of the Buddha, the Buddha would have confirmed the awakened status of his disciples or disproven wrongful claims of sainthood. With the absence of a generally acknowledged authority in this matter, the attribution of sainthood in modern Buddhism has become ambiguous and contested.

In this chapter, I will demonstrate and investigate the difficulties of defining what it means to be a saint in modern Thai Buddhism—or, maybe more accurately, to be recognized as such. In other words, what are the criteria for the behavior or actions of an individual or the biographical elements that make Thai people regard and revere someone as a Buddhist saint? What are the typical manifestations or evidence for sainthood in the eyes of Thai Buddhists? In considering these questions, one may juxtapose definitions and concepts of sainthood in the Pali literature with social constructions and contestations of Buddhist sainthood in modern Thai Buddhism, in particular with regard to female sainthood. As will be demonstrated, there exist a number of particularities in the attribution of and belief in female sainthood as a consequence of the gender of the saint.

Sainthood according to Indian Pali Literature

In the Pali canonical and postcanonical texts, the mental qualities of those who have achieved the four stages of awakening are clearly and elaborately specified. Arguably, one of the most often referenced canonical sets of criteria for the different stages of awakening is the presence or absence of the ten fetters (*saṃyojana*) in the mind of the Buddhist practitioner.[1] In accordance with their level of supramundane attainment, successful practitioners would abandon once and for all specific mental attributes, as shown in the following table. In the table and following discussion, I refer only to those canonical and postcanonical criteria, attributes, and issues of sainthood that frequently occur as topoi in contemporary Thai Buddhist hagiographical material and are thus important for an understanding of modern Thai conceptions of Buddhist sainthood.

Table 1. Levels of awakening, fetters, and spiritual attributes

Level of awakening	Fetters (*saṃyojana*) that have been abandoned	Spiritual attributes
Stream-enterer (*sotāpanna*)	1. Personality-view (*sakkāyadiṭṭhi*) 2. Doubt/uncertainty (*vicikicchā*) 3. Clinging to rules and rituals (*sīlabbata-parāmāsa*)	• Possesses unshakable confidence in the Buddhist teaching (*acalasaddhā*) • Accepts the Buddha as the highest spiritual teacher, finding it impossible to convert to another religion • Will be reborn seven times at most • No longer subject to falling into the lower realms of existence of the hells, animal realm, or ghosts (*avinipātadhammo / khīṇanirayo*)[2]
Once-returner (*sakadāgāmī*)	Attenuated greed (*rāga*), hatred (dosa) and delusion (*moha*)	Will be reborn once into the human world or a heaven
Nonreturner (*anāgāmī*)	4. Sensual craving (*kāma-rāga*) 5. Repulsion (*paṭigha*)	Will not be reborn into the human world again but into the heaven *suddhāvāsa* (pure abode), where they will attain full awakening
Worthy one (*arahant*); "one in whom all influxes have been destroyed" (*khīṇāsava*)	6. Craving for fine-material existence (*rūpa-rāga*) 7. Craving for immaterial existence (*arūpa-rāga*) 8. Conceit (*māna*) 9. Restlessness (*uddhacca*) 10. Ignorance (*avijjā*)	

The four types of beings listed in the table are referred to as *ariya-puggala* (noble person) or *dakkhiṇeyya-puggala* (person worthy of offerings) and belong to the noble *saṅgha* (Thai, *ariyasong*),[3] irrespective of whether they have actually been ordained or not. According to Pali scriptures, an arahant or *khīṇāsava*, however, is utterly liberated, as he or she does not cling to anything. In addition to, or maybe rather as a consequence of, the eradication of the ten fetters, the mind is cooled (*sītibhūta/nibbuta*) and free from any impurities (*viraja*). There is nothing further that needs to be done for such a person; they have "done what needed to be done" (*kata-karaṇiya*).

As a result of this ultimate spiritual attainment and the absence of self-worry, an arahant is able to be "friend to all" (*sabba-mitta*) and "kind-hearted toward all beings" (*sabba-bhūtānukampaka*).[4] Also, a fully awakened being does not experience any fear or have any concerns, however subtle, even when related to one's very own existence. Lambert Schmithausen writes that "in contrast to ordinary living beings, saints (i.e., fully liberated persons, arhats) do *not* regard their biological life as something valuable and are indifferent to it" for "the ultimate value is obviously not (biological) life but nirvāṇa."[5]

Thus, the Pali texts tell us that as a result of their full awakening the monks Adhimutta and Upasena and the novice Saṅkicca[6] were free from fear, even when facing death. As shown, the absence of any clinging to life as an indicator of advanced spiritual attainment has also been an important hagiographical element in the biographies discussed in the previous chapter. For example, a prominent episode in Mae Bunruean's hagiographies is when she was asked by her students to prolong her life by using her supernatural powers but refused to do so, saying that this "would mean I want to be alive, want to be happy, want to meet new things in the world [*phi phop*]. This all [however] would be [an expression] of mental defilements [*kilesa*]. I cannot do this."[7]

Even though there may be some bodily manifestations as a result of one's attainment of full awakening, as will be discussed in some depth in the subsequent chapter, according to the Pali scriptures all the crucial attributes or qualities of an arahant are of a nonphysical nature, thus not visible and therefore difficult to authenticate. In fact, only an *ariya-puggala* is said to be able to recognize another noble person (of either the same or a lower level of awakening) without any doubt.[8] But even here there is the canonical case, where the arahant monk Sāriputta is reported to have been unaware of the fully awakened status of his interlocutor.

Be that as it may, ordinary people (*puthujjana*)—that is, those people who have not attained levels of awakening—are not able to know for certain if a specific practitioner has achieved *ariya-puggala* status. However, the ascertaining of an individual's spiritual perfection has been a topos in Buddhist literature since the time of early Buddhism. The *Chabbisodhana-sutta* of the *Majjhima-nikāya*,[9] for example, contains a "series of investigations" according to which "someone claiming to have become an *arahant* should be cross-questioned on various aspects of his or her alleged purity."[10] The *sutta* provides questions that should be put to a person who "makes a declaration of final knowledge" (*aññaṃ byākaroti*) together with the "nature of [the] answer" (*ayamanudhammo hoti veyyākaraṇāya*) a fully awakened being would give to these questions.[11]

The commentary text of the *Chabbisodhana-sutta* explains further that "the practice of some ordinary people [*puthujjana*] is similar to that of fully awakened ones."[12] The method of ascertaining actual arahant status proposed in the commentary text is to frighten the person in question: "For it is normal that when a thunderbolt falls down on top of his head, a *khīṇāsava* will not have fear and will not be frightened; nor will his bodily hair horripilate. For a *puthujjana* this is the case, even if only to a small extent."[13]

The commentary text then also gives cases in which the spiritual attainments of individual monks were examined (*pariggahetuṃ*). Thus, when a monk was taking a bath in the estuary of the river Kalyāṇī, another monk grasped his feet. When the former monk thought he had been touched by a crocodile and started to make a loud noise, it was then clear that he was not an arahant.

In another case, a king wanted to "investigate" a senior monk with weak eyesight; he silently approached the monk and grasped his feet "like a snake." The monk, however, remained "motionless like a stone pillar" (*silāthambho viya niccalo*) and asked, "Who is here?" This entirely equanimous reaction of the senior monk was perceived as evidence for the monk's full awakening.

The commentary text also explains, however, that some *puthujjanas* may be very brave and fearless. In these cases, pleasant sense objects should be used as a means of investigation; when King Vasabha crushed a jujube fruit in the presence of a senior monk whose spiritual level he wanted to ascertain, the monk's mouth watered (*kheḷo cali*).[14] Since for an arahant there is no craving for taste—even divine taste (*dibbesupi rasesu*)—the physical reaction as a consequence of craving made it clear that the monk was not an arahant.

Thus, the commentary text concludes that when fear or craving for taste (*rasataṇhā*) arises, it is clear that "you are not an arahant."[15] What the methods (*imehi upāyehi*) proposed in this commentarial text seem to allow for is to establish with certainty only as to who is *not* an arahant. What they do not allow though is to ascertain with certainty as to who is an arahant or an *ariya-puggala* of a lower level. In the words of Guillaume Rozenberg,

> From the doctrinal point of view, there are no positive criteria that allow one to establish without possibility of contestation the spiritual perfection of a person. . . . The absence of a lineage of recognized saints going back to the Buddha's time, whose present representatives could possibly judge sainthood, renders the principle vain.[16]

Sainthood in Modern Times

Despite the statement in canonical literature that during the time of the Buddha there was a huge number of fully awakened saints, within the Theravada tradition there is the belief that after the Buddha's death arahantship was increasingly difficult to achieve. In fact, many have regarded the attainment of arahantship in current times as an extremely rare event or even as simply impossible. But, as will be shown in this chapter, in Thai Buddhism there are a variety of sometimes conflicting beliefs in this regard.

The decreasing number of recognized saints in Buddhist history was very often seen as a part of an inevitable decline and eventual disappearance of Buddhism. "For centuries, nearly everybody in Southeast Asia believed that there were no more Arahants."[17] It has been believed that only with the arrival of the next Buddha, Buddha Metteyya, would attainment of arahantship be possible again. However, only in a remote future will this buddha, currently living in the Tusita heaven, come to earth to realize Buddhahood and reestablish the religion, which will have died out.

In the textual and living tradition of Theravada Buddhism there is plenty of evidence pointing toward the belief in the disappearance of the possibility of achieving full awakening after the Buddha's death. In his influential magnum opus, the *Visuddhimagga*, the great fifth-century Theravada scholar Buddhaghosa described the attainment of arahantship as an extremely remote goal.[18] Richard Gombrich mentions that in Sri Lanka many Buddhists of the twentieth century believe that attainment of arahantship is no longer possible and that there "is a popular tradition in Sri Lanka that the last Enlightened person in the country died in the first century BCE."[19] Thus, the "last *arhat* is commonly said to have been Maliyadeva, though most people are very vague about when he lived."[20] However, Gombrich also refers to Sri Lankan Buddhists who "say that there *may* still be human *arhats*, but it is unlikely and/or undiscoverable. (One monk pointed out that an enlightened person is not supposed to boast about it.) . . . A monk who knew the Canon unusually well told me that it was a grave mistake to state that no *arhats* now exist."[21] Michael Carrithers reports that "received tradition of Sinhalese origin holds that the last [arahant] . . . died a long time ago."[22]

These beliefs in the unattainability of arahant status in modern times seem to be in line with, or even to have been nurtured by, teachings about the disappearance (*antaradhāna*) of the Buddhist religion.[23] There are several different versions of the *antaradhāna* teachings in the postcanonical literature, and these seem to have developed based on the well-known canonical story of the foundation of the nun order (*bhikkhunī-saṅgha*).

According to a passage in the Pali *vinaya* texts, the Buddha allowed female ordination with the condition that his stepmother, Mahāpajāpatī Gotamī, who asked to go forth in the Buddha's religion, accept eight special rules (*aṭṭha garudhammā*). After she had done so, the Buddha then said to the monk Ānanda,

> If, Ānanda, women had not gotten [the opportunity of] going forth from home into homelessness in the *dhammavinaya* [the doctrine and discipline] proclaimed by the Thus-Gone one, the holy life [*brahmacariya*], Ānanda, would have lasted long, the right teaching [*saddhammo*] would continue for a thousand years, but now, Ānanda, since women have gone forth from home into homelessness in the *dhammavinaya* proclaimed by the Thus-Gone one, now, Ānanda, the holy life will not last long, now, Ānanda, the right teaching [*saddhammo*] will continue only for five hundred years.[24]

The Buddha subsequently explained further that he had laid down (*paññattā*) the eight special rules "just like a man in his foresight erects a dam for a reservoir in order to prevent the water from overflowing."[25]

In the fifth-century commentary text *Samantapāsādikā*, it is explained that if the Buddha had not laid down the *aṭṭha garudhamma*s, the religion would have lasted only five hundred years. But since he laid down the rules, the "right teaching" (*saddhammo*) will last another five hundred years—altogether one thousand years (*vassasahassaṃ*). One thousand years of existence of the right teaching is explained here as meaning that the ability of an arahant to attain the ability of "analytical knowledge" (*paṭisambhidā*) will disappear after one thousand years. After another thousand years, the possibility of reaching ordinary arahant status will have vanished. During the next one thousand years, the highest possible supramundane attainment will be that of a nonreturner (*anāgāmī*). Then, with the disappearance of this possibility there will be the possibility of reaching at most the spiritual status of a once-returner (*sakadāgāmī*) during the next one thousand years. During the period between four thousand and five thousand years, however, the highest supramundane achievement possible will be that of a stream-enterer (*sotāpanna*).[26]

This explanation would imply that arahant status is not possible any longer in the present day. However, the commentary of the *Dīgha-nikāya* seems to be in conflict with this explanation, as it states that the attainment of such status is possible until four thousand years after the Buddha's death (during this period the ability of attaining extra special abilities of arahants will gradually disappear with each one thousand years).[27]

This difference in view about the possibility of full awakening, as apparent in the postcanonical texts, can also be seen in the variety of beliefs with regard to the (un)attainability of arahant status in modern times. Based on her fieldwork in central Thailand in the 1960s, Jane Bunnag writes that

> none of the Thai monks to whom I spoke appeared to consider *Nirvana* [i.e., attainment of arahantship] a relevant goal for which to strive; those who considered that Salvation was attainable in modern times, believed that only after billions of years of tireless effort could they or their contemporaries achieve this state.[28]

A well-known case where a Thai Buddhist in premodern Thailand claimed to have achieved *ariya-puggala* status is that of King Taksin, who reigned from 1767 to 1782. King Taksin (1734–82) seems to have believed that thanks to his meditation practice he had achieved the *ariya-puggala* level of a *sotāpanna*. When senior monks refused to pay homage to him, he punished them. The monks argued that "although a layman can be a [*sotāpanna*], he is still in a defective, inferior guise [*phet*]. A monk, even though he may come from the common classes, is in a complete, superior guise because he wears the yellow robes."[29] This rationale is of course in line with the respective canonical principles of the Theravada tradition (see chapter 6).

King Taksin's ill-treatment of the senior monks and thus challenging of the traditional hierarchy between lay and ordained was then one of the major reasons for his downfall and subsequent execution in 1782.[30] Here it is interesting to note that it was not King Taksin's claim of having achieved *ariya-puggla* status that was perceived as being problematic "but the propriety of requiring monks to worship him."[31] As expert of Thai Buddhism Sulak Sivaraksa put it in an interview, "[The claim of having achieved levels of awakening] is very political, because the king of Thonburi claimed to be an *ariya-puggala*. From then on this [has become] a taboo."[32]

In his study of modern Thai Buddhism, Tambiah mentions that "certain 'orthodox' Buddhist circles believe the *arahants* are exclusively heroes of the past; they maintain that present times are incapable of producing *arahants*."[33] Taylor also notes this:

> At the time of the ordination of the forest saint Ajaan Khao Anālayo (1888–1983) [a prominent disciple of Luang Pu Man] in 1919, he was discouraged from taking to the ascetic forest way of life. He was told that the arahant way was no longer possible and that the practice of meditation makes people go mad.[34]

At one point in his monastic life, Luang Pu Thet, also an important student of Luang Pu Man, had doubts too about the possibility of attaining arahant status in modern times: "I had some doubts about the *Dhamma-Vinaya* thinking that: 'The purity of the Path, Fruit and Nibbana—which form the culmination and ultimate goal of Buddhism—probably can no longer be attained.'"[35]

The American scholar monk Ṭhānissaro Bhikkhu reports that the great Buddhist scholar King "Mongkut himself [who was ordained as a Buddhist monk for twenty-seven years before becoming king of Siam in 1851] was convinced that the path to nirvana was no longer open."[36] The belief in the impossibility of arahantship in the modern Thai era was reportedly also held by King Mongkut's sons King Rama V (r. 1868–1910) and Prince Patriarch Wachirayan (Pali, Vajirañāṇavarorasa; 1860–1921).[37] However, in contrast to this, according to Luang Ta Thongkham Cāruvaṇṇo, one of Luang Pu Man's direct disciples and also main hagiographers,[38] Luang Pu Man believed that Prince Patriarch Wachirayan was the first arahant of the Bangkok era (1782–). Luang Ta Thongkham tells us that Prince Patriarch Wachirayan had achieved the level of stream-enterer in a former lifetime, when he was born in northern India during the time of the Buddha. In his final rebirth, which was his seventh rebirth as an *ariya-puggala*, he then attained full awakening.[39] Also, it must be noted here that already during his lifetime or not long thereafter, there were people who seem to have believed that the abbot of the Bangkok monastery Wat Somanat Wihan and famous meditation master Somdet Phra Wanarat (Thap Buddhasiri, 1806–91) was a fully awakened one (arahant).[40]

The way Prince Wiwitwanpricha (1860–1932), an acknowledged Buddhist scholar of his time and son of King Mongkut, put it may well reflect the beliefs held in scholarly circles of that time: "Nowadays, noble persons [*ariya-puggala*] do not appear in the world [*mai prakot nai lok*]. Even if there are any, there is no one capable of recognizing them."[41] During a sermon he gave at the Ho Phra That Monthien (which is in the Grand Palace complex) in 1912, the widely respected scholar-monk Somdet Phra Buddhaghosacariya (Jaroen Ñāṇavaro), however, was somewhat more affirmative in this regard when he stated, "Those who have achieved *ariya-puggala* status [*dai makphon*] do exist at the moment [*diao ni ko mi*], but no one dares confirm this, as it is no one's duty to do so."[42] Thus, similar to what Gombrich observed in Sri Lanka, despite the widespread Thai belief in the gradual disappearance of the "true religion" according to the teachings of the *antaradhāna*, there seems to have been a diversity of beliefs with regard to the (un)attainability of arahant status in modern times.

The seemingly increasing number of monks and female monastics in contemporary Thai Buddhism who are explicitly and publicly referred to and also widely believed to have achieved sainthood (*ariya-puggala*) is obviously in contrast with the described beliefs in the unattainability or indiscernibility of sainthood. Luang Pu Man and Luang Pu Sao certainly belong to the first generation of modern saints who are widely believed to have have been arahants[43] and are as a consequence of this belief revered translocally on a significant scale. As already discussed, the belief in their sainthood has been expressed in a variety of ways, such as written biographies, amulets, posters, and the building of museums and memorials. Also, a large number of their disciples have been publicly declared arahants. In fact, the majority of publicly and explicitly declared *ariya-puggalas*/arahants are found among the monastics of the Thai forest tradition who spent a significant amount of time in the jungle, caves, or cemeteries following the example set by Luang Pu Man.[44]

Here a comparison with Burmese Buddhism is interesting. According to a late eighteenth-century Burmese chronicle there were no arahants "flourishing" later than the fourteenth century. However, according to the 1861 text *Sāsanavaṃsa*, "persons possessed of extraordinary meditative attainments flourish in the present age, and should anyone choose to take up the practice of *vipassanā*, it is surely possible that that person could attain *arahant*ship in a single lifetime."[45]

Furthermore, when discussing the Burmese *vipassanā* movement in the twentieth century, Pranke argues that the "heyday of the associated cult of living *arahants* was really the mid-twentieth century. . . . This cult of charisma was part and parcel of the optimistic fanfare surrounding newly won national independence in 1948, and the 2,500th anniversary" of the Buddha's death; it was then believed that "the world had entered upon a new 'age of enlightenment,' that at this halfway point of the *sāsana*'s decline there was a sudden upsurge in the capacity of individuals to attain liberation, and that all this was the fulfillment of an ancient prophesy [*sic*]."[46]

So far, I have not come across a similar belief or prophecy in Thai Buddhism that people would refer to in order to explain the "sudden upsurge" of widely acknowledged arahant saints.[47] Here, we should, of course, also keep in mind that in contrast to Burma, Thailand has not experienced direct colonization, and its Buddhism has been influenced by and has reacted to different political and social developments. Anyhow, what is interesting is Pranke's argument that "historically, conditions of uncertainty and unrest have often prompted religious thinkers across cultures to reappraise their traditions in pursuit of truths and benefits more relevant for a world in crisis."[48]

As I will discuss below, the rather recent development of widespread, translocal veneration of Thai arahant saints does not necessarily imply that before that time there were no practitioners who were revered as *ariya-puggalas* or arahants. There may always have been these kinds of saints in Thai Buddhism who were revered on a local level, but we simply lack the evidence to confirm this.

However, the enormous social changes and political instability in post–World War II Thailand may have played a significant, or at least auxiliary, role in the growth of the cult of charisma and increasingly widespread belief in individuals' supramundane attainments.[49] This argument is confirmed by Chalong Soontravanich's study of the historical development of Thai Buddhist amulets. Chalong perceives a direct relationship between the rapid increase in crime and violence on the one hand and the dramatic intensification of the Buddhist amulet cult in Thailand's post–World War II period on the other. He argues that

> many highly respected "local" monks, living or dead, whose sanctity and amulets had previously been known largely to a closed circle of local followers now became more widely known. The prestige of the local saints grew and expanded beyond their local communities, encompassing a wider geographical region. The period saw what one may term the regionalization of local Buddhist saints in Thailand.[50]

It must be noted here though that Chalong does not define a saint as someone who has achieved supramundane states of mind in accordance with the aforementioned criteria of sainthood found in the Pali literature. Rather, for the purpose of his study, a saint is primarily understood as a source of "magical power" that can provide fortune and protection, in particular in times of social instability and crisis.

Conceptual Indefiniteness of Thai Buddhist Sainthood

As shown, the Pali canonical and commentarial criteria for verifying or disproving the claims of supramundane attainments in an individual's mind are difficult, if not impossible, to apply in an incontestable way in current times. Thus, it is not surprising that these criteria of "invisible" attributes of the mind of an *ariya-puggala* do not play an important—if indeed they play any—role when sainthood is ascribed to an individual in modern Thai Buddhism. Rather, visible or material features are often taken in order to ascribe or authenticate sainthood.

The anthropologist Keyes writes,

> A man can be recognized as a Buddhist saint only insofar as his actions are seen to have been movements along the path first exemplified in the life of the Buddha himself and later taught by him as part of the message regarding the attainment of the cessation of suffering for oneself and for others.[51]

While the perceived conformity of a practitioner's actions with Buddhist soteriology is certainly relevant, other elements are perceived as equally, often even more, relevant visible manifestations of sainthood. Unusual occurrences during the death or the funeral of a supposed saint (e.g., rain atypical for the season, sudden rain, unusual phenomena in the sky, animals behaving strangely, etc.) may be interpreted as signs or even evidence of sainthood. Another unusual postmortem manifestation suggesting sainthood is when the remains of supposed saints do not decay but may emit fragrant odor. This feature of sainthood is not unique to Buddhism but has also been observed in medieval Christianity too, a famous example being the remains of the English saint Cuthbert. Another powerful tangible marker of Thai Buddhist sainthood that plays a prominent part in almost all of the hagiographies discussed in the previous chapter is the crystallization of bones. Due to its importance I will investigate the transformation of relics in more depth in the subsequent chapter.

In 1982, in the same article just referred to, Keyes argued that

> a "saint" must be a person whose qualities of exceptional holiness are known not only to the person himself but are also manifest in signs that are interpreted by others as implicating the sacred. In Theravada Buddhist societies such as Thailand only those men (and, at least until quite recently, they were exclusively men) whose actions are believed to have led to their attainment of the highest goals of the path (*magga*) taught by the Buddha can be counted as saints.[52]

I want to qualify two aspects of this statement. First of all, as I demonstrate with my case studies in this book, albeit in a relatively inconspicuous way, female sainthood has been existent in Thai Buddhism for much longer than is normally assumed in scholarship. At the very least, there is evidence that during the time belief in Luang Pu Man's sainthood became popular—but even possibly before then—there were Thai women who were believed to have achieved supramundane states of mind (and were revered accordingly). These women may not have been widely believed to have achieved supramundane states of mind or may not have had a large group of followers; nonetheless, there were even monks who were convinced of the actuality of these women's exceptional spiritual achievements. In fact, it has been reported that Luang Pu Man's own mother was believed to have achieved the spiritual level of an *anāgāmī*.[53]

Second, I argue that often sainthood is not as straightforwardly ascribed as the definition above seems to imply. The belief that a specific practitioner has permanently eradicated some or all of the mental defilements (*kilesa*)—that is, in the words of Keyes, has attained "the highest goals of the path (*magga*)"—is often of minor importance. Rather, supernatural occurrences or feats are taken as indications of sainthood, whereas supramundane attainments may somehow be assumed but are often not clearly defined or are not understood in accordance with the scriptural criteria discussed at the beginning of this chapter.

Thus, there is often a significant gap between canonical description and actual conceptualizations of sainthood. In this way, Thai people may use the word *ariya* (noble one) in order to express deep respect or veneration without being necessarily aware of the Pali scriptural definition of this term.[54] At the same time the word arahant is, as Phra Payutto explains, sometimes used with a meaning that hardly has any connections to Pali canonical definitions.[55] Also, as Louis Gabaude has already observed, "As for the feeling of the Thai public . . . the frontier between the saint and the magician is not clear, simply because the public considers monks who have supernatural powers to be saints."[56] The way the possession of supernatural powers and attainment of supramundane states of mind are seemingly inextricably combined or confused is nicely exemplified by the following anecdote from the hagiography of one of Luang Pu Man's major disciples, Luang Pho Li (Dhammadharo, 1907–61):

> It has been recounted that after having been to a battle, a group of soldiers in the province of Lopburi wanted to challenge Luang Pho Li in their overconfidence; as the people claimed that he was an arahant and possessed marvelous supernatural powers [*abhinihāra*], they wanted to ascertain the truth [of these beliefs]. In their hubris [*khit utari*], the soldiers took a pistol to Luang Pho Li and shot at him as soon as [they saw him]. Thanks to Luang Pho Li's powers the bullet shot at the Venerable did not cause any injury whatsoever to him. From that day onward, many of the

> evil-minded soldiers became severely ill, and some of them died. Only when they felt remorse about what they had done and asked Luang Pho Li for forgiveness did all the symptoms of their illness disappear entirely.[57]

Another typical example for this conceptual entanglement is the following passage from a hagiographical text on Mae Bunruean: "Possessing *abhiññā* [superknowledge] and various miraculous powers [*itthirit*] are things that indicate in a concrete way the attainment of the reality [*dhamma*; i.e., supramundane states]."[58]

The confusion between the attainment of a supramundane mental state and the possession of supernatural powers as a result of spiritual practice is a recurring motif that can already be found in the Pali canonical and postcanonical texts. One of the most famous stories in this respect is that of the arahant Piṇḍolabhāradvāja and his public display of supernatural powers. In the *Dhammapada* commentary we can read that when a rich merchant from Rājagaha obtained a piece of sandalwood, the thought occurred to him that "there are many men living in the world who say, 'We are Arahats, we are Arahats.' For my part, however, I know not a single Arahat." He had a begging bowl made from the sandalwood and put it on a bamboo stick, more than twenty meters above the ground. He then made the following proclamation: "If any in this world be an Arahat [arahant], let him fly through the air and take this bowl." Over the course of six days, several "heretics" (*titthiyā*) tried to fly up to the bowl but were unable to do so. It was then concluded, "To-day we know for certain that there are no Arahats in the world." On the seventh day, however, two of the Buddha's foremost disciples, Mahāmoggallāna and Piṇḍolabhāradvāja, happened to learn about this contest and agreed that Piṇḍolabhāradvāja should use his supernatural powers in order to obtain the bowl. However, after he had successfully done so, he was reprimanded for this by the Buddha. As a consequence of this event, the Buddha even laid down a monastic rule that forbade his monks to show supernatural powers in front of laypeople. The Buddha said that the performance of supernatural powers was not conducive to the development of faith in those who do not possess faith. He in fact compared the display of these powers with a woman showing her private parts for the sake of money.[59]

However, in the canonical book *Therī-Apadāna*, we find a passage in which the Buddha asks his stepmother, Mahāpajāpatī Gotamī, shortly before her death to perform supernatural feats: "Gotamī, in order to eliminate their wrong views, show your supernatural powers to the stupid ones who are doubting the full realization of the *Dhamma* by women!"[60] Thus, it seems that in Pali literature there are different attitudes toward the performance of supernatural powers as visible indication of awakening.[61]

Furthermore, in Thai hagiographical literature one may also come across attributions of sainthood that are not compatible with Theravada Buddhist principles as outlined in its scriptures. For example, the highly revered northern monk Khruba Siwichai is referred to as *ariyasong*, a noble one, but at the same time is believed to have been a *bodhisatta* (Buddha-to-be). According to the normative conception of the *bodhisatta* path, however, it is precisely the condition of not having attained any of the standard four levels of awakening that is a crucial component of the *bodhisatta*'s progress to eventual Buddhahood. From this viewpoint, the notion of a *bodhisatta* who at the same time is believed to be a noble one (*ariya-puggala*) would appear to be a contradiction.

Assertion of Sainthood

In his study on sainthood in contemporary Burmese Buddhism, Rozenberg states,

> Due to the serious and delicate nature of such an assertion, the Burmese do not ordinarily employ the term saint (*yahanda* [arahant]) when describing a monk, however worthy of veneration he may be. An individual who openly declares the sainthood of a figure would claim to possess a faculty of discernment that he could not even aspire to and that no one would be ready to recognize. Spiritual perfection is suggested through anecdotes and commentaries governed by an implicit code of signs of sainthood of which the meaning is generally understood without ever having to be stated.[62]

In Thai Buddhism we find a wider spectrum with regard to the assertion of sainthood. At least three different attitudes can be identified. First, the assertion of sainthood is to be explicitly avoided, as to do so could be perceived as dangerously undermining important principles of the monastic code and Buddhist doctrine.[63] The following conversation between the famous Abhidhamma teacher Ajan Naeb Mahaniranon and one of her devotees may serve as a typical example of on the one hand the need for and on the other the avoidance of assertion of sainthood:

> Devotee: "You are a stream-enterer [*sotāpanna*], aren't you?"
> Ajan Naeb: "Why do you ask?"
> Devotee: "Because if I know for sure that you are a *sotāpanna*, as many people believe, I will be able to have confidence in the correctness of your method of Buddhist practice and intensify my own practice."

Ajan Naeb refused to give him an unequivocal answer but said,

> "Why do you not practice meditation yourself instead of insisting on getting an answer to this question? People do not give this kind of information. It is the Buddhist practice, however, that will provide you with an answer."[64]

Secondly, more or less implicit language or visual indications may be used to ascribe or express sainthood. For example, pictures of specific monks depicted with halos are widespread in Thai Buddhism. Also, in hagiographical texts, one may come across phrases that represent implicit and more or less unequivocal assertions, such as the following:

> She was not a normal person [*bukkhon thammada*]; her comportment was not that of an ordinary person [*puthujjana*].

> He relinquished his life [*la sangkhan*] peacefully and finished the long journey in the cycle of rebirth [*saṃsāra*].

> The venerable father had no body odor, despite the fact that he took showers infrequently. We regard this is as something that is beyond [the bodily features of] an ordinary person [*puthujjana*].

> She had made the mental resolution: "If the venerable father is actually an arahant, may he greet me first!" . . . A large crowd assembled around the venerable father. . . . After a long silence, he pointed his hand at her . . . asking her to get close to him . . . and said . . .[65]

Thirdly, on the other end of the spectrum, Thai Buddhists, both monks and laypeople, may openly, confidently, and unequivocally ascribe arahantship to specific Buddhist practitioners. The previous and subsequent chapters contain multiple examples of this attitude. Even more problematic, however, is the self-assertion of sainthood. After all, in addition to the problems of the verification of such claims discussed above, there are two rules in the monastic code (*vinaya*) that render the assertion of one's possession of supernatural powers and supramundane states of mind problematic. The fourth *pārājika* rule forbids all conscious lies with regard to one's possession of supernatural powers and supramundane states of mind.[66] The breach of this rule entails the heaviest possible penalty: the irrevocable expulsion from the order of fully ordained monks. A *pācittiya* rule forbids monks from revealing their actual spiritual attainments to laypeople and novices.[67] Here it is interesting to note that even though for many Thai Buddhists and direct disciples Luang Pu Man's advanced supramundane states of mind were apparent and beyond any doubt, according to Luang Ta Mahabua's hagiography of him Luang Pu Man himself did not claim to be an *ariya-puggala*.[68]

Mistaken Belief in Sainthood: The Case of Mae Chi Tat

In connection with the assertion of sainthood, be it one's own or that of another practitioner, a recurring topos in Thai Buddhist hagiographical literature is the mistaken belief in the attainment of supramundane states of mind.[69] As a result of deep and powerful meditative experiences, such as perceiving a bright light (*obhāsa*), practitioners of meditation may develop the conviction that they are *ariya-puggala*s. This misperception may be so convincing that only a very experienced teacher may be able to convince the meditators of their error. The letting go of these mistaken beliefs can take many years.[70]

The following story about Mae Chi Tat, who was locally revered (*khaorop lueamsai*) as an arahant, exemplifies a number of pertinent issues in relation to the attribution of sainthood. It also contains interesting elements related to issues of gender that are relevant to the major arguments in this book. This story can be found in the biography of the highly revered forest monk Luang Pu Fan Ācāro (1899–1977), one of Lung Pu Man's most prominent disciples.[71] The following summary draws on this telling of the story, which was written down by Luang Pu Suwat (Suvaco) based on the oral account by Luang Pu Fan. Even though there is a scarcity of circumstantial data in the narrative, it can be determined that the events must have taken place in Thailand's northeastern province of Nakhon Phanom in the 1930s.

Mae Tat, having a strong wish to renounce the life of a laywoman, became an eight-precept-keeping *mae chi*. She was strongly committed to her meditation practice, which included prolonged walking, standing, or sitting meditation sessions. Making significant progress in her meditation, she was able to remember one of her former lifetimes during which she was the son of her current monk meditation teacher. When her meditation teacher asked her for evidence of this, she told him that he had a disc-shaped figure on the sole of his foot. When she then saw the disc on his sole, she was convinced that her recollection of this past life must be authentic.

Her meditation teacher believed her and accepted her as his son. He "gave permission to his son in the female body of a *mae chi* to reside in a monastic dwelling near his own dwelling." He instructed Mae Chi Tat on how to "to gradually abandon the *saṃyojanas* [the ten fetters that bind men to the cycle of rebirth]" and achieve the various levels of awakening. As a result of her meditation practice it was revealed to her that during the life when she had been the son of who now was her meditation master, she had been ordained as a Buddhist monk whose "benevolent radiance" (*metta maha niyom*) had made his followers love and revere him. But the closeness to his followers was the cause of his downfall: becoming too entangled with his followers, he became overwhelmed by sensual desires and raped a female follower with whom he had become infatuated.

This most serious deed for a monk (*pārājika*) was kammically so grave that he was reborn in a hell, as a hungry ghost (*peta*), and as an animal for an extremely long period of time, enduring much suffering and pain. Eventually, another kammic consequence of the awful deed he committed was that he was reborn as a woman in the current lifetime.[72] She also carried a physical marker of her grave deed in her current lifetime: a skin abnormality on her leg.[73]

Meditation enabled Mae Chi Tat to have other supernatural experiences; she was, for example, able to visit hells and heavens, foresee the future, and listen to teachings given by the Buddha himself. Using her supernatural abilities, Mae Chi Tat looked into the former lives of others in order to explain to them the kammic consequences of action they had performed during their previous lifetimes. The story has it that she was also able to serve as a medium for the Buddha to give sermons to the local community.

Due to her presumed supernatural abilities people started to believe that she had attained arahantship, and her reputation as a fully awakened *mae chi* spread "in all directions." Mae Chi Tat herself also believed in her fully awakened status. She decided to wear robes tailored like those of monks, with the only difference being that hers were white instead of saffron.

However, when Mae Chi Tat accused a local layperson of intending to kill her and her meditation master, that layperson denied the allegation and asked a senior monk in Nakhon Ratchasima for help. Luang Pu Fan was then asked to investigate this matter. Having observed Mae Chi Tat's behavior, Luang Pu Fan concluded that

> she has been misled by her mental defilements into the belief [that she is an arahant]. . . . Her mind is not yet strong enough and her mindfulness and wisdom too weak to eradicate her defilements and ignorance. For this reason, she is still afraid of Māra [the Buddhist evil one] and of dying. For those who have

> really eradicated their defilements are not afraid of anything. . . . Arahants have never died nor are they afraid of death.[74]

Luang Pu Fan thus explained to Mae Chi Tat's meditation master that Mae Chi Tat's "mind has gone astray due to the imperfections of insight [*vipassanūpakilesa*] and is subject to a distorted perception of reality [*saññāvipallāsa*]" and that "even though Mae Chi Tat may possess much special [supernatural] knowledge, this is only worldly knowledge and does not mean that she attained the [supramundane] knowledge of having eradicated mental defilements [*āsava*]."[75]

Here it is important to note that, according to this story, it is not doubted at all that arahantship is possible for women in current times. Many people in the local community, including Mae Chi Tat herself and her monk meditation master, were actually convinced that she had attained arahantship. This belief was challenged neither due to her gender (see below) nor because it was thought to be impossible in current times. Rather, it was contested because it was based on Mae Chi Tat's performance of her supernatural feats. Supernaturality, Luang Pu Fan argued, cannot be taken as a criterion for the attainment of supramundane states of mind. The crucial point in Luang Pu Fan's argument was that Mae Chi Tat was still experiencing fear (of dying): "As Mae Chi Tat is still afraid of dying and concerned about life, how could she have achieved arahantship?"

Mae Chi Tat's current gender is purportedly related to the bad *kamma* she performed an incalculable number of lifetimes ago. The story does not, however, depict her femaleness as a negative thing or hindrance in her spiritual practice. In fact, for Mae Chi Tat's meditation master her biological sex was perceived only as an outward form (*phet rang*). He regarded and treated her as his son. Even though kammically determined, biological sex is depicted as something fleeting and rather insignificant. The "most ignoble deed in the practice of the holy life [*brahmacariya*]" was actually performed by Mae Chi Tat when she was a male monastic. Be that as it may, the story is presented as a case study whose major objective is to demonstrate the dangers of a mistaken Buddhist practice that both male and female practitioners can encounter in their meditation practice. The story about Mae Chi Tat concludes with a "profound" sermon by

Luang Pu Fan on the workings of the mind, meditation, the possible dangers thereof, and the relation between mundane and supramundane knowledge.

Female Sainthood in Present Thai Buddhism

As we have seen in the discussion of Mae Chi Kaew's hagiographies and devotional practices in the previous chapter, the belief that Mae Chi Kaew has achieved full awakening (arahantship) has been expressed without any uncertainty in a variety of ways. Her teacher Luang Ta Mahabua has arguably contributed most to this belief as he repeatedly declared in public that Mae Chi Kaew was a fully awakened one.[76] The fact that Luang Ta Mahabua recognized Mae Chi Kaew as an arahant lends particular weight: not only may Luang Ta Mahabua have well been one of the most famous and influential monks in modern Thai Buddhism,[77] but many Thais also believe that Luang Ta Mahabua himself had undoubtedly been a fully awakened one (arahant) for more than five decades (and, as mentioned above, it is believed that only a "noble one" can absolutely identify another). The respect Luang Ta Mahabua received from the Thai royal family, in particular from the youngest daughter of the late King Rama IX, has added to the enormous personal charisma that Luang Ta Mahabua had built up over the course of his long monastic career.

Another remarkable and powerful signifier of Mae Chi Kaew's highly advanced spiritual attainment can be seen in the monastery of Wat Yanasangwon (Chon Buri Province), the building of which was presided over by the late Thai *saṅgha* supreme patriarch. This monastery is a highly prestigious "royal monastery of the highest level" (*phra aramluang chan ek*). At the center of this monastery, in the middle of a beautifully arranged garden, is a building with the name *ariyakhan* (literally, the building of/for *ariya*s). In this building, fiberglass statues of ten prominent deceased Thai monks of the nineteenth and twentieth centuries, such as Luang Pu Man, Luang Pu Sao, and Luang Pu Khao, are placed on each flank of a Buddha image that is positioned in the middle of the large room. In the right corner are statues of two female figures in sitting posture: Upāsikā Ki Nanayon (Ko. Khao Suan Luang) and Mae Chi Kaew.[78] The presence of these two female practitioners in this room among some of the most highly revered saints of modern Thai Buddhism seems to suggest that they are perceived to have attained, at the very least, the first level of Buddhist sainthood (*sotāpanna*).

When the veneration and hagiographical literature of Mae Chi Kaew are compared to those of Mae Bunruean, some meaningful differences can be recognized. In the case of Mae Bunruean, the attribution of arahantship, or in fact achievement of any supramundane states of mind, has been done much less unequivocally and rather inconsistently. As already mentioned above, while most, if not all, hagiographical sources on Mae Bunruean unanimously celebrate that she has successfully developed the first four *jhāna*s, it is remarkable that many of them are rather vague when they mention Mae Bunruean's achievements of *abhiññā*s: while some explicitly say that she—long before her death—achieved all six *abhiññā*s, others simply state that she achieved "*abhiññā*s," without further specifying how many and which ones exactly.

For example, one hagiography notes, "She achieved many results with regard to the *abhiññā*s" and "she achieved the fourth *jhāna* and mastered *abhiññā*s, of which there are supernatural powers, divine ear, divine eye, and so forth."[79] Another states, "She was able to enter [the meditative level of] *nirodha-samāpatti* [attainment of extinction] which shows that that she was an *ariya-puggala* of a high level . . . for those who can enter *nirodha-samāpatti*, must be an *anāgāmī* or arahant with mastery of the eight *jhāna*s [*dai samabat paet*]."[80]

Thus, it is often not clear whether she was in possession of some or all of those with supernatural powers (the first five) or whether she mastered all six *abhiññā*s. In fact, at least one hagiographer writes that "she lacked only one [of the six *abhiññā*s]. This is the 'divine ear'. . . . The reason for this is that she suffered from a hearing disability from a young age."[81]

While a number of early sources state explicitly that she achieved full awakening, as we have seen in the previous chapter, many other sources do not even mention possible supramundane achievements, at least not explicitly. This vagueness and inconsistency in the hagiographical literature on Mae Bunruean is quite surprising, given that according to the Pali canon, the sixth *abhiññā* (i.e., the attainment of full awakening) is the summit of Buddhist ideals, aspiration, and practice and by far the most respected spiritual achievement possible in Theravada Buddhism (apart from achieving *sammāsambuddha* status, or "perfect awakening," of course).

Even those hagiographical texts that state that Mae Bunruean was fully awakened do so with relatively little attention to this, at least when compared to the hagiographies of Mae Chi Kaew or other saints of modern Thai Buddhism. In this way, Mae Chi Kaew is often referred to as "Mae Chi arahant" or *ariya-sāvikā* ("noble follower" of the Buddha), and her hagiographies clearly describe the moment of her full awakening (at dawn on November 1, 1952). Mae Bunruean's hagiographies, however, are far from being clear on how and exactly when she achieved supramundane states of mind.[82] For them, stories evidencing her supernatural abilities, her healing powers, and her enormous altruism seem to be of much more importance.

Why then do the hagiographies not devote more attention to the highly advanced supramundane achievements, which many believe she had? It seems that there are a number of possible reasons for this. First of all, according to the biographies, it may be that Mae Bunruean herself only very reluctantly, and only when urgently needed, talked about or demonstrated the spiritual attainments that people believed she had. In line with the Buddha's regulations for his monastic community (*saṅgha*) in this respect, she perceived "boasting about superhuman attainments [*uat uttari manutsayatham*]" as "doing wrong to the *dhamma* [*kanphit tham*]."[83] While it is reported that she often made use of her supernatural powers in order to help people by curing their illnesses, she may have seen no convincing reason to talk about or demonstrate personal supramundane achievements, which in Buddhism are regarded as something "to be known by the wise him/herself" (*paccattaṃ vedittabo viññūhi*).[84]

Indeed, it seems that she never directly claimed to have achieved the spiritual level of a nonreturner (*anāgāmī*) or full awakening. She apparently mentioned, at least according to one letter ascribed to her, that in her meditation she was able to enter *nirodho* (*nirot*; extinction), which probably means the highly advanced level of meditation *nirodha-samāpatti*, a state that according to Pali doctrine only *anāgāmī*s or arahants are capable of attaining.[85]

Here it should be noted, however, that, according to her hagiographies, Mae Chi Kaew also did not want to talk about her spiritual achievements, at least not to laypeople, and when prompted refused to do so. Only after her death did the belief in her arahantship become more widespread. In one of her books, Khunying Yai notes generally that "an *ariya-puggala* . . . would not reveal his/her advanced state of mind [*guṇadhamma*] anyway."[86] As far as we know, this reflects also her basic attitude in this regard, as in all her texts she did not refer to her own spiritual experiences (at least explicitly). It is reported, though, that in a conversation with a monk Khunying Yai was close with, she mentioned her deep meditative experiences. But this must have been a private conversation.[87]

A second reason for the absence of more frequent direct statements about Mae Bunruean's assumed supramundane achievements may be seen in the fact that female saints, in contrast to male saints, have only recently been acknowledged as such on a large scale in Thai Buddhism; this was after most of Mae Bunruean's main hagiographies had been written or compiled.[88] As already mentioned, I believe that Mae Bunruean may well have been the first Thai female saint to be venerated as an *ariya-puggala* translocally on a significant scale. Many—but as we have seen not all—of her early hagiographers may have been careful to enter new terrain in this respect. This possible reason is of course in addition to other likely reasons: the problems about the verification and assertion of sainthood, as discussed above. Still another reason may be related to a Thai belief according to which the status of someone not properly ordained would be too weak "to bear the [exalted] mind of an arahant."[89] One of the hagiographical texts on Mae Bunruean actually makes this problem quite explicit:

> It is assumed that Mae Bunruean at least reached the level of a nonreturner [*anāgāmī*]. The reason for this belief is that she was a layperson, and laypersons are not able to bear the completely perfect purity [*khwam borisut mot jot doi sin choeng*] of an arahant. If she had achieved arahantship, this must have happened during or near the time of her death [*ton la thing khan*], as arahantship as a layperson is only possible for no longer than seven days.[90]

Similar statements have also been made in relation to Mae Chi Kaew's arahantship. It was reported that some Buddhists, even monastics, might have doubts (*kangkha*) as to why "Mae Chi Kaew had such a long life after her awakening" as "according to the principles of the Pali canon, [one would have expected that] a layperson dies within seven days of his/her attaining arahantship."[91] As Mae Chi Kaew continued to live after her full awakening for nearly another forty years and was not ordained as a *bhikkhunī*, some seem to have had doubts regarding the possibility of her attaining full awakening.

Had ordination into a Theravada *bhikkhunī* order been available to Mae Bunruean and Mae Chi Kaew, such statements may not have been made. In fact, it seems that in the eyes of some Thai Buddhists, the absence of a Theravada *bhikkhunī* order appears to present a soteriological dilemma in cases of women who want to achieve or are believed to have achieved full awakening (i.e., arahant status).

The question of how women can attain long-term arahantship in the absence of a female Theravada order is a question that has repeatedly—directly or indirectly—been discussed in hagiographical literature, on Buddhist websites and blogs, and in connection with recent attempts to revive the vanished Theravada *bhikkhunī* order.[92] It was even argued that there is the belief in Thai Buddhism that "the experiencing of *nibbāna*" or "the attainment of the *dhamma*" would not be possible for women, at least in their current life (first a woman would have to be reborn as a man).[93] These beliefs seem to show that the possibility of becoming ordained as a *mae chi* is not necessarily regarded as an equivalent or satisfactory alternative to the *bhikkhunī* order.[94]

These beliefs and "theological" problems seem to have originated from the exegesis of Pali canonical and postcanonical literature. There are numerous examples in the Pali texts, both canonical and postcanonical, that could be seen to support the belief that arahantship of a layperson beyond one day is not possible. For instance, we can read that the Buddha's own father, Suddhodana; one of his most outstanding disciples (*etadagga*), Bāhiya; and the minister Santati died as lay arahants shortly after having reached full awakening. Furthermore, the Buddha explained to King Bimbisāra immediately after his wife Khemā attained arahantship that she "either ought to be ordained or pass into *nibbāna* [here meaning death]."[95]

At the same time, while there are a number of Pali canonical stories of long-term lay *ariya-puggala*s who have attained one of the first three levels of awakening (such as the famous laywoman Visākhā, the learned layman Citta, and the wealthy male lay follower Anāthapiṇḍika), it is not reported in the Pali canon that lay arahants lived longer than seven days beyond their attainment of full awakening. In addition, Pali literature tells us that both Yasa, one of Buddha's first disciples, and the acrobat Uggasena achieved full awakening as laypeople but were ordained immediately after.[96]

In the influential postcanonical text *Milindapañha*, it is even explicitly stated that there are only two options for a layperson who attains arahantship: either to become ordained on the very same day or to die, as it is not possible for a lay arahant to stay alive for another day.[97] In a commentarial text it is explained that "once having, however, attained [arahantship, one] cannot stay in the lower class of a layperson [*gihilingaṃ nāmetaṃ hīnaṃ*], since [this class] is not able to bear the highest qualities [that are those of an arahant; *uttamaguṇaṃ*]."[98]

Whereas many seem to believe that ordination and death in this context have to be taken literally, some contemporary Thai Buddhist thinkers have proposed a variety of interpretations that aim to reconcile the tension that emerges due to the postcanonical exegesis of Theravada tradition, the absence of a Theravada *bhikkhunī* order, and the possibility for women to attain *nibbāna* and stay alive. For the famous Buddhist thinker Buddhadāsa Bhikkhu (1906–93), having attained arahantship means "to have transcended both the status of a layperson and that of an ordained one."[99] The Thai Buddhist studies scholar Watchara Ngamchitcharoen understands that "to die" (*tai*) in this context may possibly be interpreted as "the dying of the mental defilements [*kilesa*]" or "to vanish [*tai*] from being a layperson."[100] Both Buddhadāsa's and Watchara's arguments here point to the Buddhist dichotomy of "conventional truth" (*sammuti-sacca*) and "ultimate truth" (*paramattha-sacca*) which has often been referred to in debates and discussions about the role of women in Thai Buddhism (see also next chapter). Asked about the absence of a Theravada *bhikkhunī* order in Thailand, the scholar monk Phra Thepdilok put it thus:

> An ordained one [*nak buat*] is not [only defined as] a *bhikkhunī*, but anyone who has the intention to abstain [*jetana wirati*] from demeritorious action [*bap*] is called an "ordained one." . . . Why should you choose a form of abstaining from demeritorious action when this outward form [*rup baep*] is not realizable [*nok wisai thi ja tham dai*]?[101]

How are the apparent "theological" problems dealt with in the concrete case of Mae Chi Kaew? This question seems to be important as it points to apparent tensions between the possibility for women to attain arahantship in present times and the refusal of the Thai *saṅgha* to recognize full (Theravada) ordination for women. In the case of Mae Chi Kaew it is believed that her being a *mae chi* was equivalent to being an ordained one (*nak buat*); through keeping the eight precepts she left the "lower life form" (*hina phet/phet tam*). The decisive characteristic of being an ordained one (*nak buat*) is thus in this context not perceived in whether someone has been formally accepted as a member of the conventional Buddhist *saṅgha* (*sammuti-saṅgha*) during the ordination act. Rather, the level of Buddhist practice and spiritual attainment is crucial. In this way, one can become ordained "internally" (*buat khang nai*) or in one's heart/mind (*buat jai*) and leave the "camp of the lay women" (*khai ubasika*) by, among other things, avoiding unchaste conduct (*abrahmacariyā veramaṇī*).[102] In connection with this point, in one of his sermons Luang Ta Mahabua said that

> Having attained arahantship and not undergone [formal] ordination, does this mean you have to die within seven days? Does this mean that the pure *dhamma* [*wisutthi tham*] or pure mind [*wisutthi jit*] act as an executioner [*phetchakhat*] of the five *khandhas*[103] [i.e., of a living individual]? This is certainly not the case! An arahant knows what he/she is supposed to do and what not.[104]

Moral or righteous behavior (*sīla*) is practiced "as a matter of course" (*doi attanomat*) by *ariya-puggalas*.[105] As for Mae Chi Kaew specifically, Luang Ta Mahabua explained in another sermon that if Mae Chi Kaew "had lived during the time of the Buddha, she would have been called *bhikkhunī*."[106]

According to these beliefs, the awakened status ascribed to Mae Chi Kaew not only points to the possibility that contemporary Thai women have the spiritual potential to attain *nibbāna* but also shows that it is not necessary to undergo the *bhikkhunī* ordination procedure as prescribed in Pali canonical texts in order to stay alive longer than seven days after the event of full awakening. In the words of Khruba Jaeo, "*Mae chi*s are a form of ordained practitioner [*nak buat*] that did not exist during the time of the Buddha. . . . [But] being a *mae chi* enables one's mind to bear [*rong rap*] the [exalted] mind [*thamma*] of an *ariya-puggala*."[107]

As for Mae Bunruean, she was ordained as a *mae chi* twice in her life, each time probably for not a very long time. In the absence of a Theravada *bhikkhunī* order and apparently not entirely satisfied with the socioreligious structures in which Thai *mae chi*s are embedded, Mae Bunruean developed her own religious identity of being a female practitioner, which she also expressed in her appearance: a shaved head and clothing in shades of green, yellow, and brown.

When once asked why she did not dress entirely in white, Mae Bunruean said that she "adheres to the normal precepts and only slightly differs from laypeople in that she shaves her head like an ordained one [*pen nak buat*], but she is *not* a *mae chi*."[108] Quite interestingly, even though Mae Bunruean did not want to be a *mae chi* permanently and was ordained as a *mae chi* for two probably rather short periods of time, she has often been referred to as "Mae Chi Bunruean." In fact, many of her more recent hagiographies carry Mae Chi Bunruean or *mae chi* in their title. Two examples of this are *Mae chi number one* and *The amazing "mae chi": The excellent female* nakbun *[person endowed with merit]; Beyond the world*. In one hagiographical text it was argued that as a *mae chi* she would have been under the jurisdiction of the Thai Saṅgha Supreme Council, and this would have made it difficult for her to use her "supernatural powers and knowledge as means to help people."[109] It has been reported that she followed the five Buddhist precepts on normal days and the eight precepts on holy days (*wan thammasawana*).[110] One of her hagiographers interestingly argued,

> The fact that even though Mae Bunruean followed only the five precepts but was able to be so successful in her practice that she attained the supramundane [*magga-phala*], superknowledge, and the ability to perform miracles [*pāṭihāriya*] shows that Mae Bunruean was a genius of an extraordinary level, an extraordinary person worthy of veneration [*pūjā*]. [It also shows that] she should very much and genuinely be taken as a role model for people who may not easily be able to become ordained as a monk or as a *mae chi*.[111]

However, it should also be noted here that according to canonical and common understanding, an *anāgāmī* or arahant would automatically not engage in sexual activities. For these two types of *ariya-puggala*s, their high supramundane attainments would entail the permanent eradication of any sensual craving (*kāma-rāga*) in their mind (see table 1 near the beginning of this chapter). Thus, as many have believed that Mae Bunruean attained one of these two highest levels of awakening, she consequently would have also naturally followed the precept of chastity rather than only refraining from sexual misconduct (the third of the five precepts).

Moreover, her devotees, who "had received her permission" to do so, donated money to her on a monthly basis. After all, Mae Bunruean did not have any income, as she provided all her work for free. In this way, "many thousand" baht were given to her each month. Mae Bunruean used this money "only for buying food for herself, those who looked after her, and her visitors." The rest she used for "various merit-making activities." Devotees also donated "expensive" items, such as Buddha statues, a TV set, and a fridge. Mae Bunruean, however, "did not want to have any external possessions [*khong nok kai*]." For this reason, the hagiography tells us, Mae Bunruean would donate all these things to others.[112] Also, we know from her own texts that she increasingly enforced her *vinaya* (discipline/monastic code of discipline) practice toward the end of her life. In fact, her practice in this respect seemed to resemble more and more that of the monks; in order to avoid physical contact with the opposite sex, she decided not to touch men older than seven years of age. For the same reason, she would also not accept objects that were handed to her by men. In addition, "so that consumption of various [things] is in line with the *vinaya* [*phra winai*]," she would not ask other people for help to obtain any consumer goods.[113]

Both Mae Bunruean's and Mae Chi Kaew's life accounts and veneration not only challenge a sharp dichotomy between being "fully" or "properly" ordained and laity but also are powerful statements regarding women's spiritual potential in present Thai Buddhism, where female saints had hitherto been unreported with such assertiveness on such a scale. While Mae Chi Kaew's status as an "ordained one" was indicated by her ordination as a *mae chi* and her life in a remote monastic setting, Mae Bunruean established herself as a spiritual leader whose charisma was based primarily on personal spiritual achievements, supported by and in proximity to, but ultimately outside, the Thai monastic community (*saṅgha*). Her hagiographies depict her as someone who has successfully integrated nonmonastic life with enormous charisma, altruism, supernatural powers, and spiritual insights—attributes more typically ascribed to a forest monk. According to her hagiographies, her sainthood has quite atypically been achieved within the turmoil of urban social life and not in the seclusion of a forest.[114]

Chapter 4

Material Expressions of Female Sainthood

> The Buddha: Ānanda, these four are worthy of a *stūpa*. What are these four? A Tathāgata who is an arahant and perfectly awakened Buddha is worthy of a *stūpa*, a *pacceka-buddha*, a realized disciple of a Tathāgata, and a wheel-turning king are worthy of a *stūpa*.
>
> *Mahāparinibbāna-sutta*[1]

As McDaniel put it, "Beliefs are articulated through objects."[2] Similarly, John Kieschnick in his study of Chinese material culture argues, "Objects are often the most expressive means for conveying religious ideas and sentiments. In short, material culture is as much a part of religion as language, thought, or ritual."[3] Thus, it is not surprising that beliefs in the sainthood of Thai women have not only affected but also been influenced by Thai Buddhist material culture of the modern era. A study of material culture in this respect allows us to understand better the ways in which these beliefs have influenced Thai religious life and belief systems. As already noted in chapter 1, the material expressions of the beliefs connected to female sainthood, in particular of contemporary women, can be found only on a rather modest scale, at least when compared to the ubiquitous and manifold expressions of the veneration of both Pali canonical and contemporary male Buddhist saints. Nonetheless, the material impact of beliefs in the sainthood of contemporary female practitioners is significant and reveals gender-related issues pertinent to my study. As relics, *stūpa*s, and amulets are key elements of Thai Buddhist culture, in this chapter I will focus on relevant attitudes and practices in relation to them.

Objects have made female accomplished practice more powerful than hagiographical texts. While texts refer to, celebrate, and describe sacredness, the objects investigated in this chapter are sacred themselves, being "repositories of sacred power."[4] Often it is only because of these sacred objects that a larger number of people learn about and develop faith in a specific (female) practitioner. This can be demonstrated to various degrees with the women of my study, but it can arguably be best shown in the development of the devotional practices and the hagiographies of Mae Chi Kaew.

Relics

In his impressive study on the ideology of relics in Buddhism, Peter Skilling has argued that

> the cult of relics is shared by all Buddhist traditions and societies. The cult is both intensely spiritual—relics inspire devotion, visions, chronicles, and rhapsodies—and unabashedly material—relics are carefully encased in precious containers, which are in turn enshrined in caskets to be installed within *stūpas*, pagodas, and images. Extraordinary amounts of wealth, of exchequer, have been and still are lavished upon relics by devotees, monastics and rulers.[5]

Unsurprisingly, the cult of relics forms an important part in the veneration of many modern Thai Buddhist saints, both male and female, too. However, for many Thai Buddhists, relics of modern saints are not only significant for their veneration of a specific saint but are at the same time material proof that sainthood is still possible in current times. Or in the words of the Thai monk Amaradevo Bhikkhu, an expert on relics of saints of modern Thai Buddhism, "The practice of the Buddhist *dhamma* really bears fruit, for there is still physical evidence [for the validity of this statement]: relics [*phra that*]."[6]

In Thai, relics are called *phra that*, which translated literally means "venerable/holy element." One of Thailand's leading relic experts, Tossapol Jangpanichkul, defines *phra that* as

> bones [*aṭṭhi*] or other body parts, such as wisps of hair, body hair, nails, teeth, skin, and blood, that have features different from those of normal people. They have characteristics resembling those of *dhātu* [literally "elements"], which when not properly studied look like pebbles, stones, glass, diamonds, and so forth.[7]

The belief is that the relic contains the essence of sacredness of the saint from which it derives. A part of the saint's dead body, however small, represents the whole saint. This understanding bears striking similarities to ideas in early Christendom: "Where there is a part, there is the whole [*Ubi est aliquid ibi totum est*]."[8] This applies not only to parts of the saint's body but may also be valid for any object that the saint was in contact with.

There are a variety of different relics (*phra that*):

1. Historical Buddha relics are those relics that are believed to be the actual remains of the historical Buddha. For example, it is believed that some of them are enshrined in the *stūpa* of the Golden Mountain Temple (Wat Saket) in Bangkok. These relics were given to King Rama V after they were excavated in northern India in 1898.
2. Nonhistorical relics of the Buddha Gotama, other *buddha*s (including *pacceka-buddha*s), and other saints mentioned in the Pali literature: these kinds of relics often look like small stones, precious stones or jewels and may be found in caves or "manifest themselves" (*sadet*). Many relics of this type possess specific visual features that allow their identification as to which saint they are believed to belong to. The relic of the Buddha's personal attendant, Ānanda, for example, has the form of a heart, while the relic of the nun Uppalavaṇṇā looks like the "backbone of a snake." These relics may also miraculously multiply. In the northeastern monastery Wat Pa Wiwekwatthanaram, for example, there were as of 1999 nearly fourteen kilograms of Buddha relics.[9]
3. The relics of Thai saints include body parts and sometimes other materials that the saint had been in contact with and as a consequence of which have transformed into crystal-like objects (see below). In most cases, these transformations take place after

> the death of the saint, but this may also happen while the saint is still alive. Thus, devotees may keep a tooth that has fallen out or betel that a saint had spit out, and put it in a small glass *stūpa* in order to observe if the relic transforms after a while. Arguably, one of the most famous examples for the emergence of *phra that* in a living saint is the case of Luang Pu Waen Suciṇṇo (1888–1985) of Wat Doi Mae Pang in northern Thailand; during an operation in a hospital, a part of one of his bones had to be removed. It was discovered that this part was a transmogrified *phra that*.[10]

Towels that had been used to wipe the body of a saint may also be carefully stored and venerated, as the sweat or blood contained in the towel may transform after a while and thus confirm the person's sainthood. Even the excrement or urine of a saint may turn into crystallized relics, according to local beliefs.[11] However, relics of Thai saints may also be created or provided by deities (*thep nimit*). This is, for example, believed to have happened with the relics of Luang Pu Thuat and Somdet To. In these cases, the relics are called *phra that thep nimit*.

There also exist numerous whole-body relics in Thai Buddhism,[12] but these relics are usually not called *phra that*. Whole-body relics are the corpses of monks that neither decay nor emit a bad smell but look as if asleep, even a long time after the death of the saint. These corpses are said not to have been preserved in any artificial way and are often displayed in glass coffins. In some cases, growth of the fingernails or hair of these corpses has been observed, and this may then be interpreted as a sacred or miraculous event. In some cases it is believed that the dead body may open its eyes on a specific day of the year—for example, when the monk's robes are exchanged. These incorruptible bodies are believed to be sources of wholesome energies. Thus, people may, for example, crawl underneath the coffin in order to receive these energies.

For my investigation, whole-body relics are not relevant as the corpses of nearly all of the women of my study were cremated fairly soon after their death. However, the corpse of Mae Chi Prathum Choti-Anan, whose autobiography I refer to several times in this book, was not cremated after her death in 1995. Her body, which did not decay (*mai nao mai pueai*) and looks "as if she were asleep," is on display in a glass coffin at her monastic residence in Pak Chong. It is believed, though, that relics (*phra that*) have manifested themselves on top of her head.[13]

Importance of Relics in Thai Buddhism

The strong veneration of Buddhist relics is attested to in Thai history since at least the thirteenth century. On the famous Ram Khamhaeng inscription we can read that

> In 1207 saka, a Year of the boar [AD 1285], . . . [the ruler of Sukhothai, King Ram Khamhaeng,] caused the holy relics to be dug up so that everyone could see them. They were worshipped for a month and six days, then they were buried in the middle of Ṣrī Sajjanālai, and a cetiya was built on top of them which was finished in six years.[14]

Terwiel nicely summarizes the importance of Buddhist relics, their miraculous abilities and the effect these miracles have had on Thai people:

> [Relics] were seen to perform miracles, usually described as the shooting forth of coloured rays (reminiscent to us of the effect that a prism emits when it is hit by sunlight). The finding of a relic and its emitting rays were apparently events that were charged with deep emotions. It appeared to many observers at the time as a cosmic event. It seemed to them a heavenly confirmation that the country was governed by the proper Buddhist ruler. The ruler himself may well have felt at the time of the miracle that he stood at the very centre of the universe and received overwhelming blessing.[15]

More recent Thai kings also seemed to have believed in the supernatural qualities of Buddha relics. Thus, it has been reported that Rama IV (r. 1851–68), Rama V (r. 1868–1910), and Rama VI (r. 1910–25) have seen miraculous manifestations of the Buddha relics believed to have been enshrined in the Pathom *cetiya* in Nakhon Pathom, which is one of

Thailand's most ancient and famous sacred sites.[16] It has also been argued that Buddha relics have played a significant role in the creation of cultural and political integration.[17]

Even for the casual observer of present-day Thai Buddhist practices and beliefs, the ubiquity and importance of the veneration of relics becomes easily manifest not only in the numerous *stūpa*s throughout Thailand. Small glass *stūpa*s can also be purchased all over the country in amulet shops and malls. These small, transparent containers are used for holding and venerating bones and other body parts of a saint and are often placed on an altar or a shrine at monasteries or private houses. As a part of veneration practice, the relics are studied on a regular basis, either to ascertain the stage of their possible transformation or to see whether the number of relics has miraculously multiplied, which is regarded as an auspicious event. It is believed that the transformation and multiplication of relics take place in households in which the Buddhist precepts are consistently being followed.[18] The general religious practice and faith (*sattha*) of those who keep the relics of an arahant may also have an impact on the pace with which they transform into *phra that*.[19] During their transformation relics may emit a pleasant odor. Also, in bookstores one can purchase numerous books on relics, often containing short biographies and pictures of the saints together with their crystallized bones or other body parts, as evidence for their sainthood.

The ongoing importance of relics can also be demonstrated by one of the most conspicuous events in recent Thai Buddhism. On March 5, 2011, the cremation of Luang Ta Mahabua's body took place in the car park in front of his monastery Wat Pa Ban Tat, near the northeastern city of Udon Thani. The cremation ceremony was initiated by Queen Sirikit. The then prime minister, many other high officials, and numerous high-ranking monks were present at the ceremony as well. Some estimates had it that up to a million people attended the cremation of Luang Ta Mahabua's body.

Shortly after the cremation many Thai Buddhists were seen crawling on their knees on the area where the cremation had taken place, trying to find relics in the form of ashes or small pieces from the funeral pyre. Something similar is reported to have taken place after the funeral of Luang Ta Mahabua's teacher, Luang Pu Man, in 1950. Tambiah writes that devotees "rushed to the remains of the pyre and gathered all the dust and cinders that remained. They regarded the dust and ashes as a treasure, which they pressed 'to their bosoms with a triumphant smile.'"[20] In the case of northern saint Khruba Siwichai, "when the cremation was over, a large contingent of policemen had to be posted around the cremation site to prevent the faithful from taking away all the remains."[21]

After the cremation of Luang Ta Mahabua's body, his remains were placed in a metal coffin that had been especially built for this purpose. Altogether eight locks were fitted to the coffin, each of which had a different key. Each of the eight keys was looked after by a different monk. Afterwards, the remains of Luang Ta Mahabua were then divided into five parts to be distributed all over the country.[22] A few days after the cremation, one of the major daily newspapers of Thailand, *Matichon*, reported on its front page headline that "People Believe That Luang Ta Distributed His Bones [*aṭṭhi*] for Them to Collect and Venerate [*pūjā*] Them." On a second *Matichon* front-page spread that same day, pictures of small body parts of Luang Ta Mahabua were shown together with a

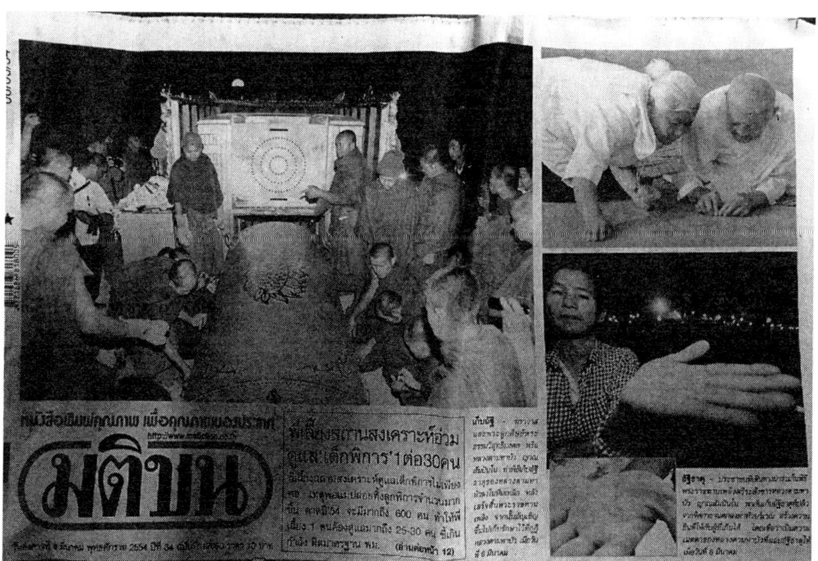

FIGURE 10. *Matichon*'s front page on March 8, 2011, showing devotees trying to find bone relics [*aṭṭhi that*] of Luang Ta Mahabua, and a picture of the metal coffin in which the remains of Luang Ta Mahabua were kept

headline in large type that read, "Bones [*aṭṭhi*] of Luang Ta [Mahabua] Are *Phra That*."[23]

Transformation of Relics

In the Pali canon there are numerous descriptions of the Buddha's unusual body. This bodily unusualness is understood to derive from and be the physical manifestation of the Buddha's supreme mental purity. The Pali canon itself does not, however, seem to contain any reference to unusual visual characteristics of his relics or those of other awakened beings. In later Pali literature, though, there are numerous descriptions of miracles performed by relics, and their unusual appearance.[24] The commentary text to the *Mahāparinibbāna-sutta*, the fifth-century *Sumaṅgalavilāsinī* by Buddhaghosa, seems to be one of the earliest sources in Theravada history citing the unusualness of visual aspects of the Buddha's relics. Here it is said that after the cremation of the Buddha's body "the relics remained like jasmine buds, like polished pearls, like gold."[25] This passage in the *Sumaṅgalavilāsinī* is often referred to in modern Thai literature on relics. Tossapol Jangpanichkul argues that the *Sumaṅgalavilāsinī* "is regarded as the first textbook on relics [*tamra phra that*] . . . and as highly reliable."[26]

The commentary text to the *Bākula-sutta* of the *Majjhima-nikāya* also contains an interesting early reference to the unusualness of the physical remainders of an awakened being. When the fully awakened disciple Bākula (also written as "Bakkula") was about to die (*ajja me parinibbānaṃ bhavissati*),[27] he entered the meditative state of *tejodhātu* (fire element). Then flames arose from his body, and his skin, flesh and blood were consumed by the fire "like butter," and the remaining relics (*dhātu*) were like "jasmine buds."[28]

A similar transformation of bones of an arahant disciple of the Buddha is described in the commentary of the *Dhammapada*. On the day Santati, minister of King Pasenadi of Kosala, attained final *nibbāna*, and

> sitting cross-legged in the air, he applied himself to meditation on the element of fire [*tejodhātu*]; and having thus induced a state of

> trance, he entered therein and straightway passed into Nibbāna. Instantly flames of fire burst from his body and consumed his flesh and blood, and his relics [*dhātu*] floated down like jasmine flowers. The Teacher [i.e., the Buddha] spread out a pure white cloth, and his relics fell therein, and the Teacher deposited them at a crossing of four highways, caused a shrine to be erected over them and said, "By doing reverence to these relics the populace will earn much merit."[29]

What is interesting about this passage is that it not only gives a description of how the transformed relics of a fully awakened Buddha disciple should be dealt with but also states the meritoriousness of their veneration.[30]

In later Theravada literary work, such as the thirteenth-century *Thūpavaṃsa* or the sixteenth-century Thai text *Jinakālamālī*, conspicuous visible features of relics are also mentioned. In the Sukhothai Asokārāma stone inscription of 1399, a relic is described as "[in color] like crystal."[31] Thus, there is ample evidence that the belief in the corporal manifestation of sainthood in the form of bones that transform according to postcanonical descriptions has long been entrenched in Thai Buddhism.[32]

Relics as "Scientific" Proof for Sainthood

That unusual visual features of relics are taken as evidence of the spiritual attainment of a great practitioner is not unique to Thai Buddhism but can be found in other Buddhist cultures too, such as Chinese, Tibetan, and Burmese Buddhism.[33] As for Thai Buddhism, Gabaude has stated that in the eyes of Buddhists the crystallization of bones "offer[s] a kind of scientific proof that the saint was an Arahant"; they are the "ultimate certificate of Arahantship."[34] Thus, it has, for example, been argued that "Luang Pu Man is certainly a genuine arahant, for only in the cases of arahants who have attained *nibbāna* is it possible that their bones [*aṭṭhi*] turn into *phra that*."[35]

It is also believed that the longer a person had been an arahant before death, the quicker the remains of that person will turn into *phra that*. It is explained that the mind had been longer able to "purify/cleanse" (*fok*) and "refine" the body. The remains of an arahant might not necessarily turn into crystals, though, as it is believed that an arahant is able to make a resolution (*athitthan*) to prevent this from happening.[36]

Even though this belief seems to be prevalent, it should be noted that in Thai Buddhism there exists a variety of views on when the crystallization of remains may take place. Thus, some Thai Buddhists believe that full awakening (arahantship) is not a necessary condition for transformed relics to occur; advanced concentrative levels of mind (*jhāna*) or having realized one of the three lower levels of awakening may be sufficient for these transformations to take place.[37]

In his "scientific study of *phra that*" (*sueksa kiao kap phra that choeng withayasat*) that also includes the findings of a scientific analysis of the physical composition of fourteen different samples of various *phra that*, Amaradevo Bhikkhu refers to the famous first verse of the Pali canonical book *Dhammapada*,

FIGURE 11. Cover of Amaradevo Bhikkhu's book *Phra that: Marvelous things of Buddhism*

> Can the power of the human mind have an impact [on matter]? . . . *Manopubbaṅgamā dhammā* . . . [This is translated,] "All things have mind as their forerunner." . . . Thus, this very sentence by our highest teacher, the Buddha, causes us to be certain that no matter which element, be it the water, earth, wind, or fire element [*dhātu*], if the mind, which is the "forerunner," is pure, these elements can undoubtedly become pure as well as a consequence of the power of the mind.[38]

At the same time, while again referring to a Pali canonical text, Amaradevo Bhikkhu argues that the emergence of *phra that* falls into the category of *buddhavisaya*,[39] which is one of the four "inconceivable matters" that "one should not think about."[40] In the Pali canon it is explained that *buddhavisaya* is the "domain of the Buddhas [and] is an inconceivable matter [*acinteyyo*] that one should not try to conceive; one who tries to conceive it would reap either madness or frustration."[41]

Relic Museums

During the last few decades, an increasing number of relic museums have been built across the country, often inside monastery compounds.[42] In them the visitor can study relics of the Buddha, his immediate disciples, monks and nuns described in postcanonical Pali texts, and often the bones and other relic types of practitioners of modern Thai Buddhism. The visitor is invited to study the relics closely. Sometimes, magnifying glasses are provided so that the visitor can observe the stage of transformation from ordinary-looking bones (*aṭṭhi/atthi* or *atthi that*) of an (assumed) saint into crystallized relics (*phra that*). There are also temporary relic exhibitions. A temporary relic exhibition that was typical in the way the relics were arranged and presented took place in 2008 in Luang Ta Mahabua's monastery, Wat Pa Ban Tat in Udon Thani Province, one of the most important pilgrimage centers in present-day Thailand. In the main building of this monastery, in a huge and systematically arranged collection, relics were displayed largely in chronological order. Centering around numerous relics of the Buddha himself (such as relics of his blood, hair, and bones), which themselves were put around the major Buddha image in the building, this was an exhibition where the visitor could venerate and closely study relics of the Buddha's direct disciples. In several glass cabinets, relics of saints of modern Thai Buddhism were displayed (there are even relics of the deceased monk Paññāvaḍḍho, an Englishman who had been a Buddhist monk in Thailand for nearly forty years).

In an adjacent room, some 170 miniature glass *stūpa*s with relics of individual saints were displayed in three large glass showcases. The relics included those of canonical and postcanonical male and female saints, such as Sāriputta, one of the Buddha's foremost monks; the missionary monks Soṇa and Uttara; and the nun Saṅghamittā. Altogether, the *stūpa*s contained the relics of 168 arahants (144 male and twenty-four female), including relics of 103 saints who lived during the time of the Buddha (83 male and 20 female saints) and ten arahants (nine male and one female) from the time of the Indian emperor Asoka (third century BCE). In chronological sequence, the visitor would eventually also find a section with relic containers for sixty Thai saints of the Bangkok era (1782–), including fifty-seven monks and three "*mae chi*s," among them Mae Bunruean and Mae Chi Kaew. A huge signboard declared that "five *stūpa*s [in this section that are still empty] have been prepared for arahants who are of an advanced age and close to reaching [final] *nibbāna*." The signboard also informed the visitor that this collection of relics

> bears witness [*pen sakkhiphayan*] that it does not matter how much time has already passed [since the time of the Buddha], the path to *nibbāna* has not become extinct . . . This museum is considered to be a memorial of the history of the Thai nation—in fact, a memorial for the history of the world, and most auspicious for Thai people. . . . As long as there are people who are intent on pursuing mental development [*bhāvanā*], the world will not be devoid of arahants.[43]

In addition to its nationalistic undertone, the signboard's text was also intriguing in the way it explained one of the exhibition's major purposes as demonstrating a genealogy of fully awakened saints that started during the time of the Buddha and is still continuing in Thai history. What the temporary relic exhibition also reflected, in a historical perspective, were the gendered imbalances in terms of the number of acknowledged female saints relative to that of male saints. While female sainthood is celebrated, it plays a minor role.

Moreover, in the way the relics were arranged, *mae chi*s were implicitly depicted as a continuation of the vanished *bhikkhunī* order, the historically last *bhikkhunī*, whose relics were on display, being Saṅghamittā, the daughter of Emperor Asoka. The arrangement, presentation, and meaning of the relic exhibition of Wat Pa Ban Tat also corresponded to the way relics are presented not only in relic museums in other parts of the country but also on relic posters, which can be seen in many monasteries, and in the numerous relic books available commercially in Thailand's bookstores and often given away for free in monasteries. While the vast majority of space is given to the presentation and description of relics of numerous male saints, arranged in chronological order and in accordance with their respective monastic seniority, pictures of relics of a few female saints are, if at all, consistently placed at the bottom of the poster or at the end of the book, irrespective of when they lived and how much time they spent in the robes of a *mae chi*.[44] The book *Buddha relics: The relics of [members] of the noble [*ariya*] saṅgha*, for example, contains the pictures of forty-four monk saints of modern Thai Buddhism, starting with Luang Pu Sao and Luang Pu Man, together with pictures of their relics, short biographical notes, and short excerpts of their teachings. At the end of book, the reader can find pictures, biographical notes, and short teachings of only two *mae chi*s (Mae Chi Kaew and Mae Chi Phimpha Wongsa-udom). The book *Relics of [members] of the noble [*ariya*] saṅgha: Relics of disciples at the midpoint of the Buddhist era* contains the pictures of forty-eight Thai monks together with pictures of their relics and some biographical notes, but the picture of only one female practitioner together with a picture of her relics and a short biography ("Mae Chi" Bunruean). Even though the relics of female Thai practitioners are presented last, the fact that they are mentioned at all is probably meant to be soteriologically inclusive by reinforcing the possibility of female *ariya*s or arahants in current times. The soteriological inclusivity that transformed relics (*phra that*) convey is nicely expressed in the words of the Buddhist author Wuthinan Jiawitthayanan in his book on Buddhist relics:

> When I was a child, I had the understanding that it is only men who achieve levels of awakening. The reason for this was that I was only aware of men who were able to be ordained. . . . [But] nowadays women who achieve the highest level of awakening still do exist. One can be confident and certain of this, as we have the bones of [a woman] which turned into very clear and pure relics [*phra that*]; this [woman] is Mae Chi Kaew Sianglam.[45]

Mae Chi Kaew's Postmortem Famousness

While alive Mae Chi Kaew had only very limited and locally confined impact on the Thai Buddhist landscape. In fact, it seems that she was hardly known outside her local area. On the translocal level, only monks belonging or close to the forest tradition might have known or heard about her. From her ordination onward, Mae Chi Kaew was able to build up personal charisma within her local community thanks to what was perceived as convincingly authentic Buddhist practice and inspiring teaching.

In contrast to other famous religious figures of modern Thai Buddhism, however, Mae Chi Kaew did not gain fame and wide recognition through homiletical skills. She left a rather small textual corpus of her teachings. Also, she is reported to have been a quiet person (*phut noi*) who gave only a rather small number of teachings.[46] In this aspect, too, she seemed to have shared a characteristic with many of the forest monks who have been "mainly interested in mental and ascetic practices transmitted by word of mouth. They were not naturally inclined to publish their teachings."[47] Also, due to the lack of formal education, Mae Chi Kaew was unable to write. Moreover, she spoke only her native Phu Thai language and not the standard central Thai.[48] Despite its linguistic closeness to standard Thai, the Phu Thai language is rather difficult to understand for most non–Phu Thai speakers. Furthermore, her teachings have largely been transmitted orally by her close disciples. It seems that there are no audio recordings or notes of her teachings, which would have helped to preserve her teachings more systematically, completely, and efficiently. The teachings of Mae Chi Kaew were only systematically compiled in 2003, more than ten years after her death.[49]

Another reason Mae Chi Kaew was not translocally well-known during her lifetime is that she did not establish a movement or organization as many other charismatic figures in Thai Buddhism have done. Instead she preferred to use the remoteness of her nunnery to pursue the practice of intensive meditation.[50] Furthermore, it is reported that she did not encourage reporters of national magazines on the supernatural to write more about her, despite the interest these magazines had in her biography (see chapter 2). She also consistently refused to use her assumed superhuman abilities to attract more followers.[51] In contrast to other Thai Buddhist practitioners who are believed to possess supernatural powers, she refused to use these presumed supernatural abilities to produce or consecrate (*pluk sek*) amulets.[52] Her personal nature seems to have been that of one who rather preferred a secluded lifestyle.

Here some notable differences to the biography of Mae Bunruean can be observed. Even though she was also reluctant to use her assumed supernatural powers, Mae Bunruean is reported to have done so numerous times based on altruistic motivations, such as when she sought to relieve people from their physical suffering. In particular, her ability to provide effective cures was one of the reasons Mae Bunruean achieved a significant degree of popularity while she was still alive; or as one of her main hagiographers put it,

> There were numerous people who participated in merit-making activities with her . . . People whose illnesses could not be cured by modern medical care asked her for help, and there were lots of people whose illnesses disappeared [because of Mae Bunruean]. They saw the sacred effects [*phon saksit*] of practicing the *dhamma* with her. For this reason, there was a great number of people who became her students [*sit*]. . . . When they listened to her Buddhist teachings and practiced accordingly, they experienced spiritual happiness in marvelous ways.[53]

There are other reasons why Mae Bunruean, in contrast to Mae Chi Kaew, gained fame while still alive: she traveled to provinces in all parts of the country in order to heal people, she produced a large number of amulets, and she was involved in fundraising and building projects for famous temples. She also delivered a number of sermons, some of which were printed with a circulation figure in the thousands. In 1956, one of her followers even erected a large house for Mae Bunruean in Bangkok so that she could "practice the *dhamma*" there.[54] This was the second house that was built for her by devotees. Out of her group of devotees developed the Pure Community Spirit Association (*samakkhi wisutthi*), which met regularly in order to pursue various religious activities together with and led by Mae Bunruean. It is clear from her hagiographies that even during her lifetime Mae Bunruean must have had a significant number of devotees from all walks of life.

Mae Chi Kaew, however, was restricted in her mobility as she had to depend on the material support of her teachers[55] or the donations of her supporters in her village. As a consequence of the charisma they gain through their ordination, monks may quite easily obtain free shelter, food, and financial support in most places in Thailand, even if they are strangers. In contrast, as pointed out in chapter 1, for *mae chi*s it can be relatively difficult to find places to stay and receive support from laity in places other than those where they are already known. Also, the resources available in her local community would not have allowed Mae Chi Kaew to support a large number of *mae chi* residents at her nunnery.[56]

If she never really became widely popular during her lifetime, was unable to write, and rarely gave sermons, then why I am I mentioning her here? She became well known after her death mainly through material culture. Though she is nowadays best known in the Northeast, Mae Chi Kaew's reputation has continued to spread, particularly within the last fifteen years or so, on both a national and an international level.[57] Why did her reputation grow so significantly only after her death? There are several interrelated reasons for this rather late, albeit rapid, growth in reputation and veneration. The most important one, it seems, is related to the discovery that her remains had crystallized. One of her hagiographies explained,

> The life story of Mae Chi Kaew would have nearly faded away gradually from the memory of people if there was not the

> occurrence of a marvelous event: the transformation of her bones into clear and pure relics [*phra that*], as happened in the case of the remains of Mae Chi Kaew's first monastic meditation teacher, Venerable Luang Pu Man.[58]

Spurred by this metamorphosis of her remains, the belief in Mae Chi Kaew's sainthood has been expressed in a variety of ways, such as the building of *stūpa*s, the publication of numerous hagiographies, many of which contain pictures of her *stūpa* in Khamcha-i and her relics, and the production of amulets and statues of Mae Chi Kaew. Thanks to an increasing number of hagiographies[59] that have been widely circulated in print and are partly published online, the patronage of one of Thailand's most famous and influential monks, Luang Ta Mahabua, and the late supreme patriarch Somdet Phra Ñāṇasaṁvara, and the spreading of her relics across the country, she has been increasingly recognized, venerated, and celebrated on a national level. This extended to the international level through a hagiography published in English in 2009 with a circulation figure of 30,000 copies. This hagiography was distributed not only in Thailand but also in Europe and the United States.[60] Another way her reputation has been spread is via the medallion amulets that bear her image; some 10,000 such amulets were produced to commemorate the

FIGURE 12. Mae Chi Kaew medallion amulet distributed at the opening of the Mae Chi Kaew stūpa in Khamcha-i in May 2006

opening of the Mae Chi Kaew *stūpa* in Khamcha-i in May 2006.[61] Since her death, through books, relics, amulets, and the internet her life story has become much more easily accessible, widely known, and influential than during her lifetime.

Relics of Mae Chi Kaew

After the cremation of her body, which took place five days after her death in June 1991, Mae Chi Kaew's remains were collected from the cremation site and divided among "many people" so that they could venerate (*kep wai sakkara bucha*) them. The largest part of them, however, was put into a jar (*tho*) and stored in the northeastern monastery of Wat Pa Kaew Chumphon and later in a safe in Wat Pa Na Kham Noi before it was eventually enshrined in the Mae Chi Kaew *stūpa* in Ban Huai Sai. It has been reported that "many people" who were in possession of her relics had "reliably" (*chuea thue dai*) and "independently" confirmed that their parts of the remains had crystallized into albeit not perfectly clear roundish crystals.[62]

Over the years, Mae Chi Kaew's bones and crystallized relics have been disseminated in other parts of Thailand. I was thus able to find her crystallized relics not only in the two huge and well-designed *stūpa*s in her nunnery in Ban Huai Sai and the forest monastery Wat Pa Kaew Chumphon (see below) but also in the influential Dhammayuttika-nikāya monastery Wat Jedi Luang in the northern city of Chiang Mai. There her relics are on display in a large, beautifully ornamented glass case in which the crystallized remains of a large number of other saints of the modern Thai era are venerated in small glass *stūpa*s. Another portion of Mae Chi Kaew's relics is kept in the Dhammayuttika-nikāya monastery Wat Santitham in Chiang Mai, on whose grounds a relic museum has been built. It is very likely that further portions of her relics are venerated and stored in private houses and other monasteries in many parts of Thailand.[63] This shows that Mae Chi Kaew's relics have been taken physically beyond the actual places where she lived and worked during her lifetime; moreover, pictures and accounts of the crystallization of her relics have also been electronically disseminated on numerous Thai Buddhist blogs and websites.[64] This has further enhanced the multiplication and dissemination of Mae Chi Kaew's relics and with it the effective spreading of her life story, reputation, and veneration.

With regard to Indian Buddhist saints, Reginald Ray remarks that

> while they were alive, the saints often have been relatively inaccessible: they spent much of their time in remote places. . . . But when the saints had passed beyond and their relics were enshrined in stūpas, they finally became available to all and could become the objects of an ongoing cult.[65]

A similar phenomenon seems to have happened in the case of the veneration of Mae Chi Kaew. During her lifetime, due to the remoteness of her nunnery and several other factors that were discussed above, her veneration seems to have taken place largely in her local area. However, the "post-mortem charisma"[66] of Mae Chi Kaew has been increasing significantly over the years and has become especially visible through her crystallized relics, in which her charisma has become objectified and through which "Mae Chi Kaew" has been made more easily and widely accessible. Robert Sharf has remarked with regard to Buddhism more generally that "there is, in fact, considerable evidence that the mobility of relics contributed to the success of Buddhism as a missionary religion."[67] Similarly, it can be argued that in the case of Mae Chi Kaew, her paradigm-setting example has become much more effective postmortem than while she was alive. Also, as John Strong has observed, "relics are also *extensions* of the Buddha's biography. It is perhaps possible to think of this as an assertion of the ongoing 'presence' of the Buddha, but it is preferable to think of it as the further development of a powerful narrative."[68] Similarly, the dissemination in various parts of Thailand, the relic crystallization, and the putting of Mae Chi Kaew's relics into specific frameworks with powerful meanings can be regarded as some kind of extension of her biography that is affecting and transforming the Thai Buddhist landscape much more profoundly than Mae Chi Kaew ever did during her lifetime.

There is another interesting aspect of the metamorphosis of Mae Chi Kaew's bones into crystalline objects. As shown in chapter 2, her meditational study of the ephemerality (*aniccatā*) and nonsubstantiality (*anattatā*) of life figure prominently in her life accounts. Thus, seemingly quite paradoxically, while alive Mae Chi Kaew had been using her body and bones as objects to contemplate the Buddhist principles of impermanence (*aniccatā*) and suffering of being (*dukkhatā*), and to develop the "perception of loathsomeness" (*paṭikūlasaññā*). She perceived her body as "disgusting and repulsive."[69] Through attainment of spiritual perfection and cremation, however, this very body, or rather the remains of it, has turned from something "repulsive" into something beautiful and attractive, serving as the focus of veneration and motivation for pilgrimage and Buddhist practice.

*Stūpa*s for the Veneration of Thai Women

While *stūpa*s built for the veneration and commemoration of male practitioners and their relics are relatively ubiquitous in Thailand, so far there are only a few Thai *stūpa*s for the veneration of women.[70] The largest of the three *stūpa*s in the northern monastery Wat Kukut (also known as Wat Cāmadevī) in Lamphun must be mentioned as an example here: it is believed that one of the two sons of the eighth-century Queen Cāmadevī built this quadrangular and cascaded *stūpa* made from laterite for enshrining the remaining bones (*aṭṭhi*) of his mother.[71] Nowadays, this *stūpa* is the object of veneration for many Thai Buddhists. This is visible by the many elephant statues, flowers, and incense sticks that are offered in front of the *stūpa*, in particular during the anniversary of Queen Cāmadevī's birthday (believed to be in August). In connection with the *stūpa* veneration, it should be mentioned that, in particular in northern Thailand, statues and pictures of Cāmadevī showing her not only as a queen but also as a white-clad celibate are widespread—the latter arguably much less than the former, however.

Another famous *stūpa* built for a Thai woman is a *stūpa* in the Ayutthaya monastery Wat Suan Luang Sop Sawan. This *stūpa* is believed to contain the ashes of the legendary and heroic Queen Suriyothai (sixteenth century) of Ayutthaya. In this context, I should also mention the Phra Ariya Sawika Phiksuni Sangkha Maha Cetiya on the grounds of the

Grand Palace in Bangkok, whose apparent purpose is to commemorate noble *bhikkhunī*s.

However, in line with what I have observed in chapter 1, it must be noted that all the *cetiya*s/*stūpa*s mentioned here have been built for the veneration of heroic women (Queen Cāmadevī and Queen Suriyothai) or of *bhikkhunī*s who have traditionally not existed in Thai history. It is not widely believed, if it is believed at all, that Queen Cāmadevī and Queen Suriyothai attained levels of awakening.

In the temple compound of the controversial Wat Phra Thammakai movement in Pathum Thani, however, a huge golden hexagonal pyramidical construction was completed in 2003 for the veneration of one of the founding figures of this movement, Mae Chi Chandra Khonnokyoong (1909–2000). This construction, which is twenty-nine meters tall, has been built for the enshrinement of the *mahā ratana aṭṭhi dhātu*, the "great gem bone elements," of Mae Chi Chandra. Similar to the architectural style of many of the forest tradition *stūpa*s (see next section), this construction is surrounded by water and has two floors; while the first floor houses a museum displaying personal items and information about the life and achievements of Mae Chi Chandra Khonnokyoong, on the second floor the visitor finds a statue of her in meditation posture.[72] On the temple's official website it is stated that "the second floor is reserved for meditation. Housed here are her relics and a pure gold statue cast in her image situated at the center of the room. The statue of the Master Nun is one and a half times the actual size of the Master Nun and weighs about two tons."[73] The symbolism makes clear that Mae Chi Chandra Khonnokyoong is venerated as a highly accomplished practitioner.[74]

The Mae Chi Kaew *Stūpa*s

The building of memorials for male Thai saints of the forest tradition must have commenced sometime during the second half of the twentieth century, probably during the 1970s.[75] In Thai these memorials are often called *jedi phiphitthaphan*, (*cetiya* museums). While these museums may have different architectural structures, their purpose and meaning have developed out of traditional *stūpa*s. Many of these Thai "saint museums" also resemble traditional *stūpa*s in their architecture. What most if not all of these museums have in common, though, is that they contain one or more images of the revered saint together with a number of personal objects the saint used. These may include robes, alms bowls, monk identification booklets, books, glasses, towels, scales, walking sticks, false teeth, urine containers, unused medicine, and pictures. The most important items of the museum, though, are the saint's relics, which are normally displayed at the center of the construction.

The two *stūpa*s built for the veneration of Mae Chi Kaew certainly belong to the first Thai *stūpa*s ever built for the veneration of a Thai Buddhist woman believed to be and explicitly celebrated as an arahant. In fact, the one built for her in the monastery Wat Pa Kaew Chumphon in 1996 might well be the first ever. This memorial was erected beside the *stūpa* of Phra Ajan Singthong Dhammavaro (1924–80), who was a close disciple of Luang Ta Mahabua and is also widely believed to have attained arahantship. This *stūpa* of Mae Chi Kaew cost some two million baht. The second *stūpa* for Mae Chi Kaew was built next to Mae Chi Kaew's nunnery in Khamcha-i between July 2005 and April 2006. The costs for

FIGURE 13. Mae Chi Kaew *stūpa* in Wat Pa Kaew Chumphon

FIGURE 14. Mae Chi Kaew *stūpa* in Ban Huai Sai, next to her nunnery

this construction were nearly twenty million baht, while the whole site on which the *stūpa* is located cost some thirty million baht altogether, including all the buildings, landscaping, and parking places.[76]

The Mae Chi Kaew *stūpa* in Ban Huai Sai has been described as a contribution to the material cultural landscape of northeastern Thai Buddhism, as it augments the religious map of highly venerated pilgrimage sites. It has become one of the major sightseeing points in the whole province of Mukdahan.[77] There are numerous road signs and posters throughout Mukdahan Province that make visitors aware of the Mae Chi Kaew *stūpa*. But not only spatially has the *stūpa* had an impact on the region; on the last Sunday of March every year since the completion of the Mae Chi Kaew *stūpa* in Khamcha-i, an annual commemoration day is held at the *stūpa*.

Descriptions and designations of Mae Chi Kaew as a *thūpārahapuggala* ("a person who is worthy of a *stūpa*") can be found frequently in her life accounts. In this way, the *stūpa* in Khamcha-i has been built to demonstrate that in current times the realization of *nibbāna* is still achievable for laywomen and is not restricted to the male monastic community. Other objectives of this *stūpa* are to "celebrate Mae Chi Kaew as an example for female lay followers [*sāvikā*, literally "(female) hearer"] in the present era [*yuk patjuban*]"[78] and to "encourage [*hai kamlangjai*] women to pursue the path toward *nibbāna*."[79]

While there are numerous similar edifices for male saints, the Mae Chi Kaew *stūpa* in Khamcha-i was unprecedented in that the construction explicitly celebrated the arahantship of a contemporary Thai woman. Thus, it is perhaps not surprising that the Mae Chi Kaew *stūpa* in Khamcha-i does not appear to have been an unproblematic undertaking. Phra Ajan Inthawai Santussako, who was the driving force in the building of the *stūpa*, initially had concerns about the project:

> My decision to construct a *cetiya* for a *mae chi* was not a straightforward one and was made only after careful consideration, for people may argue that this is something fatuous [*ngom ngai*]. But I went ahead with it, as our great master confirmed, and I have seen with my own eyes that her bones turned into crystallized relics [*pen phra that pen kaeo*], as a matter of fact.[80]

Due to the uniqueness and enormous paradigmatic significance of the Mae Chi Kaew *stūpa* in Khamcha-i, further discussion of particularities of its meaning and architectural features is due. In like manner to some of the *stūpa*s erected for male saints of the Thai forest tradition, the first floor of the *stūpa* houses a museum in which personal items of Mae Chi Kaew, such as a water kettle, glasses, scissors, a toothbrush, a mat, and towels, are displayed in glass cases. In the middle of the museum and surrounded by the glass cases, there is solid white life-size statue of Mae Chi Kaew, showing her practicing walking meditation. On the walls of the museum bilingual (Thai and English) tables invite the visitor to study the life, work, and spiritual achievements of Mae Chi Kaew.[81] On the first floor of the *stūpa* the visitor can enter a room where a life-size statue and relics are kept. The figure shows Mae Chi Kaew in a sitting meditation position with open eyes that seem to look more to the inside than at the onlooker. She is holding a colored handkerchief in her hands. Around the statue there are baskets containing utensils and tools for the preparation of betel. The verisimilitude of her likeness together with the baskets and the cuspidor make her appear present and alive.

Parts of her relics are displayed in two glass urns on small white stone pillars on the left and right in front of her statue. These glass urns are placed in such a way that they seem to invite the visitor to lean over them in order to study the relics closely. The glass of the urns seems to have a magnifying effect. The two urns contain numerous relics in many colors and shapes; while some of them are white or translucent, others are pink, yellow, or green. Many of them look like various gemstones, such as lapis lazuli or quartz.[82] Unlike in many or maybe even all traditional Thai *stūpa*s where the "relics are buried deep within a *stūpa* and are never seen,"[83] in most of the recently built *stūpa*s for monks of the Thai forest tradition the relics are made easily visible for the visitor; sometimes even magnifying glasses are provided so that a closer study of the relics is possible, as, for example, in the case of Luang Pu Waen's relics displayed in the Luang Pu Waen Suciṇṇo Museum in Wat Doi Mae Pang, north of Chiang Mai.[84]

The design of the Mae Chi Kaew *stūpa* was quite obviously inspired by the architectural structure of the famous and highly revered Phra That Phanom *stūpa* in Nakhon Phanom Province, a very important pilgrimage center in northeastern Thailand.[85] In addition to the common symbolism of traditional *stūpa*s, the outward architectural features of the Mae Chi Kaew *stūpa* in Khamcha-i are remarkably pregnant with soteriological meaning in a variety of particular ways. The *stūpa* is surrounded by water basins, which demarcate the sacred and pure (*parisuddhi*) inner area from the outside worldly sphere. These basins are filled with cool and clear water in which lotus flowers float on the surface. A further remarkable feature of the Mae Chi Kaew *stūpa* is that the then Thai *saṅgha* supreme patriarch Somdet Phra Ñāṇasaṁvara gave the *stūpa*'s name (*thawai nam*): *Cetiya* in Commemoration of the Triple Gem—that is, the Buddha, the *dhamma*, and the *saṅgha*.

In addition, the supreme patriarch also provided relics of the Buddha (*sārīrika-dhātu*) for enshrinement in it. Together with relics of fully awakened disciples of the Buddha (*arahantasawok*) and of some Thai Buddhist saints (such as Luang Pu Man, Luang Pu Sao, and Luang Pu Khao), the Buddha relics were enshrined in the spire of the Mae Chi Kaew *stūpa*.[86] No relics of *bhikkhunī*s from the time of the Buddha were enshrined in the *stūpa*. Initially, it was planned to place crystallized remains of Mae Chi Kaew in the spire of the *stūpa*, too. This plan was abandoned, though. One of the reasons was that there apparently were people who disapproved of this idea. It was also felt that it would "not be appropriate" (*khong ja mai mo som*) or "not correct/right" (*khong mai thuk tong*) to do so. Phra Ajan Inthawai Santussako explains that "we are still living in a world of conventions, and Mae Chi Kaew was a woman."[87] For this reason, the relics of Mae Chi Kaew that people initially wanted to store in the spire were eventually enshrined on the *stūpa*'s second floor underneath the statue that shows her in a sitting position. According to the available sources, it seems that Mae Chi Kaew herself adhered to the concept of a gender hierarchy without ever challenging it. In fact, it is reported that when a layperson took pictures of her, Mae Chi Kaew ordered the pictures burned, explaining, "Pictures of women for veneration cannot be put on the same level as pictures of monks. This would be a demeritorious thing [*pāpa*] for the one who does this."[88]

Here it is interesting to note that Mae Bunruean seems to have had a similar understanding; she reportedly ordered that images of her (which have become highly sought-after items in Thai Buddhism) should not be venerated in shrines with Buddha images.[89] It was argued that Mae

FIGURE 15. Phra That Phanom *stūpa* in Nakhon Phanom Province

Chi Kaew's understanding of her hierarchical relation with monks is one reason it was decided that her relics not be enshrined in the spire with the other relics. This, it was argued, reflected one aspect of her own spiritual practice; she consistently paid high respect to the "saffron robes" (*pha lueang*) and placed herself on a lower level in the presence of monks, practicing modesty and humbleness (*on nom thom tua*). "No matter how physically demanding it would have been, Mae Chi Kaew would always sit on the floor if a monk passed by, no matter if the ground she sat on was dirty or not. "[90]

Another reason for the decision to place Mae Chi Kaew's relics on the second floor and not in the spire was that it was felt that if revered male monastic teachers would visit the *stūpa*, Mae Chi Kaew's relics would be placed too high if enshrined in the *stūpa*'s spire. This gender hierarchy expressed in the *stūpa*'s design, so it is explained, conforms to the first rule of the eight *garudhammas* (the special rules for *bhikkhunī*s that clearly subordinate them to the monks),[91] which stipulates that a *bhikkhunī* must show deference to monks, regardless of their relative seniority. In this regard, the question must be raised as to why or how the *garudhamma* rules apply to her, as she was not a *bhikkhunī*. It may be that the decision was not entirely based on gender but also on the divide between lay and monastic, where gender of course implicitly plays a role, as Mae Chi Kaew could not take the *bhikkhunī* ordination. Be that as it may, it is interesting to note that Lisa Battaglia in her ethnographic study on contemporary Thai *mae chis* found that "virtually all of the *mae chis* I interviewed were not only aware of the Eight Special Rules, but also adhered to them in practice."[92]

While being soteriologically irrelevant, socioculturally Mae Chi Kaew's gender remains relevant, even after her death and even in her relics, which seem to be both gendered and genderless at the same time. But the dichotomy of conventional and ultimate truth is not only seen in relation to gender. A monk involved in the construction of the Mae Chi Kaew *stūpa* argued that the placing of Mae Chi Kaew's relics on a lower level of the *stūpa* is to be understood as an expression of monks' rigor of following monastic practices as described by the canonical *vinaya* and not as an expression of "disrespect for women." After all, "on a spiritual level monks would respect women [*hai kiat*]; on this level there are no differences between men and women."[93]

The way Mae Chi Kaew's relics were enshrined in her *stūpa*, together with these accounts, points at the fundamental Buddhist concept of the two truths: "conventional truth" (*sammuti-sacca*) and "ultimate truth" (*paramattha-sacca*). This concept, which can be traced back to Pali canonical texts, is often invoked in debates and discussions about the role of women in Thai Buddhism (see chapter 3).[94] Here it has been used as an interpretative strategy to explain the apparent contradiction between Buddhist "soteriological inclusiveness" and "androcentric tendencies" that has been observed in Pali canonical scriptures.[95] In this way, on the level of *paramattha-sacca*, gender from a soteriological point of view is irrelevant and is to be overcome as an essentialized concept and cause of attachment. This idea is nicely expressed in the speech that Luang Ta Mahabua gave on May 20, 2006, during the opening ceremony of the Mae Chi Kaew *stūpa*: "Being an arahant means to have transcended the gender differentiation in female and male."[96] The *sammuti-sacca*, however, represents social convention and reflects specific sociocultural contexts and values. In the context of the Mae Chi Kaew *stūpa*, it seems to point at the widespread worldly convention (*lokasammuti*) of the socioreligious subordinate status of women.

Spatial Sanctification

Being the most potent physical affirmation of Mae Chi Kaew's sainthood, the *stūpa* undoubtedly constitutes the most sacred center of Mae Chi Kaew's nunnery, or indeed of her entire veneration. However, there are also a number of specific sites within the nunnery that have become sanctified by the fact that crucial events in Mae Chi Kaew's biography are believed to have taken place there. Thus, the pathway where she practiced walking meditation shortly before her awakening on November 1, 1952, has been fenced off with barbed wire so that no one else can use it. Her monastic dwelling (*kuṭī*) can be visited for paying respects but is no longer occupied. The spot on which her body was cremated has been encircled by stones too heavy to be moved by hand. On the site where the cremation took place a *phayom* tree has been planted "in remembrance of liberation [*vimutti*]," according to a sign that was erected there. In this way, the layout of the nunnery spatially marks key events of Mae Chi Kaew's biography with the purpose of causing deep emotion in the numerous visitors and pilgrims, prompting them to contemplate Buddhist soteriology, and inspiring their faith.[97] This spatial element of her veneration is strongly reminiscent of the four *saṃvejanīyaṭṭhānas* (places to rouse emotion/sense of urgency) found in the Pali canon: the Buddha's birthplace, the place where he attained awakening, the place where he preached his first sermon, and the place where he died. These four sites are mentioned in the *Mahāparinibbāna-sutta* where the Buddha says that "there are four places the sight of which should arouse emotion in the faithful . . . the faithful monks and nuns, male and female lay-followers will visit those places. And any who die while making the pilgrimage to these shrines with a devout heart will, at the breaking-up of the body after death, be reborn in a heavenly world."[98] Thus, the spatial layout of the whole site of the Mae Chi Kaew memorial and the adjacent nunnery potently reconnect Mae Chi Kaew's life story to the Buddha's own biography, while also localizing and making tangible key elements of the Buddha's paradigmatic life and soteriology.

Commemoration Hall and Museum for the Veneration of Mae Bunruean

Even though one can also find accounts of the transformation of Mae Bunreuan's remains into *phra that* in her hagiographies,[99] these accounts do not have such a prominent role as they do in the hagiographies and veneration of Mae Chi Kaew. This is despite the fact that according to some accounts the transformation of Mae Bunruean's remains into *phra that* took place unusually quickly—already during the cremation of her body in 1964.[100] As already observed in chapter 3, her assumed supramundane attainments, of which transformed relics are believed to be the physical evidence, do not play a particularly prominent role in her hagiographies or in devotional practices. Thus, so far, no *stūpa*s similar to those of Mae Chi Kaew, Mae Chi Chandra Khonnokyoong, and Mae Chi Soda have been erected for the veneration of Mae Bunruean.[101]

However, there are several shrines of various sizes in or near Bangkok where devotees can venerate statues or relics of her, such as in Wat Saranat in Rayong, Wat Sangkhathan in Nonthaburi, the nunnery Sala Santisuk in Nakhon Pathom, and Wat Samphanthawong in Bangkok. The most important site of veneration, however, is in the Bangkok monastery Wat Awutwikasitaram. Not more than two years after Mae Bunruean's death in 1964, the abbot of Wat Awutwikasitaram gave permission for a commemoration hall (*sala*) to be built in the monastery compound, next to the main entrance.[102] Nowadays, at the center of the hall there are several statues of Mae Bunruean, in front of which devotees show respect by prostrating themselves. On the walls there are several photographs of Mae Bunruean. The visitor can also inspect parts of her relics that are on display in a glass showcase. On a large table in front of the central Mae Bunruean statue, devotees place not only fruits, such as coconuts, pineapples, apples, and bananas, but also water and other things in the belief that Mae Bunruean's "miraculous [*itthi patihan*] powers that are still effective to the current day" will endow these things with curative and protective power:

> Even though Mae Bunruean passed away many years ago, the statues of her in the memorial hall in Wat Awutwikasitaram . . .

> still contain enormous sacredness [*khwam saksit ying yai*] just as when Mae Bunruean was still alive. Thus, if you suffer from any physical pain or illness and prostrate yourself in front of [and show respect to] her statue while making a solemn wish [*tang athitthan jit*], you can ask for healing salve . . . or other things from Mae Bunruean in order to cure your illness. If your *kamma* is not too heavy, the illness can disappear.[103]

Devotees may also place small objects, such as coins, into the clasped hands of a Mae Bunruean statue and attach them there with sticky tape in the belief that positive energies will be transferred from the statue into these objects. Furthermore, the hall is used for endowing Mae Bunruean amulets with positive energy. Posters in the monastery advertise Mae Bunruean amulets, for example, as "supremely auspicious things—heritage of the monastery, heritage of the *dhamma*." In front of the hall, a small amulet shop was built a number of years ago. Another amulet shop is located inside the area where the monks live. Both of these shops sell Mae Bunruean amulets, some of which cost up to 25,000 baht each. In front of the commemoration hall there is also a shrine with a golden Buddha image at the center. At this shrine devotees can ignite incense sticks, light candles, and donate flowers. On the right side of the shrine, positioned slightly below the Buddha image, there is a statue of Mae Bunruean. On the left side there is a statue of the Buddha's personal physician, Jīvaka-Komārabhacca. The Pali canon depicts Jīvaka as an unusually gifted physician who achieved the first level of awakening (*sotāpanna*). The way the statues are arranged seems to suggest that Mae Bunruean was an accomplished disciple of the Buddha with outstanding abilities to heal, comparable to those of Jīvaka.

Another important construction of veneration is the Khun Mae Bunruean Tongbuntoem Museum in the royal monastery of Wat Samphanthawong in Bangok, built with financial support from the Thai Department for Tourism. The museum opened in 2014. Even though the museum displays a number of Mae Bunreuan's personal items, letters, pictures of her, and a number of first editions of her texts, it is obvious that the main purpose of the museum is neither to store knowledge nor to educate but to prompt veneration of Mae Bunruean. At the center of the

FIGURE 16. Statue of Mae Bunruean next to those of the Buddha and the physician Jīvaka-Komārabhacca, in Wat Awutwikasitaram

museum the visitor finds a true-to-life statue of Mae Bunruean. Behind the figure parts of her relics are on display, enshrined in glass *stūpa*s that are placed in beautifully and elaborately carved miniature pavilions made of gold-colored wood. Some visitors have reported seeing rays miraculously emerge from the relics. The museum is being used for consecration rituals. During these elaborate rituals, amulets, pictures, or statues are endowed with positive, protective powers. This is done by monks who sit around the objects to be consecrated. Each of the monks holds in his hands the end of a white cotton cord (*sai sin*) that is connected to and extends over a web running along the museum's ceiling to the statue of Mae Bunruean and her relics. With the help of the white thread, the power inherent in the participating monks, the chanting of Pali texts, and of course the power

FIGURE 17. Khun Mae Bunruean Tongbuntoem Museum in Wat Samphanthawong

believed to be inherent in Mae Bunruean's statue and relics, sacred power is transferred to the amulets, pictures, or statues that are to be consecrated in the ritual. In this way, large numbers of statues and pictures of Mae Bunruean, in addition to new editions of her Phra Phuttho Noi amulets, have been consecrated in the museum.

The purpose of both the commemoration hall in Wat Awutwikasitaram and the museum in Wat Samphanthawong is clearly not only to preserve and make available biographical knowledge. In fact, it seems that this is a minor objective of these places of memory. In contrast to the Mae Chi Kaew *stūpa*, neither of these two places provides a substantial amount of biographical data. It appears that the main objective of the commemoration hall and the museum is to serve as source and storehouse of Mae Bunruean's benevolent supernatural powers, which, so it is believed, can be activated, manipulated, and distributed. These two sites are first of all not for the preservation of knowledge about the past but are used as living centers for veneration and generation of protective powers. In this way, they are also sources of income through the production and selling of amulets and other devotional items.

The Amulets of Mae Bunruean

Anthropologists have described various restrictive cultural practices and prohibitions in Thailand that manifest beliefs about women's bodies having the power to pollute sacred objects or areas. For this reason in some temples women are not allowed to enter specific areas deemed vulnerable to the magically polluting powers of menstrual blood. Terwiel writes that "a woman should not possess an object charged with protective power; inadvertently she is likely to spoil its magical value."[104] In addition, the consecration of amulets has been described as an exclusively male domain. It is normally done either by individual monks when they are believed to possess enormous "mind powers" (*phalang jit*) or by a group of monks. Here meditation and often incantations (*khatha*) are used to endow amulets with magically efficacious powers.[105]

In this cultural context, Mae Bunruean's biography brings out a conspicuous gendered feature that is arguably the most well known and effective of Mae Bunruean's contributions to Thai Buddhism; between September 11 and 13, 1951, Mae Bunruean performed the consecration (*athitthan*) of one hundred thousand amulets called Phra Phuttho Noi. The amulet depicts the Buddha in meditation posture. The majority of these amulets, which are made of different ingredients, such as parts of plants, powder from other amulets, and clay, were given to Wat Awutwikasitaram. The monastery subsequently gave these amulets to people who donated money for the development of the monastery. Mae Bunruean's powers to consecrate amulets must have been believed to be considerable, for it is reported that even monks asked Mae Bunruean for help consecrating highly sought-after amulets depicting the deeply revered Ayutthaya monk Luang Pu Thuat.[106]

FIGURE 18. Phra Phuttho Noi amulets

Over the years, the Phra Phuttho Noi amulets have become increasingly popular and valued. While they had initially been given away for free, some twenty-five years after Mae Bunruean's death some of them were sold for up to 50,000 baht each. It has been reported, however, that for a while the amulet dropped quite significantly in value and was temporarily worth less than 10,000 baht in the amulet market when a well-known amulet magazine reportedly criticized (*jomti*)—together with another matter—the fact that it was consecrated by a woman. Their value has risen again, however, and nowadays some Phra Phuttho Noi amulets are valued at more than 200,000 baht (some 6,400 USD) each.[107] It has also been reported, for example on the internet and in Thai newspapers, that a number of well-known amulet collectors, such as Boy Thaphrajan, who made his fortune trading amulets, was wearing Mae Bunruean's amulets.[108] This has certainly contributed to their recent increase in reputation. Due to the currently enormous popularity of Phra Phuttho Noi and the scarcity of amulets still available, the monastery Wat Awutwikasitaram even decided to produce new amulets following Mae Bunruean's method and using the same ingredients (along with the substance of damaged original Phra Phuttho Noi amulets).

FIGURE 19. Amulet magazine with a picture of a Phra Phuttho Noi amulet on its front page

In the huge and booming Thai amulet market, Mae Bunruean is now widely considered a unique exception in being a female source of the enormous charisma (*barami*) required to produce amulets that are so highly sought after and valued.[109] Mae Bunruean's Phra Phuttho Noi amulet is certainly an exception as well; in my many interviews with professional amulet collectors, it has often been stressed that she is the only woman widely acknowledged as having been able to effectively consecrate amulets with supernaturally efficacious powers. It is even believed that the amulets she consecrated are more powerful (*phalang di kwa*) than some consecrated by male monks who are famous for their amulets (*keji ajan bang ong*).[110] But not only are her Phra Phuttho Noi amulets attributed these powers; even photographs—sometimes as small as postage stamps—and small statues of Mae Bunruean are worn as amulets in the belief that they contain supernatural powers. In addition, statues of her, with relics of her enshrined in the pedestal, have also become sought-after items of veneration. According to my research it seems likely that medallion amulets depicting Mae Bunruean as a highly revered female practitioner may well be the very first of their kind for a woman in Thai Buddhism, having first been produced in 1968 only four years after her death.

Some twenty years after her death, a monk who was a close disciple of Mae Bunruean produced thirty thousand amulets with the same name and form of Mae Bunruean's original amulet, Phra Phuttho Noi,

FIGURE 20. Medallion amulet with the effigy of Mae Bunruean

FIGURE 21. Small statues of Mae Bunruean

FIGURE 22. Small statue of Mae Bunruean, made in 2016

containing parts of Mae Bunruean's relics (*phra that*). Another amulet—this time produced in a quantity of ten thousand—was produced in 1988 and given the name Phra Phuttho Ariyasap. The amulets contain "relic powder" (*phong phra that*) and ashes from the cremation of Mae Bunruean's body together with powder from amulets of Mae Bunruean's original Phra Phuttho Noi amulet made in 1951.[111]

Thus, while Mae Chi Kaew's relics are depicted and by many perceived first of all as a physical representation of the ultimate aim of Buddhist soteriology, *nibbāna*, and as evidence for the possibility of achieving *nibbāna* in current times, it seems that the primary purpose of the relics of Mae Bunruean is the generation and dissemination of supernatural powers.

Other female practitioners of my study produced amulets too, albeit in significantly smaller numbers and with far less impact than Mae Bunruean. Mae Chi Nari, for example, is reported to have consecrated (*pluk sek*) some 400–500 medallion amulets and 300–400 "powder amulets," all carrying an image of her.[112] The powder samulets contain wisps of Mae Chi Nari's hair. She gave these amulets out to her devotees. It is also reported that Mae Chi Soda consecrated one thousand locket amulets carrying her effigy.[113] There are also amulets that carry the image of female practitioners other than Mae Bunruean. For example, the locket amulet of Mae Chi Bunmi Wetchasan of Wat Samphanthanwong carries her image and contains wisps of her hair. This amulet too was probably produced in a relatively small number. Also, as already mentioned above, for the opening ceremony of the Mae Chi Kaew *stūpa* in Ban Huai Sai ten thousand medallion amulets carrying the image of Mae Chi Kaew were produced and distributed. However, so far none of these amulets has achieved anything near the value and popularity of Mae Bunruean amulets.[114] In fact, Mae Bunruean's amulets have become so popular and valuable that counterfeits of her amulets have emerged, at least within the last twenty years or so.

It is clear that, with the exception of the amulets of Mae Bunruean, amulets consecrated by or carrying the effigy of female practitioners have so far not become nearly as popular, widespread, and valuable as those consecrated by or carrying the image of a male practitioner. Most of these amulets have been produced for a rather small group of devotees of the

FIGURE 23. Amulet of Mae Chi Nari Karun that contains wisps of her hair

FIGURE 24. Locket amulet with the effigy of Mae Chi Nari Karun, from the year 1986

female practitioners. As Mae Chi Prathum Choti-anan, who produced the medallion amulet Phra Khotsetthi, explains in this regard in her autobiography, "I produced only 285 amulets—a small number. I did not dare to produce a large number. I was concerned that no one would have any faith [*sattha*] as I am only a *mae chi*. There are only a few people who have faith in a *mae chi*."[115] Thus, female practitioners are generally not believed to be a source of supernatural potency for the consecration of amulets, even if they had spent a significant amount of time on intense spiritual practice. So far, Mae Bunruean and her amulets are unique in this respect.

Material Objects as Catalysts for the Veneration of Female Saints

In his study of Buddhist sainthood in contemporary Burma, Rozenberg argues that with the cremation of the body of a saint "things almost stop here.... The figure ceases to be the motor and the heart of a system of social relations. His saintliness is no longer effective."[116] This happens despite the fact that transmogrified relics are not uncommon in Burma and may be found among the ashes of the saint's cremated body. However, in contrast to relics of the Buddha, "which are national palladiums venerated by every Buddhist in the country, the cremated relics of Burma's modern *arahants* are relatively neglected."[117] Similarly to the Thai beliefs I describe above, Burmese Buddhists may also interpret these transformed relics as evidence for sainthood. Nonetheless, in contrast to the Buddhism of Thailand, in Burma the "intense ritual veneration that the aspiring saint was at the heart of vanishes after his funeral. . . . [T]he physical passing of the aspiring saint generally signifies the almost complete dissolution of his charisma."[118]

In Thai Buddhism, the material forms of relics, *stūpa*s, and amulets in which the charisma of the saint has become objectified play a significant role. These objects continue the life story of the saints beyond their physical demise. In fact, in the case of Mae Bunruean one could argue that her relics and, more importantly, her amulets have been crucial in the spreading of her veneration and fame. Moreover, her amulets, pictures, statues, and other items, such as prints of the markings on the sole of her foot (see chapter 2), have been effective even after her death. Since these objects can be duplicated without a loss of the efficacy of their inherent supernatural powers, this has led to large numbers of new stories of Mae Bunruean's altruism and effective powers to cure and protect. These stories have taken place after Mae Bunruean's physical demise. The supernaturally efficacious objects and the stories of their effectiveness sustain or even intensify interest, fascination, and faith, and as a consequence and reflection of this have significantly increased the commercial value of Mae Bunruean's amulets. In this way, a number of "updated" hagiographies of Mae Bunruean with stories about the postmortem effectiveness of her persisting powers have been produced and widely disseminated.

In the case of Mae Chi Kaew, her transmogrified relics have been crucial for the emergence of her translocal veneration and the preservation of knowledge of her remarkable life story, as evidenced by the increasing number of hagiographies and the building of her *stūpa* museum. As noted earlier in this chapter, without the realization that her physical remains had turned into crystalline relics Mae Chi Kaew's life story "would have nearly faded away . . . from the memory of people."

At the same, one could argue that through the transmogrification of their remains, Mae Chi Kaew and other *mae chi*s have become part of the pantheon of the highly and widely revered saints of the Thai forest tradition, albeit taking, due their gender, a marginal position, as expressed in the many relic posters and relic books. However, despite their marginal position, these *mae chis*' transformed relics complete the soteriological message, namely that *nibbāna* is equally realizable by men and women in the current time.

In the study about Burmese sainthood referred to above, Rozenberg also states that at the site where the living saint's charisma was effective, after the death of the saint the "forest takes over."[119] In Thai Buddhism, the exact opposite may happen. Here, the postmortem events in the case of Mae Chi Kang Thephin are instructive as they further underscore and exemplify the differences between Burmese and Thai veneration of deceased Buddhist saints while demonstrating again the importance of relics as a catalyst for increased veneration and a desideratum for the preservation of biographical data. The discovery of Mae Chi Kang's bones/relics made people clear forests some fifty years after her death to provide land where a future generation could erect a *stūpa* for veneration.

Not much is known about the life of Mae Chi Kang. The few biographical fragments we have stem primarily from the hagiographies of Luang Pu Man.[120] Luang Pu Man spent the last five years before his death in 1949 in the monastery Wat Pa Ban Nong Phue at the small northeastern village of Ban Nong Phue. During this time he instructed Mae Chi Kang in meditation; she was already about eighty years old. She was highly praised by Luang Pu Man for her meditative insights, and when she had conversations with the great master, monks and novices would come in large numbers in order to listen to their dialogues. Mae Chi Kang passed away in the 1950s. But it was only around the year 2005 that people started to look for and eventually found the buried and cremated remains of Mae Chi Kang in the cemetery of Nong Khaoji not far from the village Ban Nong Phue.[121] Elderly villagers were able to remember that her bones had been buried near a termite hill in the cemetery. Even though the location was unmarked, the villagers were convinced that the bones must be hers as they were found near a betel cassette that belonged to Mae Chi Kang. Fragments of her bones were put in two transparent reliquaries, which were then put on display in a glass shrine at the local monastery, Wat Pa Ban Nong Phue, next to the relics of Luang Pu Man and a number of his disciples. The two relic containers of Mae Chi Kang's relics (and

FIGURE 25. Miniature glass *stūpa*s with the relics of Luang Pu Man, Mae Chi Kang, and those of other practitioners of the Thai forest tradition, in the monastery Wat Pa Ban Nong Phue

next to her those of another *mae chi*)[122] appear small and inconspicuous in comparison to the elaborately ornamented reliquaries in which the miniature glass *stūpa*s of the relics of the monks are presented. The relic containers of the two *mae chi*s are placed on two silver-colored pedestals. These two pedestals stand on a piece of white cloth on the floor while the relic containers of the monks are placed on three significantly larger wooden pedestals of different height and size, obviously in accordance with the degree of respect given to the monks. The relics of Luang Pu Man are placed on the largest pedestal. Thus, as with the gendered arrangement of the relic posters and books and the placement of Mae Chi Kaew's relics in her *stūpa* in Ban Huai Sai described above, the intended message of the way the relics are presented here appears to be soteriological inclusiveness while maintaining gendered hierarchy.

On the spot in the cemetery where the bones of Mae Chi Kang were discovered five decades after her death is a wooden sign saying that in this place her remains were cremated in 1955. In a sermon he gave to laypeople at his monastery, Wat Pa Ban Tat on June 6, 2005, Luang Ta Mahabua said, "I have learned that the bones of [Mae Chi Kang] have turned into *phra that*. I certainly believe and . . . immediately accept this [*yom rap thanthi*]."[123] In the cremation volume of Luang Ta Mahabua one can read that "[Mae Chi] Kang is an example of a woman who attained the supramundane during the time of Luang Pu Man."[124] The immediate area around the ground where Mae Chi Kang's cremation is believed to have taken place has been cleared of bushes in the middle of an otherwise densely vegetated area with many old, large trees. This was done "in case people in a future generation decide to erect a *stūpa* [for the enshrinement of Mae Chi Kang's relics] here."[125] It seems that in the case of Mae Chi Kang the hagiographical process is at a very early stage and, if it further unfolds more than five decades after her death, this would largely be due to the discovery of her bones and their transmogrification into relics.

However, the material manifestations of sainthood are ambiguous. Despite, or perhaps because of, its high effectiveness in the spreading of saints' reputations, the objectification of sainthood may cause discomfort to those who are interested in the preservation of the saints' life stories and their exemplary soteriological messages. As one of the main hagiographers of Mae Chi Nari stated in an interview,

> There is a dilemma. It goes against my feeling but [on the one hand] I want to spread the biography of Mae Chi Nari. [I want people to learn about] her goodness and virtues. But this may have to involve business. . . . For if you want to sell [her biography and build a museum for her], you need to have auspicious objects [*watthumongkhon*]. Even though I do not want people to be interested in amulets, I may have to do it.[126]

Here, material objects are perceived as potentially distracting from the soteriological ideal that the saint represents; at the same time, they are regarded as a necessary means to preserve memory of the saint's exemplary biography and to help spread and make meaningful its soteriological implications. The concern here, however, is that instead of inspiring devotees to develop detachment, the saint's charisma may become a source for material enrichment and attachment.

With this chapter, I tried to demonstrate the importance of studying material culture for our understanding of beliefs about the roles and spiritual aspirations and potential of female practitioners in modern

Thai Buddhism. My investigation has shown that even though Buddhists have tried to find legitimacy for or challenge specific material practices by juxtaposing them with normative texts, material manifestations and expressions of belief are often more powerful than authoritative texts or doctrinal arguments. This has become especially clear with regard to the belief in the possibility of achieving sainthood in current times, in particular for women. Objects, such as *stūpa*s and transmogrified relics, have often had a much wider and deeper impact on religious practices, emotions, and beliefs than Pali canonical texts or sermons by contemporary figures. At the same time, objects have also been able to prompt the production of new texts. Consider, for example, the many hagiographical texts that emerged as a result of the transformation of Mae Chi Kaew's remains and the assumed supernatural efficacy of Mae Bunruean's amulets and other consecrated objects. Thus, in the words of David Morgan, "belief should be studied as taking place in material practices. Belief should not be understood as coming only before such things as the veneration of relics or the ecstatic drudgery of pilgrimage, but as being constituted by them." In this way, one sees "that materiality *mediates* belief, that material objects and practices both enable it and enact it."[127]

Chapter 5

The Importance of Orality and Memory in Spiritual Practice

> Better than a thousand useless verses
> is one useful verse,
> hearing which one attains peace.
>
> *Dhammapada*, verse 101[1]

In her study of the "History of Women's Education and Activism in Thailand," LeeRay Costa argues that "as women were barred from the monkhood by virtue of their sex, they were denied learning at the *wat* [monastery] and, as a result, prohibited access to an enormous body of knowledge considered to be culturally and socially valuable."[2] She also writes,

> In 1915, the government initiated another education plan [that] attempted to give girls more educational opportunities. But prevailing cultural attitudes slowed such advancement for a number of reasons. First, the general public still believed that women should care for the home and family and that book learning was unsuitable for girls. Second, the majority of schools were located in provincial monasteries, and it was thought indecorous for women to attend school in these principally male religious spaces.[3]

Similarly, Darunee Tantiwiramanond argues that

> the most important consequence of banning women from the order, however, was to deprive women of literacy. Prior to the early 20th century, literacy was imparted solely in Buddhist monasteries. Female education was suppressed by religious

> mechanism: physical contact between the lay female and (male) monks was considered sinful. Consequently, women were barred from knowledge.[4]

Referring to sermon texts and biographical texts of both male and female monastics, I show in this chapter that both Darunee's and Costa's statements appear to be too simplistic with regard to women's access to (text-based) knowledge, the relationship between monks and women, and the roles of women in Thai Buddhism; if nothing else, they certainly require qualification. A shortcoming of Darunee's and Costa's statements is that they overlook the importance of orality and memory in Buddhist learning environments, at the very least when it comes to the transmission of Buddhist knowledge. As the case studies in this chapter demonstrate, Buddhist women had access to (sometimes high-ranking) monk teachers; they also suggest that, in the study of Buddhist teaching, literacy did not often play a decisive role in the pedagogical relationships between a Buddhist master and his students, and this applies to both male and female students.

This chapter thus focuses on how Thai female practitioners conceived of knowledge and their acquisition of it. In this way, I want to make a contribution to the study of Thailand's educational history by investigating these women's access to Buddhist teachings and practice. I want to emphasize, though, that I will deal neither with formal public education[5] nor with formal monastic education in Thai history; nor will I directly engage with arguments regarding gendered differences in the acquisition of reading and writing skills. However, referring primarily to the experiences and ideas of individual female practitioners, this chapter demonstrates and investigates the importance and persistence of orality and memorization in Buddhist learning environments before and after compulsory education was introduced in Thailand in 1921.

The Persistence of Orality and Memorization

There is ample evidence that in Thailand there has long been a strong oral/aural culture, as monks have committed large amounts of Pali texts to memory for giving blessings or for liturgical purposes, as a part of their meditation practice, or as part of their preparation for Pali language exams. For example, the Thai historian and educational reformer Prince Damrong Rajanubhab (1862–1943), son of King Rama IV, reports that according to "an ancient custom" over the first five years of their monastic career, new monks were expected to gradually memorize a large number of Pali texts, such as the texts for the daily chanting sessions, Abhidhammic texts, protection texts (*paritta*), the lengthy canonical texts *Dhammacakkappavattana-sutta* and *Mahāsamaya-sutta*, and then finally, before the end of the fifth year after their ordination, the *pāṭimokkha*, which consists of the 227 monastic rules for monks.[6] Also, in order to pass the second-highest level of the Thai monastic Pali language exams, monks may memorize a text of more than 160,000 words, and "preparation for the exam . . . requires word-perfect memorization of the entire set Pali text."[7] Also, interestingly, the Pali language translation examinations were held until 1912 entirely in oral form; only then was the written examination for Pali language gradually introduced.[8]

It has been argued that during the reign of Rama IV (1851–68), the acquisition of knowledge through reading started to become increasingly important.[9] Also, with the arrival of print technology and the proliferation of printed books in Thailand during the nineteenth century, oral transmission of knowledge certainly decreased in importance.[10] Nonetheless, it seems that the increasing availability of printed texts and the arrival of a modern educational system have not eclipsed the importance of orality and memory.

Thai historian Nidhi Eoseewong believes that "it is possible that the majority of Thai people are still in a culture of listening rather than of reading, and the very reason Thai people read little is that we are not familiar with this form of receiving information."[11] Nidhi argues that a considerable amount of old (*boran*) Thai literature was to be read out so that people could listen to it. Even nowadays, he observes, Thai bestsellers still have an oral character: "[Authors] for example create texts that are like a conversation with the reader."[12]

Thai scholar Chetana Nagavajara also underscores the importance of orality and memory in traditional textual practices when he notes that

> texts were written down in an effort to safeguard them against oblivion and at the same time to constitute a kind of literary trust for the benefit of the general public and posterity. But this quest for permanency does not preclude dissemination through the oral tradition. Those who could read continued to commit the fruits of their reading to memory.

He recalls how his grandmother,[13]

> who was among a small number of women in those days who could read and write, . . . [g]rowing up in the oral tradition . . . [n]aturally . . . was endowed with an extraordinary memory (which was common to her contemporaries) and possessed a very large repertoire of literary works that she could recite. It was perfectly natural for her to recite . . . for a continuous period of a few hours.[14]

The following case studies, which not only include relevant practices and ideas of the major women of my study but also those of some further female practitioners, lend further support to Chetana's observations on the importance of orality and memory in Thai culture.

Case Study 1: Khunying Damrongthammasan (Yai Wisetsiri)

Much of what is known about Khunying Yai's acquisition of Buddhist knowledge comes from the recollections of the abbot of Wat Sattanatpariwat in Ratchaburi, Phra Thepsumethi (Yuak Cattamalo, 1914–2002), who as a young monk listened to Khunying Yai's explanations of Buddhist teachings; this information has been augmented by interviews with her adopted son, Prasop Wisetsiri.[15] Phra Thepsumethi reported, "She had an excellent memory and was able to recollect the content of long-ago discussions with a high degree of precision."[16] He also tells us that "she was able to memorize a large number of *dhamma* principles/teachings (*lak tham*); she was even able to memorize all [423] verses of the *Dhammapada* from a young age." Her ability to memorize a large number of texts must have been regarded as remarkable. Somdet Phra Buddhaghosacariya, who himself was able to memorize a huge amount of Buddhist texts, starts the foreword of Khunying Yai's cremation volume with the following sentences:

> From a young age until her death, [Khunying Yai] had faith in Buddhism. She was able to recite from heart the [entire] *Mahāsatipaṭṭhāna-sutta*, which has a length of thirty-and-a-half pages as printed in the chanting book. She was also able to recite the entire translation [of this *sutta*]. Also, she was able to recite all sixteen questions of the *Soḷasapañha* [*Pārāyana-vagga*[17]], both in Pali and its [Thai] translation. In addition to this, she was able to recite other Buddhist texts.[18]

It has been reported that even highly educated monks were in awe of Khunying Yai's vast and precise knowledge of Buddhist teaching. However, according to available sources, it seems that despite her enormous Buddhist eruditeness she hardly gave any public teachings. She taught monks at her monastery Wat Thammikaram and gave private instruction to friends. Evidence of her comprehensive knowledge and deep understanding of Buddhist scriptures are her texts, most of which, as discussed in chapter 2, were published anonymously during her lifetime.

Khunying Yai's major prose texts, which consist of dialogues between two interlocutors, contain numerous interesting features, both in terms of formal structure and also content. One of the most important features for the purpose of my investigation in this chapter is the many lists that can be found throughout Khunying Yai's texts, such as the ten *saṃyojana*s (fetters that bind human beings to rebirth), the four *vesārajja*s (types of self-confidence), the ten *bala*s (types of power), the six *dhātu*s (elements), the four Noble Truths, and the fifteen *caraṇa*s (practices/conducts). There are also numerous quotations in Pali with their translations given in Thai. The way that these lists and quotations are embedded in these dialogues makes clear that they had been learned by heart by the people involved in these dialogues,[19] and their function was to trigger discussions and explanations. The content of the texts demonstrates that Khunying

FIGURE 26. Picture hanging on the wall of the ordination hall of Wat Thammikaram showing Khunying Yai as a laywoman

Yai must have had a close familiarity with Abhidhammic teachings. The popular tenth- or eleventh-century Abhidhamma compendium *Abhidhammatthasaṅgaha* is referred to and seems to have been an important source text for Khunying Yai's understanding of the Buddhist teaching.[20] Also, another prominent feature of Khunying Yai's texts is the comparison between different *dhammas*. Often *dhamma* teachings are explained by showing the differences from seemingly similar teachings.

The structure of Khunying Yai's texts is also quite obviously similar to the textual structure of the Pali canonical *sutta*s, incorporating numerous repetitions and embedding *dhamma* lists in a narrative.

In addition, there are numerous references to oral modes of transmitting knowledge. Thus, rather than being read, a book is "listened to" (*fang nangsue*), and the study of *dhamma* teachings is often described with the word *fang* (to listen) rather than with "to read" or "look at." The word "listen" (*fang*) is mentioned more than eighty times in her five major prose texts,[21] often in the sense of listening to an explanation, speech, teaching, sermon (*thet*), specific *sutta*s or "verses from the Buddha" (*tam khatha phra phutthaphasit*), the *dhamma*, or "*dhamma* expositions" (*thammapariyai*). In addition to this, *sadap*, which also has the meaning "to listen to," occurs eight times in these texts. "Write" (*khian*) and "read" (*an*), however, are not mentioned once. In her answers in *Aṭṭhadhammapañha* (*Eight questions on the* dhamma), probably her only prose text not published anonymously during her lifetime, when not familiar with a specific phrase in one of the questions, she replies literally, "I have never heard and never listened to this within the tradition."[22] Another typical statement can be found in her text *paṭipattivibhāga*, where she states, "We are very fortunate in that we were born [into a time period during which] the Buddhist teaching is available; this enables us to *listen* [*fang*] to the *dhamma*."[23] The abundance of references to oral modes of learning in Khunying Yai's texts is strikingly similar to authoritative Pali texts of the Theravada tradition, in which most of the words in connection to teaching and learning relate to hearing and speaking.[24]

Moreover, in her texts Khunying Yai often refers to memorization, using words like "recollect/recall" (*raluek*) and "memorize" (*jam song wai*). Her texts make it abundantly clear that for Khunying Yai there is a close connection between (right) memory, (real) knowledge, and (right) Buddhist practice. This is also evidenced in the following dialogical passage:

> *Tho.*: I am a [Buddhist] practitioner, which means I observe the precepts and lead a virtuous life [*mi tham*]. I also possess an understanding of numerous *dhamma* teachings. Why then am I still affected by worldly conditions [*lokadhamma*]?

> *To.*: Your knowledge is only on the level of *saññā* [perception, recognition]. You have not gained insight [*ru hen*] on the level of *paññā* [wisdom], but you understand that you know because when thinking about a specific *dhamma* teaching you have memorized [*jam song wai*] you gain clarity about it on the level of *saññā*. But this is not really knowing, which would be knowing on the level of *paññā*, like the knowing of a noble disciple [*ariya-sāvaka*]. . . . Remembering numerous *dhamma* teachings is called *pariyatti*.[25]

Elsewhere Khunying Yai gives the following explanation:

> *Tho.*: Paying homage [to the Triple Gem], using flowers, incense, and candles, and saluting the Triple Gem, reciting holy texts [*suat mon*], such as the daily morning and evening chanting and the chanting of other texts that are the words of the Buddha [*buddhabhāsita*], does this all not [simply] constitute worship by offering material things [*āmisapūjā*], as it is not [the practice of] *sīla*, *samādhi*, and *paññā*?
> *To.*: Do not misunderstand this point. For example, when showing respect to and prostrating oneself in front of the Triple Gem, this constitutes right action [*sammākammanto*]; to recite the virtues of the Buddha, *dhamma*, and *saṅgha* constitutes *sammāvācā* [right speech]; both of them are parts of the *sīla* group. As for the mind that recollects the virtues of the Buddha, *dhamma*, and *saṅgha*, this should be seen as a part of the *samādhi* group. As for the morning chanting that describes the five *khandha* as impermanent [*anicca*] or not-self [*anattā*] and the reciting of other *sutta*s that contain the teaching of the three characteristics [*tilakkhaṇa*], when recited with a focused and attentive mind [*jai kamnot tam*], clarity about impermanence, unsatisfactoriness, and nonself will arise. Thus, when reciting [in this way] this should be seen as a part of the *paññā* group. This means that the threefold training is complete and thus constitutes *paṭipattipūjā*, worship through practice.[26]

These and other passages in her texts make clear that for Khunying Yai reciting Buddhist texts with a correctly focused and attentive mind constitutes mind development (*citta-bhāvanā*) in accordance with the spiritual path. This is in line with early Buddhist ideas about recitation, as observed by a number of Buddhist studies scholars. Thus, Bhikkhu Anālayo, for example, argues that

> early Buddhist oral tradition also served as a way of meditating or reflecting on the *Dhamma*. . . . Recitation undertaken for its own sake does seem to function as a means of mental development (*bhāvanā*) in a wider sense, and as such could become a tool for progress on the path to liberation.[27]

Similarly, Collins states that "the oral/aural dimension of Buddhist texts is not only a matter of learning and public performance: it plays a role in meditation also."[28] Or as expressed in the words of Rupert Gethin, "mindful recitation of a text . . . operates as a kind of recollection of Dhamma (*dhammānusati*), a traditional subject of meditation."[29]

It is also notable that Khunying Yai did not only know the Pali canonical text *Pārāyana-vagga*,[30] which forms the last part of the canonical book *Suttanipāta*, by heart; this text also served as one major source for her own literary work. These two facts are noteworthy for several reasons. First of all, like the structure of all her prose texts, *Pārāyana-vagga* too has the format of questions and answers: sixteen Brahmin students approach the Buddha with questions, which he answers. What is also interesting is that in the *Nandamātā-sutta* of the *Aṅguttara-nikāya* it is said that one day the female lay follower Veḷukaṇṭakī Nandamātā recited this very text in the morning hours. The deva king Vessavaṇa, who happened to overhear her chanting, praised her for this with the words *sādhu, sādhu* ("well done, well done!").[31] Also, in the *Aṅguttara-nikāya*, we find a passage where the Buddha praised Veḷukaṇṭakī Nandamātā along with Khujjuttarā as a model female lay follower.[32] In the commentaries she is described as an *anāgāmī* (nonreturner; that is, someone who has achieved the third level of awakening) and able to recite the Pali canon.[33]

It is of course difficult, if not impossible, to tell if the textual structure of *Pārāyana-vagga* and the fact that this text was recited by an outstanding laywoman had an impact on Khunying Yai's decision to rote learn and avail herself of this text so frequently. What is certainly worthwhile though is to point out the striking similarities in textual practices. In fact, there are other canonical elements Khunying Yai incorporated in her texts that combine outstanding spiritual practice by women with the status of a lay disciple. In her text *Aṭṭhadhammapañha*, apart from referring to the Buddha she refers to only three other persons mentioned in Pali texts, all of whom are female lay followers.[34] Khunying Yai describes these three female figures as examples of persons with "unshakable confidence" (*acalasaddhā*) in the *dhamma*. One of these three women is Mallikā, the wife of the *senāpati* (general) and also later judge, Bandhula. The other one is Uttarā, who hired the prostitute Sirimā for her husband so that she could keep the eight precepts. The third one is Queen Sāmāvatī, who was the mistress of another remarkable canonical female figure, Khujjuttarā. Khujjuttarā is said to have been able to memorize sermons by the Buddha, which later became the canonical book *Ittivuttaka*.[35] She memorized what the Buddha taught so that she could repeat it for Queen Sāmāvatī and her five hundred ladies-in-waiting. The Buddha praised Khujjuttarā as the foremost of his laywomen disciples in terms of her learning.[36]

These biographies of Pali (post)canonical figures clearly resemble a number of elements in Khunying Yai's own biography. In particular, the similarities in terms of memory, orality, and recitation of Buddhist texts as an important part of female Buddhist teaching and learning should be pointed out here. However despite briefly referring to these female canonical figures in her *Aṭṭhadhammapañha* text, Khunying Yai does not discuss matters related to gender at all, at least not in the texts available to us. (For more on this see chapter 6.)

From an account by Phra Thepsumethi we know that at a very early age Khunying Yai was a student of Somdet Phra Wanarat (Thap Buddhasiri, 1806–91), a former abbot of the prestigious Bangkok temple Wat Somanat Wihan and still highly revered meditation master. As Khunying Yai was born in 1882, she must have been extremely young when she became a student of Somdet Phra Wanarat Thap. Given that we know from other sources that Khunying Yai had great enthusiasm for the study of Buddhism and at the same time possessed what seems an unusually advanced receptivity, this apprenticeship at such a young age was certainly possible. Even though I do not have a source at the moment to confirm this, it seems certain that she must have received her instruction from the great master in oral form. Later in life Khunying Yai became a student of another highly revered and high-ranking monk: Somdet Phra Buddhaghosacariya (Jaroen Ñāṇavaro), abbot of the Bangkok monastery Wat Thepsirin. He became her main teacher; she received a significant amount of her knowledge through listening to his teachings. For probably several years she visited him in his monastery almost daily in order to learn from his oral instruction and explanations.

From our interviews with her adopted son we know that Khunying Yai composed her major prose texts to a large extent, if not entirely, orally;[37] she dictated these texts to her servant Phueng Chuenjit. This is remarkable in that even though she must have possessed at least basic writing skills and was able to read, she preferred to compose these rather complex texts in her mind and then dictate them. That this method of text production seems to have been quite normal for her is also supported by the fact that Khunying Yai even dictated private letters.[38] Of course, we do not and probably never will know exactly how she produced her texts, and it seems likely that Khunying Yai read the texts (or had them read out) once Phueng Chuenjit had noted them down, and edited them. At least one of her major texts (*paṭipattivibhajana*) that was orally composed was proofread by Somdet Phra Buddhaghosacariya before publication. In the foreword of one edition of this text, Somdet Phra Buddhaghosacariya mentions that he "made minor corrections" to the text.[39]

However, the significance of orality and memory becomes clear not only in the way Khunying Yai produced her texts and received instruction from monastic teachers. Khunying Yai possessed a large number of books, among them a collection of Pali canonical scriptures—possibly the entire canon. She had her many books moved from Bangkok in numerous boxes to her southern monastery Wat Thammikaram when she took up permanent residence there after her ordination as a *mae chi* in 1933. However, instead of reading the books herself she had a servant read out Buddhist texts to her, sometimes for large parts of the day.[40]

Despite the enormous memory the oral production of Khunying Yai's prose texts would require, in light of what I have described above this does make perfect sense. Khunying Yai grew up in an oral culture in

FIGURE 27. Statue of Somdet Phra Buddhaghosacariya (Jaroen Ñāṇavaro) in the Chon Buri monastery Wat Khao Bang Sai

which the memorization of long texts seems to have been rather common. Many people she knew or must have been close to seemingly naturally memorized long texts as an integral part of their Buddhist practice.

Case Study 2: Somdet Phra Buddhaghosacariya (Jaroen Ñāṇavaro)

In order to investigate further the importance of orality and memory in the context of Buddhist teaching, learning, and practice, I would now like to explore relevant ideas and practices in the biography of Khunying Yai's main teacher, Somdet Phra Buddhaghosacariya (Jaroen Ñāṇavaro). Somdet Phra Buddhaghosacariya has been celebrated not only as an expert on the Pali canon and Pali language but also as an accomplished administrator of the monastic community.[41] His admirers also often refer to his strict adherence to the monastic rules (*vinaya*), describing him as an exemplary monk.[42] He was the editor of eleven books of an influential Thai edition of the Pali canon and also edited fundamental Thai textbooks for the monastic study of the Pali language and Buddhist teachings.[43] Some people believed him to have achieved the state of a noble person (*ariya-puggala*), or saint.[44]

Phra Dunlayaphaksuwaman, a judge who was also student of Somdet Phra Buddhaghosacariya, writes that Somdet Phra Buddhaghosacariya was "very strict" (*khreng khrat mak*) with monks of his monastery in requiring them to attend the communal recitation of Buddhist texts twice a day, in the morning and in the evening.[45] Only newly ordained monks were allowed to use chanting books as a memory aid. In this context Phra Dunlayaphaksuwaman also refers to one of Thailand's most famous monks, Buddhadāsa Bhikkhu, who "said that 'to attend the daily chanting is like meeting the Buddha.'"[46]

Somdet Phra Buddhaghosacariya's *dhamma* teachings have been described as "profound" and "impressive" (*truengjai*) but at the same time "easily accessible"[47] and "pleasant sounding."[48] Somdet Phra Buddhaghosacariya even gave *dhamma* teachings to King Rama VII, who praised him for his sermons.[49] Phra Dunlayaphaksuwaman, paraphrasing (or directly quoting?) Chaokhun Dhammatrailokajan, a close student of Somdet Phra Buddhaghosacariya, writes that

> the *dhamma* teachings [of Somdet Phra Buddhaghosacariya] were organized in a system and pleasant sounding from the beginning to the end. [He distinguished clearly] different aspects of a *dhamma* teaching and then provided appropriately detailed explanations of each. This was done in a way that avoided confusion [in the minds of the students] and allowed the listeners to gain clarity on what he presented. Sometimes he translated Pali quotations from the *Tipiṭaka* [*phra bali*] into rhyme with the aim of helping his listeners to memorize [what they had heard].[50]

In a small book titled *Questions and answers about* sīla, samādhi, *and* paññā, which Somdet Phra Buddhaghosacariya edited (*truat kae*) and whose content he approved (*hen chop duai*), the foreword indicates that the thirty-two questions and answers the book comprises are for the memorization of the Buddhist teaching: "Once the different *dhamma* points have been memorized, their content can be contemplated."[51]

For the author of this foreword these questions and answers seem to serve as a kind of key when listening to (!) *dhamma* sermons (*dhammadesanā*) or discussions (*dhammasākacchā*). This key is to facilitate understanding of what was heard. The reader of the book is addressed, "I ask you . . . to diligently memorize this book, for once you can remember its content you will see the benefits through your own mind."[52] The questions of the book then trigger numerous *dhamma* lists, such as the five *khandha*s, forty *kammaṭṭhāna*s, twelve *āyatana*s, and the six *viññāṇa*s.

Thus, what is clear from the texts of both Khunying Yai and Somdet Phra Buddhaghosacariya is that the memorization of *dhamma* lists is not only to be understood as an exercise to gain and retain knowledge. There are two further important objectives of this exercise. Similar to what Gethin observed with regard to early Buddhism, the learning of lists is "to learn the Dhamma with a view to its inner structure and dynamic."[53] Thus, the way lists are used is creative,[54] or expressed in the words of the enormously influential monastic educator Prince Patriarch Wachirayan, a contemporary of Khunying Yai and Somdet Phra Buddhaghosacariya:

> [When] the student has understood the dhammic topics with its characteristics and then learns them as lists [*muat*] arranged into categories, he will easily gain understanding. He may even be able to employ [*khum*] the lists and categories resourcefully [*doi patiphan*]. This is comparable to a student of pharmacy who, having studied the medical textbooks, will be able to prepare [a new medical formula] effective [*mo*] for usage with [different] individual [patients].[55]

Both Khunying Yai's and Somdet Phra Buddhaghosacariya's literary outputs well exemplify the creative application and adaptation of dhammic lists in their production of new texts. The second further objective of the memorization of *dhamma* lists that is apparent in the texts of Khunying Yai and Somdet Phra Buddhaghosacariya is that memorization has a transformative aspect; the text, once memorized, becomes a part of one's life.[56]

Uposathasīla, another book by Somdet Phra Buddhaghosacariya, is also revealing in this regard. Writing in 1929, he states that this book forms a part of "the curriculum for female and male householders and is to replace [monks'] *vinaya*" studies in the case of laypeople's studies.[57] This text was developed as a textbook for the newly created *dhamma* learning system for laypeople and offers a translation of the *Uposatha-sutta* in the *Aṅguttara-nikāya*.[58] In the first paragraph of his translation into Thai, Somdet Phra Buddhaghosacariya highlights twice the oral character of the sermon and emphasizes that the Buddha wanted his monks to listen attentively—that is, with mindfulness. His translation is followed by a commentary that, similar to Khunying Yai's prose texts, consists of questions and answers, starting with a short explanation of the word *uposatha*, and then gives the eight precepts in a list "in order to facilitate their memorization [*jam ngai ngai*]."[59] One of the initial questions is,

> When the one who knows this content recites this text and does so with a mind that focuses on the content, this may very effectively make his mind peaceful and [make him] experience wholesomeness [*kusala*], positive qualities, and benefits. It may even sometimes allow the temporary suppression of the

> hindrances [*nīvaraṇa*], which is called *tadaṅga-pahāna* (the momentary abandoning of [*kilesa*; mental defilements]). Can this be regarded as the meditative development of the recollection of morality [*sīlānussati*]?

And the answer to this question is "yes!" (*dai*).[60] Albeit in slightly different terms, this certainly is in line with Khunying Yai's understanding of proper recitation and the objective of it as described above.

The pervasiveness and importance of orality and memory in Buddhist education of that time also become clear in Somdet Phra Buddhaghosacariya's scholarly work. The story behind Phra Buddhaghosacariya's translation of the *Dhammacakkappavattana-sutta* in 1931 is revealing in this context. Somdet Phra Buddhaghosacariya did this translation at the request of a female lay follower; when she listened to the chanting of the *sutta* in Pali, "confidence/faith arose" in her:

> She thought that this was an important *sutta* as it was the first sermon of the Perfectly Awakened One. If a translation could be made available so that the meaning could be accessed while reciting the text, it would increase the faith and very much facilitate right practice among Buddhists. For this reason she asked me to translate this *sutta* as well as the *Mettānisaṁsa-sutta*, so that she could print and disseminate these translations as a wholesome act on the occasion of her birthday. . . . For this reason I agreed to undertake this translation and asked a [Pali scholar] monk to write down the translation that I dictated to him.[61]

Somdet Phra Buddhaghosacariya's translation of the *Mahāsatipaṭṭhāna-sutta*, another major Pali canonical text, had emerged in a similar way more than three decades earlier. When he learned that Noi Paurohitya, another female lay follower, was able to recite the entire *sutta* by heart, he prepared a Thai translation of the text by asking the son of this Thai woman to note down his oral translation: "I thought that if Ms. Noi could study the translation as well, it would increase her faith [in Buddhism] enormously." Somdet Phra Buddhaghosacariya completed the translation for Noi Paurohitya in 1896. Noi Paurohitya then also learned the translation by heart. (The Pali text of the *Mahāsatipaṭṭhāna-sutta* comprises some twenty-seven pages.) In the preface to the translated text, Somdet Phra Buddhaghosacariya writes that Noi Paurohitya was then not only "able to recite the complete *sutta* both in Pali and Thai by heart but also practice in accordance with it until her death [in 1931]."[62]

Noi Paurohitya must have built up an impressive knowledge of the Buddhist teaching, for in the cremation volume printed for her in 1931, the widely celebrated expert on Thai language Phra Sanprasoet (Tri Nakhaprathip) writes about her,

> There are female lay Buddhists [*upāsikā*] with firm faith in Buddhism who possess knowledge of advanced *dhamma* teachings and practice accordingly as *sammācāriṇī* [those who practice in the right way]. The elderly monks of Wat Thepsirin who are still alive know one among these *sammācāriṇī* well and have always respectfully called her Khun Nai Noi [Noi Paurohitya]. At that time, I was a junior monk and had the opportunity to discuss the Buddhist teaching with Khun Nai Noi. For this reason, I have known her and have had faith in her advanced understanding of the *dhamma* since then.[63]

What the background of Somdet Phra Buddhaghosacariya's translations of the *Dhammacakkappavattana-sutta* and the *Mahāsatipaṭṭhāna-sutta* also shows is that writing was perceived as a means to facilitate memorization. Here, memorization is understood to enable "real" understanding of these texts by internalization, contemplation, and ultimately realization.

We can see then that the texts of Khunying Yai and Somdet Phra Buddhaghosacariya are strongly influenced by early Buddhist texts. Both of these practitioners and authors aimed to accurately preserve the textual content and form, and also followed a variety of textual practices characteristic of text production and preservation in early Indian Buddhism.[64] At the same time, Khunying Yai's and Somdet Phra Buddhaghosacariya's texts give evidence of textual practices that were firmly established in the second half of the nineteenth century and first half of the twentieth century. These textual practices allowed women to develop an in-depth understanding of Buddhist teaching that was regarded as quite impressive. The following shorter case studies lend further weight to my arguments and show that Khunying Yai and Somdet Phra Buddhaghosacariya were not exceptions in their pursuits and understanding.

Case Study 3: Upāsikā Ki Nanayon

The scholar monk Ṭhānissaro Bhikkhu correctly observes of Upāsikā Ki Nanayon (1901–78) that she is "one of the best-known Dhamma teachers, male or female, in Thailand,"[65] and Buddhadāsa Bhikkhu praises her as an "extraordinary woman" whose "objective was genuine understanding of the *dhamma*."[66] Upāsikā Ki, also known under her pen name Ko. Khao Suan Luang, was born into a family of Chinese merchants in the province of Ratchaburi. Like Khunying Yai and other women of my study, she developed a strong interest in Buddhist teaching from a young age. Even though not ordained as a *mae chi*, Upāsikā Ki started to observe the eight precepts from the age of twenty-four. In 1945, together with her aunt and uncle, she moved to a remote hill in Ratchaburi Province in order to devote her life entirely to the practice of meditation. This hill, Khao Suan Luang (hence her pen name), has now become one of the most famous meditation centers for female practitioners in the whole country. During the second part of her life, Upāsikā Ki gave many sermons. These were recorded, transcribed, and then printed or disseminated as audiotapes. In the course of the last nine years of her life, once her sermon texts had been transcribed and edited by her followers, they were read out to Upāsikā Ki so that she could then approve the content. In this way, four large volumes of her texts emerged.[67]

In an autobiographical text, Upāsikā Ki recounts how her mother taught her how to memorize and recite Buddhist texts when she was only three or four years old: "Before going to bed, my mother taught me how to recite holy texts every night. If I forgot to recite the Buddhist texts before falling asleep, I had to get up again and do the chanting before I was [allowed] to sleep."[68] Only at the age of eleven or twelve did Upāsikā Ki start to practice reading in lessons at home.[69] After her eyesight deteriorated, she started to compose *dhamma* poems in her mind. Her biography reports that "it was amazing that she was able to compose long poems entirely in her mind . . . altogether flawlessly. These poems consist of internal and external rhyme and are pleasant to listen to. In addition, one will receive deep and impressively profound *dhamma* teachings."[70]

Case Study 4: Mae Chi Kao Saetan

Mae Chi Kao Saetan (1870–1968) was ordained as a *mae chi* at the age of forty at one of Thailand's most famous and historically significant monasteries, Wat Phra Pathom Jedi, Nakhon Pathom. Three years later, together with four or five other *mae chi*s, she moved to the newly founded monastery Wat Saneha, also located in Nakhon Pathom. There, in the afternoon, when monks were instructed in meditation practice, the female practitioners would listen to the instruction too. During the night they then put it into practice.[71] Mae Chi Kao was to a large extent involved in the construction of the ordination hall (*uposathāgāra*) of Wat Saneha, which is regarded as one of the most beautiful in the area. She contacted laypeople and encouraged them to make donations.[72] Her biography tells us that she must have had a very influential position in her temple; she is described as an advisor (*khu khit*) to the abbot.[73] According to her biography she was like an elder sister to the abbot.[74] The success of Wat Saneha in terms of Buddhist practice, numbers of monastic residents, and education has been ascribed to the successful teamwork of Mae Chi Kao and the abbot. She is described as self-confident and speaking with a firm voice. Mae Chi Kao was not only famous in the local area but also known among senior monks in Bangkok, which is some sixty kilometers away. She was in charge of a community of about eighty *mae chi*s.[75] She is consistently described as outspoken and would admonish monks and novices when she perceived them showing "inappropriate" behavior.[76]

Women wishing to become ordained as *mae chi*s at Wat Saneha had to first undergo intensive training in order to internalize the rules of the female monastic community. Once ordained, they were required to pursue meditation practice during the night. They were also required to participate in the recitation of Buddhist texts twice a day. Mae Chi

Kao regularly took other female practitioners to the cemetery to practice meditation there.[77] The biography reports that in its early years Wat Saneha was visited by a respected and experienced meditation teacher who gave daily instruction in meditation to the female monastics. Some of the highest-ranking monks and famous meditation masters of her time, such as Chaokhun Upāli Guṇūpamācariya (Jan Siricando, 1857–1932), also visited the monastery and taught meditation there. Her biographer also mentions that Somdet Phra Buddhaghosacariya often frequented Wat Saneha and knew Mae Chi Kao. It is not clear, though, how far she also received *dhamma* teachings from him.[78] Mae Chi Kao's spiritual practice also consisted of daily meditation with a focus on mindfulness of breathing (*ānāpānasati*). Her biography says that due to her regular meditation practice she was able to develop and maintain until old age an extraordinarily precise and vast memory.[79]

Case Study 5: Upāsikā Nu-nueang Thapmeng

Upāsikā Nu-nueang's (1887–?) life account[80] was published by the accomplished Pali scholar Phra Chodok Ñāṇasiddhi (1918–88), one of Thailand's most influential teachers of insight meditation (*vipassanā*) in the Burmese style. Already a high-ranking monk, in 1968 Phra Chodok praises her highly in the foreword of this biography (when Upāsikā Nu-nueang was still alive), arguing that Upāsikā Nu-nueang

> has consistently tried to establish herself in the noble quest [*ariyapariyesanā*; the quest for *nibbāna*]. She should be very much congratulated [*anumodanā*] on this by the sages; there is only a rather small number of people who consistently lead their lives in accordance with the *dhamma*, being able to reach the other shore.[81]

Her life account tells us that Upāsikā Nu-nueang was the daughter of farmers and had no opportunity to go to school. From a young age she had the intention of becoming a *mae chi*, but lamented, "I cannot read. How then can I memorize and recite texts [*thongbon*]?"[82] She asked her uncle to teach her how to read and divided her time between developing her reading skills and working in the rice fields. Her life account describes her as having a good memory.[83] At the age of seventeen, when eventually able to read, she intended to become ordained as a *mae chi*. When she told her friends about her wish, they mocked her, saying that someone so young could not do so. However, around 1905 she "often had the opportunity to visit the local monastery in order to listen [*fang*] to Buddhist teachings [*dhamma*], and this increased her familiarity with the religion."[84] She pursued intensive meditation practice. At the age of nineteen, together with a *mae chi*, she wanted to practice a specific set of austere practices (*dhutaṅga*), which are widely followed by monks of the forest tradition. These practices may involve dwelling in the jungle or in cemeteries and sleeping in the open air. But she was told by her teacher that "for young women this is demeritorious [*pāpa*]."[85] This was why she continued her practice of keeping the precepts and meditation in a monastery. Only when she nearly died of cholera, and her father had made a vow that if she escaped death he would allow her to become a *mae chi*, was she finally able to be ordained. This must have happened around the year 1906.[86]

Mae Chi Talap, who, the life account tells us, had been a minor wife of King Rama IV (r. 1851–68) and ordained as a *mae chi* after the king's death, became Mae Chi Nu-nueang's mentor.[87] Mae Chi Talap took her student to numerous monasteries to study the *dhamma*. It is noteworthy that Mae Chi Talap studied and practiced the *dhamma* as a student of the famous meditation master Somdet Phra Wanarat (Thap Buddhasiri), who, as mentioned above, was also the teacher of Khunying Yai.[88] Mae Chi Nu-nueang's life account describes Mae Chi Talap as "an advanced master who has *listened* a lot to higher *dhamma* [teachings]."[89]

What is also of interest is the way that Mae Chi Talap's teaching is described: "Mae Chi Talap taught [Mae Chi Nu-nueang] a lot; first, on a basic level she taught her to have faith in the qualities of the Buddha, of which there are three." What then follows are other *dhamma* lists. It seems that Mae Chi Talap wanted her student to memorize these lists in order, not only to learn the Buddha's teaching but also to increase faith and confidence in the *dhamma*.[90]

Mae Chi Talap must have been an effective teacher, as many influential people (*phu yai*) and *upāsikās* (here meaning female devotees) from

Bangkok followed her instruction.[91] Mae Chi Talap also took Mae Chi Nu-nueang to practice *dhutaṅga*. Mae Chi Nu-nueang studied the *Abhidhammatthasaṅgaha*; she actually was literally "chanting/reciting" this text.[92] In her fourth year as a *mae chi* she was able to recite the entire translated version of the *Mahāsatipaṭṭhāna-sutta*. She also managed to complete the study of "five Pali grammar books" (which must have happened around 1910).[93] Further noteworthy features of her biography are the extensive travels she undertook as a *mae chi* in order to study the *dhamma*, and the (probably informal) networks of male and female practitioners of which she was a member.

On her journeys, Mae Chi Nu-nueang was even able to study the *dhamma* with the great meditation teacher Luang Pu Man.[94] In addition, she often visited Wat Saneha in Nakhon Pathom; there Phra Khru Winai-sangwon[95] "paid a lot of attention" to teaching female lay followers. "When he wanted to learn about the level of understanding of the *upāsikā*s he would use the technique of asking them questions," and assessing the answers.[96] His questions, so Mae Chi Nu-nueang's life account tells us, were on the highest level of the formal monastic *dhamma* studies (*nak tham ek*), and the *upāsikā*s gave their answers based on their understanding of the famous Theravada manuals *Visuddhimagga* and *Abhidhammatthasaṅgaha*.[97] The knowledge of Pali language, Buddhist doctrine, and meditation that Mae Chi Nu-nueang was able to accumulate over the course of her ordained life must have been impressive, in particular when taking into account that she had had no access to formal education. But even though it contains many distinctive biographical features, Mae Chi Nu-nueang's biography makes it clear that she was not exceptional in being a female Buddhist with an extraordinarily advanced level of understanding of the Buddhist doctrines, as there were other Buddhist women whose knowledge of Buddhist teachings was no less impressive.

Case Study 6: Mae Chi Kaew Sianglam

Mae Chi Kaew's extraordinary biography also contains some relevant information on how she obtained her knowledge. As mentioned in chapter 2, in her teenage years, Mae Chi Kaew received individual instruction from Luang Pu Man and was able to achieve some unusually quick successes in her spiritual development. However, despite her deep interest in monastic life, due to her gender her ordained life began relatively late, only when she was already thirty-six years old; before then she was several times denied permission to become ordained. At the age of seventeen she was married, and her husband forbade her to practice meditation at the temple; he allowed her to recite Buddhist texts, though. In the then-remote area of northeastern of Thailand where she lived, there was no local school. One of her major biographies devotes a section to telling about how she learned:

> **She was not able to study; learning how to write and read was even more out of reach for her**
> The only thing she could do was to memorize the teachings of her teachers. She was [however] able to memorize all [she learned from her teachers]. She committed it to memory and then recited it until it entered her mind. Formerly, when she observed others reading and writing she was jealous, thinking, "In this lifetime I was born a stupid hillbilly who has no opportunity to acquire literacy." But now as she had become old, she understood that being literate or illiterate did not make any difference. It was just the same, for her Buddhist practice was an ingenious approach in following the wise teachings of her highly revered masters.[98]

For Mae Chi Kaew's *mae chi* community at her home village, Ban Huai Sai, recitation and memorization of Buddhist texts were of central importance for their monastic life. It has been reported that when villagers were not satisfied with the quality of funeral chanting performed by local monks, they invited the *mae chi*s to do the chanting and were pleased with it. As a consequence, one of the local monks "became jealous of the *mae chi* community headed by Mae Chi Kaew, complaining to Mae Chi Kaew that by performing the chanting they had gone beyond the precepts of *mae chi*s [*tham koen sin mae chi*]—beyond the remit of *mae chi*s."[99]

*Mae chi*s who had been close to Mae Chi Kaew reported that Mae Chi Kaew established a strict and regular practice of chanting and memorization of Pali texts in her monastic community. Mae Chi Kaew herself was able from a young age to recite large numbers of texts. Once ordained, her ability to memorize texts increased even more. But "not only was she able to chant [from memory] numerous texts [such as different *sutta*s, funeral texts, and protection texts], she was also able to translate each text and explain its meaning."[100]

Case Study 7: Mae Bunruean Tongbuntoem

In Mae Bunruean's biography, in terms of knowledge acquisition and text production there are numerous similarities to other women of my study. As with other female practitioners investigated in this book, Mae Bunruean's interest in the study of Buddhist doctrine began at a young age, and she also received support in this from a well-known and respected monk. Her biographer assumes that the teachings of the famous and highly revered Luang Ta Phring, abbot of the monastery Wat Bangpakok, were the catalyst for her spiritual career. "It has been told that [Mae Bunruean] started to frequently offer food and other donations to Luang Ta Phring [whom she highly respected]. This allowed her to become familiar with the Buddha's teaching . . . and develop faith."[101]

There is a noteworthy account by Mae Bunruean's main teacher, the eminent monk and abbot of the famous Bangkok monastery Wat Samphanthawong, Phra Maharatchamangkhalajan (Thet Niddesako). Written a month after her death, it tells of how she was able to gradually and systematically develop her thorough knowledge of Buddhist teaching (*dhammavinaya*) in a monastic learning environment and how she herself eventually became a skilled Buddhist teacher who made "a large number of people interested in Buddhism." Phra Maharatchamangkhalajan also wrote that during the period before 1927 Mae Bunruean together with numerous other women received *dhamma* teachings on a regular basis for up to more than an hour, the level of teaching gradually and substantially increasing.

> Once the *dhamma* teachings were finished, the women were asked questions in order to assess their understanding and check what they had memorized [*tham khwam khaojai lae khwam*

> *kamnot jotjam*]. They also received instructions in the general practice of the *dhamma*, and once [these women] had attended these teachings for a longer period of time, they would gradually receive teachings on more intricate [aspects of the] *dhamma*.[102]

Some of her many supporters, so Phra Maharatchamangkhalajan informs us, would also "listen to her reading of Buddhist texts."[103]

Her followers built a house for her in Bangkok. In this house they regularly met her, listened to her teachings, and discussed what she had presented. Mae Bunruean has also been praised for her pedagogical skills: "She applied a variety of different, individualized methods [even including physical methods] by using her special knowledge to read her students' mental dispositions in order to adjust her teachings [most effectively]."[104] From her biographies it seems clear that Mae Bunruean not only gained her knowledge of Buddhist teachings mostly through oral teachings from various well-known and highly revered meditation masters of her time, but she herself also transmitted Buddhist knowledge largely orally. Her transcribed sermon texts give clear evidence of the advanced and precise memory she must have developed from acquiring much of her knowledge aurally.

On the occasion of the celebrations of the Buddhist year 2500, her disciples implored her "to compile [her] *dhamma* [teachings]" with the intention of donating 7,500 copies of the compilation to monks. This book came into existence by Mae Bunruean dictating the text. Like Khunying Yai, Mae Bunruean also dictated private letters. Her signature, which she added to the letters, reveals that her writing abilities were not very developed. Even though she probably received some very basic education in the Thai language when young, at the age of around sixty she declared, "I can only write my name. I am not educated [*mai dai rian nangsue*]."[105]

"Appropriate" Physical and Mental Distance

Even though the case studies above consider female educational experiences in the period between 1880 and 1950, the teaching and learning practices and relations between male monastics and the female Buddhists discussed seem to represent the continuation of much older practices and ideas. We know that in the 1850s Western visitors observed *mae chi*s reciting Buddhist texts.[106] In addition, accounts by Western travelers from the seventeenth century confirm that *mae chi*s were regularly listening to sermons. Nicolas Gervaise, for example, who visited Siam in 1683, wrote that *mae chi*s "listen to sermons every day and they spend much time praying in the temples."[107] Praying here probably means reciting holy texts. Given that these Western observers did not give very detailed descriptions of *mae chi*s, it seems that *mae chi*s' reciting of Buddhist texts must have been perceived as an important characteristic of their ordained life. This is of course fully corroborated by the evidence given above.

It seems likely that for Siamese women practicing Buddhism, the recitation and memorization of Pali texts are not just a recent phenomenon but have long been an important part of their spiritual practice. Thus, due to the existence and importance of oral modes of teaching and learning in Thailand before and after compulsory education was introduced in 1921, women's access to knowledge and the gender relations between monks and women seem to have been much more complex than presented by Darunee and Costa at the outset of this chapter. Despite the customs in place to ensure "appropriate" physical distance between monks and women, female Buddhists from different social strata had the opportunity to gain access to culturally significant knowledge in a monastic environment and with the help of (often high-ranking or famous) monks. While this knowledge was to a large extent text-based, as it derived from canonical or other influential Theravada texts, it was often transmitted orally. This type of knowledge has been regarded as the most valuable and desirable type of knowledge.

The case studies above also suggest that intensive pedagogical relationships between monks on the one side and *mae chi*s and laywomen (*upāsikā*) on the other existed well before the significant increase in literacy among Thai women during the first half of the twentieth century. It is true that various restrictive cultural practices and gendered prohibitions, such as the refusal to ordain women as *bhikkhunī*s, had an impact on women's access to knowledge, as confirmed by some of the case studies above. For example, from Mae Chi Kaew's biography we learn that as a girl she was allowed to go to the monastery only when accompanied by her parents.

In addition, she had to sit as far away from the monks as possible.[108] Also, as mentioned above, her gender was the reason Luang Pu Man did not accept her as his monastic student and forbade her to continue her meditation practice. At the same time, we also know from her biography that Mae Chi Kaew nonetheless had access to "great teachers," such as Luang Pu Man and Luang Ta Mahabua, and received individualized and direct teachings from them.

As Mae Chi Kaew's biographies show, illiteracy did not prevent her from gaining access to the knowledge she and her community deemed the most valuable; this was possible because she was relying on oral modes of teaching and on memory. Moreover, note that Luang Pu Man's practice has been described as very strict in terms of avoiding associating with women, in line with the instructions the Buddha gave to his monk attendant Ānanda in the *Mahāparinibbāna-sutta*, advising his monks if possible to avoid looking at and speaking with women.[109]

Nonetheless, for monks of the forest tradition and other teachers introduced in this study, keeping the "right" distance from women did not preclude intensive and regular teaching of female students. Thus, Mae Chi Kaew was not the only female disciple whose spiritual progress Luang Pu Man paid a lot of attention to. During the last five years of his life, Luang Pu Man stayed at a forest monastery in northeastern Thailand near the village of Ban Nong Phue. There he was teaching meditation to local villagers. In this community, even before his arrival, many female villagers had decided to take the robes and become *mae chi*s. Once ordained, they were living in a separate monastic residence close to the main monastery so that they could "listen to the *dhamma* sermons by Ajan Lui Candasāro [a monastic disciple of Luang Pu Man] whenever the opportunity to do so arose." Following his instructions, they also practiced meditation in cemeteries. Whenever they encountered problems in their meditation they were able to consult the master about these. Female practice included not only intensive meditation and listening to sermons but also reciting Pali texts.[110] Throughout this book I have repeatedly referred to one of the *mae chi*s of the Ban Nong Phue community; Mae Chi Kang Thephin was praised for her advanced meditation and is believed to have achieved *ariya-puggala* status.[111] Luang Pu Man often gave her instruction on her meditation, and monks were "eager to hear her questions and his answers. Because her questions arose directly from her own experiences in meditation, these exchanges fascinated the monks."[112] It is reported that up to fifty monks listened to Mae Chi Kang's conversations with Luang Pu Man.[113] Luang Ta Mahabua even states that one of the reasons Luang Pu Man stayed unusually long at this place was because of this woman's practice.[114]

This account together with other biographies examined in my study show that even though there was no established institutional route of monastic education for women, many of them received individualized and intensive instruction from their monastic teachers (*phra ajan*). Rather than excluding women from Buddhist practice and knowledge, the major concern of these monk teachers seems to have been the "appropriate" physical and mental distance and the strict adherence to the *vinaya* rules in these pedagogical relationships between monks and women. This is nicely exemplified by the manner in which Somdet Phra Buddhaghosacariya taught Khunying Yai. For a certain period of time, probably several years, Khunying Yai went almost daily around noon to the monastic dwelling of Somdet Phra Buddhaghosacariya in his Bangkok monastery Wat Thepsirin. Somdet Phra Buddhaghosacariya would ask a novice to be present as well in order to avoid being alone with Khunying Yai, for he perceived being alone with a woman as in conflict with the monastic code. Had the novice not arrived yet, Somdet Phra Buddhaghosacariya would hide behind a pillar in order not to violate the monastic code (*phra winai*).[115]

Thus, I want to argue that while for monks teaching women may sometimes have posed a challenge to them in terms of their monastic discipline, this did not stop them from doing so. The issue here was not whether women should be taught or whether they have the spiritual potential to understand the *dhamma*. In the biographies investigated in my study these two points were not doubted. However, the major concern was rather to keep intact the monks' monastic code and to avoid the emergence of any rumors that could have a negative impact on their reputation as celibates and thus harm their monastic community or even the religion as a whole. Also, another concern in this respect concerns male monastics who have not yet established themselves in celibate life, as expressed in the words of Luang Ta Mahabua:

> Monks are especially vulnerable to the sounds of the opposite sex. If their *samādhi* is not strong enough, concentration can easily be destroyed. I must apologize to women everywhere because my intention here is not to criticize women in any way. It is the unsuccessful meditator that I am addressing here so that he may arouse mindfulness as an antidote to counter these influences and not merely surrender meekly to them.[116]

Importance of Orality and Memory

In addition to the case studies provided above, the importance of orality and memory in Thai Buddhist learning environments can also be demonstrated by the way in which Luang Pu Man taught monks. It is reported that he had an astonishingly high number of monastic students—more than eight hundred. Most of his teachings were passed on to them directly, without the use of any written notes. "The reason for this may be sought in the fact that the teaching and studying of the *dhamma*, according to the insight meditation lineage, does not regard books or manuals as important or necessary for the realization of the truth as one's own practice."[117] Indeed, we have only one rather short text that is believed to have been written by Luang Pu Man himself. Moreover, Luang Pho Wiriyang, one of Luang Pu Man's major direct disciples, writes, "[Luang Pu Man] never allowed anybody to write down his sermons. These have only been memorized, committed to one's heart. If anybody tried to write down his sermons, he would have certainly scolded and reprimanded him for that." In fact, one major text of Luang Pu Man, *Muttodaya*, came into being only because Luang Pho Wiriyang "secretly" and "thievishly" wrote down sermon texts by Luang Pu Man after having committed their content to memory.[118] Luang Pu Man himself was able to memorize numerous texts both in Thai and Pali.[119] At night, he regularly chanted Buddhist texts, such as the *Dhammacakkappavattana-sutta* and *Mahāsamaya-sutta* on his own.[120] As a teenager, when ordained as a novice, Luang Pu Man "memorize[d] various *sutta* from local teaching monks."[121]

Luang Pu Man also required those who wanted to study with him to learn by heart numerous *dhamma* lists and specific Pali texts together with the *pāṭimokkha* (the 227 training rules of the *bhikkhus*) within three years. "If they were not able to achieve this, they were not allowed to stay with him in the same monastic residence."[122] Many of Luang Pu Man's pupils were illiterate or semiliterate.[123] Some of Luang Pu Man's more famous male monastic disciples were not able to read or write, as they had not attended school. Luang Pu Kongma Cirapuñño (1900–1962), for example, had to learn by heart the *pāṭimokkha* rules orally (*pak to pak*) "word by word" (*kham to kham*) before he was allowed to receive his ordination as a monk of the Dhammayuttika-nikāya (the Thai Buddhist congregation Luang Pu Man belonged to).[124]

This and the examples above make it very clear that orality and memory were regarded as of the utmost importance and seen as an integral part of both male and female spiritual practice.[125] These concepts of Buddhist knowledge are in line with Khunying Yai's definition of Buddhist learning (*pariyatti*), which nicely demonstrates that *pariyatti* is to be understood as learning not necessarily directly from written texts but first of all and most importantly from orally transmitted texts:

> The method to reach the *dhamma* is by *pariyatti*, because one has listened to the teachings of the Buddha. These teachings include numerous points, and all are *niyyānikadhamma*—that is, they can lead the practitioner to the release from *dukkha* [unsatisfactoriness] and cause the arising of faith and respect; this is called reaching the level of *pariyatti*.[126]

In many of the biographies discussed above, writing was not perceived as being crucial for spiritual development. Only in Mae Chi Nu-nueang's biography—and to some extent in Mae Chi Kaew's—was the inability to write initially a concern. But what is significant in Mae Chi Nu-nueang's biography is that even though literacy was initially thought to play a significant role in Mae Chi Nu-nueang's spiritual life, for her it was instrumental only in getting access to the texts she wanted to learn by heart. As for Mae Chi Kaew, later in life she understood that for her spiritual practice, reading and writing skills were not important at all; what was a far more important concern than having *direct* access to written Buddhist texts was access to teachers. She was able to develop a vast memory of Buddhist knowledge, which many regarded as impressive, through oral means. Despite being able to read and write because of her privileged social background, Khunying Yai preferred not only to listen to texts and instructions by her teachers but also to dictate her own texts. At the same time, her texts consistently emphasize the importance of orality and memory as an integral part of Buddhist practice.

Also, as shown above, in many cases repeatedly listening to sermons or sometimes even to one specific sermon may have been the catalyst for deep interest in the study of Buddhist teaching. This happened, for example, in the case of Mae Chi Sali Thomanakon (1880–1945). Around the year 1898, when she was only eighteen years old,

> she felt weary of the life of a layperson [*khrong ruean*]. For this reason she asked her mother for permission to listen to a sermon at the monastery Wat Pho, where Mae Chi Jamroen was giving instruction to those who came to Wat Pho to listen to sermons. Having listened to the sermon, in Upāsikā Sali faith arose, and she wanted to take the white robes and become a *mae chi* in that monastic residence. At that time, her younger sister Upāsikā Jan, being only fourteen years old, followed her older sister and [also] became a white-robed *mae chi* in the monastic residence of Wat Pho.[127]

Later, the mother of the two sisters became a *mae chi* as well, living in a monastic dwelling that she had built in the important Bangkok monastery Wat Phichaiyat. The older sister Mae Chi Sali together with four or five other *mae chi*s moved to Ratchaburi Province, where they established their own *mae chi* nunnery and pursued intensive meditation practice. Mae Chi Sali's strict practice together with her charismatic appearance attracted a lot of people "who wanted to become her students."[128]

Furthermore, there are instances where it was only due to the memory of female Thai Buddhists that texts by famous monks were preserved. For instance, based on what she remembered from listening to sermons given by the famous meditation master Luang Pho Li Dhammadharo,

Mae Chi Abhivaṇṇā made notes. These notes were later published.[129] Similarly, Princess Vapi Busbakara (1891–1982), a daughter of King Rama V (r. 1868–1910), committed to memory the teachings of Somdet Phra Buddhaghosacariya of Wat Thepsirin, which she had listened to and noted down later. Somdet Phra Buddhaghosacariya corrected and made further comments on these notes. These handwritten texts have been published in three volumes[130] and are now an important source text for the study of the teachings of Somdet Phra Buddhaghosacariya. Princess Beatrice Bhadrayuvadi (1876–1913), also a daughter of Rama V, is another good example. She "was very pleased to listen to *dhamma* sermons." She wrote down what she remembered so that others could read and benefit from it.[131] In fact, when she listened to a sermon given by Somdet Phra Buddhaghosacariya, first "when listening to the sermon, I did not intend to remember it, but as [Somdet Phra Buddhaghosacariya] was talking slowly and clearly and the sermon was not too long, once it had finished it appeared that his words arose in the correct sequence in my mind."[132]

Conclusion

Between 1880 and 1950 there was a significant number of Thai women who possessed a remarkable knowledge of Buddhist teaching. This is also confirmed by Narin Phasit, who has become famous for his unsuccessful attempt to reestablish the *bhikkhunī* order in Thailand in the 1920s.[133] In 1929 he wrote that "in fact, based on my observations and experience I believe that in our time there are numerous women with Buddhist knowledge and authentic Buddhist practice comparable to that of men; there are even women who are better than men in these regards."[134] He then also praises a number of individual *mae chi*s in various parts of the country for their knowledge of Buddhist teaching or outstanding spiritual practice. One of those he mentions is the aforementioned Mae Chi Sali Thomanakon, adding that "there are likely to be many more [remarkable] *mae chi*s whom I do not know of."[135]

The case studies above, which include female practitioners from various social strata, reveal the extensive networking between their subjects, allowing them to exchange knowledge and experiences. They were traveling the country extensively as part of their ascetic practice (*dhutaṅga*) or in search of a teacher. Wat Saneha in Nakhon Pathom, Wat Sattanatpariwat in Ratchaburi, Wat Thammikaram in Prachuap Khiri Khan, and the Bangkok temples Wat Somanat Wihan, Wat Prok, and Wat Thepsirin, to name only a few, have been important monasteries for female practice, knowledge exchange, and networking. In these monastic centers, sometimes large groups of female practitioners were actively supported by monks in their pursuit of Buddhist knowledge (*pariyatti*) and spiritual practice (*paṭipatti*). There are possible links between the outstanding female practitioners and teachers Khunying Yai, Upāsikā Ki Nanayon (Ko. Khao Suan Luang), Khunying Rabiap Sunthornlikhit, and Ajan Naeb Mahaniranon.[136] But these links need to be the subject of a separate study.

I want to conclude this chapter by arguing that the women in my study had access to what they deemed to be (the most) valuable knowledge, despite the fact that many of them were illiterate or semiliterate. However, for many of these women literacy did not play an important role in their quest for knowledge—if, indeed, it played any role at all. The women of my study received their knowledge in or near monasteries, often with the support of or directly from monks. In fact, there existed intensive long-term pedagogical relationships between monks on the one side and *mae chis* and laywomen (*upāsikā*) on the other.

In these cases, Buddhist knowledge was often conveyed regularly, systematically, interactively, progressively, and effectively. Thanks to the possession of what was perceived as great and precise Buddhist knowledge, the women of my study were highly revered not only by laymen and laywomen but also by other female monastics and often by monks.

Chapter 6
Experiencing Gender

> We establish the habit of being a good person so that we will be reborn again as a human being. Having come across the Buddha's teaching means we have had enormous luck. [The teaching] wants us to focus on the internal by focusing on the mind, solely on one's own mind. This is to allow our mind to be in the present only, so that it does not wander about, being attracted by external sense objects [*ārammaṇa*]. [In this way, the mind] will understand and realize the present only.
>
> From a dhamma text by Mae Chi Phimpha Wongsa-udom based on her understanding of the instruction of her teacher Luang Pu Thet Desaraṅsī[1]

Aside from presenting, contextualizing, and analyzing the biographies and autobiographies of the women of my study, so far this study has mainly focused on how these women were perceived by others as a result of their assumed spiritual achievements and gender, and how female practitioners conceptualized and gained their Buddhist knowledge. This chapter, however, will focus on how and to what extent Thai female practitioners themselves have expressed and reflected on issues related to gender. In this way I will investigate how they experienced their own gender's implications in various ways, such as in their relationships to monks, laypeople, and family, in ideas about the female body, and in forms of religious practices that in Thai Buddhism are primarily associated with men. Unfortunately, of the six women central to my study only in the cases of Khunying Yai, Mae Bunruean, and Mae Chi Phimpha do a substantial number of relevant texts authored by them remain extant. Thus, while also referring to other women's experiences, in this chapter I will predominantly discuss and base my arguments on texts composed by these three women.

The Complexities of Religious Hierarchy and Gender

In academic literature, Thai *mae chis* have often been described as hierarchically inferior to male monastics. Susan Fulop Kepner, for example,[2] writes that *mae chis* possess "a vastly different and immeasurably inferior status when compared with the monkhood."[3] Marjorie Muecke has reported that there are people who argued that if *mae chis* "ask people for support . . . they are inferior even to lay persons."[4] Bhikkhunī Dhammanandā (then Chatsumarn Kabilsingh) wrote in 1991 that *mae chis*' "lack of self-esteem, coupled with negative social attitudes, have resulted in their extremely low status."[5]

While I do not deny that *mae chis* are in a subordinated position, they may nevertheless perceive their embeddedness in the gender hierarchy quite differently. This is shown in the ethnographic study of Cook. Positing the necessity "to examine the meaning of monastic hierarchy and ascetic duty for *mae chee* themselves," she argued that for *mae chis* in the monastery in which she worked "the rationale of monastic practice is never understood in terms of resistance to male authority or the equality of women *vis-à-vis* men."[6] Referring to Alan Sponberg's influential 1992 study "Attitudes Toward Women and the Feminine in Early Buddhism," she also suggests that

> the hierarchy of gender prevalent in the monastery [she lived and worked in] is effectively sidestepped by *mae chee* and monks through ascetic practice. They thereby employ the ideals of soteriological inclusiveness, without engaging in either institutional androcentrism or ascetic misogyny. While such views are present in the monastery and reflected in spatial separation, hierarchical duty and domestic performance, they are understood as irrelevant to the non-gendered narrative of spiritual achievement.[7]

Even though these statements are based on the study of only one monastic community in (northern) Thailand, they give further evidence pointing to the complexity of gender relations in present-day Thai society for which scholars have so far failed to provide concordant explanations. With regard to *mae chis*' own perceptions in terms of subordination and gender hierarchy, in her ethnographic study of *mae chi*s, carried out as part of a PhD, Lisa Battaglia came up with results similar to Cook's. Battaglia identifies "an underlying tension between the practices, motivations, and goals of Thai *mae chis* and Western liberal feminist assumptions, commitments, and objectives."[8] Thus, she concludes that "approaching the study of *mae chi*s through liberal feminist agendas emerges as ineffective and misleading; these agendas are based on western experience and derive from Western values, and have little relevance to the aims and motivations of Thai Buddhist nuns."[9] She even argues that "hierarchy—as exemplified in the act of nuns' compulsory bowing to monks and to each other based on seniority—can, in fact, be interpreted and experienced as spiritually enriching and even liberating."[10]

While mentioning the diversity of monastic practices with regard to gendered hierarchy Ṭhānissaro Bhikkhu states,

> One major drawback to nuns' communities affiliated with monasteries is that the nuns are relegated to a status clearly secondary to that of the monks, but in the better monasteries this is alleviated to some extent by the Buddhist teachings on hierarchy: that it is a mere social convention, designed to streamline the decision-making process in the community, and based on morally neutral criteria so that one's place in the hierarchy is not an indication of one's worth as a person.[11]

Discussing Thai religious gendered hierarchy with me in 2013, a Theravada Buddhist monk who had been ordained for over three decades argued that reverential behavior of women toward monks has to be understood as "etiquette." He pointed out to me that their advanced hierarchical position with the accompanying respect may actually be "seductive" for monks, and they may become "enchanted by prestige"; monks from a rural and poor background with hardly any education may become revered by highly educated, rich people from Bangkok. This can lead to "illusions" in these monks' minds, whereas female Thai monastics "live with the reality of monastic life," that monk argued. A *mae chi* interviewed by Cook underscores this view: "Mae Chee Pon responded to my concern about inequality in the monastery by suggesting that she actually felt quite sorry for monks: 'after ordination their status is so high that they have a really hard time to be humble. They don't have the experience of *mae chee* to help them.'"[12]

In July 2012 I interviewed a highly revered female Buddhist practitioner and *dhamma* teacher in northern Thailand. Most of the laypeople know of and visit the monastery she lives in because of her. The second edition of her autobiography, of which three thousand copies were printed with the help of financial donations from more than 260 people, had just been released. After my interview with this *mae chi*, I also interviewed the abbot of the monastery. He told me, "Even though she [the *mae chi*] prostrates herself in front of me, I respect her as my teacher [*khruba ajan*]."

In his magnum opus *Buddhadhamma*, in which he provides a systematic presentation and explanations of Pali canonical core teachings, the scholar monk Phra Payutto argues,

> According to Buddhism the showing of respect [between laypeople and monks and among monks themselves based on seniority] is not an expression of superiority and inferiority of fame, of external authority, or of inner virtues . . . but is to create orderliness and harmony of the *saṅgha* or society.[13]

The views and experiences discussed above show that, while being gendered to a significant extent, religious hierarchy in Thai Buddhism is conceptualized and engaged with in diverse and complex ways. Needless to say, hierarchy is not only determined by religious belief or gender but often also by a number of other factors, such as income, education, power networks, and political ideology. These factors further increase the complexity of gendered relationships in the hierarchical structure of Thai Buddhism.

Be that as it may, even though a gendered religious hierarchy is regularly referred to in studies about *mae chi*s and Thai Buddhist women more generally, often the way in which these women themselves perceive and experience their embeddedness in hierarchical structure is not discussed.[14] In addition, further discussion or mention of the complexities of the Thai religious hierarchy are frequently also missing. It should also be pointed out, for example, that certain men are also hierarchically superior or inferior to other men, while certain women are hierarchically superior or inferior to other women. Both men and women face challenges and rewards, albeit usually in different ways and to different degrees, as a consequence of their hierarchical embeddedness. Thus, there are other inequalities than those related to gender. At the same time, men, including Thai monks, may show respect to Thai women they regard as spiritually or otherwise superior. If a Thai monk shows respect to a woman, this normally does not happen through prostration or raising one's hands, as this is forbidden by their monastic codes (*vinaya*; see below).[15] But they may do this in a variety of other ways—for example, verbally, in writing, or through the building of places of veneration for these women. This I have amply shown in this book. Also, both Thai Buddhist men and women, monastics and lay, perceive the prostration in front of a high-ranking or highly revered monk not only as an act of subordination but also, and maybe more importantly, as a meritorious act. Having the (sometimes rare and thus precious) opportunity to prostrate oneself in front of, or even serve, an assumed saint or otherwise outstanding practitioner or monastic is often perceived as a manifestation of one's good *kamma* (*mi bun*), while creating more merit (*tham bun*) at the same time. Therefore, while not denying that *mae chi*s are subordinated to monks, are often discriminated against in various ways, and often live in hardship because of their gender, what I want to argue here is that a more nuanced understanding of how the religious hierarchy works and has been conceptualized is needed. In fact, when examining religious hierarchy in Thailand it is more insightful to talk about "hierarchies" than "hierarchy," as in Thai Buddhism there are a number of religious hierarchies at work, often simultaneously. These hierarchies are interrelated, dynamic, and often affecting one another. This approach will allow us to understand better how respect is conceptualized and expressed within the parameters of gendered hierarchical relationships.

Five Hierarchies in Thai Buddhism

Gabaude has argued that "Thai Buddhism is structured by three separate hierarchies, which are supposed to measure Buddhist achievements."[16]

There is what he calls the *vinaya* hierarchy; this "is the only hierarchy admitted by the Buddha, that which should come out of his *Vinaya* rules. . . . [I]f the criteria of imperfection are well described in the *vinaya*, the actual realization of perfection by such and such a monk is only well known in his community."[17] According to Gabaude there is also the administrative hierarchy. This

> virtually government-appointed hierarchy is made up of monks who are responsible for the day-to-day routine of what is "order," not only in the eyes of the Buddha (or his *Vinaya*) but in the eyes of the political authorities. . . . This hierarchy is parallel to the civilian administration, from the patriarch who plays the role of a kind of religious king (*saṅgha-rāja*) down to the head of a temple who serves as a kind of village chief.

Except on formal occasions or exceptional cases, the "public is not generally concerned with this network of religio-political hierarchy." Thirdly, and in line with my respective observations in this book, the

> popular hierarchy is made up of monks who are considered extraordinary in one way or another by the general public: they give winning lottery numbers through enigmas; they "read" minds; they perform miracles; they prevent individuals from dying in car crashes; they live ascetic lives; they produce potent artefacts (medallions, Buddha images, phalluses) with special protective powers; or they preach well. There is no specific body to decide who will be a part of this hierarchy and who will be at the top. Often, it begins with local fame, which spreads throughout the country by word of mouth.

While I find Gabaude's categorization of these three hierarchies quite useful, I want to introduce two further hierarchies. In addition, I would also like to define the *vinaya* hierarchy differently. In contrast to Gabaude, I understand *vinaya* hierarchy to refer to the status of monks not only within their monastic community but also in society, gained through the length of time spent uninterruptedly in the robes since their higher ordination (*upasampadā*) to the status of a fully ordained monk (*bhikkhu*). My definition here is in line with what Kate Crosby calls the "*vassa*-age hierarchy"; she explains, "No matter what positions monks may hold in the Sangha or even the government, their hierarchy within the Sangha is based solely on their monastic age" as a fully ordained *bhikkhu*.[18] That means that the longer a monk has held full ordination without having lost it through a major violation of the code of discipline, the higher he automatically rises within this hierarchy.[19]

Anyhow, the length of uninterrupted time spent in the robes decides the relative seniority between monks. Taking spiritual perfection as a criterion for seniority within a monastic community may be problematic (see also chapter 3). This is already clearly expressed in the Pali canonical *vinaya* texts.[20] Furthermore, another problem with a hierarchy based on levels of supramundane attainments is that, even for fully awakened monks, the spiritual level of a fellow monk may not be obvious.[21]

In addition to the *vinaya*, administrative, and popular hierarchies, I want to add the hierarchy of ecclesiastical ranks (*samanasak*) and the hierarchy of educational achievement. Monks enter or are promoted within the hierarchy of ecclesiastical ranks by receiving a monastic title conferred by the king of Thailand.[22] In present-day Thai Buddhism, ecclesiastical titles are conferred for outstanding achievements in the field of monastic administration, fundraising, or education, or when monks are highly revered for their spiritual practice by a significant number of Thai Buddhists.[23] Monks receive a title, a fan (*phat yot*), and a certificate that indicate their rank. These fans and certificates are often lavishly displayed at the monk's monastic cell or central places in the monastery.[24]

The hierarchy of educational achievement consists of two systems: the *nak tham* and, more importantly in this context, the *parian tham*. By passing exams on Buddhist doctrine and monastic regulations monks can achieve up to three levels, the highest of which is *nak tham ek*. In the *parian tham* system monks have to demonstrate advanced knowledge of the Pali language in order to receive a title. When they have passed grade three, monks are called *phra maha* (great venerable). There are altogether nine grades; the level of achievement is expressed in *prayok*. Candidates who successfully passed the level *prayok* 3 or higher will also receive a fan that shows the level of their academic achievement. Monks and novices who have passed the grade of *prayok* 3 are regarded as having achieved a "*samanasak* of [Pali] studies."[25]

It needs to be noted, though, that the five hierarchies introduced here can overlap and may influence one another in complex ways. Thus, a high position in one hierarchy may cause one to rise in another hierarchy as well.[26]

Due to the absence of an officially recognized *bhikkhunī* order, Thai women have not had the opportunity to practice within a system of *vinaya* hierarchy established by the Pali canonical *pāṭimokkha* (until recently, when female groups started attempts to revive the order). However, I should mention here that in 1971 the Thai Mae Chi Institute published the "rules of practice" (*rabiap patibat*) that are to be adopted by *mae chi*s nationwide. These rules, which obviously took the canonical *pāṭimokkha* as a model, establish a *vassa* hierarchy among *mae chi*s and also say that "*mae chi*s should not (due to the power of the precepts they practice) prostrate themselves in front of [*krap*] or *wai* laypeople; *mae chi*s should receive [*khuan ja rap*] their *wai* and give blessings when appropriate."[27] It should be noted here, though, that even though probably first propagated nationwide in the 1970s in the form of a manual of regulations, in practice these hierarchy rules for *mae chis* seem to have been in existence for a long time before then.

Furthermore, as another consequence of their gender and the absence of an officially recognized *bhikkhunī* order, *mae chi*s have not been able to become part of a *samanasak* and administrative hierarchy, as careers in these two hierarchies are possible for fully ordained monks (*bhikkhu*) only. As for the hierarchy of educational achievements, women were initially excluded from the *nak tham* system, in existence since 1915, and for a long time from the *parian tham* system, which has complexly evolved from its precursors since premodern times.[28] Since 1929, however, laypeople, both male and female, have been allowed to take exams similar to the *nak tham* exams but following a different curriculum for nonmonastics (called *thamma sueksa*).[29] Furthermore, since 1963, the Thai Buddhist monastic university Mahamakut has provided courses in Pali studies for *mae chi*s (and laypeople), using the same curriculum as that for monks. This system is called Pali Studies (*bali sueksa*) instead of *parian tham* and allows *mae chi*s to study up to level nine as well.[30] In contrast to monks, however, *mae* *chis* who have achieved the highest level of grade nine do not receive a monthly allowance (*nitthayabat*) from the government. In addition, since the late 1990s the monastic educational career opportunities for *mae chis* have improved significantly.[31] Concurrent with these changes, there has been an increasing number of *mae chis* and female nonmonastics who have become widely regarded as erudite Buddhist scholars and teachers.[32]

At the same time, as already observed in chapter 1, female practitioners may perceive their position outside religious hierarchical systems as an opportunity for freedom due to the flexibility this gives them. As mentioned, Mae Chi Thotsaphon Bunthewaphithak, for example, uses the supernatural powers her followers believe she possesses in order to help people to "correct their [negative] *kamma*." As monks are required to follow their 227 *pāṭimokkha* rules, they may find pursuing such practices problematic. As shown in chapters 2 and 3, Mae Bunruean used her assumed supernatural powers in order to heal (albeit only when deemed necessary). At the same time, she seems to have created her own *vinaya* rules suitable to her spiritual practice and work as a healer. In her autobiography Mae Chi Phimpha Wongsa-udom tells us that she enjoyed the freedom of her simple monastic life outside the ecclesiastical hierarchy with its obligations and constraints.[33]

Female Perspectives on Hierarchy and Gender

Like the other women central to my study, Mae Bunruean does not appear to have challenged existing structures of (gendered) hierarchy in Thai society. Mae Bunruean's homiletic texts, which are obviously based on a rather profound and comprehensive understanding of Buddhist doctrines and narratives and are eloquently delivered, deal predominantly with the way of overcoming internal defilements and are largely not related to gender. She emphasized, though, that both men and women can equally attain full awakening:

> If you practice seriously, it doesn't matter whether it is the mind of a woman or the mind of a man; they are similar. If one's mind is firmly established in the virtues [*guṇa*] of the Triple Gem, all

> the five mental hindrances [*nīvaraṇa*] can be eradicated and all the ten fetters [*saṃyojana*] can be abandoned [which means full awakening can be attained], and one can truly reach the virtues of the Triple Gem.[34]

Elsewhere she says, "Both women and men, may you attain *nibbāna* in the present, in your current rebirth" and, "The *dhamma* pervades the world and does not favor specific age or gender."[35] At the same time, she admits that women have to face certain constraints due to their gender when they want to practice meditation. She continues, however, by arguing that this would not bar women from Buddhist practice as the noble path has to be developed internally and can be practiced under any circumstances:

> Those who do not possess understanding about the internal practice [of the *dhamma*] and have not yet reached the genuine Triple Gem still have to look for seclusion [*viveka*] in the mountains and other places in order to escape from the unpleasant noise of the world and pursue their personal practice, [following the footsteps of] the monks wandering the forests and mountains in search of seclusion. But as we are women, we have many duties. We are not able to look for seclusion in such a way. As we have a different gender, looking for such external seclusion poses many dangers. . . . Thus, it is necessary to pursue morality [*sīla*], concentration [*samādhi*], wisdom [*paññā*] . . . mental seclusion and physical seclusion and make them arise in one's mind by practicing concentration with eyes open and insight meditation internally. We will have to drive away the mental defilements that make our mind depressed, and by doing so achieve mental seclusion. Having established mental seclusion, we will be successful no matter what we practice. . . . If we have perseverance in our practice, and even if we are not able to find physical seclusion, our mind can still find seclusion. For example, with the husband gone to work and the children to school, being at home one can try to bring one's mind to seclusion, by practicing meditation with open eyes, which constitutes insight meditation

> [*vipassanā*]. Cleaning the house, one establishes mindfulness [*sati*] internally, focusing on cleaning one's house like purifying one's mind internally, as the mind does not get attached to the body's external activities.[36]

Mae Bunruean does not appear to have perceived gender and social status as significant potential obstacles to spiritual practice. What Mae Bunruean repeatedly emphasizes in her texts, however, is the importance of being born as a human being.[37] Being born as a human being is "most excellent" and allows the individual, through the study of Buddhist teaching, to attain *nibbāna*: "Rebirth can take place in any form [*rūpa*] and name [*nāma*], . . . but rebirth as a human being is extremely difficult."[38] Rebirth as a human being into a time period when Buddhist teaching is accessible is believed to be even more difficult. In their texts, both Khunying Yai and Mae Bunruean strongly emphasize the rarity, and thus extreme preciousness, of the coalescence of rebirth as a human being and accessibility to Buddhist teaching within the vast cosmic cycle of rebirth.[39]

Khunying Yai explains,

> We have to realize the perils of the cycle of rebirth and the perils of rebirth into a woeful existence [*duggati*], being [for example] reborn as an animal [*tiracchāna*]. Those who are negligent [*pamāda*] will have to be reborn constantly into the three realms of the rebirth cycle [*vaṭṭa*], being captured in the realm of the king of death [*maccurāja*]. That means they will endlessly experience rebirth, aging, pain, and death. Floating around in these three realms of rebirth, one is subjected to extreme hardship. When humans, however, have the chance to learn from righteous people [*sappurisa*] and listen to the Buddha's teaching [*dhamma*], pursuing meritorious acts, they will consequently be reborn into a blissful state of existence [*sugati*]. . . . We can practice [the *dhamma*] only as long as we are alive. Once we have passed away we may not have the chance to create goodness. No one can predict when one's last breath will take place. For this reason, we should persevere in order to achieve the supramundane [*mak*

> *lae phon*] and thus escape from the perils of unhappy existences [*apāya*] and the perils of the rebirth cycle.[40]

The extremely rare and fortunate opportunity of human rebirth allows soteriological perfection and is thus not to be carelessly wasted. According to this thinking, due to the "perils and hardship of the cycle of rebirth" and the unpredictability and constant possibility of one's death, there is an immediate urgency to attain *ariya* status in order to escape the unceasing cycle of rebirths, dying and hardship in the various planes within Buddhist cosmology. As expressed by Mae Chi Phimpha in her autobiography,

> Those human beings [whose life is governed by ignorance (*avijjā*) and craving (*taṇhā*) and only know greed (*lobha*) and anger (*kodha*)] waste their rebirth and thus their capital [as human beings] in vain. . . . As the nights, days, months, and years pass, our life is coming to an end. We die every moment, every time we are breathing in and out. All in this world is ephemeral, uncertain, and not lasting.[41]

In none of the available texts authored by the women of my study are female Pali canonical figures explicitly referred to as particular role models or inspirational figures due to their gender. When referring to Pali narratives in which female Buddhist practitioners figure predominantly, it is done in order to exemplify a specific Buddhist teaching.[42] Even though rather different in their styles and emphases, the homiletic texts of both Khunying Yai and Mae Bunruean do not contain a gender-specific focus. While Mae Bunruean discusses gender to a larger extent than is the case in the texts of Khunying Yai, the texts of both are characterized by a kammic-cosmic perspective and, closely related with this, a deep concern with mental states and activities (*cetasika*) and, of course, the spiritual path toward soteriological perfection. In Mae Chi Phimpha's autobiography a similar focus and perspective can be identified:

> [While practicing] walking meditation or sitting meditation I was unrelentingly thinking only about one thing: the mind which

> travels [through the cycle of rebirth] constantly creating *kamma* and [thereby new] becoming [*bhava*] and rebirth [*jāti*]. Doing so made me continuously watch [the workings of] my own mind.[43]

In both Khunying Yai's and Mae Chi Phimpha's texts, social hierarchy is hardly discussed. When Khunying Yai refers to social hierarchy, it is looked at as something kammically conditioned. Referring to the famous *Cūḷakammavibhaṅga-sutta* of the *Majjhima-nikāya*, Khunying Yai explains that "beings [*satta*] are different" due to "the fruition" of their *kamma*.[44] Wealth, influence, and social position (among other things) are kammic results of one's own past deeds. After all, as Khunying Yai and Mae Bunruean repeatedly point out in their texts, beings are the "owners" and "heirs" of their own *kamma*.[45]

In contrast to Khunying Yai and Mae Chi Phimpha, Mae Bunruean refers in her texts rather frequently to contemporary Thai society, its social structure, and the Thai nation-state and monarchy. In her texts, Mae Bunruean makes clear that for her, social hierarchy is not something to be challenged but something to be maintained:

> Virtuous people, possessing faith [*saddhā*]—and faith is like an amicable teacher of the practitioner . . . , know in specific situations who is superior to whom. People have to respect one another in accordance with their status. The inferior has to respect the superior and the Thai people have to respect their religion like [their] father.[46]

This is not a defeatist or deterministic view. Mae Bunruean argues that despite (relatively) unfavorable rebirth within the human realm, significant social and spiritual advancement is possible through perseverance (*khwam phian*). No doubt, what is perceived as most important is spiritual advancement:

> Even if reborn into the countryside without any access to education, if your wisdom lets you turn to Buddhism and you study Buddhist teaching with the help of a teacher . . . until you

> reach the supramundane accordingly, this should be regarded as "coming from the dark into the light" [*ma muet pai sawang*].[47]

Thus, it can be argued that for Khunying Yai, Mae Bunruean, and Mae Chi Phimpha[48] (and from the available sources, we can assume that this is also the case for the other women central to my study), gender is rather insignificant in view of the uncertainties of the rebirth cycle within the vast Buddhist cosmology and the extreme hardships that constant rebirth within it entails. What really matters is that being reborn as a human being, no matter as man or woman, affords the extremely rare, potentially short-term and thus extraordinarily precious opportunity to escape from the cycle of rebirth, or at least "to close the gates to the woeful states of existence" (by becoming an *ariya-puggala*).[49]

Ephemerality and Insubstantiality of Gender

While Khunying Yai and Mae Bunruean explain social position, influence, and wealth as being connected to one's past *kamma*, so far I have not found any reference in their texts identifying maleness or femaleness as the result of deeds performed in previous lifetimes. One reason for this lack of gender-specific explanations of kammic law may be that their main source for the teaching on how *kamma*'s fruition becomes visible in body, social status, and so on seems to have been the Pali canonical texts, such as the *Cūḷakammavibhaṅga-sutta*, in which this topic is not mentioned.[50]

In the cases of Khunying Yai, Mae Bunruean, Mae Chi Kaew, and Mae Chi Nari, there are biographical references to their former lifetimes. According to Phra Thepsumethi, Khunying Yai recounted that when pursuing meditation with a deeply concentrated state of mind of one-pointedness (*ekaggatā*) she was able to recollect former lifetimes. According to Phra Thepsumethi's account, her previous gender is only clear in one lifetime, when she was a female human being.[51] The three previous rebirths that are recounted in Mae Bunruean's hagiographical texts took place each time as a female human being, too. In Mae Chi Kaew's hagiographical texts we can read that when seven years old she was able to remember a former lifetime in which she was reborn as a mother chicken that looked after her many chicks. Two of her chicks, so oral transmission has it, were reborn as human beings in her current lifetime and became famous teachers of the Thai forest tradition. In another lifetime, so it is reported, she was reborn as a female human being.[52] Sex or sex change across lifetimes is not discussed in the major Thai biographies of Khunying Yai, Mae Bunruean, or Mae Chi Kaew.

Mae Chi Nari's story is somewhat unusual in this respect in that it contains a reflection on sex as determined by *kamma* from a former life. However, she commented on this topic only, so it seems, because in an interview her (male) hagiographer prompted her to do so. Mae Chi Nari's hagiographies tell us that she was able to remember numerous former lifetimes, when she was, for example, reborn as a human being in different countries, having been a king, a soldier, a farmer, and more. She also is reported to have remembered her former lifetimes as various animals. When her hagiographer asked, "How does the mind [*jit winyan*] that is constantly reborn differ in terms of maleness and femaleness?" she answered,

> The mind [*jit winyan*] does not have a gender at all. Being reborn as a male or female human being is a result of how *kamma* divides us up to be. Take me, for example: in each former lifetime I have been reborn as a man. It was only in my current life that I have come back as a woman.[53]

Another hagiographer explains this sex change by noting that when she was a man in a former life, she wanted to know how it felt to give birth: "This minor interest caused her to be reborn as a woman and to gain deep understanding of motherhood."[54]

In chapter 3 I related the story of how Mae Chi Tat and her monk meditation master believed she had been his son in a former lifetime. This belief made the monk

> respect her as his son. . . . The son, in the body of a *mae chi*, had respect and was dutiful, following all the instructions of the monk master. That she treated her monk father in the same way

> a boy would treat his master made the monk very much love his *mae chi* son.[55]

The story goes that Mae Chi Tat's actual sex as a woman was the result of *kamma* performed during a former lifetime when she, then being a monk, committed an "evil deed" (*pāpa-kamma*) by raping a female lay supporter. However, the story makes clear that for Mae Chi Tat and her meditation teacher, gender, or maybe more precisely the physical appearance (*rang*) of gender, seems to have been a superficial category and rather irrelevant to their relationship.

What the rebirth stories of Mae Chi Nari, Mae Chi Kaew,[56] and Mae Chi Tat also show is the belief that current intensive relationships may have spanned or developed across lifetimes. In various former lifetimes, all three of these women were close to famous monk teachers. Mae Chi Kaew is reported to have been the mother chicken of two famous meditation masters who had been her chicks in that lifetime. Mae Chi Nari's hagiography tells us that in a former lifetime she was the younger brother of Luang Pu Man and also (probably in another lifetime) the father of the famous meditation master Luang Pu Lui Candasāro. Here, I should point out that the idea of links between individuals across lifetimes can also be found in Pali canonical literature.[57]

The major objectives of the rebirth stories of these women seem to be to demonstrate the validity of kammic law within the many realms of Buddhist cosmology, the hardships of unfavorable rebirths, the effectiveness of Buddhist practice and teaching, and, again, the preciousness of human rebirth. With regard to gender and rebirth, Phra Payutto explains that

> according to Buddhist principles, each person is sometimes reborn as a woman and sometimes as a man. This changes depending on one's *kamma*. [In being human, however], no matter whether female or male, all have the same potential to achieve supramundane states of mind [*banlu tham*]. Our way of differentiating between female and male is a short-term and temporary way of looking at it. But, in fact, everyone has both femaleness and maleness, which can constantly change.[58]

Elsewhere Phra Payutto further explains that according to Buddhism, sex change between rebirths can happen "quite easily, depending on how the mind's inclinations, desires and doubts condition [the future] life."[59] Corresponding to Phra Payutto's scriptural explanations, in the texts by or about the women central to my study, sex change across lifetimes is certainly possible, and sex is presented as being soteriologically irrelevant. However, as Naomi Appleton has observed about early Indian Buddhism, sex across lifetimes is depicted as generally stable.[60]

The perceptions of the ephemerality and soteriological irrelevance of gender do not, however, mean that for the women of my study their femaleness did not impose a number of gender-specific challenges, experiences, and constraints on their spiritual path. This has already become abundantly clear in the previous chapters of this book. However, gender-related issues, as perceived by the women themselves, are particularly prominent when the textual material discusses renunciation, possession of formal Buddhist knowledge, and the pursuit of austere practices. In the following sections I will not give a comprehensive presentation and analysis of gender-specific experiences in this regard; given the vastness of the material, this would be too ambitious for the purposes of this book. Rather, I will demonstrate and discuss the spectrum of relevant experiences expressed in the biographies. This I will do by providing a number of biographical elements that are representative of larger issues of gender differences in the soteriological quest.

Female Renunciation within Patriarchal Power Structures

An important element in many of the biographies of Thai *mae chi*s that I investigated is the strong and often long-held wish to renounce lay life. While the ordination of Thai men as monks is normally strongly encouraged and supported by family members and society at large, women who wish to become ordained as *mae chi*s may face a number of gender-specific obstacles in their quest for or embracing of ordained life. This also becomes clear in the biographies of some of the women who are central to my study.[61]

As already shown above, in her texts Khunying Yai consistently expresses and argues for the urgency of pursuing Buddhist practice in one's present human rebirth. In one of her major texts, published in 1932, she has one of the two interlocutors say

> I am still worried about my duties that I have to myself and others. . . . I am afraid that I cannot fully pursue [my spiritual training], or do I have to go to a tranquil place [in order to do so]? [But even though] I am truly committed to my practice, at the moment I do not yet have the opportunity to escape [from my current situation].[62]

It was one year after the publication of this passage, in 1933, that Khunying Yai became ordained as a *mae chi* by Somdet Phra Buddhaghosacariya of Wat Thepsirin, having asked her husband for permission to do so first.[63] From the autobiography of her adopted son, Prasop Wisetsiri, we learn that when he was nine years old Khunying Yai gave him into the care of other people: "My mother's concerns in having to look after me came to an end. She therefore shaved her hair and was ordained as a *mae chi* . . . for the rest of her life."[64] As Khunying Yai does not explicitly refer to herself in her texts, it is difficult, if not impossible, to say how far her texts reflect her own biography and experiences.[65] But, given her understanding of and devotion to Buddhist teaching and practice, it seems reasonable to conclude that Khunying Yai had held the wish to become ordained for a while before she eventually felt able to do so. The "duty" to look after her adopted son had prevented her from becoming a *mae chi* and devoting her life more intensively to spiritual practice sooner.

In the hagiographies I studied, the sense of duty toward husband or children was often referred to as a reason for delaying the renunciation of lay life.[66] For some *mae chi*s this would even entail, at least temporarily, a hybrid life of being a layperson and a monastic. Mae Chi Kaew, for example, performed her household chores despite being ordained, while for Mae Chi Nari "it was necessary to stay at home after her ordination as a *mae chi* so that she could look after her two-year-old child for a while." When she visited Luang Pu Man in order to listen to his teachings and ask him questions about her practice, she would take her family with her.[67]

Not long after her ordination as a *mae chi*, Khunying Yai was sued for insolvency.[68] In the course of the hearing, her ordained status as a *mae chi* and the question of whether she was still legally married to her husband became the decisive matter in the case. In the then-applicable Laws on Husbands and Wives (*Kotmai laksana phua mia*), which forms a part of the Three Seals Law (compiled in 1805 during the reign of King Rama I), it says that "when a wife who departs from her husband becomes ordained [*buat*] and the husband has allowed her to become ordained, wife and husband are no longer married."[69] The plaintiff's lawyer in this case argued that the word "become ordained [*buat*]" in this law text should be understood as referring to the ordination as a *bhikkhunī* or *sāmaṇerī*. As Khunying Yai was ordained as a *mae chi*, however, the plaintiff argued that she was still legally married to her husband and thus, in the context of this case, liable to pay her debts. While the Civil Court agreed with this reasoning, the Supreme Court eventually agreed with the argument of the Court of Appeals that "to become ordained [*buat*]" in the Laws on Husbands and Wives means "ordination as a *mae chi*" as "presently, women can be ordained as *mae chi*s only" and "in the old laws there is no mention of *bhikkhunī* or *sāmaṇerī*, whereas [*mae chi*s] are mentioned in monastic law [*kotmai phra song*]."[70] Thus, the Supreme Court decided in favor of Khunying Yai and the case was dismissed. What is also noteworthy here is that in the equivalent law applicable for when men become ordained, it does not mention that a man needs to have permission from his wife. This means that according to these two laws a married woman who had become a *mae chi* but had not received permission from her husband to become ordained would still be regarded as legally married. With his ordination as a monk, however, the marriage of a man was automatically legally terminated, irrespective of whether he had received prior permission from his wife to do so.[71]

That women were subject to and dependent on their husbands' will when they wanted to become ordained is not only apparent in the Laws on Husbands and Wives but also in many of the biographies of the women of my study, as well. In actual social relationships the implications of patriarchal hierarchy may become manifest even more forcefully, as some of the renunciation stories of the women of my study vividly show. As detailed in chapter 2, Mae Chi Phimpha strongly wished to become a *mae chi* but was anxious that her husband might not allow her to do so. In her autobiography she writes,

> I raised my hands, making a vow by asking for the [positive] fruits of [my] moral behavior and I asked the goodness [*guṇa*] of the Buddha, the *dhamma*, and the *saṅgha* for help—"May my husband not change his mind!" . . . I couldn't eat . . . as I felt constantly utterly repressed in the fear that my husband may change his mind and not become ordained.[72]

It has also been noted that if not for her gender Mae Chi Kaew's monastic career may have started much earlier than it actually did, as Luang Pu Man had declined to ordain her because he was concerned that it would be problematic with regard to the teachings and monastic regulations of the Buddha if he had a girl accompanying him. She had to wait until she was in her thirties before she was able to become eventually ordained as a *mae chi*. After seventeen years of marriage, "for a period of two years she persevered in asking her husband for permission to become ordained."[73] Mae Chi Kaew vividly described the strong wish to renounce the world and how she experienced lay life prior to her ordination:

> I was utterly weary and exceedingly experiencing *dukkha* in the life of a layperson. On those days that I thought about the *dhamma* and the teachings of Luang Pu Man late in the night while lying, I would cry, sad and feeling bad about myself. Lying on my side, I was crying and crying. When working in the rice field, I would hide and, being on my own, cry. I was thinking about ways of how to escape [from this]. My husband did not allow me to go to the monastery; he [only] allowed me to donate food to the monks. He did not give me permission to visit the *mae chi* community in the monastery, and meditation practice at home I was not able to do. He allowed me to recite Buddhist texts [*suat mon*]. Whatever my husband told or forbade me to do, I had to surrender to his will. The weariest thing in the world is the married life. I was so weary of this life that I could not find any joy in it at all. Even wearing the clothes of a layperson I disliked.[74]

As related in chapter 2, it was only with the intercession of an uncle that her husband finally allowed her to become a *mae chi*, and when she returned home after the agreed-upon period, she did not disrobe but tried to hide her *mae chi* robes and soon fled back to the monastery. Similarly to Mae Chi Phimpha, she perceived herself "to be the possession" (*yu nai kammasit*) of her husband.

Although much less dramatic, the female sense of duty toward husband and family is also evident in the biographies of Mae Chi Nari, Mae Chi Phimpha, and Mae Chi Soda. Mae Chi Nari was the one who even offered "to find three new wives" for her husband if he would let her ordain,[75] and when Mae Chi Phimpha felt the wish to become ordained as a *mae chi*, she told her husband to remarry. Mae Chi Soda had to wait for a long time for her ordination as she was worried about her son, but once he had a regular job, she asked him for permission to become ordained.[76]

It is, however, not their gender alone that may have significantly impeded and delayed the monastic spiritual practice of women. The female aspirant's age may also have played a role. This is exemplified in the story of Mae Chi Bunmi Wetchasan (1938–2016) of the Bangkok monastery Wat Samphanthawong (the same monastery in which important episodes of Mae Bunruean's spiritual career took place).[77] Mae Chi Bunmi was a meditation student of the famous Burmese *vipassanā* meditation teacher Phra Bhaddanta Āsabha (1911–2010). She herself became a meditation teacher with a large number of students. It has been believed that she achieved the supramundane level of an *ariya-puggala*.[78] Mae Chi Bunmi was initially so strongly interested in trade that she even left primary school after only two years in order to pursue a career in trade. One day she happened to enter a monastery where a meditation teacher monk persuaded her to practice meditation. When the monk recognized that Mae Chi Bunmi was talented at meditation, he encouraged her to practice more intensively. She made rapid progress; within only five days she experienced powerful mental images (*phap nimit*) and on the seventh day, having experienced extraordinary bodily lightness (*bao*) and having perceived multiple colors emanating from her body, she even believed that she had already reached the supramundane (*mak phon nipphan*). Her meditation teacher clarified, though, that these were only appearances of bright light (*obhāsa*)[79] and that "there are many more, better things [that result from meditation practice] than these [phenomena]." These events triggered in her an extremely strong desire to become ordained (*khit ja buat luea koen*). But her meditation teacher did not give her the permission to do so. Her biography explains, "The reason for this is that [Mae Chi Bunmi] was still young. In former times, those who wanted to become ordained as a *mae chi* were rather old. When one is ordained as a *mae chi* at a young age, so senior people [*phu yai*] argued, one may be the reason why monks disrobe."[80] In the monastery where she sought ordination, there were only very old *mae chi*s, and despite being already thirty-eight years old at that time, Mae Chi Bunmi was told that "young [*sao sao*] *mae chi*s [like you] cannot be ordained [here] at all. They may cause monks to disrobe. This would damage the reputation [of our monastery]." But her meditation practice caused her to feel "depressed and [at the same time] have a feeling of urgency [*salot sangwet*]." She thought,

> I constantly have to experience rebirth and dying; when will this finally stop? Why should I spend my life as a lay? . . . The following thought arose in my mind: "Will this mean that I have to waste this lifetime as a human being [*sia chat koet*] as I am not able to study the teachings of Lord Buddha?"[81]

When she failed to get permission to become ordained, Mae Chi Bunmi then decided to continue with her practice at home. She closed her business and dedicated her time fully to the practice of meditation. Then one day Luang Pho Thuam (Phra Khrubaidikaphayakon, Vesārajjo) of Wat Saensukwisutthiwararam in Chon Buri Province, who was famous for his accurate foretelling, told her that she had to become ordained; otherwise she would die. Being afraid of dying, she consented, and Luang Pho Thuam, having secured two sets of robes for her, ordained her.[82]

Here, I should point out that in the biographies of female practitioners that I investigated, *mae chi*s are never depicted as the agents in undermining male monastic celibacy. As already argued in chapter 5, it is rather the feeble and insufficiently trained mind of the male monastic that may allow itself to be seduced by close or long-term exposure to the body or "external form" of women. Thus, it is the monk's mind that sexualizes the female body and may, in this way, succumb to sexual desire.

Apart from concerns about women living in monastic community with monks as being potentially dangerous for male monastics' celibacy, intactness of the *vinaya*, and the reputation of the monastery, Upāsikā Nu-nueang Thapmeng's biography shows another idea that could make *mae chi* ordination for younger women difficult. When she was only seventeen years old, Upāsikā Nu-nueang had the strong wish to become a *mae chi*. She then shaved her hair and made preparations for her ordination.

> At that time, I was very much afraid of [rebirth into] a hellish realm. I thought about dying every day. *Dukkha* had become very clearly manifest to me. I thought I would not be able to remain in the world; my mind was only preoccupied with the wish to become ordained as a *mae chi*. . . . When working in the rice field with my young female friends, I told them that I will become ordained as a *mae chi*. However, they teased me, saying, "Hey, she will become a *mae chi*!" They could not believe that someone at my age would be able to become ordained as a *mae chi*. Normally, most people believe that those who renounce lay life and are able to become ordained as a *mae chi* are people who must have experienced [some form of deep] disappointment, such as in love, and therefore turn toward the being [*phet*][83] of a *mae chi* in order to avoid the gaze of people.[84]

Dangers and Fears in the Pursuit of Ascetic Practices

Another gender-specific aspect in female spiritual practice is the obstacles and dangers women have to face when pursuing spiritual practice in seclusion, in particular in the forest. As a *mae chi* who had been ordained for numerous years put it in an interview, "[Even though] women and men are the same when it comes to spiritual practice, we women cannot go into the forest; here, we are disadvantaged. . . . The forest is dangerous for the female gender."[85] As shown above, for Mae Bunruean, too, female practitioners' spiritual practice in seclusion may be dangerous and thus not possible. However, in numerous hagiographies of male practitioners intensive practice in the seclusion of the forest is depicted as a crucial part of their soteriological journey. The austere practices (*dhutaṅga*; *thudong* in Thai), which were widely practiced by monks of the forest tradition, may involve dwelling in the jungle or in cemeteries and sleeping in the open air. In Thai, *thudong* is commonly understood as wandering in the forest with a special umbrella with a mosquito net attached to it (*klot*), with the aim of spending lengthy times in solitude. Monks may spend a significant amount of time in the forest or in cemeteries on their own in order to test their determination and develop their minds in line with canonical ideals. In this way, "deep forest and the forest cemetery" have been perceived as "training grounds" for the monks' practice toward spiritual perfection.[86]

Even though some of the women of my study only hinted at the constraints, challenges, and dangers they faced in this regard due to their gender without giving further elaboration, in some of the biographies of the female practitioners I studied, the fear of becoming a victim of male physical violence is directly discussed. The hardly known Mae Chi Prachumphon Jaksurak, whom I already mentioned in chapter 2, gave a particularly vivid account in this regard. In an interview with Luang Pho Jaran Ṭhitadhammo of Wat Amphawan she recounts how she only narrowly escaped being sexually assaulted or even raped.

Mae Chi Prachumphon became "fully weary of family life" and "ran away in order to become ordained," leaving behind her four young children. Not long after her ordination as a *mae chi*, she started to practice meditation by regularly contemplating corpses. Over the course of her ordained life of thirty years, she practiced in altogether twenty-two different cemeteries. Even though she was made aware that "the Lord Buddha forbade women from being alone,"[87] she was determined to continue her practice in solitude near corpses in cemeteries in order "to achieve liberation." One of her admirers states that the practice of contemplating the unattractiveness (*asubha*) of corpses may have allowed her to gain valuable insights into the reality of life.[88] She spent the last fourteen years of her life in solitude in a cemetery in Saraburi Province, where she died in January 1983. When her children tried to convince her to give up solitary practice and asked her to stay with them, she only replied, "It is better to die in the field than to live on as a loser [in the quest for liberation]. What is the benefit of living, when having lost?"[89] One day, her determination was tested in an extreme way. While practicing in solitude in a cemetery, a young man aged about twenty, who during a previous visit had already stolen Mae Chi Prachumphon's clock, returned again. He forced her to lie down. Mae Chi Prachumphon says she thought,

> Today I will [be forced] to terminate my life of chastity [*brahmacariya*]. I will die for sure. But once I thought about dying, I thought about the Buddha. And when I thought about the Buddha [*phra*], I immediately raised my hands in order to show my respect to the Lord Buddha. [But when that young man saw that] I was raising my hands [in order to pay respect to the Lord Buddha], his hands, which were forcing me down, stopped pressing me down. He seized the clock [he had stolen from me] from his pocket and returned it to me. See! This is the power of the Lord Buddha!

Despite this incident Mae Chi Prachumphon decided to go for alms (*piṇḍapāta*) the following morning, after having had to rest for a while as a consequence of the physical harm she had experienced in this assault and what may have been attempted rape.[90]

Due to their gender, female practitioners were sometimes not allowed to pursue their spiritual practice outside a monastery. As mentioned in the previous chapter, Mae Chi Nu-nueang, still in her teenage years, was told by her teacher that going on *thudong* at her age was demeritorious (*pāpa*). She writes, "As my teacher forbade it, I had to stop and practice meditation and keep the precepts in [a] monastery."[91] Mae Chi Bunmi, however, reports that she went on *thudong* many times in her monastic life, sometimes for several months: "I saw monks who went on *thudong*, so I asked myself, 'Why can't I do this? I have feet and hands, so I must be able to do this too. I want to go too.' . . . So I went with a *klot*, an alms bowl, and a bag for clothes."[92] Mae Chi Bunmi went for *thudong* to the North, South, and Northeast of Thailand over the course of ten years.[93] She reports that she was not the only *mae chi* to go on *thudong*, even though the number of *mae chi*s, at least when compared with the monks, was small. Mae Chi Bunmi also practiced in the wilderness and in cemeteries. She described her experiences in the cemetery as enormously valuable for her spiritual practice:

> A monk helped me [to practice] in a cemetery. He prepared the *klot* and some candles for me. . . . [During the daytime] I was not afraid, but during the night I was very afraid. . . . The wind was blowing; the dry leaves caused a noise that made me feel startled; I shed tears. . . . [Sitting] in front of a grave I [first believed] that I was afraid of the ghosts [of people who had passed away] . . . but then I [found out] that I was not afraid of ghosts but rather of dying. . . . And being in a cemetery [helps] to establish mindfulness [*sati*]. . . . When you [feel safe in your monastic hut] you cannot establish mindfulness as well as in a cemetery, because fear helps you to establish mindfulness.[94]

The ideas expressed in this account remarkably resemble concepts of early Buddhism; fear is here considered as a valuable means, or "goad," rather than as an obstruction in spiritual practice.[95]

In some of the biographies we can read that laypeople perceived *mae chi*s as authentic practitioners of *thudong*, giving them respect and support in a similar way they would to monks. Both Mae Chi Phimpha and Mae Chi Bunmi recount how villagers generously supported them when they were practicing meditation intensively in remote places. In her autobiography Mae Chi Phimpha writes that, together with a group of sometimes up to thirty other *mae chi*s, she "pursued spiritual practice with extreme effort day and night" on a mountain for some two years. This mountain "is a suitable place for Buddhist practice; in addition to being a remote, uninhabited place, it offers other things that provide delight and fearsomeness, such as various kinds of birds, rabbits, fierce tigers, dangerous people, and ghosts [*phi*]." Local villagers invited the *mae chi*s to ask for (*pavāraṇā*) food, which they would bring up the mountain in order to offer to the *mae chi*s. Even though the *mae chi*s had decided that under no circumstances would they ask for anything as a part of their spiritual practice, there was no lack of food for the whole two years. Mae Chi Phimpha writes that the villagers' support was "truly amazing." The intensive meditation on that mountain allowed Mae Chi Phimpha "to achieve amazing results. I was able to understand the language of birds; my mind was resolute and not afraid of anything."[96] Similarly, Mae Chi Bunmi reports that during her long renunciate life she received plenty of support and respect:

> The people showed great respect [*nop nom*] to me. . . . The villagers would dismount from their bicycles, take off their hats, and show respect [*wai*]. . . . They regarded me as truly ordained one [*okbuat tem roi*] to whom you should show respect and salute by raising your hands. . . . When I was sleeping in cemeteries, villagers would come to respectfully donate [*on nom nop nom*] things to me. . . . If they had any questions with regard to the Buddhist teaching, I would discuss these with them.[97]

Access to Buddhist Knowledge

In chapter 5 I described how female practitioners were able to develop what was regarded as impressive knowledge of Buddhist teaching by primarily relying on memory and oral means of textual transmission. However, the fact that Thai women did not have the same educational opportunities to gain Buddhist knowledge in a systematic and progressive way as Thai men is sometimes referred to and reflected upon in the biographies I studied. As described in the previous chapter, Upāsikā Nu-nueang, still in her teenage years, wanted to become ordained as a *mae chi* sometime around the year 1900. However, she thought,

> I have not learned how to read. . . . How then can I memorize and recite texts [together with other *mae chis*]? I therefore begged my uncle to teach me as well as possible under the circumstances. I learned, while I had to work in the rice field. As I had to work a lot, there was little time to learn. But with the help of my good memory I was able to remember things easily. . . . [Even though] after the harvest season I was able to read . . . my spelling was not really good, as my uncle . . . busy with the work in the rice fields, was not able to devote adequate time to teaching me. Thus,

> I practiced how to read and write in accordance with what my merit [*puñña*] and *kamma* [enabled me to].[98]

Once able to read, Upāsikā Nu-nueang started to prepare for ordination. This account shows that there were ordinary Thai women who had been able to develop reading and writing skills before compulsory education was first introduced in the 1920s. However, as they normally did not have the chance to do so within monastic learning environments—unlike boys and men—for ordinary Thai women learning how to read and write would normally have been impeded significantly or not possible at all. What is also noteworthy in Upāsikā Nu-nueang's account is that she relates educational opportunity to *kamma*.

Mae Chi Phimpha's autobiography contains a passage that tellingly expresses how she experienced the lack of scriptural knowledge (*pariyatti*) when conversing with monks. Even though she felt overjoyed that she had the chance to study Buddhist teaching with the great meditation master Luang Pu Thet Desaraṅsī, at the same time she

> was very much afraid of him. Even though I had been devoting my full energy to the practice of meditation for the whole time, I was afraid that he might ask me questions about it. I did not know how to express myself, and did not dare answer his questions. If a teacher monk would ask me about my meditation practice, my mind wanted me to prostrate myself in front of him, and immediately escape [from this situation]. If a monk would ask me about my thoughts, I would say that I have never had the chance to study and that I was not able to read or to write—"I am only able to speak and understand local language." I was very much afraid of scriptural knowledge [*pariyatti*]. I was afraid that a monk teacher might use sophisticated terms [*kham plaek plaek*] I would not be able to recognize or understand and would not be able to respond to. For this reason, I usually avoided meeting monk teachers.[99]

This is remarkable, for Mae Chi Phimpha herself had already given Buddhist instruction to other laypeople before her ordination; she also had spent several decades in the robes of a *mae chi*, rigorously pursuing spiritual practice. Surely she must have been regarded as a relatively advanced Buddhist practitioner. Yet she felt trepidation due to her inability to communicate in Buddhist professional jargon. Elsewhere in her autobiography she reports that once she was asked by a monk to help another monk who "was mentally ill," probably due to meditation gone awry: "I felt unable to help—how could I be able to help? This monk is a Pali scholar of an advanced level [*pen thueng maha*]. I am a woman—from where should I get the knowledge to help him?"[100]

Conclusion

The texts examined in this chapter show that within the patriarchal power structures of Thai society, women have had to face a number of gender-specific obstacles in their quest for their spiritual practice. These obstacles have been experienced in diverse ways and to various degrees, often depending on the women's individual social and educational background and local specifics. However, despite and maybe also because of the sometimes substantial obstacles, the women studied here were strongly determined in their spiritual practice; their motivation and determination were based on and derived from their understanding of and belief in Buddhist doctrine. In fact, I would argue that the biographies of these women often express experiences and feelings in a way that is very much in line with respective concepts of early Buddhism. Thus, in the words of Giuliano Giustarini in his study of the role of fear in Pali texts, "*saṃvega*, an uncomfortable stirring factor . . . and *nibbidā*, the healthy disenchantement towards the lures of *saṃsāra*" are depicted as "important stimuli" to proceed on the spiritual path toward soteriological perfection.[101] Also, "Buddhist texts generally describe fear as a pernicious aspect of the mind, to be scrutinized and eventually overcome. . . . On the other hand, in numerous Pāli passages fear is also described as a fundamental instrument, especially when referred to in the early stages of the practice."[102] As shown above, female practitioners in modern Thai Buddhism perceived and instrumentalized the negative consequences of their hierarchical position in society and family as motivating factors for their spiritual journey. The negative aspects of their hierarchical embeddedness they had to experience made the "weariness of life" in the rebirth cycle manifest and were thus seen as a powerful motivational source for their spiritual development.

As a consequence of their gender, the women of my study were excluded institutionally from the monastic community, and this disadvantaged them in many respects. They lacked the charisma that monks automatically possess as a result of their ordination into the "unbroken lineage" believed to have been established by the Buddha. They were not able to rise within and profit from the rewards of the *vinaya*, administrative, *samanasak*, and educational hierarchies. While lack of educational opportunities is sometimes described as a significant obstacle, as shown in this and previous chapters, none of these hierarchies were challenged by the women of my study. The opposite is the case. Religious hierarchical structure was rigorously maintained by these women. In particular, the perpetuation of the *vinaya* hierarchy was regarded as crucial, as it was seen as directly connected to—or even a basis for—the longevity of Buddhism.

While they had to face numerous gender-specific challenges and obstacles, the women of my study also received significant support and respect both from laypersons and monks who regarded them as practitioners with the awakening potential equal to that of male practitioners. Receiving support from laypeople and monks, these women were able to develop their meditation and build up the charisma of accomplished practitioners, thus advancing in the popular hierarchy. When compared to the careers of monks, however, this usually happened on a rather modest scale and often only on a local level, at least while the saintly women were still alive. In this respect, Mae Bunruean's trajectory to sainthood is unique among the women of my study, as she was venerated by a large number of people on a national level even during her lifetime.

In none of the texts examined in this chapter is rebirth as a woman seen as something negative. Rebirth as a human being, no matter whether male or female, is by far the most important thing as it allows for the realization of soteriological perfection. Perceiving the world with the kammic-cosmic view, described above, these women's primary aim was the attainment of liberation from the cycle of rebirth, thus making gender ultimately irrelevant. The texts investigated in this chapter describe identification with one's gender as a secondary or rather superficial concern for these women. In fact, social or gender equality is not a concern at all in these texts.

There are a number of famous and influential Thai monks who publicly referred to these women as role models for other women. The highly revered monk Luang Pu Sangwan (Khemako, 1916–2004), who had been quite close to Mae Bunruean, for example,

> held the view that women . . . can equally bear the supramundane if they have internalized the principles of the Pali canon. They are able to develop body and mind into that of a monastic [*phra*] just like the male gender. [Luang Pu Sangwan] gave all women the advice to take Mae Bunruean as an example.[103]

Here, it is noteworthy that when still a layperson Luang Pu Sangwan started to practice meditation after a *mae chi* had encouraged him to do so.[104] The well-known and highly revered saint of the forest tradition Luang Pu Thet Desaraṅsī writes in his foreword of Mae Chi Phimpha's autobiography, "Mae Chi Phimpha is a woman with the heart of a lion . . . All *mae chi*s should take her life as an example."[105] The famous meditation master Luang Pho Pramote (Pāmojjo) writes that Mae Chi Phimpha is "an excellent example for the general Buddhist practitioner."[106] Phra Ajan Inthawai Santussako said of the Mae Chi Kaew *stūpa*,

> It is very appropriate to build this *stūpa* [*jedi banju aṭṭhi that*] so that it encourages [*hai kamlangjai*] women to pursue the path toward *nibbāna*. For not only monks and men can achieve *nibbāna*. If women pursue the right practice [of the *dhamma*], they too are capable of achieving *nibbāna*. There is no doubt about this. Mae Chi Kaew is an example [for this statement].[107]

Here it is interesting to note that in the Pali canonical collection *Saṃyutta-nikāya*, the Buddha recommends that female lay followers should take the lay followers Khujjuttarā and Veḷukaṇṭakī Nandamātā as role models (see chapter 5). *Bhikkhunī*s, so the Buddha continues, should take his foremost disciples Khemā and Uppalavaṇṇā as role models.[108] As mentioned above, according to the available texts the women of my study did not refer explicitly to specific female canonical figures as role models for their own spiritual practice. It is possible that they may have taken inspiration from the lives and teachings of accomplished female figures of early Buddhism as described in the Pali canonical texts or the Pali commentaries. But if so they seem to have preferred not to express this in their writing and speeches that were aimed at a wider audience. Alternatively, it is also possible that the somewhat ambiguous position of the women of my study between the lay and the monastic world made it difficult for them to take as their model either a lay follower or a *bhikkhunī*, the former being below and the latter above their own position and lived reality.[109] As mentioned in chapter 5, Khunying Yai refers in her texts to three Pali (post)canonical figures who clearly resemble a number of elements in Khunying Yai's own biography. However, she does not explicitly mention them as role models for her own spiritual practice.

Be that as it may, not only the women themselves but also their male monastic fellows and teachers seem to have had the same kammic-cosmic perspectives that I discussed in this chapter. Thus, the female practitioners and their male monastic fellows and teachers shared the same view, which was nicely expressed by Richard O'Connor: "the Dhamma of the Buddha applied equally to all beings. Universalistic in its opportunities and philosophy, it was hierarchical in its consequences and practice, for as surely as their past actions had differed, all beings differed in their present karma."[110]

Conclusion

> Historiography, not history, is at fault in the omission of the contributions of women. . . . It is important to include the ways in which women have been oppressed, but it is perhaps more important to extend one's purview to include what women *have* accomplished, especially when they do so in spite of oppressive circumstances.
>
> Paula Arai, based on her research on Japanese Buddhist nuns[1]

The historical absence of an order of fully ordained Theravada nuns (*bhikkhunī*) has undoubtedly had a major impact on women's religious roles, statuses, and identities in Thai Buddhism. Thai Buddhist women have had to face barriers, obstacles, and challenges in their religious learning and practice that men have not had to confront. Nonetheless, in modern Thai Buddhism there have been numerous women who have pursued the path to awakening while being highly revered for their deep knowledge of the *dhamma* and rigorous spiritual practice by sometimes large numbers of Thai Buddhists, both male and female. The biographies I have studied show women who were not deterred by their "gendered form" and socially constructed gendered constraints and expectations. Rather, they were active and creative agents who were highly committed to their spiritual practice, in many cases from a young age. Because of their gender, they were barred from upward social mobility within a number of socioreligious hierarchical structures and the numerous special privileges that are available to monks. Thus, while monks may gain their religious authority and significance through a career in ecclesiastical structures, the women of my study achieved their outstanding religious position primarily through charisma that emerged as a consequence of their rigorous spiritual practice. On a conventional level they have always been perceived as inferior to monks, even after the spreading of their reputation as accomplished practitioners of meditation, erudite Buddhist scholars, effective healers of seemingly incurable diseases, or saints (*ariya-puggala*), and even postmortem when in most cases their sainthood has become tangible in the form of transmogrified relics.

However, these women's reflections and actions did not aim at abolishing or even questioning the religious hierarchical structure that subordinated women. Rather, these women perceived the adoption of religious hierarchy as a part of their spiritual practice and thus supported and employed it accordingly. In some cases, as we have seen, female subordination was even reinforced by these women, for example by following "the spirit of the *garudhammas*" despite the nonexistence of a *bhikkhunī* order. In none of the texts that I studied is it reported that the women of my study aspired to become *bhikkhunī*s. Nor did they wish to be reborn as men. Probably convinced that the (re)establishment of a Theravada *bhikkhunī* order is impossible, they seem to have believed that being a *mae chi* (or in the case of Mae Bunruean, a renunciant in a new form) was sufficient for their practice toward spiritual perfection. In fact, their biographies make clear that overcoming mental defilements (*kilesa*) had for them much greater significance than fighting against gender inequality and the existing social disadvantages connected to it. Their biographies depict the struggles these women had to face as a consequence of their gender as being to them of considerably less significance than the task of realization of sainthood.[2] Strongly motivated by a kammic-cosmic view and dhammic sense of urgency, their major aim was the attainment of *nibbāna* as quickly as possible. At the same time, these women were intensively and generously supported by (often high-ranking) monks in a variety of ways. In fact, my research allows me to conclude that in many respects, albeit to varying extents, the biographies of the women discussed in this book contain numerous elements that seem to be remarkably similar to textual and spiritual practices of modern Thai Buddhist male practitioners revered as Buddhist saints, as well as "noble beings" (*ariya-puggala*) of early Buddhism as described in Pali literature. I have also shown that there is a high number of remarkable similarities between the biographical themes and modes of expression in the texts I studied on the one hand and corresponding themes and language in the Pali canonical and commentary texts on the other.

This is particularly well exemplified in the hagiographical literature of Mae Chi Kaew. The different versions of her biography not only are replete with hagiographical elements that are evocative of various Pali canonical narratives, in particular the accounts of the Buddha's life, death, and postmortem events, but also incorporate a number of hagiographical themes of famous Thai saints, which themselves are partly reminiscent of these very Pali narratives.[3] These hagiographical elements include many supernatural occurrences, encounters with supernatural beings, superhuman powers generated by meditational practices, the mention of a final teaching (*pacchimā vācā*) before death, rain unexpectedly extinguishing the funeral pyre (compare this to the Buddha's funeral and that of the northern saint Khruba Siwichai),[4] the distribution of relics (as in the case of the Buddha, Luang Pu Man, and many other male saints of modern Thai Buddhism), remains enshrined in *stūpa*s, the development of hagiographies and devotional practices, the production of amulets, and so forth.[5] The hagiographies also mention that, due to her advanced meditation, Mae Chi Kaew was able to come into contact with different beings from various levels of heavens or from the lower realms of the rebirth cycle of Theravada Buddhist cosmology. Such superhuman experiences allowed her to study and understand the working of the kammic law. These hagiographical elements resemble the Buddha's own progress toward *nibbana*: during the night of his awakening (*bodhi*), after having explored cosmological and kammic aspects of reality, the Buddha attained arahantship. Also, similar to the other women of my study, the oral aspects of Mae Chi Kaew's religious learning and spiritual practice strongly resemble practices of early Buddhism (see chapter 5).

Even though Mae Bunruean's hagiographies also contain many elements that depict her as being in line with Pali canonical and postcanonical paradigms of noble persons (*ariya-puggala*), the hagiographical emphasis is more on her supernatural powers and the altruistic way she used them in order to relieve people from their hardships. While her homilies often dealt with awakening and the spiritual practice thereto, Mae Bunruean became more famous for the possession of supernatural powers rather than because of the belief that she had achieved supramundane states of mind.

Still, her hagiographies are unique collections of powerful statements not only about the possibility of female magical powers to heal rather than to pollute but also about spiritual potential in a sociocultural context that in terms of gender has too often been described and evaluated in male terms.

The hagiographical processes in the cases of the women of my study are ongoing and at different stages of development. In the cases of Mae Bunruean and Mae Chi Kaew, the hagiographical process is certainly much more developed than with the other women, albeit in rather different ways. In contrast, despite having died well before all the other women who are central to my study, Khunying Yai was hardly known and revered as an outstanding Buddhist practitioner and scholar until quite recently.[6] Also, the trajectories toward and socially constructed definitions of sainthood differ quite significantly in the cases of the women whose biographies and veneration I studied. As shown in this book, the reasons for this are complex and idiosyncratic but often closely related to questions of gender.

Yet I want to argue that the hagiographies of all the women of my study and the attendant devotional practices can be understood as an actualization and localization of ideals outlined in the Pali canon. However, similarly to the Pali canon, the ideals that these women represent and have made manifest for their followers and admirers are embedded in texts and contexts that incorporate a multivocality with regard to Buddhist attitudes toward women. In this way we can discern, in the words of Alan Sponberg, not only "soteriological inclusiveness" but also "institutional androcentrism."[7]

Even though still only rather modest—at least when compared with established and equivalent devotional practices of male saints—the scale and pervasiveness of veneration for women who are believed to be accomplished practitioners seems to have increased significantly over the last two decades or so. When compared with the number of widely revered male Thai saints, the number of female saints is small. However, while there is a seemingly "ever increasing number of [male] saints,"[8] there also seems to be a growing number of female practitioners who are widely revered for their supramundane achievements. This change in scale is not only evidenced by an increasing number of hagiographical texts on female practitioners, which are being more widely distributed (in the case of Mae

Bunruean a hagiography of her has been sold in Thai 7-Eleven shops; or in the case of Mae Chi Kaew, a hagiography written in English has been distributed internationally for free) but also in material culture, visible through amulets depicting female practitioners or relatively large shrines and *stūpa*s conveying powerful meanings of women's spiritual potential and achievements. It seems to me that visible markers of accomplished female Buddhist practice have occurred recently and conspicuously on a scale that does not appear to have ever been witnessed before in Thai Buddhism. I should here also mention the increasing number of hagiographical documentary films on these women, available on YouTube or broadcast on Thai TV. Thus, the suggestion that women's spiritual potential is equal to that of men is more widely explicitly expressed and celebrated. Such gaining of religious space for women has been perceived by many as a continuation and natural consequence of Thai social and cultural norms and approaches. As a consequence, these new phenomena—which though not part of any single organized movement still represent an important trend in contemporary Thai Buddhism—do not face much, if any, resistance in Thailand; rather they are actively and generously supported by a huge number of laypeople and many monks (many of whom are famous or influential). To many Thai Buddhists, this is perceived as a confirmation that women are able to practice Buddhism successfully without having to challenge what are popularly held to be traditional Thai religiocultural practices and values, for example by pushing for the revival of the vanished *bhikkhunī* order.

However, although the widespread interest in the relics, amulets, and biographies of female saints may have begun only relatively recently with the veneration of Mae Bunruean and Mae Chi Kaew, as shown in this book, we cannot infer from this that earlier there have been no outstanding female Buddhist practitioners. In fact, the sources examined in this book suggest that there would have been eminent female renouncers for a long time in Thai history; they may have been revered only on a local level, though. Some of these were spiritual teachers. A good example here is Mae Chi Talap (mentioned in chapter 5), with whom "a large number of female practitioners [*upāsikā*] practiced meditation,"[9] around the year 1900. Mae Chi Nu-nueang's and Khunying Yai's biographies also contain ample evidence for intensive and extensive informal networks of female practitioners across the country. These networks need further scholarly attention in order to learn more about the popularity of meditation within and outside monasteries and the belief in the attainability of the supramundane before the "revival" of *vipassanā* meditation in twentieth-century Thai Buddhism.[10]

The major problem is that we lack the textual sources that would allow us to gain a more comprehensive understanding of female renunciation and practice from a historical perspective. As discussed in chapter 2, Buddhist female practitioners usually wrote little or nothing at all, especially about themselves, and were often reluctant to teach.[11] Only in exceptional cases do we have a substantial amount of texts by or about female practitioners before the mid-twentieth century. Successful female practitioners might be mentioned only parenthetically in the hagiographies of male saints. Material things, such as relics, statues, and amulets, may sometimes help to preserve hints of revered female practitioners.[12] However, scarcity or lack of sources on female practitioners does not imply their historical absence. I believe that with this book I am able to show that in Thai Buddhism there were more women rigorously engaged in soteriological practice and teaching—and they were more influential—than is often assumed.

Abbreviations for Pali Texts

A	*Aṅguttara-nikāya*
Ap	*Apadāna*
D	*Dīgha-nikāya*
Dhp-a	*Dhammapada-aṭṭhakathā* (commentary on Dhp)
Dhp	*Dhammapada*
Kv	*Kathāvatthu*
M	*Majjhima-nikāya*
Mil	*Milindapañha*
Mp	*Manorathapūraṇī* (commentary on A)
Pj I	*Paramatthajotikā I* (commentary on *Khuddakapāṭha*)
Pj II	*Paramatthajotikā II* (commentary on *Suttanipāta*)
Ps	*Papañcasūdanī* (commentary on M)
S	*Saṃyutta-nikāya*
Sv	*Sumaṅgalavilāsinī* (commentary on D)
Th	*Theragāthā*
Thī	*Therīgāthā*
Ud	*Udāna*
Vin	*Vinaya*
Vism	*Visuddhimagga*

Notes

Introduction

1. More literally, "You have now been promoted to the high rank of chaokhun" (in the Thai ecclesiastical ranking system).

2. Phimpha 2553, 78–79.

3. For example, Mae Chi Sansanee Sthirasuta (1953–), a former fashion model, who is famous for her many social activities and creative methods of teaching the *dhamma* and meditation; Mae Chi Thotsaphon Bunthewaphithak (1958–), who is well-known for her ability to look into the former lives of others; or Khun Mae Dr. Siri Krinchai (1917–2011), a lay teacher of *vipassanā* meditation who had a huge number of students.

4. I found some short mentions in English translations of hagiographies of Thai monks. Also, Taylor mentioned Mae Chi Kaew in a footnote in his 1993 book on Thai forest monks (277n22). In 2006 Suniwan Tangphaithunsakun (2549) completed a comprehensive and detailed MA thesis in Thai on the life of Mae Chi Kaew Sianglam. She collated a wide range of sources, such as printed biographies, pictures, teachings, and interviews with key informants. Suniwan also quotes extensively from various hagiographical accounts. Her thesis has therefore been a valuable source for my own research. Unfortunately, the thesis has so far not been published in its complete form and is rather difficult to access, though some sections have been published in a hagiography (*Lok ni lok ha dai* 2550). I only found the thesis by chance.

5. Samuels 2010, xxix–xxx.

6. Phanom Phaetkhun 2532, issue no. 15,521, p. 16.

7. See, e.g., Bunnag 1973, 187. See also Tannenbaum 1999.

8. Cook 2009, 349.

9. Olson 1992, 279; see this article for more on the genre of Thai cremation volumes.

10. Ibid., 288.

11. As Olson (1992, 287–88) put it, because "the distribution of books is often chaotic, tracking down older publications can become a full-time job."

12. Adapted from a translation by Robin Moore of my interview in Thai with Phra Paisal Visalo on August 9, 2015.

Chapter 1. The Female in Thai Buddhism

1. Thepjetiyajan 2551, 183–85. For the four different levels of awakening, see chapter 3.

2. Prathum Choti-Anan 2539, 10.

3. In 1980 there were 357,040 *bhikkhus*; in 1987 there were 292,080; in 1994 there were 279,790; in 2004 there were 265,355; in 2007 there were 258,163 (Channarong Boonnoon 2551, 12–13 and the statistics available at the website of the Thai National Office of Buddhism (http://www.onab.go.th, accessed October 2, 2015). The official statistics of the year 2014 says that there were 290,015 *bhikkhus* and 58,418 *sāmaṇeras* in Thailand during that year, while in 2016 there were 298,580 *bhikkhus* and 59,587 *sāmaṇeras*. (Thailand had a total population of 65,729,098 in that year, of whom 61,746,429 were Buddhists.) On the issue of nuns (*bhikkhunī*) in the Theravada ordination lineage, see Seeger 2006.

4. *Mae* means mother in Thai. It is not quite clear, though, where *chi* derives from (Chatsumarn Kabilsingh 1991, 36–37). De Bernon researched the origin of the word *chi*, and according to him it is likely to derive from Khmer, where it is used to convey respect (de Bernon 1996, 87–89). According to the Regulations of the Thai Mae Chi Institute, *mae chis* are required to follow many more training rules than "just" the eight or ten precepts, such as the seventy-five *sekhiya* rules, for example (see Thai Mae Chi Institute 2547).

5. It is difficult to ascertain the exact number of *mae chis* in Thailand since, unlike monks and novices, they do not appear in official monastic records (see Lindberg Falk 2007, 2). What can be found in the statistics of the National Office of Buddhism is the number of foreign *mae chis* in Thailand, of whom there were not more than fifty in the year 2015. The Thai scholar Veerachart Nimanong (2545, 29) reports that the Department of Religious Affairs conducted a survey in 1997 that established that there were 14,690 Thai *mae chis*. In his study of 2002, Manop Nakkanrian (2545, 94), however, says that there are approximately 45,000 *mae chis* in Thailand. This figure seems rather high (unfortunately Manop does not mention how he reached this number). See also Bessey 1991, 312: in 1979 there were officially 12,083 *mae chis*. There are however some reports that ordinations of female novices (*sāmaṇerī*) have taken place in northern Thailand, Rayong, and Nakhon Pathom, but these ordinations are still officially not acknowledged. More recently, there was an ordination of eight women as *bhikkhunī* in southern Thailand on November 29, 2014. This ordination has been widely debated in Thailand, and the Mahatherasamakhom (Thai Saṅgha Supreme Council) only a few days after this ordination reiterated that it is forbidden for "monks and novices of all *nikāyas*" to ordain women as *bhikkhunī* (See, e.g., "Mahathen yam ham buat samaneri phiksuni nai thai" [Sangha suupreme council repeats its prohibition on ordaining *sāmaṇerī* and *bhikkhunī* in Thailand], *Daily News*, December 11, 2557, http://www.dailynews.co.th/education/286849).

6. See B. D. Dipananda, "The Thai Bhikkhuni Order: From One to One Hundred and More to Come," *Buddhistdoor Global*, September 25, 2015, http://www.buddhistdoor.net/news/thai-bhikkhuni-order-from-one-to-one-hundred-and-more-to-come.

7. See, e.g., Channarong Boonnoon 2551.
8. Lindberg Falk 2002, 119, 123, 141–43.
9. Lindberg Falk 2007, 53.
10. Kritsana Raksachom and Martin Seeger 2556. See also Seeger 2009a.
11. See Tannenbaum 1999.
12. Swearer 2009, 192; see also Tannenbaum 1999, 244–48.
13. Kulavir Prapapornpipat 2548, 37–38.
14. Van Esterik 2000, 74. See also Kabilsingh 1991, 31; Lindberg Falk 2010, 162–63; and Peach 2009, 310.
15. Terwiel 2007. See also Lindberg Falk 2007, 106–9; Bowie 2011.
16. As Collins (1998, 278) notes, however, "the concept *cetiya* is wider than that of *stūpa*. Any Buddha-shrine is a *cetiya*, whereas a *stūpa* must contain a relic; and relics can also be kept in other containers. Both *thūpa* (*stūpa*) and *cetiya* (*caitya*) are from verbs meaning 'to pile up,' and seem originally to have referred to burial grounds." In the following I will use *stūpa*/*thūpa* or *cetiya* respectively in the way they are used in the original sources or when I want to indicate that I am referring to a relic-containing shrine (*stūpa*; I use the Sanskrit *stūpa* instead of the Pali *thūpa* because it is more widely used and understood).
17. See also Anālayo 2016a, 22–27.
18. According to the statistics of the Thai National Office of Buddhism, in 2016 there were 40,580 monasteries (*wat*) in Thailand (see latest statistics at http://www.onab.go.th).
19. See S I 124: *Atha kho taṇhā ca arati ca ragā ca māradhītaro yena bhagavā tenupasaṅkamiṃsu; upasaṅkamitvā bhagavantaṃ etad avocuṃ 'pāde te, samaṇa, paricāremā'ti.*
20. Collett 2016, 227
21. Murcott 2006, 79. Anālayo wrote in some detail on Māra as a tempter of nuns (2014a).
22. *Itthī malaṃ brahmacariyassa* (S I 43).
23. A III 260–61. I thank Mudagamuwe Maithrimurthi for making me aware of these passages.
24. This passage is discussed in Anālayo 2016b, 140ff.
25. *Dukkho itthibhāvo* (Thī 216).
26. See, e.g., Collett 2016; Murcott 2006. See also Anālayo 2014b.
27. See, e.g., Sponberg 1992.
28. Anālayo 2016b, 145; see also Collett 2016.
29. As far as I am aware, my research outputs are the first English academic publications in which amulets depicting or made by female practitioners are discussed (Seeger 2013). The first medallion amulet depicting a contemporary monk seems to be the amulet produced for the cremation of Phra Chonlathopamakhun (Phut Puṇṇakathera) of the Chon Buri monastery Wat Khao Bang Sai. This amulet was produced in 1907 (see Thirachai Thongthammachat 2554, 192). The first medallion amulet depicting a woman highly revered for her Buddhist practice may be the one produced for Mae Bunruean in the 1960s. See chapter 4.
30. Jory 2008.

31. Lindberg Falk 2007, 106–9. See chapter 4 for a more detailed discussion of amulets consecrated by Thai women.

32. At the time of my visit (August 2008) there were still a number of vacant niches in the statue gallery, and it might be possible that statues of female saints have now or will be placed there.

33. See Gabaude 2003a; Gabaude 2003b.

34. Pattana Kitiarsa 2005, 480. See also Jackson 1999b.

35. Swearer and Sommai Premchit 1998, 26.

36. See, e.g., Nilsen 2011.

37. See Taylor 2008, 4–7.

38. See, e.g., Scott 2012.

39. Phanthakan Kimthong, n.d.

40. Thiaranan 2550.

41. https://youtu.be/AjRjRaEkCpE, accessed August 8, 2017.

42. https://youtu.be/UreJQ-FyIIU, accessed August 8, 2017.

43. Lindberg Falk 2000a, 47.

44. See Seeger 2009a.

45. Wirat Thiraphanmethi and Thongbai Thirananthangkun 2546, 459.

46. See, e.g., Seeger 2006; see Seeger 2010a.

47. Thanissaro 1995.

48. See, e.g., Anālayo 2013, 2014c, 2017.

49. See, e.g., Seeger 2006; Ito 2012.

50. See Skilling 1995.

51. See, e.g., Payutto 2554.

52. Tomalin 2006, 386.

53. See also Seeger 2009a.

54. Tavivat Puntarigvivat 2543, 101.

55. Muecke 2004, 227.

56. See Seeger 2009a.

57. Cited in Duan Kamdee 2551, 76.

58. Cited in Montri Suepduang 2551, 328.

59. Lindberg Falk 2000a, 47.

60. Lindberg Falk 2000a, 51–52; 2000b, 69–70; 2002, 24–25; 2007, 81–82, 146–51.

61. See Lindberg Falk 2000b; Varaporn Chamsanit 2006, 70; and Kritsana Raksachom and Seeger 2556.

62. Collins and McDaniel 2010.

63. Lindberg Falk 2000a, 54; see also p. 52.

64. Paisal Visalo 2546, 191; see also Lindberg Falk 2000a, 53; Muecke 2004, 227; Apinya Feungfusakul 2544; Paisal Visalo 2544, 2.

65. Lindberg Falk 2002, 13.

66. Here I am referring to the eight *garudhammas* ("weighty principles," "important/heavy rules," or rules of hierarchy) that the Buddha imposed on women as a condition for their ordination (Vin II 253–56). See Juo-Hsüeh Shih 2000, 463–64. See, e.g., Seeger 2009a; Collins and McDaniel 2010.

67. Here, it must be noted that in this context I use the terms "traditionalist" and "traditional" out of convenience in order to refer to Thai thinkers who prefer to continue more commonly recognized forms of Buddhist practice with regard to the *bhikkhunī* ordination controversy. The use of these terms does not imply, however, that proponents of the *bhikkhunī* ordination are not traditional with regard to other ideas or practices or that opponents of the *bhikkhunī* ordination are traditional in every respect.

68. See Seeger 2006.

69. See Sanitsuda Ekachai 1999, 227–34; 2001, 218–27; see also Varaporn Chamsanit 2006, 280.

70. *Phiksuni nai rup mai* (interview with Phra Payutto, July 15, 2002). See also Paisal Visalo 2546, 360–62; Sipariyattimoli et al. 2544, 90.

71. Seeger 2005, 206.

72. A well-known Thai Buddhist monk who requested anonymity gave this explanation.

73. See Ito 2007 and 2012b, pp. 216–38.

74. Gabaude 1988; Pracha Pasannathammo 2535, 467–87.

75. Dhammadāna Foundation 2544; Phikun Wiphatprathip 2547, 36–37; interview with Jitsai Phadungrat, April 8, 2007; see also Ito 2007.

76. Chao Asok 2529, 60–76; interview with Sikkhamata Paniya, April 5, 2007. See also Lindberg Falk 2002, 77–79. See also Heikkilä-Horn 2000.

77. When there are over 100 *samaṇas*, the ratio is 1 to 3. As of April 2007, there were twenty-seven *sikkhamats* and 103 *samaṇas* (email from Sikkhamata Paniya).

78. Sunai Setbunsang 2534, 336. Here, Sunai is probably referring to Vin II 256. See also under "Sainthood in Modern Times" in chapter 3; and Anālayo 2016b.

79. Somchai Maitree et al. 2546, 131–32.

80. Cited in Veerachart Nimanong 2545a, 25. For more on Phra Payutto and his command of the Pali canon, see Seeger 2005; Seeger 2009a.

81. For more details, see Sanitsuda Ekachai 1999, 227–34; Sanitsuda Ekachai 2001, 218–27; interview with Phra Payutto, July 15, 2002, and January 4, 2005, Veerachart Nimanong 2545a, 25; Payutto 2547, 72–73. See Payutto 2554.

82. See Seeger 2006.

83. On people in favor, see, e.g., Paisal Visalo 2544, 2. On resistance or indifference, see Pramuan Pengjan 2544; Rabiebrat Pongpanith 2546; Somchai Maitree et al. 2546; interview with Luang Pho Khanong Dhammadhīro, July 19, 2012. See also Terwiel 2007.

84. Lindberg Falk 2000a, 46, 47, 55; Lindberg Falk 2002, 6, 92, 233, 250; Seeger 2006, 12; Apinya Feungfusakul 2544; Sopha Onophat and Aphichat Siwirot 2546, 27; Laddawan Tamafu 2548, 142; Laddawan Tamafu 2549, 120–21; Kritsana Raksachom and Seeger 2556; Collins and McDaniel 2010; Battaglia 2015.

85. Interview with Phra V. Vajiramedhi, April 4, 2007.

86. Interview with Bhikṣuṇī Nirāmisā, April 5, 2007.

87. Somchai Maitree et al. 2546, 3, 147; interview with Sikkhamata Paniya, April 5, 2007.

88. See, e.g., Itoh 2013; Delia 2014.

89. Van Esterik 1996, 33–41; Muecke 2004, 221–38; Laddawan Tamafu 2548, 67.
90. Lindberg Falk 2002, 127–38; Laddawan Tamafu 2548, 50.
91. Ratchabanditayasathan 2546, 365; Payutto 2538, 56; *Matichon Dictionary* 2547, 274.
92. Supreme Court of Thailand 2480, 375–80.
93. See, e.g., "Kritsadika chi chat 'mae chi' pen 'nak buat' mai mi sitthi lueak tang" [The Office of the Council of State makes clear: "Mae chi" are "ordained ones" and thus do not have the right to vote], *Thai Rath Online*, March 3, 2014, http://www.thairath.co.th/content/407400. See also "Mai hai lueak tang chi sathana: 'Kon phom hom khao' pen 'chi' pen 'nak buat'" [Not allowed to vote—clarifying the situation: 'Shaving one's head and wearing white robes' as a 'mae chi' makes you an 'ordained one'], *Daily News*, March 7, 2014, https://www.dailynews.co.th/article/220857.
94. So. Chanasongkhram 2544, 7.
95. Muecke 2004, 225; Laddawan Tamafu 2549, 119; Thai Post 2545, 12.
96. Parichart Suwanbubbha 2003, 70.
97. Veerachart Nimanong 2545b, 23.
98. Narumon Hinshiranan 1993; Laddawan Tamafu 2548, 51.
99. Narumon Hinshiranan 1993; Apinya Feungfusakul 2544; Laddawan Tamafu 2548, 140–41.
100. See, e.g., *Phra Ratchamethaphon khunanuson* 2542, 153.
101. Lai 2011, 7.
102. See, e.g., Battaglia 2015; Cook 2010; Collins and McDaniel 2010; Lindberg Falk 2007.
103. Gross 2013, 667; King 1996, 411; Muecke 2004; Heinze 1994, 661. See also Gosling 1998, 124.
104. See, e.g., Narumon Hinshiranan 1993; Laddawan Tamafu 2548, 55–56.
105. The Thai Mae Chi Institute (Sathaban Mae Chi Thai) has "the objective of assisting and uniting *mae chii*s from all over the country, and its central goals are to help them develop intellectually and spiritually. Its organisation is modelled upon that of the monks' *sangha*. The Institute is hierarchically organised with offices and heads . . . at regional, provincial and district levels. The Institute has introduced rules and regulations for the *mae chii*s that are influenced by the monks' rules. It also promotes the foundation of the *mae chii* communities and the streamlining of *mae chii* practice and its efforts have strengthened *mae chii*s as a distinct category and today growing numbers have tasks similar to those of the monks" (Lindberg Falk 2007, 177). On the institute's material support of *mae chi*s, see Lindberg Falk 2002, 149–52; Sopha Onophat and Aphichat Siwirot 2546, 21, 26, 33, 34.
106. See next chapter and, e.g., Kamala Tiyavanich 1997, 281.
107. Tomalin 2006, 388.
108. See Apinya Feungfusakul 2544; Somchai Maitree et al. 2546, 2, 124–25; see also Bell 2000, 9.
109. Apinya Feungfusakul 2544.
110. Gabaude 1997, 158.
111. Holt 1995, 130.

112. *Vinayo nāma buddhasāsanassa āyu. Vinaye ṭhite sāsanaṃ ṭhitaṃ nāma hoti* (Sv I 11). See also Vin I 98 where it is said, *Pamuṭṭhamhi ca suttante, abhidhamme ca tāvade; vinaye avinaṭṭhamhi, puna tiṭṭhati sāsanaṃ.* (Even if the *suttas* and the Abhidhamma are forgotten, when the *vinaya* is not lost, the religion will remain.) See also Channarong Boonnoon 2545, 2547a, 2547b.

113. Interview with anonymous Thai *sāmaṇerī*, March 24, 2007.

114. Dhamma practice center [anon.], n.d., 2.

115. Nidhi Eoseewong 2545, 61–62; see also Somchai Maitree et al. 2546, 22–23 ; Laddawan Tamafu 2549.

116. Muecke 2004, 221, 231.

117. Even in their appellation there are regional differences; in northeastern Thailand, *mae chis* are called *mae khao* (white mother) instead of *mae chi*. Women who do not shave their hair and eyebrows but keep at least the eight precepts temporarily are known under a variety of different names, like *chi phram*, *phramajarini*, *thammajarini*, and *silajarini* (Somchai Maitree et al. 2546, 120–21).

118. Phra Payutto is referring to the *odātavasanā brahmacārinī* (M I 491), i.e. the "white-clad women living in sexual abstinence" (Payutto 2544, 16–17); see also Veerachart Nimanong 2545a, 26.

119. Laddawan Tamafu 2548, 73, 97.

120. Thai Maechi Institute Foundation 2547, (4), 11; see also Lindberg Falk 2002, 48–52.

121. Laddawan Tamafu 2548, 143–44; see also Laddawan Tamafu 2549, 122–23.

122. Lindberg Falk 2000b, 62–63; Sopha Onophat and Aphichat Siwirot 2546, 28.

123. Laddawan Tamafu 2548, 110.

124. Interview with Mae Chi Arun Phet-urai, April 3, 2007.

125. Mae Chi Thotsaphon is known under several different names as she has changed her name repeatedly.

126. Thotsaphon Bunthewaphithak 2550, 170; see also Thotsaphon Chaiprakhong, n.d., and Scott 2012.

127. See, e.g., Seeger 2006. Needless to mention, due to the wealth of available literature on women in Thai Buddhism, the following consideration of sources is far from being a comprehensive literature review but only contains a discussion of what I regard as significant studies that indicate trends and set important parameters in this area of scholarship and that are relevant to the major arguments developed in this book.

128. Bessey 1990, 311. He also argued that "the phenomenon of women meditation teachers in Thailand has received little attention among western scholars" (Bessey 1990, 319). He mentions John Van Esterik's 1982 article as an exception to this, though. See below.

129. Ibid., 312.

130. Lindberg Falk 2000a, 51–52; 2000b, 69–70; 2002, 24–25; 2007, 81–82, 146–51.

131. Collins and McDaniel 2010; McDaniel 2008, 251.

132. In particular, I want to mention the impressive work done by Laddawan Tamafu (2548) for her MA thesis submitted at Chiang Mai University.

133. Brown 2001, 144.

134. Cook 2010, 151.

135. I should also mention here the detailed and thus interesting study by Nerida Cook, who studied many aspects of the rather atypical *mae chi* community of the famous Bangkok monastery Wat Pak Nam as part of her MA degree, submitted in 1981. Unfortunately, this study has not been published as a book and was only recently published online. Being an early study of Thai *mae chis*, the major argument of her thesis was that "ideologically, ritually and economically, maechii in Thailand occupy an ambivalent status in most respects, poised somewhere between monks and laity" (p. 228).

136. However, see Cook 2009; Thanissaro 1995; van Esterik 1996; Seeger 2009a, 2010, 2013. In his book *Civilisation et Femmes Célibataires dans le bouddhisme en Asie du Sud et du Sud-Est*, published in 2011, Steven Collins discusses the lives of some Thai female Buddhist practitioners. This discussion builds on work done by Rachelle Scott, Bhikkhu Sīlaratano, Ṭhānissaro Bhikkhu, myself, and others.

137. Van Esterik 1996, 40. See also Kornfield 2007, 137–65.

138. Thanissaro 1995.

139. Ibid. Tomomi Ito has also to some extent discussed the life of Upāsika Ki Nanayon (see, e.g., Ito 2012, 220–26).

140. See, e.g., Tambiah 1984; Gabaude 1988; Jackson 1999a, 2003; Kamala Tiyavanich 1997; Taylor 1993, 2008; Taylor 2537

141. Cook 2009, 349.

142. However, there do exist now a small number of shorter studies on this topic (see, e.g., Cook 2009; Scott 2012; Collins 2011, 86–89). Peter Skilling (1995) has written an important article on *mae chis* as institution in the premodern era, without discussing individual *mae chis*.

143. Tambiah 1984, 95.

144. Taylor 1993, 256. In a short footnote, however, Taylor mentions Mae Chi Kaew, one of the women my study is based on. He wrote that she was "known for her meditative accomplishments and praised by [Luang Pu] Man himself" (277n22).

145. Kamala Tiyavanich 1997, 281.

146. Ibid., 282, 283.

147. Sīlaratano 2009.

148. Collins and McDaniel 2010, 1399.

Chapter 2. Biography and Hagiography: Female Practitioners in Modern Thai Buddhism

1. Bua Ñāṇasampanno 2541, 256–57.

2. Despite this, Thai people often refer to her as Mae Chi Bunruean. See also next chapter.

3. Bua Ñāṇasampanno 2541, 344. See also Seeger 2009.

4. Some of these kinds of hagiographical elements have, unsurprisingly, also been contested in Thai Buddhism. See, e.g., Seeger 2009, 10; Taylor 1997, 302–3.

5. Reynolds and Hallisey 1987, 323.

6. Harvey 2013, 14. See also Williams 2000, 22–27

7. The eminent Buddhist studies scholar Erich Frauwallner has argued that a biography of the Buddha, complete up to not long after his awakening, was already composed around one hundred years after the Buddha's death but is now lost (see Reynolds and Hallisey 1987, 323)

8. Keyes 1982, 151.

9. For Thai cremation volumes and their origin (about which there are different views), see Olson 1992. In an email to me, Justin McDaniel elaborated on this point: "There might have been more in manuscript form. Indeed, manuscripts do contain stories of famous donors and *seṭṭhi*s [wealthy persons]. Moreover, oral histories and *tamnan* [relic, image, and temple histories] from temples, especially in northern Thailand discuss the works of famous monks. Pali *tamnan*, commentarial texts and chronicles in Burma and Thailand also discuss the lives and acts of famous monks and kings. While the biographies have become more popular as printing has become cheaper and more widespread in Thailand, hagiographies may not be a completely modern genre in Thailand" (email from December 23, 2010).

10. Tambiah 1984, 128–31; see also Taylor 1997, 290.

11. Taylor 1993, 2; Seeger 2015.

12. Cremation volume of Luang Ta Mahabua 2554, 26.

13. Interview with Phra Paisal Visalo, August 9, 2015, quoted in the introduction.

14. This new genre in Thai hagiographical literature certainly deserves a separate study.

15. Nattha Kamonrattanakun 2554, *Kham nam* [foreword]. Another popular example of these cartoon hagiographies is *Luang Pho Khun: Cartoon version*, published in 2015, and in its presentation similar to that of Luang Ta Mahabua.

16. Gyatso 1998, 115.

17. Blackstone 2000, 116–17.

18. See Walters 2013; Collett 2016.

19. Cook 2009, 349.

20. See, e.g., Sharf 1995, 236. See also Kamala Tiyavanich 1997, 13–15.

21. Olson 1989, 34.

22. Tate 1997, ix–x.

23. See also the historically and otherwise very valuable diaries of Luang Pu Lui Candasāro (1902–89). Clearly, more systematic research into the historical development and contexts of Buddhist autobiographical activities in Thailand is needed.

24. Sujarit Thawonsuk 2507, 263–64. Despite continued attempts, I have still not been able to obtain copies of these two texts.

25. An example of an amulet auction website is http://uauction3.uamulet.com/.

26. Interview with Luang Pho Khanong Dhammadhīro, July 19, 2012.

27. Sathuean Suphasophon 2526, 12.

28. The life account of Mae Chi Nu-nueang Thapmeng (1887–?) printed in 1968 seems to consist of one of the first autobiographical texts of significant length authored by a Thai woman revered for her spiritual practice. This text, however, tries to avoid the use of the first person. It is also not clear to what extent the text may have been edited. The autobiography of Mae Chi Prathum Choti-anan, first printed

in 1996, had a circulation figure of 5,000 copies. Mae Chi Phimpha Wongsa-udom's remarkable autobiographical text has been published at least twice: in 2006 with a circulation figure of 5,000 copies and in 2010 as her cremation volume—again 5,000 copies. I strongly suspect though that there was at least one earlier edition. There is also the first-person life account of Mae Chi Nai Chaemchoi, which was first printed in 2007 with a circulation figure of 3,000 copies. More systematic research into the historical development of hagiographical literature in Thailand is needed.

29. There are some texts authored by members of the royal family that give fragmentary insights into female perspectives on female renunciation and Buddhist practice. See, for example, texts authored by Chao Chom Mom Rajawongse Sadap Ladavalya (1891–1983), a concubine of Rama V, and Princess Beatrice Bhadrayuvadi (1876–1913), a daughter of Rama V.

30. Phimpha Wongsa-udom 2553, 86–87.

31. Pramot Santayakon in Phimpha Wongsa-udom 2553, *Kham nam* [foreword].

32. For more on these scandals, see, e.g., Keyes 1999.

33. Interview with Luang Pho Khanong Dhammadhīro, July 19, 2012.

34. See also, e.g., Prathum Choti-anan 2539, 123.

35. Sujarit Thawonsuk 2507, 263–64.

36. Interview with Luang Pho Khanong Dhammadhīro, July 19, 2012.

37. See Sulak Sivaraksa 1993.

38. Cited in *Lok ni lok ha dai* 2550, 17

39. Ibid., 17.

40. Prachumphon Jaksurak, n.d.

41. Seeger and Naris 2559a. For more on the scarcity on sources on her life, see below and introduction.

42. Damrongthammasan 2559, 57.

43. Translation by Acharya Buddharakkhita (1985, 51).

44. For more on this see chapter 6.

45. Gyatso 1998, xiii.

46. I will discuss literacy or the lack thereof of female Buddhist practitioners in some detail in chapter 5.

47. Wanjai Chukon 2549, 25–28.

48. Tambiah 1984, 124.

49. Sulak Sivaraksa 1993, 6.

50. Mellick Cutler 1994, 2. See also Walters (1995) who calls the life stories of the *Apadāna* "moral biographies."

51. Sīlaratano 2009, 20.

52. See also, e.g., Kleine 1998, 327.

53. See also Sulak Sivaraksa 1993, 6–7.

54. Williams 2000, 26–27.

55. I conducted these interviews together with Naris Charaschanyawong during the summer of 2012. We interviewed many monks, *mae chis*, and laypeople in Prachuap Khiri Khan, Ratchaburi, Bangkok, and Phetchaburi Provinces. For more on Khunying Yai's life, see Seeger and Naris 2559a. See also Seeger and Naris 2556a, 2556b, 2558; Seeger 2016.

56. Some sources give 1886 as the year of her birth, but our research has shown that this is extremely unlikely.

57. Dhammayuttika-nikāya is one of the two major Thai Buddhist monastic congregations. It was founded by Prince Mongkut during the time he was a monk (1824–1851), before he became king Rama IV in 1851. The other congregation is Mahānikāya; the vast majority of Thai monks belong to the Mahānikāya congregation.

58. Cremation volume of Khun Mae Thang Khotchasut 2477, ฆ–ฉ.

59. Based on recent findings, as my co-researcher on this project, Naris Charaschanyawong, and I will argue in a forthcoming publication, it may be possible that Khunying Yai authored other dialogical texts when she was in her twenties.

60. Seeger 2015, 516.

61. "Aramphabot" [introduction], 2552.

62. Cremation volume of Pacha Siriworasan, November 12, 2526, (ก).

63. According to one source, Khunying Yai's texts were distributed at Luang Pu Man's funeral in January of 1950. This may be another reason for this wrong attribution of authorship.

64. See Seeger 2015; Seeger and Naris 2559a.

65. Although see note 59 above.

66. Khana Samakkhiwisutthi 2507; Buai Siwaphruek 2496; Bunruean Tongbuntoem 2528; Phanom Phaetkhun 2532; "Sutyot watthumongkhon" 2549; Saithip 2548a, 2548b; Phisit Jansi 2549; *Chiwit lae ngan Luang Ta Sawai* 2540; Sittha Chetawan, n.d. Many of the hagiographies that I have been using do not contain bibliographical details. I also used a number of websites, such as the *Lan thammajak* forums, May 25, 2007, http://www.dhammajak.net/board/viewtopic.php?t=12567; "Prawat Mae Chi Bunruean Tongbuntoem [History of Mae Chi Bunruean Tongbuntoem], *Web-Pra*, September 19, 2010, http://www.web-pra.com/Article/Show/611; and others.

67. I conducted these interviews in northern, northeastern, and central Thailand between 2008 and 2011. In addition to this, I also conducted telephone interviews.

68. Between 2007 and 2015 I repeatedly visited Wat Awutwikasitaram, where the main site of her veneration is located; here followers have erected a building called Sala Khun Mae Bunruean, exclusively for her veneration (see chapter 4). During these visits I talked to visitors of the shrine and people living and working nearby. On July 27, 2008, I joined the weekly chanting that takes place at this shrine every Sunday at 1:00 p.m. In addition to this, I twice visited Wat Sangkhathan in Nonthaburi Province, where a shrine has been built for her veneration. Over the last six years, I also frequently visited Wat Samphanthawong and conducted several informal interviews there.

69. As I was not always able to obtain explicit permission to use specific information, in such cases I am not able to reveal the sources.

70. Sujarit Thawonsuk 2507, 175.

71. A report says that Mae Bunruean covered a distance of eight kilometres on foot in only thirty minutes (Sujarit Thawonsuk 2507, 236).

72. It is not always clear which of the "witness accounts" published in her cremation volume and *The History of Phra Phuttho Yai and Phra Phuttho Noi:*

Upāsikā Mae Bunruean Tongbuntoem, edited by Buai Siwaphruek in 1953, were submitted as a result of Phra Maharatchamangkhalajan's request. However, many, and perhaps most, of the accounts published in 1953 and 1964 seem to have been written early in the 1950s.

73. Phanom Phaetkhun 2532, issue no. 14,515, p. 6. No exact references to Pali scriptures are given here. It is only said that "many stories can be found in the commentaries [*aṭṭhakathā*], such as . . ." Then, a number of disciples of the Buddha together with miracles they performed are mentioned.

74. This information is derived from my many conversations with followers of or people who have faith in Mae Bunruean during the last eight years, including people visiting her shrine at Wat Awutwikasitaram, amulet collectors, and taxi drivers. This topic also came up in my interview with Boy Thaphrajan, August 6, 2010.

75. Sujarit Thawonsuk 2507, 321. This statement is also based on my participant observation on July 27, 2008 during the weekly chanting that takes place at the Mae Bunruean shrine at Wat Awutwikasitaram every Sunday at 1:00 p.m.

76. This information derives from my participant observation (July 27, 2008) and many visits to Wat Awutwikasitaram. See, e.g., Sharf 1999, 75–99; Swearer 2004, 108–15.

77. Sujarit Thawonsuk 2507, (108).

78. *Chiwit lae ngan Luang Ta Sawai* 2540, 23–24.

79. See D III 281, A III 280–81.

80. Sujarit Thawonsuk 2507, (115).

81. Borrowed from Wilson 1996, 78. Wilson uses the phrase with regard to early Indian Buddhism.

82. See, e.g., Buddha's sixth disciple Yasa, the pampered son of a wealthy man, whose 'mind was established in weariness' (*nibbidāya cittaṃ saṇṭhāsi*; Vin I 15). See also Wilson 1996, 77–82.

83. *Tena saccena sotthi te hotu, sotthi gabbhassā'ti.* M II 103. Translation by Ñāṇamoli and Bodhi (1995, 714).

84. *Mahākassapattherabojjhaṅga-sutta* (S V 79), *Mahāmoggallānattherabojjhaṅga-sutta* (S V 80), and *Mahācundattherabojjhaṅga-sutta* (S V 81). See Phaiyon Kasi, n.d., 41–50; see also Payutto 2551, 209–20; Tambiah 1970, 195–222.

85. Phanom Phaetkhun 2532, issue no. 14,515, p. 7; Buai Siwaphruek 2496, 50–51.

86. Dhp-a III 206–8. So far I have found only one temple mural in Thailand depicting this episode. This mural can be admired at Wat Phochai (Wat Phra Sai) in Nong Khai. Also, conversations with Thai Buddhist monks and laypeople confirm that this episode does not seem to be widely known in contemporary Thai Buddhism.

87. Sujarit Thawonsuk 2507, (122).

88. Ibid., 211.

89. "Prawat lae ngan khong Khun Mae Bunruean Tongbuntoem 7" 2556.

90. Tate 1997, 243.

91. See, e.g., Saipan Puriwanchana 2555, 120, 210–11. When one of Thai Buddhism's most famous and widely revered saints Somdet To (see McDaniel 2011) was only one month old, his body revealed unusual bodily markers which were interpreted as auspicious signs. For this reason his grandparents, "donated" (*thawai*)

the baby to a monk for him to look after as an "adopted child" (*but buntham*). This monk then interpreted these bodily markers as meaning that when grown up, the baby will be someone with an excellent store of merit and a vast number of people will have faith in and respect him; and he will also have long life (Saipan 2555, 76).

92. Mrozik 2007, 66. See D III 141–79.

93. D III 157. See also *Brahmāyu-sutta* (M II 136): *Sukhumattā chaviyā rajojallaṃ kāye na upalimpati.*

94. Vin I 40: *Parisuddho chavivaṇṇo pariyodāto*. See also Crosby 2014, 35–39.

95. Sujarit Thawonsuk 2507, 237.

96. Dhp-a III 309–11.

97. See Sujarit Thawonsuk 2507, (131).

98. Ibid., (132).

99. Tate 1997, 115. See also, e.g., the cases of the famous monks Chaokhun No (Dhammavitakko) of Wat Thepsirin, Luang Pho Kai of Wat Bophitphimuk, Luang Pho Iam of Wat Nang, and Luang Pu Phu of Wat Inthrawihan (Saipan Puriwanchana 2555, 81–84, 87).

100. Schmithausen 1997, 14. See D II 155–57 and S IV 40–41, respectively.

101. See, e.g., "Phra that patihan" [Miraculous relics], *RelicsofBuddha.com*, http://www.relicsofbuddha.com/page7.htm, accessed December 10, 2011.

102. Group and individual interviews with long-term followers of Mae Bunruean on October 22, 2009.

103. *Ariyasawika Khun Mae Chi Kaew Sianglam* 2551; *Duai det phra metta*, n.d.; *Lok ni lok ha dai* 2550; Phensi Makaranon 2549; *Phu banlu chuai luea juea jun* 2552. The sermons and talks by Luang Ta Mahabua can be found in the online archive at http://www.luangta.com. I would like to thank Bhikkhu Sīlaratano, who provided me with a collection of Luang Ta Mahabua's sermon texts that refer to Mae Chi Kaew.

In April 2009, an English-language biography of Mae Chi Kaew written by the American Theravada monk Bhikkhu Sīlaratano was published. This publication contains some information that is not mentioned in the Thai sources I had consulted. Suniwan Tangphaithunsakun's (2549) comprehensive and detailed MA thesis in Thai on the life of Mae Chi Kaew Sianglam collates a wide range of sources, such as printed biographies of Mae Chi Kaew, pictures, teachings of Mae Chi Kaew, and interviews with key informants. Suniwan also quotes extensively from various hagiographical accounts of Mae Chi Kaew. Unfortunately, the thesis has so far not been published in its complete form and is rather difficult to access, though some sections have been published in a hagiography (*Lok ni lok ha dai* 2550). There appears to be only one copy available for public perusal, namely in the library of the Mahidol University College of Religious Studies.

104. My in-depth interviews with Khruba Jaeo Sianglam of Wat Pa Wiwekwatthanaram, who has been involved in the writing and dissemination of many (hagiographical) texts on Mae Chi Kaew, and with "Khruba Ajan," who is an expert on Mae Chi Kaew, included a semistructured questionnaire. (Khruba Ajan is a respectful term of address for a revered, knowedgeable monk. This particular monk

asked me to use this appellation in order to not reveal his real identity.) In other cases where informants requested anonymity, the sources are not further specified.

105. Mukdahan only became a province in 1982; the village was previously located in the Nakhon Phanom Province.

106. See Kirsch 1967. After the Phu Thai entered Siam from Laos during the reign of King Rama III (1824–51), they were first "an isolated and semi-autonomous ethnic enclave," only later becoming "assimilated within the national Thai framework" (Kirsch 1966, 371).

107. *Aññatra bhagavato sare nimittaggāhā i.* See Collins 1992, 132n36.

108. See Collins 1992, 126, 132

109. Terwiel 1994, 45. In Thai society a number of behavioral patterns have developed to ensure that physical contact between monks and women is avoided—for example, the provision of special seating for monks on public transport and the use of a cloth (*pha prakhen*) when a woman presents an object to a monk (so that the monk does not even touch the object that is touched by a woman). Thai women also avoid being close to monks in crowded places (such as at a market and on the bus) in order to minimize the risk of their touching.

110. Luang Pu Sao had already been staying in Khamcha-i for two years when Luang Pu Man arrived in 1917. Another source, however, reports that Luang Pu Sao had already left when Luang Pu Man arrived.

111. *Ariyasawika Khun Mae Chi Kaew Sianglam* 2551, 6.

112. There are altogether thirteen of these austere practices in Theravada Buddhism; see Buddhaghosa 1976, 59–83.

113. Another source says that it was her father who was unwilling to grant permission, though the same reason for this refusal is given.

114. *Duai det phra metta*, n.d., 47; Suniwan Tangphaithunsakun, 2549, 26.

115. *Duai det phra metta*, n.d., 48.

116. See Keyes 1982.

117. *Duai det phra metta*, n.d., 54–56. Emphasis mine.

118. Sīlaratano 2009, 163, see also pp. 174–79.

119. Ibid., 133.

120. Wilson 1996, 148–54.

121. *Duai det phra metta*, n.d., 57.

122. Tambiah 1987, 114. On *dhutaṅga* practices see Vism 59–83.

123. See, e.g., M I 287.

124. Phensi Makaranon 2549, 9–10.

125. *Ariyasawika Khun Mae Chi Kaew Sianglam* 2551, 43.

126. Suniwan Tangphaithunsakun 2549, 20.

127. Reciting texts from the seven Abhidhamma scriptures, or *sattappakaraṇābhidhamma*.

128. "Uplifting crown of the cetiya," *Dhamma* talk in Thai by Phra Ajan Inthawai Santussako, CD-ROM. These happenings are reminiscent of the account of Buddha's passing away (see D II 164; see below).

129. Interview with Phakdiphuri, July 22, 2012.

130. Thaidam 2527; Phakdiphuri 2554, 2555a, 2555b. The account of 2015 clearly depended significantly on the account of 1984. The hagiography of 1984 contains numerous passages that are probably more or less direct quotations from the interview. In fact, some parts read like a transcript. Sometimes quotation marks are used to indicate direct speech.

131. Interviews with Samorn Thophaengjan took place in person on August 12, 2012, and via telephone on May 17, 2016. The interview with Phakdiphuri took place on July 22, 2012. In 2012 Phakdiphuri had been a hagiographer for some ten years and authored at least twenty texts on highly revered Buddhist figures.

132. Phakdiphuri 2554, 86.

133. Thaidam 2527, 88.

134. Ibid., 89.

135. Ibid., 89.

136. With regard to the time spans she spent at various monasteries, there seem to be some inconsistencies in the hagiographies. I was not able to resolve these.

137. Phakdiphuri 2554, 88.

138. From the viewpoint of Theravada Buddhist doctrine, this statement may be perceived as problematic as arahants who have entered final *nibbāna* cannot be met anymore, even in meditation. Compare with Seeger 2009, 10.

139. For more on the metamorphosis of bones into crystalline relics, see chapter 4.

140. This sermon was recorded in MP3 format and given to me by Phra Ajan Inthawai Santussako, abbot of Wat Pa Na Kham Noi. This sermon was later also made available online and can be downloaded from the website of his monastery, Wat Pa Na Kham Noi (http://www.watpanakamnoi.com/sound.html, sermon no. 23/18, accessed June 4, 2016).

141. Interview with Phra Khru Wisanpanyakhun (Bunmi Sumaṅgalo), July 20, 2011.

142. Phimpha 2553, 23.

143. Ibid., 32.

144. See, e.g., Tate 1997, 123.

145. Phimpha 2557, 7.

146. Sermon of Phra Ajan Inthawai Santussako, no. 23/18, http://www.watpanakamnoi.com/sound.html, accessed June 4, 2016. For the transmogrification of bones as indicator of sainthood, see chapter 4.

147. Interview with Phra Khru Wisanpanyakhun (Bunmi Sumaṅgalo), July 20, 2011.

148. See, e.g., *Palungjit* web board, May 3, 2010, http://palungjit.org/threads/คุณแม่พิมพา-ชีใจสิงห์รัตตัญญูแห่งหินหมากเป้ง-เขาว่าท่านเป็นแม่ชีอรหันต์. 237823; *Larndham* forums, June 15, 2010, http://larndham.org/index.php?/topic/39578-ขอเชิญร่วมสร้างเจดีย์คุณแม่/; *Larndham* forums, May 11, 2010, http://larndham.org/index.php?/topic/39203-สรุปยอดและรายละเอียดการทำบุญ/. See also Narirat Whiphat 2554, 161–63.

149. *Khun Yai Chi Soda Sosut* 2552.

150. Tambiah (1984, 280–83) gives a description of this impressive monastery.

151. *Khun Yai Chi Soda Sosut* 2552, 7.

152. Ibid., 21.

153. Ibid., 49.

Chapter 3. Female Sainthood in Modern Thai Buddhism

1. See, e.g., S V 61; see also Tambiah 1984, 13–14. In the Pali canon there are slightly different variations of these ten fetters. Thus, one may find as the fourth fetter *kāma-chanda* (sensual desire) and as the fifth, *byāpāda* (ill-will) instead of *kāma-rāga* (sensual craving) and *paṭigha* (repulsion), respectively.

2. See, e.g., A II 80, where the Buddha says to Ānanda, "*Sotāpanno avinipāta-dhammo niyato sambodhiparāyaṇo.*"

3. However, strictly speaking this also comprises the one on the path to stream entry.

4. Th 648.

5. Schmithausen 2000, 36 and 38. See also Harvey 2013, 76–78.

6. Th 708–23, S IV 40–41, and Dh-a II 247–50, respectively.

7. Sujarit Thawonsuk 2507, (131).

8. See, e.g., Sirimane 2016, 38–49.

9. M III 29–37.

10. Anālayo 2008a, 242.

11. Translation by Ñāṇamoli and Bodhi (1995, 903).

12. *Ekaccassa hi puthujjanassāpi sato khīṇāsavapaṭipattisadisā paṭipadā hoti* (Ps IV 97).

13. *Khīṇāsavassa nāma asaniyāpi matthake patamānāya bhayaṃ vā chambhitattaṃ vā lomahaṃso vā na hoti, puthujjanassa appamattakenāpi hoti.* See also A I 77: "Bhikkhus, there are these two that are not terrified by a bursting thunderbolt. What two? A bhikkhu whose taints are destroyed and a thoroughbred elephant. These are the two that are not terrified by a bursting thunderbolt" (translation by Bodhi [2012, 168]). The commentary to this passage explains that "the arahant is not terrified because he has abandoned personal-existence view (*sakkāyadiṭṭhiyā pahīnattā*); the thorough-bred elephant, because his personal-view is very strong (*sakkāyadiṭṭhiyā balavattā*)" (translation by Bodhi [2012, p. 1631]; Mp II 151). See also *Dhammapada* verse 397, where it is said, *Sabbasaṃyojanaṃ chetvā, yo ve na paritassati.*

14. While the Chaṭṭha Saṅgāyana CD-ROM edition has *maddamāno* here, meaning that the king himself crushed the fruit, in the Budsir 7 for Windows version of Mahidol University the causative form *maddāpesi* is used, which means the king had someone else crush the fruit.

15. Ps IV 97.

16. Rozenberg 2010, 149.

17. Gabaude 2003a, 117.

18. Bond 1988, 164. See also Bond 1984.

19. Gombrich 2006, 168.

20. Gombrich 1971, 285

21. Ibid., 286.

22. Carrithers 1983, 222.

23. See also Nattier 1991.

24. Vin II 256; adapted from the translation by Krey (2010b, 59), and the translation by Anālayo (2016b, 233). See also *Gotamī-sutta* (A IV 274–79). See also Anālayo 2016b.

25. Vin II 256; adapted from the German translation of the Pali by Hüsken (1997, 363).

26. Hüsken 1997, 361n78; see also Gombrich 1971, 284–85.

27. Payutto 2555a, 74–76.

28. Bunnag 1973, 19–20.

29. Translation by Reynolds (1973, 33).

30. See Terwiel 2011, 72–79 and Reynolds 1973, 31–34.

31. Reynolds 1973, 34.

32. Interview with Sulak Sivaraksa, March 25, 2013. Quoted with permission.

33. Tambiah 1987, 112. See also Mettiko 2014, 84.

34. Taylor 2008, 142.

35. Tate 1997, 80; see also Thiaranan 2550, 60.

36. Thanissaro 1999.

37. Taylor 2008, 141; 1993, 134. Ṭhānissaro writes, "As for the question of the possibility of the noble attainments, Rama V had ordered his Dhammakaan Ministry to conduct a survey of the meditation monasteries known to them, to see if any monks could provide convincing claims that they had reached such attainments. The official report found evidence of none. Thus the implicit position of the Fifth Reign reforms was that these attainments were no longer possible. This position was rarely stated explicitly, for fear of sparking controversy, but the implicit message is scattered throughout Prince Vajirañana's writings. For instance, in the introduction to the first volume of the *Vinayamukha*, he states that he will explain only those rules that are relevant to the present. When he reaches Pacittiya 8—the rule forbidding monks to make true claims to superior human attainments (jhana and the noble attainments)—he leaves the rule unexplained [*Vinayamukha*, vol. 1, p. 128]. The message is that the rule is no longer relevant inasmuch as no such claims could be true" (Thanissaro 2005, 11–12). See also Paisal Visalo 2546, 13.

38. See Seeger 2015, 520–22.

39. Thongkham 2552, 131. See also Taylor 1993, 147

40. Interview with Sulak Sivaraksa, March 25, 2013.

41. Wiwitwanpricha 2524, 71

42. Buddhaghosacariya 2558, 2; see also p. 11.

43. See, e.g., Taylor 1997; Keyes 1982, 150.

44. Nonetheless, there is also the belief that sainthood is possible in village or urban settings. Chaokhun No (Dhammavitakko 1898–1971), for example, has been called "the arahant in the middle of the city" (*phra arahan klang krung*); from 1936 until his death in 1971 he did not leave the compound of his monastery, Wat Thepsirin, in the middle of Bangkok. Chaokhun No's teacher, the abbot of Wat Thepsirin, Somdet Phra Buddhaghosacariya (Jaroen Ñāṇavaro), was also believed to have achieved *ariya-puggala* status, even though his biographies primarily depict him as a scholarly and high-ranking administrative monk with thousands of students. Both of these monks have been highly revered by a large number of Thai Buddhists for their "genuine" Buddhist practice.

45. Pranke 2010, 459.

46. Ibid., 466. See also Tambiah 1984, 344–45.

47. See, however, the millenarian or Holy Men movements in Thai history (e.g., Tambiah 1984, 293–320; Bowie 2014; Keyes 2014, chapter 3).

48. Pranke 2010, 456.

49. See also Taylor 1997, 293. Compare with Tosa (2009, 248) who argues that "the growing number of saint cults in Burma is surely related to the rapid social changes of the 1990s."

50. Chalong 2013, 179.

51. Keyes 1982, 152.

52. Ibid., 149.

53. Thepjetiyajan 2551, 184. See also epigraph of chapter 1. Luang Pu Juan's mother was also believed to have achieved the noble level of *anāgāmī*. It is reported that this happened in the late 1940s (Thiaranan 2552, 60–63).

54. Interview with Phakdiphuri, July 22, 2012.

55. Payutto 2552, 10.

56. Gabaude 2003a, 110. Kawanami (2009, 225) observes something similar in Burmese Buddhism, as "there is a certain amount of confusion among the Myanmar public as to the notion of [arahant] and *weikza* [a type of male practitioner who strives for the attainment of magical powers and an extraordinarily long life]." See also Payutto 2556, 32.

57. Tossapol Jangpanichkul 2548, 176.

58. Bunruean Tongbuntoem 2528, (1).

59. Dh-a III 200–204. Translation by Burlingame (2005, 3:36). See also Vin II 110–12. See also Fiodarlis 2008, 41–43; Strong 1979, 71–75; Ray 1994, 151–62; Anālayo 2008b, 462–65.

60. Ap II 535. Translation by Krey (2010a, 18).

61. Anālayo (2008b, 465) argues that "early Buddhism recognizes the ability to perform supernormal feats and, according to the early discourses and the *Vinaya*, the Buddha himself and various disciples repeatedly availed themselves of such abilities. Yet, the public display of such abilities for worldly motives is censured as unbefitting." According to Strong (1979, 73), Piṇḍolabhāradvāja's decision to levitate to the bowl "is intended to overcome this doubt [that there are no arahants in the world]—to show that among the Buddhists (i.e., *only* among the Buddhists) there are indeed enlightened individuals."

62. Rozenberg 2010, 150. Similarly, in her study of arahantship in present-day Burmese Buddhism Kawanami reports that specific monks are "rumoured to be *arahants*" and "people would nod and whisper that he was indeed an *arahant*" (Kawanami 2009, 228).

63. See, e.g., Seeger 2005, 135ff.; Seeger 2009, 7ff.

64. Cremation volume of Ajan Naeb Mahaniranon 2526, 40–41. It is reported that when Chaokhun No of Wat Thepsirin was asked by the intellectual, writer, and politician Kukrit Pramoj (1911–95) if he was an arahant, he replied "you crazy guy [*ai ba*]!" (Sulak Sivaraksa 2542, 278)

65. *Jak jai* [2555?]; unidentified hagiography of a Thai monk; Bunlong Thamkhamfu 2549, 12; Bunlong Thamkhamfu 2459, 225.

66. Vin III 91.

67. Vin IV 25. During the last few decades, there were a number of high-profile cases where Thai monks were reported to have made self-assertions of sainthood. Two of the most famous examples are Luang Ta Mahabua's and Samana Phothirak's public speeches during which they were understood to have made claims to sainthood. In both cases, this has led to numerous discussions about their validity and appropriateness. For Luang Ta Mahabua, see his sermon given at Wat Burapharam in Surin on February 3, 2541 (http://luangta.com/upload/ThammaTalk/pdf/Sep3surin.doc.pdf); see also, e.g., Luang Ta Mahabua's sermon of June 17, 2002, titled "Pen phra arahan thammai nam ta ruang" [Why does an arahant shed tears?], https://youtu.be/6yjN8QeFjko; Taylor 2008, 161–62. For Samana Photirak, see, e.g., Phatharaphon Sirikanjana 2540, 110–12; Seeger 2005, 138ff; Seeger 2009, 11ff; Mackenzie 2007, 183. See also Samana Phothirak's sermons where he makes this claim (https://youtu.be/XcsssNSgM9U and https://youtu.be/AnnomLIxYmo).

68. See, e.g., Keyes 1982, 160. On Luang Pu Man's practice in this regard, Bua Ñāṇasampanno 2541, 109; Taylor 1993, 75.

69. See, e.g., Thepjetiyajan 2551, 115–16, 201–5; Mettiko Bhikkhu 2015, 48; Tate 1997, 42, 251, 257. See also Phimpha 2553, 75–76. In Buddhaghosa's *Visuddhimagga* (Vism 634–35) there is an interesting story exemplifying the mistakenly held belief in one's own awakening. This story has it that the arahant monk Dhammadinna wanted to help his former teacher Mahānāga to attain awakening. Mahānāga mistakenly thought he had attained arahantship sixty years previously. Using his supernatural powers to visit Mahānāga, he greeted him respectfully (!) and asked him a thousand questions, which Mahānāga was able answer instantly. Afterwards Dhammadinna asked Mahānāga to use his supernatural powers to create the mental image of an elephant. When the master perceived the image of the elephant he became frightened, sprang up, and wanted to run away. Dhammadinna, however, grabbed his master's robes. This made Mahānāga realize that he had wrongly believed he was an arahant (*attano puthujjanabhāvaṃ ñatvā*), for fully awakened beings would not be afraid of anything. Eventually, Dhammadinna gave Mahanāga instruction in meditation; this then allowed Mahānāga to truly achieve arahantship (see also Ñyāṇamoli 1976, 740–41). For a more recent example of the mistaken belief in one's sainthood, see the case of the controversial monk Phra Kasem Āciṇṇasīlo (now Kasem Duangphaengmat) of Wat Pa Samyaek in Phetchabun Province, which received broad attention in Thai society; see, e.g., the interview with the former monk at https://youtu.be/5N4HcBZEnWc.

70. In Thai Buddhist jargon this "mental disturbance" is called *wipatsanu* and derives from the Pali term *vipassanūpakilesa* (imperfections/defilements of *vipassanā* meditation).

71. *Luang Pu Fan Ācāro, Wat Pa Udomsomphon*, n.d., 288–331.

72. For more on the perceived connection between *kamma* and female rebirth see chapter 6.

73. In contrast to Mae Bunruean's kammic bodily manifestation (see previous chapter), Mae Chi Tat's kammic marker was the result of a demeritorious deed.

74. *Luang Pu Fan Ācāro, Wat Pa Udomsomphon*, n.d., 317.

75. Ibid., 319, 320.

76. "Uplifting crown of the cetiya," *Dhamma* talk in Thai by Phra Ajan Inthawai Santussako, CD-ROM; Luang Ta Mahabua 2549. On a table in the *cetiya* museum of Mae Chi Kaew, Luang Ta Mahabua is quoted: "Mae Chee Kaew has attained the same purity of heart that I have" (translation as given on the table; *rao borisut chen rai phuthao Mae Kaew ko borisut chen nan phuthao Mae Kaew borisut chen rai rao ko borisut chen nan*). Often Phra Ajan Inthawai speaks a hybrid of Phu Thai and standard Thai language in his talks on the CD-ROMs distributed by his monastery.

77. See, e.g., Taylor 2008, 110–68.

78. Suniwan Tangphaithunsakun (2549, 96–97) also briefly discusses this statue of Mae Chi Kaew.

79. Monastic community of Wat Samphanthawong 2553, 18.

80. Bunruean Tongbuntoem, n.d., section titled "Prawat Khun Mae Bunruean Tongbuntoem."

81. Sathuean Suphasophon 2526, 15.

82. See, e.g., Sujarit Thawonsuk 2507, (113). Here it is said that "it is not confirmed as to whether she attained the six *abhiññā*s together with the four *jhāna*s, but it is believed to have happened around the same time."

83. Sujarit Thawonsuk 2507, (119).

84. See, e.g., D II 217. See also Buai Siwaphruek 2496, 118, 318.

85. See Payutto 2538b, 270.

86. Damrongthammasan 2559, 194.

87. Somphong Suthinsak 2537, 95.

88. See Seeger 2010b.

89. *Ja rong rap jit thi lutphon dai*. This way of putting this belief is taken from Dhammanandā 2546, 21.

90. Tossapol Jangpanichkul 2553, 118.

91. "At Wat Rangsi," *Dhamma* talk in Phu Thai language by Phra Ajan Inthawai Santussako, CD-ROM; interview with Khruba Ajan, November 7, 2009.

92. Compare with Dhammanandā 2546, 21. See also e.g., *Larndham* forums, February 15–20, 2007, http://larndham.org/index.php?showtopic=24797&st=1; *Palungjit* forums, http://palungjit.org/threads/ประวัติแม่ชีแก้ว-เสียงล้ำ-แม่ชีอรหันต์-สำนักชีห้วยทราย-จ.48711/.

93. Sometimes, the formulations used in Thai in these contexts are not entirely clear on whether women in current Thai Buddhism are believed to be unable to achieve any of the four levels of awakening or only the highest level, i.e., arahantship. See Seeger 2010b, 559; also compare with Akhin Raphiphat, cited in Montri Suepduang 2551, 3–4.

94. Here it must be noted that, as already mentioned in chapter 1, the Pali canon contains many stories of *bhikkhunī*s who attained full awakening.

95. *Mahārāja, khemāya pabbajituṃ vā parinibbāyituṃ vā vaṭṭatī'ti* (Dhp-a IV 59). This story can be found in the commentaries. In the Pali canon itself, however, it is said that Khemā only attained arahantship after having been ordained for seven months (*sattamāse* according to the Thai edition of the Pali canon; however, the Chaṭṭha Saṅgāyana CD-ROM edition gives *addhamāse*, meaning half a month after her ordination; Ap II 550).

96. Vin I 17–18 and Dh-a IV 63, respectively.

97. *Tasmiṃ yeva divase pabbajati vā parinibbāyati vā; na so divaso sakkā atikkametun'ti*. Mil 264–66.

98. Ps III 196.

99. *Yu nuea khwam pen kharawat lae yu nuea khwam pen banphachit*. Buddhadāsa Bhikkhu 2537, 89.

100. Quoted in Mahahansa Dhammahāso 2548.

101. Quoted in Montri Suepduang 2551, 262.

102. Interview with Khruba Jaeo, November 3, 2009; interview with Khruba Ajan, November 7, 2009.

103. According to Buddhist teaching the five aggregates (*khandha*) constitute the individual human being.

104. Available at http://www.luangta.com/thamma/thamma_talk_text.php?ID=1022&CatID=3, accessed July 9, 2016.

105. Interview with Khruba Ajan, November 7, 2009.

106. Available at http://www.luangta.com/thamma/thamma_talk_text.php?ID=4312&CatID=2, accessed July 9, 2016.

107. Interview with Khruba Jaeo, November 3, 2009. Also, as pointed out by Phra Payutto (2555a, 51), "the fact that a layperson becomes ordained [*buat*] does not necessarily mean that he/she has to become a *bhikkhunī* or *bhikkhu*, as those who are not of the required age [that is, at least twenty years old or in the case of married women at least twelve years old] cannot be ordained as such. During the time of the Buddha, there were numerous male and female novices who achieved arahantship but had to wait for many years before they were eligible for full ordination [*upasampadā*]." For the minimum age requirement for the higher ordination of women, see Kieffer-Pülz 2005.

108. Phanom Phaetkhun, 2532, issue no. 15,516, p. 38.

109. "Prawat lae ngan khong Khun Mae Bunruean Tongbuntoem 7" 2556.

110. Sujarit Thawonsuk 2507, (110). In a previous publication on Mae Bunruean (Seeger 2013), I failed to elaborate sufficiently and provide more clarification on this point.

111. "Prawat lae ngan khong Khun Mae Bunruean Tongbuntoem 7" 2556.

112. Sujarit Thawonsuk 2507, (130).

113. Ibid., 272.

114. Compare with Kamala Tiyavanich 1997.

Chapter 4. Material Expressions of Female Sainthood

1. *Cattārome, ānanda, thūpārahā. Katame cattāro? Tathāgato arahaṃ sammāsambuddho thūpāraho, paccekasambuddho thūpāraho, tathāgatassa sāvako thūpāraho, rājā cakkavattī thūpāraho ti.* (D II 142). This translation closely follows that by Rupert Gethin (2008, 82).

2. McDaniel 2011, 162.

3. Kieschnick 2003, 23.

4. Term borrowed from Kieschnick 2003, 31.

5. Skilling 2005, 269. For relic veneration in the Theravada tradition, see Trainor 1997.

6. Amaradevo Bhikkhu 2550, *Kham prarop* [preface].

7. Tossapol Jangpanichkul 2548, 37.

8. Angenendt 2007, 154–55.

9. Sulak Sivaraksa 2550, 56–57. These relics were also on display in a glass bowl in the major *stūpa* of the monastery when I visited it in August 2008. However, I was not able to ascertain the weight of the relics. In another glass bowl there was a large number of relics of the noncanonical Theravada saint Upagupta; in still another bowl there was an even larger number of relics of "fully awakened disciples" (*arahantasawok*).

10. Amaradevo Bhikkhu 2550, 20.

11. Cremation volume of Luang Ta Mahabua 2554, 913.

12. Compare with Bingenheimer (2006) who discusses whole-body relics in Buddhism.

13. I visited the monastic residence of Mae Chi Prathum in July 2008; see also, e.g., "Phra Rae Khotsetthi Khun Mae Chi Prathum Choti-anan" [The Phra Rae Khotsetthi amulet of Khun Mae Chi Prathum Choti-anan], http://www.nutchaamulet.com/article/3/พระแร่โคตรเศรษฐี-คุณแม่ชีประทุม-โชติอนันต์, accessed September 9, 2016). The corpse of Upāsikā Ki Nanayon, whose life and work I refer to repeatedly in this study, has also not been cremated but is kept in a sarcophagus on a hill in Ratchaburi Province where she pursued Buddhist practice.

14. Translation by Griswold and Prasert (1971, 217).

15. Terwiel 2010, 48. See also Wyatt 2001.

16. Tossapol Jangpanichkul 2548, 287–92; Natthaphat Janthawit 2539, 47–48, 60.

17. See, e.g., Sisak Wanliphodom 2546; Blackburn 2010.

18. Over the years of my research, I frequently came across this belief in my many interviews on this topic.

19. Interview with Khruba Jaeo, November 3, 2009; interview with Khruba Ajan, November 7, 2009.

20. Tambiah 1984, 109. See also, Amaradevo Bhikkhu 2550, 27. It has been reported that devotees tried to get parts of Luang Pu Man's remains even before the fire of the cremation pyre was extinct. Even earth on which the cremation took place was removed with bare hands and taken away (Mettiko Bhikkhu 2014, 272).

21. Keyes 1982, 163.

22. Cremation volume of Luang Ta Maha Bua 2554, 876.

23. See the *Matichon* newspaper from March 8, 2554 (issue no. 12050).

24. See also Skilling 2005.

25. . . . *sumanamakuḷasadisā ca dhotamuttasadisā ca suvaṇṇasadisā ca dhātuyo avasissiṃsūti attho.* Sv II 604. Translation by An (2005, 206).

26. Tossapol Jangpanichkul 2548, 214.

27. M III 127.

28. *Tejodhātuṃsamāpajjitvāparinibbāyi. Sarīratojālāuṭṭhahi, chavimaṃsalohitaṃ sappi viya jhāyamānaṃ parikkhayaṃ gataṃ, sumanamakulasadisā dhātuyova avasesiṃsu.* Ps IV 196.

29. Dhp-a III 78–84. Translated by Burlingame (2005, 2:315–16).

30. In this context, it is interesting to refer to the death of the arahant monk Dabba Mallaputta, who according to the Pali canonical book *Udāna* (Ud 93) also rose into the air and autocombusted, but the marvelous aspect of this feat was that no ashes or soot remained (see Anālayo 2012).

31. Griswold and Prasert 1969, 44 and 52.

32. See also Skilling 2005; Sulak Sivaraksa 2550, 47–57.

33. For Chinese Buddhism, see, e.g., Kieschnick 2003, 34–35; for Burmese Buddhism, e.g., Pranke 2010, 482; Rozenberg 2011, 91; for Tibetan Buddhism, e.g., Martin 1994; Zivkovic 2010. See also Strong 2004, 10–12.

34. Gabaude 2003a, 116 and 118.

35. Amaradevo Bhikkhu 2550, 30.

36. See, e.g., Taylor 1993, 175–80.

37. This statement is based on my interviews with a number of Thai monks. Also see, e.g., Tossapol Jangpanichkul (2548, [introduction], 210–11) who explains that *phra that* can emerge as a result of the Buddhist practice of an *ariya-puggala*.

38. Amaradevo Bhikkhu 2550, 81

39. Ibid., *Kham prarop* [preface].

40. The Thai *mai khuan khit* is a direct translation from the *Acinteyya-sutta*: *Cattārimāni, bhikkhave, acinteyyāni, na cintetabbāni.*

41. A II 80. Translation by Bhikkhu Bodhi (2012, 463); see also Nyānatiloka 1999, 16. The commentary text gives for "domain of the buddhas" (*buddhavisaya*) only the following definition: "the procedure and spiritual might (*pavatti ca ānubhāvo ca*) of the Buddha's qualities such as the omniscient knowledge and so forth." (Mp III 108–9; translation by Bhikkhu Bodhi [2012, p. 1693]).

42. See also, e.g., Gabaude 2003a, 2003b.

43. The last statement in this quote clearly is based on a passage in the *Mahāparinibbāna-sutta* in which the Buddha says that "if the monks here live properly, the world should not be empty of arahats [arahants]." (D II 151; translated by Gethin [2008, 86]).

44. I will discuss the hierarchical embeddedness of *mae chi*s further in chapter 6.

45. Wuthinan Jiawitthayanan 2553, 114, 123.

46. Interview with Khruba Jaeo, November 3, 2009; Bhikkhu Sīlaratano 2009, 206; see also Suniwan Tangphaithunsakun 2549, 106.

47. Gabaude 2003b, 181.

48. See, e.g., Bhikkhu Sīlaratano 2009, 206; Suniwan Tangphaithunsakun 2549, 114.

49. Suniwan Tangphaithunsakun 2549, 112, 114.

50. Interview with Khruba Ajan, November 7, 2009.

51. Interview with Khruba Jaeo, November 3, 2009; Bhikkhu Sīlaratano 2009, 205; see also Suniwan Tangphaithunsakun 2549, 85, 107.

52. Interview with Khruba Jaeo, November 3, 2009.

53. Sujarit Thawonsuk 2507, (121)–(122).

54. Ibid., (126).

55. *Asai khao kon bat khong khruba ajan liang chiwit.* Suniwan Tangphaithunsakun 2549, 137.

56. See Suniwan Tangphaithunsakun 2549, 141–43.

57. This statement is based on my own observations and my many interviews with Buddhist studies scholars and Buddhists in numerous provinces in northern, northeastern, and central Thailand.

58. *Phu banlu chuai luea juea jun* 2552, 64.

59. According to Khruba Jaeo more than 5,000 copies of each biography of Mae Chi Kaew were printed (interview, November 3, 2009).

60. Bhikkhu Sīlaratano 2009. This book was produced at a cost of one million baht (interview with Bhikkhu Sīlaratano, November 7, 2009; email from Bhikkhu Sīlaratano, December, 24, 2009).

61. For the opening of the *stūpa*, some two hundred small figures of Mae Chi Kaew were also produced and given to people who were actively involved in the construction process of the *stūpa* (interview with Khruba Ajan, November 7, 2009).

62. *Mai chai kaeo thi sai jaeo pen met klom klom pen met kaeo baep khun khun*. "Uplifting crown of the cetiya," *Dhamma* talk in Thai by Phra Ajan Inthawai Santussako; CD-ROM; interview with Khruba Ajan, November 7, 2009.

63. During fieldwork in Thailand in October/November 2009 I was able to identify further possible locations of and narratives on the relics of Mae Chi Kaew.

64. See, e.g., www.watpa.com, www.santidham.com, www.dhammasavana.or.th.

65. Ray 1994, 324.

66. I borrow this term from Gifford 2003, 77.

67. Sharf 1999, 78. See also Strong 2004, 231–32.

68. Strong 2004, 7.

69. Bhikkhu Sīlaratano 2009, 133.

70. In Thailand, there is also the tradition of building small *stūpa*s for common people. These *stūpa*s, however, differ significantly not only in size but also in their symbolism from the *stūpas* mentioned and discussed in this book.

71. This *stūpa* is called *Suwannajeti Jangkot* and has a height of twenty-one metres.

72. See, e.g., the page about the memorial hall dedicated to Mae Chi Khonnokyung on the official temple website, http://www.dhammakaya.net/วัดพระธรรมกาย/มหาวิหารคุณยายอาจารย์มหารัตนอุบาสิกาจันทร์-ขนนกยูง.

73. "The Memorial Hall of the Master Nun Chand Khonnokyoong," *Dhammakaya Foundation*, http://en.dhammakaya.net/about/dhammakaya-temple/the-memorial-hall-of-the-master-nun-chandra-khonnokyoong/, accessed October 2, 2017.

74. See also Scott 2009, 70–76.

75. See, e.g., Taylor 1993, 157–58; Gabaude 2003a, 2003b; Suniwan Tangphaithunsakun 2549, 102.

76. *Phu banlu chuai luea juea jun* 2552, 24.

77. "Points to Ponder 3," *Dhamma* talk in Thai by Phra Ajan Inthawai Santussako, CD-ROM. See also, e.g., *Laeng thong thiao amphoe Khamcha-i* [Tourist sites of Khamcha-i district], August 12, 2560, http://khamcha-i.mukdahan.police.go.th/?page_id=585.

78. "The realization of *nibbāna* is still achievable for laywomen": *yom phuying . . . mak phon nipphan ko yang khoi phuak than yu*; "not restricted to the male monastic

community": *mai mi tae chapho phra song thaonan.* "Starting of *cetiya* construction," *Dhamma* talk in Thai by Phra Ajan Inthawai Santussako, CD-ROM.

79. "Points to ponder 3," *Dhamma* talk in Thai by Phra Ajan Inthawai Santussako, CD-ROM.

80. Phra Ajan Inthawai Santussako, sermon number 23/18, http://www.watpanakamnoi.com/sound.html, accessed June 4, 2016.

81. According to Gabaude (2003a, 115), the museums of Thai saints correspond to the concept of *paribhoga-cetiya*, which is one of the four classifications of *cetiya* developed in commentarial Pali texts (see, e.g., Pj I 221–22). The four kinds of *cetiya* are (1) *dhātu-cetiya*, a shrine containing Buddha relics, (2) *paribhoga-cetiya*, for things and places used by the Buddha, such as the Bodhi tree, (3) *dhamma-cetiya*, a shrine containing the Buddha's teachings (e.g., palm leaves with holy texts), and (4) *uddesika-cetiya*, a shrine containing images and other objects.

82. An informant told me that the relics displayed in the glass urns may actually not all be "real" relics. Sometimes, devotees may add gemstones to express veneration and beautifully complement the real relics. This seems to be a plausible explanation as actual bone relics and their *phra that* at the various stages of transformation are quite easily identifiable as such.

83. Veidlinger 2006, 174.

84. During my research I was repeatedly invited to hold the relics of saints in my hands or at least to have a close look at them. Several times urns with relics were opened especially for me when I showed my academic interests in them.

85. A table at the *stūpa* informs that in a previous life Mae Chi Kaew was involved in the construction of the Phra That Phanom *stūpa*.

86. Interview with Khruba Jaeo, November 3, 2009; interview with Khruba Ajan, November 7, 2009.

87. *Rao yang yu nai lok sommut khun mae pen phuying.* "Uplifting crown of the *cetiya*," *Dhamma* talk in Thai by Phra Ajan Inthawai Santussako, CD-ROM; "The Lord's Relics at Udon," *Dhamma* talk in Thai by Phra Ajan Inthawai Santussako, CD-ROM; interview with Phra Ajan Inthawai Santussako at Wat Pa Na Kham Noi, July 19, 2008.

88. Quoted in Suniwan Tangphaithunsakun 2549, 113. See also chapter 6.

89. I have repeatedly come across this information during my many informal interviews in amulet markets in Bangkok and at Wat Awutwikasitaram, where a shrine of Mae Bunruean is located.

90. Interview with Khruba Jaeo, November 3, 2009.

91. Vin II 253–55; interview with Khruba Ajan, November 7, 2009.

92. Battaglia 2007, 209. See also chapter 6.

93. Interview with Khruba Ajan, November 7, 2009.

94. The *sammuti-sacca/paramattha-sacca* dichotomy is explicitly mentioned in a relatively late canonical text, the Abhidhamma text *Kathāvatthu*. Here, the terms *sammati-sacca* in Kv 311 and *saccikaṭṭhaparamattha* and *paramattha* in Kv 1–69 appear (see, e.g., Collins 1990, 147–56). See also, e.g., Seeger 2005, 200–202; Seeger 2006, 165–66.

95. See Seeger 2005, 206–11; also compare with Sponberg 1992.

96. *Kham wa arahan mai niyom wa pen ying pen chai*. Available at http://www.luangta.com/thamma/thamma_talk_multimedia.php?CatID=2&video= (accessed December 14, 2016)

97. The two donation books at the museum on the ground floor of the *stūpa*, along with my interviews with locals, show that there were up to one hundred visitors on a weekend in November of 2009. This kind of spatial sanctification is not unusual and can be observed in the cases of other Thai Buddhist saints too. Thus, in front of the pathway where Mae Chi Soda practiced walking meditation, there is a sign that says crossing the pathway is forbidden. Also, the spot where the cremation of her body took place, in the middle of a lawn behind her *stūpa*, is fenced off. Likewise, the monastic cell of Somdet Phra Buddhaghosacariya (Jaroen Ñāṇavaro) in the monastery Wat Khao Bang Sai in Chon Buri has not been used since his death in 1951, and normally no one is allowed to enter it, as it "belongs to the superior" (*khong sung*). A sign at the monastic hut of Luang Pu Man in the monastery Wat Pa Ban Nong Phue tells the visitor that entry is not allowed. One is also not allowed to cross the pathway in front of the hut where the master practiced walking meditation.

98. D II 140–41. Translation by Walshe (1987, 263–64).

99. See, e.g., Phanom Phaetkhun 2532, issue no. 15,521, p. 17; Tossapol Jangpanichkul 2553, 190–91.

100. Interview with a respected amulet collector on August 27, 2008. See also Amaradevo Bhikkhu 2550, 16.

101. I should mention here, though, that the building of *stūpa*s for practitioners in an urban context would be quite untypical anyway, as most of the *stūpa*s, discussed above, have been built for the saints of the Thai forest tradition. The only exception of a female practitioner in this regard seems to be Mae Chi Chandra Khonnokyoong of Wat Phra Thammakai (see above and Scott 2009, 70–76).

102. It has been reported that the throwing of an egg was used in order to determine the location of the commemoration hall.

103. Sittha Chetawan, n.d., 30.

104. Terwiel 1994, 79; see also Van Esterik 2000, 78; Lindberg Falk 2007, 107; Bowie 2011.

105. Niti Kasikoson 2544, 40–41. See also, Chalong Soontravanich 2013.

106. Phanom Phaetkhun 2532, issue no. 15,522, p. 16.

107. Interview with Boy Thaphrajan, August 6, 2010; "Phra Phuttho Noi (1) Mae Chi Bunruean Tongbuntoem" [Phra Phuttho Noi (1): Mae Chi Bunruean Tongbuntoem], *Khom Chat Luek*, July 13, 2553, http://www.komchadluek.net/news/detail/66253. The value of Phra Phuttho Noi amulets also depends on the size and condition of the amulet.

108. See, for example, the daily *Khao Sot* of August 2, 2010; this also came up in my interview with Boy Thaphrajan, August 6, 2010. "Boy Thaphrajan 'sian rian' niyom hoi Phra Luang Pu To" [Boy Thaphrajan, expert in medallion amulets, likes to wear Luang Pu To Amulets], *Itthi Patihan Phra Khrueang*, sourced from *Daily News*, http://www.itti-patihan.com/บอย-ท่าพระจันทร์-เซียนเหรียญ-นิยมห้อยพระ-หลวงปู่โต๊ะ.html.

109. It was estimated that in 2007 there was more than twenty-two billion baht in the Thai amulet market and related businesses (Kaset Noithip 2550, 26; see

also Chalong Soontravanich 2013). This statement of Mae Bunruean's exceptional charisma is based on my many interviews with amulet collectors over the last seven years. Related discussions were in my interview with a respected amulet collector, August 27, 2008; and my interview with Boy Thaphrajan, August 6, 2010.

110. Interview with a respected amulet collector, August 27, 2008.

111. Phanom Phaetkhun 2531, issue no. 15,530, pp. 36-38.

112. This information on Mae Chi Nari's consecration of amulets is from my interview with Samon Thophaengjan, August 12, 2012.

113. "Phraariyajaohaeng Dong Mothong: Khun Yai Chi Soda Sosut phuthotkaithip ho nuea Phuthok" [The noble one of Dong Mothong: Khun Yai Chi Soda Sosut, the one who hovered with her astral body above Phuthok], online discussion board post on Mae Chi Soda, *Palungjit* forums, http://palungjit.org/threads/พระอริยเจ้าแห่งดงหม้อทอง-คุณยายชีโสดา-โสสุด-ผู้ถอดกายทิพย์เหาะเหนือภูทอก.224993/.

114. It has been reported that *mae chis* were involved in the production of the famous Wat Pak Nam amulet Phra Khongkhwan (see Nathathai Chattinawat 2552, 152–53). But this is not widely known and the powers the amulet is believed to contain are associated with those stemming from a monk.

115. Prathum Choti-anan 2539, 138.

116. Rozenberg 2010, 155.

117. Pranke 2010, 482.

118. Rozenberg 2010, 155–56. In a footnote referring to the studies of Keyes (1982) and Tambiah (1987), Rozenberg also makes this observation of a "striking" contrast between Thai and Burmese practices in this regard.

119. Ibid., 156.

120. The epigraph of chapter 2 of this book is such a biographical fragment of Mae Chi Kang.

121. The following account is based on my interviews with local monks and the fieldwork notes that I made when I visited the place on August 12, 2012.

122. Mae Chi Tat Janthawongsa. So far, I was not able to find any significant amount of biographical data on this *mae chi*.

123. Available at http://www.luangta.com/thamma/thamma_talk_text.php?ID=3415&CatID=2, accessed December 14, 2016.

124. Cremation volume of Luang Ta Mahabua 2554, 205.

125. Interview with a local monk, August 12, 2012.

126. Interview with Phakdiphuri, July 22, 2012.

127. Morgan 2010, 11–12.

Chapter 5. The Importance of Orality and Memory in Spiritual Practice

1. Buddharakkhita 1985, 39.

2. Costa 1997; see also Barmé 2002, 21–22. Costa (1997) notes, however, "It is clear that elite women *did* receive formal education in the palace, though subjects were gender specific."

3. Scholars have stated that only around 1921, when the Thai state made education compulsory for both genders, did the number of literate women begin

to increase significantly. See, e.g., Barmé 2002, 135. Relying on Vella (1978), Keyes (1991, 96) writes that "between 1921 and 1925 the percentage of female students throughout the country jumped from seven to thirty-eight."

4. Darunee Tantiwiramanond 1997, 172. Even though Darunee alludes to *mae chis* (see below) in this context, she does not mention their educational opportunities here but rather discusses the "inferiority" and "the derogatory status of . . . *mae chi*" (172–73).

5. A number of scholars have argued that before the introduction of compulsory education in Thailand (until 1939 known as Siam) in 1921 there were significant differences in the education of men and of women. Terwiel (2012, 104), for example, writes, "Since prior to the 1930s girls were not allowed to learn in the monastery schools, only a limited number of privileged women could read and write." Similarly, Keyes (1991, 123n3) has argued, "Some women in premodern urban settings did become literate, but rural women were, almost without exception, illiterate until after the compulsory primary education was instituted." Terwiel (2012, 106) also states that "it can be shown that traditional monastic education was remarkably effective. During the first half of the nineteenth century, when the traditional system was still operative, European and American residents remarked on the large proportion of adult Thai males who could read and write. Not only government officials and princes possessed these skills, but also ordinary workmen, farmers, and fishermen."

6. Damrong Rajanubhab 2514, 216.

7. Ishii 1986, 95.

8. *Prawat kan sueksa khong song* 2527, 44. For an interesting study on the importance of orality and memory in northern Thai Buddhism, see Veidlinger 2006.

9. Saichol Satayanurak 2546, 252.

10. See, e.g., Pathom Takhananan 2551, 14.

11. Nidhi Eoseewong 2549, 74.

12. Ibid., 74.

13. Chetana Nagavajara was born in 1937.

14. Chetana Nagavajara 1994, 33.

15. I conducted these interviews in person together with my co-researcher on this project, Naris Charaschanyawong, and on the phone between July 2013 and Prasop Wisetsiri's death in October 2014. Naris conducted one final interview with him—based on questions I had prepared—at the end of July 2014 in order to verify and clarify a number of important biographical elements of Khunying Yai's life. Prasop Wisetsiri was ninety years old when he died. During our many interviews, he consistently showed us that he had an astonishingly precise memory. He often surprised us by being able to remember numerous details from the time period when he was between ten and twenty years old.

16. Somphong Suthinsak 2537, 95.

17. In a Thai edition of 1902, this Pali text together with its Thai translation consists of more than eighty pages.

18. Cremation volume of Khunying Damrongthammasan 2489, 1.

19. As I argue elsewhere, it is not clear how far, if at all, these conversations may have actually taken place or are imaginary (Seeger 2015).

20. At that time this influential Pali text *Abhidhammatthasaṅgaha* was already available in a Thai translation.

21. I should mention that this includes the occurrences of the word *fang* when it is used in connection with the Buddhist teaching on the six senses (*āyatana*), which is referred to quite frequently throughout the texts. Here it is of course not surprising that *fang* is used.

22. Damrongthammasan 2474, 9.

23. [Damrongthammasan] 2475a, 35. My emphasis.

24. See, e.g., Collins 1992.

25. [Damrongthammasan] 2475a, 6–8.

26. [Damrongthammasan] 2475b, 15–16.

27. Anālayo 2007, 16.

28. Collins 1992, 126.

29. Gethin 1992, 166.

30. In Thai Buddhism, this text is also known as *Soḷasapañha*.

31. A IV 63.

32. A I 88–89.

33. Pj II 370.

34. Damrongthammasan 2474, 7.

35. Anālayo (2007, 19) establishes that the tradition of a laywoman having first learned the *Ittivuttaka* finds support in the peculiar opening and closing formulas.

36. A I 26.

37. This is also confirmed in the foreword Somdet Phra Buddhaghosacariya wrote for Khunying Yai's cremation volume.

38. Seeger and Naris 2556b, 142.

39. *Kae nitnoi*. Cremation volume of Khunying Damrongthammasan 2489, 1.

40. Interview with Prasop Wisetsiri, July 30, 2014.

41. See, e.g., Prasok 2554, 53.

42. See, e.g., Buddhadāsa 2554, 125.

43. Thirachai Thongthammachat 2554, 186.

44. See, e.g., Thirachai Thongthammachat 2554. The following description and discussion is based on letters written by his students and texts produced by himself.

45. These daily recitations of Buddhist texts by heart are still widely practiced in many monasteries, other monastic communities, and even private houses.

46. Dunlayaphaksuwaman 2554, 18.

47. Parinyayokhawibun 2554, 58.

48. See, e.g., Vāsana 2554, 106.

49. Vāsana 2554, 106–7.

50. Dunlayaphaksuwaman 2554, 23.

51. Buddhaghosacariya 2481, *Kham nam* [foreword].

52. Ibid.

53. Gethin 1992, 155.

54. See also Seeger 2015, 527–28.

55. Wachirayan 2537, p. ก, *Kham nam* [preface].

56. Compare with, e.g., Anālayo 2011, 857–58.

57. Buddhaghosacariya 2522, *Kham nam* [foreword].
58. A IV 248–51.
59. Buddhaghosacariya 2522, 7.
60. Ibid., 8. When providing an explanation of the first of the four "virtues that lead to welfare and happiness in the future," the *saddhā-sampadā* (accomplishment in faith), Somdet Phra Buddhaghosacariya writes that "to be accomplished by faith means to believe that the Buddha really gained true understanding of reality and that his teachings are correct. Thus, you will not have doubts, nor will you hesitate; you will attentively listen to his teachings and memorize them" (*Sam Somdet* 2523, 85–86).
61. Buddhaghosacariya 2474a, *Kham nam* [preface].
62. Buddhaghosacariya 2474b, p. ข.
63. Cremation volume of Noi Paurohitya (3) 2474, p. ก.
64. See Anālayo 2007 and 2011, 855–77.
65. Thanissaro 1995.
66. Cited in *Thammathan bucha khun* 2544, 198–99.
67. *Rom thamma rom phrueksa* 2547, 7.
68. *Thammathan bucha khun* 2544, 200.
69. Ibid., 201.
70. *Rom thamma rom phrueksa* 2547, 4–5.
71. *Prawat Ubasika Kao Saetan* 2511, 9.
72. Ibid., 14.
73. Ibid., 15.
74. Ibid., 19.
75. Ibid., 16.
76. Ibid., 19.
77. Ibid., 24.
78. Ibid., 16.
79. Ibid., 26–27.
80. In line with my observations in chapter 2 about biographical and autobiographical writing, even though the text is called "biography" (*chiwaprawat*), it seems that large parts of Upāsikā Nu-nueang's "biography" seem to be autobiographical. In her life account she is referred to as both "Upāsikā Nu-nueang" and "Mae Chi Nu-nueang."
81. *Chiwaprawat khong Ubasika Nu-nueang* 2511, ข-ค.
82. Ibid., 2.
83. Ibid., 2.
84. Ibid., 4.
85. Ibid., 5. In Thai Buddhism, such *dhutaṅga* practices often involve sleeping under a special umbrella with a mosquito net attached to it.
86. Ibid., 10.
87. It seems that the biographer may have been confused here, as another source states that the minor wife of King Rama IV by the name of Talap passed away in 1885 (Wannaphon Bunyasathit 2553, 288). If this is correct it is not possible for her to have become Mae Chi Nu-nueang's mentor. In this case it may be possible that

the biographer is referring here to Talap Ketuthat (1852–1928), a minor wife of King Rama V (r. 1868–1910). I have not yet been able to clarify this (but see next note).

88. As Somdet Phra Wanarat passed away in 1891, this fact, together with all the other significant biographical dates given, makes it more likely that Mae Chi Nu-nueang's biography is correct with regard to the biography of Mae Chi Talap (see previous note). According to Mae Chi Nu-nueang's biography Mae Chi Talap must have died around 1908 or 1909.

89. *Chiwaprawat khong Ubasika Nu-nueang* 2511, 14. Italics mine.

90. Ibid., 15.

91. Ibid., 15.

92. Ibid., 18.

93. Ibid., 19.

94. Ibid., 31.

95. This should probably read "Phra Khru Sangwon-winai" (At Jutindharo). See *Prawat Ubasika Kao Saetan* 2511, 13.

96. *Chiwaprawat khong Ubasika Nu-nueang* 2511, 25.

97. Ibid., 26.

98. *Lok ni lok ha dai* 2550, 77.

99. Ibid., 91.

100. Ibid., 91.

101. Sujarit Thawonsuk 2507, (107).

102. Maharatchamangkhalajan 2507, (13).

103. Ibid., (14).

104. "Prawat lae ngan khong Khun Mae Bunruean Tongbuntoem 7" 2556.

105. Bunruean Tongbuntoem 2528, 9.

106. Kameniar 2009, 285.

107. Cited in Skilling 1995, 57.

108. Seeger 2010b, 568.

109. D II 141. "Lord, how should we act towards women?" "Do not see them, Ānanda." "But if we see them, how should we behave, Lord?" "Do not speak to them, Ānanda." "But if they speak to us, Lord, how should we behave?" "Practise mindfulness, Ānanda." (*"Kathaṃ mayaṃ, bhante, mātugāme paṭipajjāmā"ti? "Adassanaṃ, ānandā"ti. "Dassane, bhagavā, sati kathaṃ paṭipajjitabban"ti? "Anālāpo, ānandā"ti. "Ālapantena pana, bhante, kathaṃ paṭipajjitabban"ti? "Sati, ānanda, upaṭṭhāpetabbā"ti.*) Translation by Walshe (1987, 143).

110. "Khun Yai Khao Kang tit panha" [The white-robed Khun Yai Kang faced an obstacle], June 27, 2014, http://www.luangpumun.org/watpab5.html.

111. Cremation volume of Luang Ta Mahabua 2554, 205.

112. Translation by Bhikku Dick Sīlaratano (Mahā Boowa 2003, 341–42).

113. Cremation volume of Luang Ta Mahabua 2554, 204.

114. Mahā Boowa 2003, 343.

115. Damrongthammasan 2559, 383.

116. Translation by Bhikku Dick Sīlaratano (Mahā Boowa 2003, 92–93).

117. Wirasak Jansongsaeng 2553, 48.

118. Thepjetiyajan 2551, 71.

119. Thongkham 2552, 70; see also Mahā Boowa 2003, 316–17. For more on Luang Pho Wiriyang's transcription of Luang Pu Man's sermons, see Seeger 2015.

120. Mettiko Bhikkhu 2014, 197.

121. Taylor 1993, 76.

122. Thongkham 2552, 70–71.

123. Taylor 1993, 147.

124. Thongkham 2552, 70–71.

125. See also Mettiko Bhikkhu 2014, 100, 181.

126. [Damrongthammasan] 2475b, p. 10.

127. Cremation volume of Upāsikā Jan Thomanakon 2508, ก.

128. Both of these *mae chi* sisters had interesting monastic careers during which they were supported by a number of high-ranking monks.

129. Sutthithamrangsikhamphiramethajan (Li Dhammadharo) 2552, 8.

130. Vapi Busbakara 2522.

131. Beatrice Bhadrayuvadi 2517, 13.

132. Ibid., 19. I will devote a separate publication to the investigation of the texts by Princess Vapi Busbakara and Princess Beatrice Bhadrayuvadi.

133. See, e.g., Varaporn 2006, 73–108; Sakdina Chatrakun 2536; Seeger 2006; Ito 1999.

134. Narin Phasit 2544, 10.

135. Ibid., 10–11.

136. Ajan Naeb (1898–1983) was the first famous female Abhidhamma teacher in Thailand.

Chapter 6. Experiencing Gender

1. Phimpha 2553, 141.
2. See also chapter 1.
3. Kepner 1996, 34.
4. Muecke 2004, 227.
5. Chatsumarn Kabilsingh 1991, 39.
6. Cook 2009, 350, 367.
7. Cook, 2010, 170.
8. Battaglia 2007, 289. See also Salgado (2013, 2), who argues that "renunciant narratives can be misinterpreted and misunderstood when placed, as they often have been, within a theoretical framework of liberal feminism."
9. Battaglia 2007, 278. See also Battaglia 2014, 2015.
10. Battaglia 2007, 287.
11. Thanissaro 1995.
12. Cook 2010, 159.
13. Payutto 2555b, 922–23.
14. Notable exceptions are Cook 2009 and 2010; Battaglia 2007, 2014, and 2015.
15. However, there has been a debate over whether it is permissible or appropriate for a monk to prostrate himself in front of his mother. Following the dissemination of a picture in 2015 that shows a monk doing so, this was widely discussed in Thai society. See, e.g., "Ti jot 'phra krap mae phit mai' wikhro kham to kham: Krap phra

khun rue krap rangkai" [For addressing the problem "is it wrong for monks to prostrate themselves in front of their mothers?" each word needs to be investigated: Is it to prostrate oneself in front of the goodness or the body?], *Thai Rath Online*, August 17, 2558, http://www.thairath.co.th/content/518498.

16. Gabaude 2003a, 110.

17. Ibid., 110–11. The remaining quotes from Gabaude (2003a) in this section are found on p. 111.

18. Crosby 2014, 210, and see discussion on pp. 210–12.

19. In the eyes of Thai Buddhists, it may often not be very important how strict a monk's adherence to all of these rules actually is. In this way, Thai Buddhists may in fact find specific acts or habits of monks that would be regarded as minor offences according to the *vinaya* rules as highly problematic (e.g., the consumption of alcohol), while other behavior and actions also forbidden by the monastic code may be winked at (e.g., the handling of money). Nonetheless, if a monk is believed to follow strictly all of the 227 rules of his monastic code of discipline (*vinaya*), this may of course make him rise in his position in the popular hierarchy. In present-day Thai Buddhism, the relative seniority based on monastic age becomes visible in a variety of ways—for example, in the seating arrangements of monks and the way monks greet or show respect to one another, irrespective of how strictly the other is believed to be following the monastic rules. Thus, during a ritual the monk who has spent the most time in the robes among all the monks present would usually sit closest to the main Buddha image, while all the other monks would sit on the left side of this most senior monk in a line, in accordance with the length of time that has passed since their ordination. A monk may also show respect to a more senior monk by prostrating himself in front of him. Sometimes, this more elevated status of senior monks may be expressed by the more senior monk sitting on higher chair, dais, or a rug. People who are not monks are outside the *vinaya* hierarchy and would consequently always be expected to show respect to monks by raising their hands, prostrating themselves, lowering their head, or sitting below monks.

20. See Vin II 160–62. As Phra Payutto puts it, "Taking the attainment of spiritual levels [as principle for showing respect] will cause great confusion and not really achieve its objectives. The reason for this is that spiritual achievements are invisible, and it is difficult to prove who really has attained them and who is falsely claiming of having done so. Also, those who have achieved these spiritual levels do [naturally] not publicly announce this" (Payutto 2555a, 940).

21. For even the monk Sāriputta, one of Buddha's outstanding disciples and excelling among all the monks of the Buddha in terms of wisdom (*paññā*), is said to have been unaware of the fully awakened status of a monk he was having a conversation with (Buddhaghosacariya 2558, 21–22).

22. This hierarchy has existed in Thai Buddhism for centuries, probably already during the Sukhothai era, if not even before, and has developed into a highly complex system that incorporates numerous different ranks and titles. At the top of this hierarchy is the supreme patriarch (*saṅgha-rāja*), who is also in charge of the administrative hierarchy.

23. Mahanirut (Ṭhitasaṁvaro) 2552.

24. This hierarchy can be said to be the monastic equivalent of the Royal Thai Orders and Decorations.

25. Mahanirut (Ṭhitasaṁvaro) 2552, 189. Even though these titles of Thai Buddhist scholarship give evidence of a monk's advanced knowledge of Buddhist doctrine, monks may also of course develop what is regarded as impressive knowledge of Buddhist scriptures and teachings outside, or in addition to, the Thai monastic educational system. Thus, academic degrees earned at higher education institutions outside Thailand, in particular when received from prestigious universities such as Cambridge, Oxford, or Yale, are also regarded as extraordinary scholarly achievements. Monks who are perceived as being able to display convincingly their advanced knowledge of Buddhist teaching in sermons and books may then be regarded as authoritative in that they are able to, in the words of William Graham (1993, 165), "'speak scripture' when they write or utter any words at all." A good example here is the widely revered scholar monk Phra Payutto. Due to his comprehensive and precise scriptural knowledge, he has been called "walking *Tipiṭaka*" (*phra traipidok thi doen dai*) (see, e.g., Seeger 2005, 2009).

26. For example, having risen to the level of Somdet Phra Ratchakhana Chan Suphannabat in the *samanasak* hierarchy makes a monk automatically a member of the highest body in the administrative hierarchy, the Mahatherasamakhom (Thai Saṅgha Supreme Council), no matter if the promoted monk had only been an abbot of a rather small monastery before. This was, for example, the case in the recent promotion of Phra Payutto to "Somdet Phra Buddhaghosacariya" on December 5, 2016. A monk with a high *parian tham* title may find it much easier to climb up in the administrative and *samanasak* hierarchies. Being highly revered by a large number of people may be the reason why a monk may unusually quickly be promoted in the *samanasak* hierarchy. Depending on the circumstances, one hierarchy may be more relevant than the others. In fact, one hierarchy may eclipse another hierarchy temporarily in specific situations, even though this is rather unusual. When the late supreme patriarch Ñāṇasaṃvara visited Buddhadāsa's monastery Suan Mokkh in 1989, for example, Buddhadāsa prostrated himself in front of the *saṅgha-rāja*, despite the fact that Buddhadāsa was, according to the *vinaya* hierarchy, more senior, as he had spent a longer time in the robes. The *saṅgha-rāja* was also sitting on a bench while Buddhadāsa was kneeling in front of him. Normally, even the *saṅgha-rāja* would be in a lower position in front of monks who had been ordained before his own ordination. The *vinaya* hierarchy is usually, but not necessarily always, more decisive than the *samanasak* and administrative hierarchy. Even when believed to be a fully awakened one (arahant), the *vinaya* hierarchy would be regarded as more important. This practice as we have seen above has its origin in early Buddhism.

27. Thai Mae Chi Institute 2547, 74.

28. See *Prawat kan sueksa khong song* 2527; Ishii 1986, 81–90.

29. See *Prawat kan sueksa khong song* 2527, 58–59. See also Ishii 1986, 91–92.

30. Kritsana Raksachom and Seeger 2556, 71–72; Natthahathai 2552, 256.

31. For more details on these developments see Kritsana Raksachom and Seeger 2556.

32. See, e.g., Collins and McDaniel 2010.

33. Phimpha 2553, 79. See also the epigraph before the introduction to this book.
34. Buai Siwaphruek 2496, 102, see also pp. 8, 118, 162.
35. Ibid., 118, 162, see also p. 113.
36. Ibid., 208, 215–16.
37. See, e.g., her homiletic texts (Buai Siwaphruek 2496, 257, 305). See also Bunruean 2528, 30, 41.
38. Buai Siwaphruek 2496, 213.
39. Both refer to the *Dhammapada* verse 182: "Hard is it to be born a man; hard is the life of mortals. Hard is it to gain the opportunity of hearing the Sublime Truth, and hard to encounter is the arising of the Buddhas" (*Kiccho manussapaṭilābho, kicchaṃ maccāna jīvitaṃ; Kicchaṃ saddhammassavanaṃ, kiccho buddhānamuppādo*). Translation by Buddharakkhita (1985, 51).
40. Damrongthammasan 2559, 63–64. Khunying Yai refers here to the *Bhaddekaratta-sutta* in the *Majjhima-nikāya* (M III 187–89). The passage she quotes in this context is from the *Bhaddekaratta-sutta*, which has been translated from the Pali by Ñāṇamoli and Bodhi (1995, 1039).

> Today the effort must be made;
> Tomorrow Death may come, who knows?
> No bargain with Mortality
> Can keep him and his hordes away.

41. Phimpha 2553, 90–91. See also Damrongthammasan 2559, 33.
42. See Seeger 2014a, 164–65.
43. Phimpha 2553, 44.
44. Damrongthammasan 2559, 33; see also p. 7; Bunruean 2528, 11; and M III 202–6.
45. See Damrongthammasan 2559, 143, where she refers to the well-known *Abhiṇhapaccavekkhitabbaṭhāna-sutta*, in which we can read that "a woman or a man, a householder or one gone forth, should often reflect thus: 'I am the owner of my kamma, the heir of my kamma; I have kamma as my origin, kamma as my relative, kamma as my resort; I will be the heir of whatever kamma, good or bad, that I do" (A III 72; translation by Bodhi [2012, 686]). See also Buai Siwaphruek 2496, 273; Sujarit Thawonsuk 2507, 291.
46. Buai Siwaphruek 2496, 272, see also p. 221; Bunruean 2528, 28, 33, 35.
47. Buai Siwaphruek 2496, 264–65.
48. For Mae Chi Phimpha see, e.g., Phimpha 2553, 30, 66, 96–98.
49. Damrongthammasan 2559, 64.
50. See, e.g., Anālayo 2014d, 114–15.
51. Somphong Suthinsak 2537, 95
52. Suniwan Tangphaithunsakun 2549, 219–31.
53. Thaidam 2527, 92.
54. Phakdiphuri 2554, 88.
55. *Luang Pu Fan Ācāro, Wat Pa Udomsomphon*, n.d., 290–91.
56. Suniwan Tangphaithunsakun 2549, 11, 223; Sīlaratano 2009, 227.
57. See, e.g., Mellick Cutler 1994, 15–16.
58. Payutto 2544, 26. See also Payutto 2555a, 7–14.

59. Payutto 2555a, 11.

60. Appleton 2011, 43–47. See also Walters 1995, 117.

61. The following accounts contain interesting similarities to the more recent stories of *mae chi*s presented by Lindberg Falk (2007, 55–80).

62. Damrongthammasan 2559, 68.

63. See Supreme Court of Thailand (*San dika*), case number 384, 2480 BE, 375–80.

64. Prasop Pasāro and Khunying Yai Damrongthammasan 2527, 4.

65. See Seeger 2014a, 161.

66. See, e.g., Phimpha 2553, 23; Suniwan Tangphaithunsakun 2549, 29.

67. Thaidam 2527, 89–90. See also chapter 2.

68. It is not yet clear to me why exactly Khunying Yai was sued for insolvency as she must have owned considerable wealth during that time, despite she and her husband already having divided up their wealth.

69. Supreme Court of Thailand 2480, 377. The Laws on Husbands and Wives were operative until 1935 and then replaced by the Civil and Commercial Code (*Kotmai phaeng lae phanit*). As Khunying Yai was ordained as a *mae chi* in 1933, the former were applied.

70. Supreme Court of Thailand 2480, 377–78.

71. Jaturon Chumchumpu 2557, 16–19; Mali Phruekphongsawali 2552, 190; Darunee Tantiwiramanond, 1997, 173. In the Laws on Husbands and Wives, there are further inequalities between the genders (see, e.g., Mali Phruekphongsawali 2552; Loos 2006, 130–54).

72. Phimpha 2553, 27.

73. *Lok ni lok ha dai* 2550, 8.

74. Ibid., 9.

75. Thaidam 2527, 89. See also chapter 2.

76. *Khun Yai Chi Soda Sosut* 2552, 2–3.

77. For the following account, I depended on Mahawichian et al 2553 and Mae Chi Bunmi's cremation volume, in addition to the interviews I conducted with her, in particular the interview on September 2, 2012.

78. Mahawichian et al 2553, ข.

79. See also "Mistaken Belief in Sainthood: The Case of Mae Chi Tat" in chapter 3.

80. Mahawichian et al. 2553, 251–52.

81. Interview with Mae Chi Bunmi Wetchasan, September 2, 2012.

82. Age restrictions for women who wish to become ordained as a *mae chi* seem to have existed for a long time in Thailand, at least in some monastic communities. The French Jesuit missionary Nicolas Gervaise, who visited Siam in 1683, reports that "since [*mae chis*] frequently have dealings with the monks, they are not permitted to become nuns before the age of fifty, so as to avoid all occasion for scandal" (cited in Skilling 1995, 57). A few years later, the French diplomat Simon de la Loubère visited Siam in 1687–88. He noted that "the *Siameses* do think that the advanced Age of all these Women, for there are none young, is a sufficient caution of [the monks'] Chastity" (cited in Skilling 1995, 58).

83. Depending on the context, the Thai word"*phet* may be translated as "sex," "gender," or "sexuality" but "is an exceptionally rich and productive notion in Thai"

that is often not easy to translate because of its many "diverse nuances" (Cook and Jackson 1999, 4).

84. *Chiwaprawat khong Ubasika Nu-nueang* 2511, 3–4. Compare with Muecke 2004.

85. Interview with Mae Chi Suni Saensasom on August 6, 2012.

86. Kamala Tiyavanich 1997, 79. See also Seeger 2014b, 62–65.

87. Prachumphon Jaksurak, n.d., 21.

88. Ibid., 10.

89. Ibid., p. 31.

90. Ibid., pp. 46–47. In her autobiography, Mae Chi Phimpha (2553, 48–50) gives an account of her fears of being raped or even killed by "a very vicious" man when she was living in a monastery within only two other *mae chi*s but no monks, novices, or other male monastics.

91. *Chiwaprawat khong Ubasika Nu-nueang* 2511, 5.

92. Interview with Mae Chi Bunmi, July 28, 2012, and September 2, 2012.

93. Mahawichian (Jinavaṁso) et al. 2553, 262.

94. Interview with Mae Chi Bunmi, July 28, 2012, and September 2, 2012; see also Mahawichian et al. 2553, 260–61.

95. See Giustarini 2012. Compare in particular with the *Bhayabherava-sutta* (M I 16–24) of the *Majjhima-nikāya*. Similarly, in her autobiography, Mae Chi Phimpha (2553, 57) describes how her practice in wilderness or in cemeteries was in order to face the fear of tigers.

96. Phimpha 2553, 70–72. This, as did many other episodes in Mae Chi Phimpha's life, actually took place on the Laotian side of the Mekong River, not far from Vientiane. At the time, people could quite easily cross the border.

97. Interview with Mae Chi Bunma Wetchasan, July 28, 2012 and September 2, 2012.

98. *Chiwaprawat khong Ubasika Nu-nueang* 2511, 2–3.

99. Phimpha 2553, 84–85.

100. Ibid., 75.

101. Giustarini 2012, 513n1.

102. Ibid., 512.

103. Suthep Phongphianchop 2554, 17.

104. Ibid., 11.

105. In Phimpha 2553, 7, *Kham nam* [foreword]. See also the foreword in Mae Chi Phimpha's cremation volume written by Phra Athikanphaibun Kovilo: Mae Chi Phimpha "can be a good example for all women who are interested in the practice of the *dhamma*" (Phimpha 2553, *Kham nam* [foreword]).

106. In Phimpha 2553, 8, *Kham nam* [foreword]. At the time he wrote this he was still a layperson by the name of Pramot Santayakon.

107. "Points to Ponder 3," *Dhamma* talk in Thai by Phra Ajan Inthawai Santussako, CD-ROM.

108. S II 236. See Bodhi 2000, 689.

109. It is clear that this topic would require a much more detailed investigation that also considers the importance of role models for Thai *bhikkhus*.

110. O'Connor 1978, 67.

Conclusion

1. Arai 1999, 107.
2. See also Sīlaratano 2009, 16.
3. According to Tambiah (1984), modern monastic biographies of Thai saints take the paradigmatic life of the Buddha as a model. Kamala (1997, 11), however, maintains that "these texts are diverse; they do not follow the paradigm of the Buddha's life and in fact appear to have no common denominator." See also Saipan Puriwanchana 2555.
4. Many believe that Khruba Siwichai was a *bodhisatta* (*buddha*-to-be) and therefore per definition not an *ariya-puggala* (see chapter 3). For a list of themes that are "typical" of Buddhist saints see Ray 1994, 80–96.
5. See, e.g., Keyes 1982. Also, Ray (1994, 90) observed in the cases of early Indian Buddhist saints that "it is often through receiving the darśan ["seeing"] of the Buddha and other saints that prospective saints . . . are inspired to renounce the world." Similarly, Mae Chi Kaew's spiritual journey was triggered by her encounter with Luang Pu Man, who through his authentic lifestyle of the archetypal (male) Buddhist renouncer inspired Mae Chi Kaew to pursue the Buddhist spiritual path.
6. Here it is interesting to note that the Thai historian Nidhi Eoseewong (1940–) reports that when he was young he "met at various places a number of elderly women [*khun yai khun pa khun na*] who claimed to be experts in Abhidhamma [studies] and frequently gave teachings on the mind, mental factors [*cetasika*], mind processes and so forth . . . without having had to open a textbook . . . [these women, who were contemporaries of Khunying Yai] did not belong to a higher social class but were all from the lower middle-class. Even though they had an urban background and were able to read and write, their economic status was not very good. However, they were able to find sufficient time to study what they were interested in. One of these women was even unable to read but, following ancient methods of learning, she obtained [her knowledge] through memorization" (Nidhi Eoseewong 2560, 30).
7. Sponberg 1992, 8, 12; compare with Cook 2009, 359–62.
8. Gabaude 2003a, 114.
9. *Chiwaprawat khong Ubasika Nu-nueang* 2511, 15.
10. See, e.g., Sharf 1995.
11. In addition to the women discussed in this book, see also the biographies of Mae Chi Thongsuk Samdaengpan (1900–63) and Mae Chi Chandra Khonnokyoong (mentioned in chapter 4). Both were students of the famous meditation master Luang Pho Sot Candasaro, founder of the Dhammakāya meditation school, and became themselves highly respected meditation masters with numerous students (see Singhon 2546, 176–204).
12. See the examples given in the introduction and chapter 4.

Glossary

Thai (T), Pali (P), and Sanskrit (Skt) terms.

Abhidhamma (P). The higher dhamma; the analytical teaching of the Pali canon; one of the three main divisions of the Pali canon.

abhiññā (P). Higher knowledge; super-knowledge; the six abhiññās are supernatural powers, divine ear, ability to read another's mind, recollection of former lives, divine eye, and knowledge of the ending of mental intoxicants.

acinteyya (P). Inconceivable; unthinkable.

ajan (T, P *ācariya*). Teacher; instructor; often used before a name in order to express respect.

anāgāmī (P). "Nonreturner"; someone who has achieved the third stage of awakening.

anattā (P). Not-self/no-self or nonself; Buddhist teaching that rejects the idea of a permanent self.

arahant/arahat (P, T *phra arahan*). A worthy one; a perfect person; a fully awakened Buddhist saint; one who has realized *nibbana* and is no longer subject to rebirth; Skt *arhat*.

ariya (P, T). noble; noble person; those who have attained levels of awakening; often used with other words, such as *ariyasong* (T "[member of] the noble *saṅgha*," P *ariya-saṅgha*) or *ariya-magga* (P "noble path"); see *ariya-puggala*.

ariya-puggala (P). Noble person; person who has achieved one of the four stages of awakening.

athitthan (T). To make a solemn wish; to set one's mind on what one considers sacred with the aim of obtaining a specific result.

aṭṭhi (P, T *atthi*). A bone; bones.

Ayutthaya (T). The kingdom of Ayutthaya was a Siamese kingdom from 1351 to1767.

bhāvanā (P). Mental development; Buddhist meditation.

bhikkhu (P). A fully ordained monk.

bhikkhunī (P). A fully ordained nun.

bodhisatta (P). A being intent on buddhahood; a future buddha; buddha-to-be; Skt *bodhisattva.*

brahma (P). A divine being; a god of the higher heavens.

brahmacariya (P). Holy life; often used to refer to the monastic life; celibacy.

buat (T). To go forth; to be ordained.

bun (T, P *puñña*). Merit; meritorious (deeds).

cetasika (P). Mental factors; in the Abhidhamma compendium *Abhidhammatthasaṅgaha* there are fifty-two *cetasika*s mentioned.

cetiya (P, T *jedi*). A shrine; memorial.

desanā (P). Sermon; teaching; instruction.

dhamma (P, T *thamma* or *tham*). The teachings of the Buddha; the Truth; nature; Skt *dharma.*

dhammavinaya (P). The teaching (*dhamma*) and monastic regulations (*vinaya*) of the Buddha; see also *dhamma* and *vinaya.*

Dhammayuttika-nikāya (P, T Thammayut). One of the two major Thai Buddhist monastic congregations, founded by Prince Mongkut during the time he was a monk (1824–51) before he became King Rama IV in 1851. The other congregation is called Mahānikāya; the vast majority of Thai monks belong to the Mahānikāya congregation.

dhātu (P, T *that*). Element; relic, in particular of a buddha or an arahant.

dhutaṅga (P). See *thudong.*

dukkha (P). Unsatisfactoriness; one of the three marks of existence.

etadagga (P). Foremost; the state of being regarded as the best of one's class or type.

garudhamma (P). "Weighty principle"; the eight *garudhamma*s (*aṭṭha garudhammā*) are a special set of rules/conditions that *bhikkhunī*s must adhere to. The Buddha gave permission for women to become fully ordained nuns (*bhikkhunī*) provided that they accepted the eight *garudhamma*s as conditions.

jhāna (P). Meditative absorption.

kamma (P). "Action"; "deed"; volitional action that can have pleasant or unpleasant results which are experienced in the current or a future life; Skt *karma.*

khandha (P). Aggregate; constituents of personhood; there are five aggregates in Buddhist teaching: material form (*rūpa*), feeling (*vedanā*), perception/cognition (*saññā*), volitional activities/mental formations (*saṅkhāra*), and consciousness (*viññāṇa*).

khīṇāsava (P). One whose corruptions are destroyed; one whose mind is free from mental defilements; an arahant.

Khruba (T). "Teacher"; put before the name of a monk in order to express respect (commonly used in the North and Northeast of Thailand).

Khun (T). Placed in front of the first name or appellative of a person in order to express respect or politeness.

kilesa (P). Mental defilements; impurities.

klot (T). A special, large umbrella with a mosquito net attached, used by monks when they are living and practicing meditation in the forest or in cemeteries.

kuṭī (P). Monastic cell/dwelling; lodging of a monastic, in most cases of monks and novices.

Luang Pho (T). "Venerable Father"; put before the name of a monk in order to express respect.

Luang Pu (T). "Venerable Grandfather"; put before the name of a monk in order to express respect.

Luang Ta (T). "Venerable Grandfather"; put before the name of a monk in order to express respect.

mae chi (T). Women who shave their hair, keep either the eight or ten Buddhist precepts, and wear white robes; *mae* is "mother" in Thai.

mahā (P). Great; big; often used in compounds.

Mahānikāya (P, T Mahanikai). One of the two major Thai Buddhist monastic congregations. The other congregation is called "Dhammayuttika-nikāya"; the vast majority of Thai monks belong to the Mahānikāya congregation.

nak buat (T). One who is ordained.

nak tham (T). One who is learned in the Buddhist teaching; someone who has passed the Thai ecclesiastical exams of *dhamma* studies; there are three levels of *nak tham*.

nibbāna (P, T *phra nipphan*). The extinction of greed, anger, and ignorance; escape from *dukkha* and future rebirth; the ultimate goal of Buddhist soteriology; Skt *nirvāṇa*.

nimit (T, P *nimitta*). Mental image; sign.

nirodha-samāpatti (P). "Attainment of cessation"; possible only for *anāgāmī*s and arahants; also known as *saññāvedayita-nirodha*, the cessation of perception and feeling.

pacceka-buddha (P). A buddha who discovered the truth by himself but does not teach it; a silent buddha; private buddha.

Pali. The Indic language in which the sacred texts of Theravada Buddhism have been preserved; regarded as a sacred language in Theravada Buddhism.

paññā (P). Wisdom.

pāpa (P, T *bap*). Evil; bad; demeritorious.

pārājika (P). The most serious class of monastic rules; for *bhikkhus* there are four of these rules; when breached, the monk who did so is no longer a fully ordained monk.

paramattha-sacca (P). Ultimate truth; absolute truth.

paritta (P). "Protection"; protective (Pali) chants.

pariyatti (P). Study of the scriptures.

patihan (T, P *pāṭihāriya*). Miracle, wonder.

pāṭimokkha (P). Code of monastic rules; collection of the fundamental monastic rules; for *bhikkhus* there 227 rules, for *bhikkhunīs* there are 311 rules.

paṭipatti (P). The practice of the Buddha's teaching, including the practice of meditation.

phi (T). ghost, spirit; the dead, deceased.

phra (T). A monk; a Buddha image; prefix word placed before words referring to the Buddha, divinities, ranks of nobility, ecclesiastical titles, sacred places and things, places and things associated with royalty, etc.; also used when referring to amulets.

phra that (T). Transmogrified relics.

piṇḍapāta (P). Collection of alms.

pluk sek (T). To consecrate; to sacralize; to bless; to endow with supernatural powers.

pūjā (P). Veneration; worship.

puthujjana (P). Ordinary person; worldling; someone who has not attained levels of awakening.

sakadāgāmī (P). "Once-returner"; someone who has achieved the second level of awakening.

saksit (T). Sacred, holy.

sala (T). Pavilion; hall.

samādhi (P). Concentration.

samanasak (T). Ecclesiastical rank.

sāmaṇerī (P). Female novice.

sammāsambuddha (P). A buddha who discovered the truth by himself and teaches the truth to others.

sammuti-sacca (P). Conventional truth.

samnak (T). In this book, a monastic residence that is not officially registered as a monastery (*wat*) and does not have an ordination hall

saṃsāra (P). Cycle of birth, aging, death, and rebirth.

saṃyojana (P). The fetters that bind men to the cycle of rebirth; there are altogether ten of these fetters.

saṅgha (P). Buddhist monastic community.

saṅgha-rāja (P). Supreme patriarch.

saññā (P). Perception; cognition.

sāsana (P, T *satsana*). Teaching; religion.

sati (P, T). Mindfulness; awareness.

sikkhamat (T). "Studying mother"; "mother who trains herself."

sīla (P). Moral conduct.

sotāpanna (P). "Stream-enterer"; someone who has attained the first level of awakening.

stūpa (Skt, P *thūpa*). Sacred monument erected to contain the relics of a Buddhist saint.

suat mon (T). To recite/chant the Buddha's teaching or Pali texts.

sukha (P). Happiness.

sutta (P). A discourse; sermon text believed to have been given by the Buddha.

taṇhā (P). Craving; thirst; the root cause of why beings are subject to rebirth.

thudong (T, P *dhutaṅga*). Austere practices; in Theravada Buddhism there are altogether thirteen of these practices that include dwelling in a charnel ground, eating from one's alms bowl and dwelling at the root of a tree.

Tipiṭaka (P, T *phra bali* or *phra traipidok*). The Pali canon; the most sacred scriptures of Theravada Buddhism.

Triple Gem. The Buddha, the *dhamma*, and the *saṅgha*.

upāsikā (P, T *ubasika*). Female devotee; female practitioner; female lay follower.

vinaya (P, T *winai* or *phra winai*). Monastic discipline.

vinayapiṭaka (P). The first of the three divisions of the Pali canon; the *vinayapiṭaka* contains the monastic rules for monks and nuns.

vipassanā (P). Insight meditation.

vipassanūpakilesa (P). Imperfections/defilements of *vipassanā* meditation.

wai (T). To greet someone by raising one's hands, pressed together in a prayer-like fashion.

wan phra (T). The Buddhist holy day; Buddhist observance day.

wat (T). Monastery.

References

Cremation Volumes

Cremation volume of Ajan Naeb Mahaniranon. 2526. *Anuson* [In remembrance]. Wat Makutkasatriyaram, December 14. Bangkok: Thanetwon.

Cremation volume of Upāsikā Jan Thomanakon. 2508. *Khandhavibhajana and Gahaṭṭhaka-sutta*. Translated and compiled by Somdet Phra Buddhaghosacariya Ñāṇavarathera. Wat Thepsirintharawat, April 24. Bangkok: Mahawitthayalai Mahamakut Ratchawitthayalai Press.

Cremation volume of Khun Mae Thang Khotchasut. 2477. *Ovāda-pāṭimokkha Gāthā*. By Somdet Phra Mahawirawong Sanghanayok. Wat Sattanatpariwat, Ratchaburi, November 25. Bangkok: Mahawitthayalai Mahamakut Ratchawitthayalai.

Cremation volume of Khunying Damrongthammasan. 2489. *Paṭipattivibhajana by Khunying Damrongthammasan (Yai Wisetsiri)*. October 12. Published by Prasop Wisetsiri.

Cremation volume of Luang Ta Mahabua. 2554. *Yanasampannathammanuson*. Bangkok: Siriwattha Inter.

Cremation volume of Mae Bunruean Tongbuntoem. 2507. *Khun Mae Bunruean Tongbuntoem anuson* [In memory of Khun Mae Bunruean Tongbuntoem]. Wat That Thong, October 25. Bangkok: Khana samakkhiwisutthi lae phu ruam ngan bun nai adit [Samakkhiwisutthi group and former co-merit-makers].

Cremation volume of Mae Chi Bunmi Wetchasan. 2559. Accessed at Wat Samphanthawong, Bangkok.

Cremation volume of Noi Paurohitya (1). 2474. *Aṭṭhadhammapañha: Phutthamamaka pen phu top Phra Jao Boromwongthoe Krom Muen Wiwitwanpricha song tatsin* [Eight questions on the dhamma: Buddhists gave answers, Prince Wiwitwanpricha decides (who gave the best answers)]. November 26. Phra Nakhon: Rongphim Phra Jan Tha Phra Jan.

Cremation volume of Noi Paurohitya (2). 2474. *Mahāsatipaṭṭhāna-sutta and Girimānanda-sutta*. Translated by Somdet Phra Buddhaghosacariya. November 26. Phra Nakhon: Rongphim Lahu-thot.

Cremation volume of Noi Paurohitya [Sithammarat] (3). 2474. *Shiba Luohan* [Chinese characters], *Jap poi lo han* [Thai transliteration; The eighteen arahants]. November 24. Bangkok: Thai Khasem.

Cremation volume of Pacha Siriworasan. 2526. *Putcha wisatchana wa duai kan patibat tham* [Questions and answers on Buddhist practice]. November 12.

Cremation volume of Phra Thepkhunathan (Phon Jinaputto). 2514. *Prachum phra niphon kiao kap tamnan thang phra phutthasatsana khong Somdet Phra Jao Boromwongthoe Krom Phraya Damrong Rajanubhab* [Compilation of Writings on Buddhist History by Prince Damrong Rajanubhab]. Wat Phra Phiren, March 21. Phra Nakhon: Rungruean Tham.

Sources in Thai

Amaradevo Bhikkhu. 2550. *Phra that: "Mahatsajan haeng phra phutthasatsana"* [Phra that: "Marvelous things of Buddhism"]. Chiang Mai: Wat Santitham.

Apinya Feungfusakul. 2544. "Phiksuni: Khati rue akhati [Bhikkhunīs: Tradition or prejudices?], Bhikkhuni: The controversial issue." Transcription of a lecture on February 7. Part 1 of 2. Midnight University's Buddhism Religion Issue. http://v1.midnightuniv.org/finearts2544/newpage1.html.

"Aramphabot" [Introduction]. 2552. *Dhammānudhammapaṭipatti* [Practice in perfect conformity with the dhamma]. Noppharat Printing House.

Ariyasawika Khun Mae Chi Kaew Sianglam / Ariyaka savika Ven. Khun Mae Chi Kaew. 2551. Khon Kaen: Khana sityanusit Mae Chi Kaew Sianglam.

Beatrice Bhadrayuvadi, Princess. 2517. *Nangsue phra niphon lae banthuek thammathetsana* [Writings and recordings of dhamma sermons]. 4th imprint. Bangkok: Buntham Suntharawathi.

Bua Ñāṇasampanno, Phra Maha. 2541. *Prawat than Phra Ajan Man Phurithatta Thera* [The biography of Venerable Ajan Man Bhūridatta Thera]. Bangkok: Chuan Phim.

Buai Siwaphruek, compiler and ed. 2496. *Prawat Phra Phuttho Yai Phra Phuttho Noi: Ubasika Bunruean Tongbuntoem* [The history of Phra Phuttho Yai and Phra Phuttho Noi: Upāsikā Mae Bunruean Tongbuntoem]. Bangkok: Mahawitthayalai Mahamakut Ratchawitthayalai.

Buddhadāsa Bhikkhu. 2537. *Lak tham samrap nak sueksa* [Buddhist principles for students]. Bangkok: Thammasapha.

——— [Buddhadāsa Indapañño]. 2554. "Somdet nai khwamrusuek khong kha pha jao" [Somdet in my feeling]. In *Pramuan kiatikhun Somdet Phra Phutthakhosajan Jaroen Yanawaro* [In honor of Somdet Phra Buddhaghosacariya Jaroen Ñāṇavaro], edited by Thirachai Thongthammachat, 118–48. Chon Buri: Yuwaphutthikasamakhom Chon Buri.

Buddhaghosacariya, Somdet Phra, trans. 2474a. *Dhammacakkappavattana-sutta and Mettānisa-sutta*. Phra Nakhon: Rongphim Lahu-thot.

———, trans. 2474b. "Mahāsatipaṭṭhāna-sutta and Girimānanda-sutta." Cremation volume of Noi Paurohitya (2). November 26. Phra Nakhon: Rongphim Lahu-thot.

———. 2481. *Khamtham khamtop sin samathi panya* [Questions and answers about sīla, samādhi, and paññā]. Bangkok: Mahawitthayalai Mahamakut Ratchawitthayalai.

———. 2522. *Uposathasīla*. 14th imprint. Bangkok: Mahawitthayalai Mahamakut Ratchawitthayalai.

———. 2558. *Somdet Phra Phutthakhosajan: Thi raluek nai kan bamphen kuson uthit thawai Somdet Phra Phutthakhosajan (Yanawaramahathera) lae adit jao awat Wat Thepsirintharawat thuk rup wan jan thi 8 mithunayon phutthasakarat 2558 pi thi 64* [Souvenir for the merit-making ceremony dedicated to Somdet Phra Buddhaghosacariya (Ñāṇavaramahāthera) and all the other abbots of Wat Thepsirin on Monday, June 8, 2015, year 64]. Bangkok: Thammasapha.

Bunlong Thamkhamfu, comp. 2549. *Prawat Luang Pho Kasem Khemako* [The history of Luang Pho Kasem Khemako]. Bangkok: Khunthongdi.

Bunruean Tongbuntoem, Mae. 2528. *Samakkhikatha*. 3rd imprint.

Channarong Boonnoon. 2545. "Khwamsamkhan khong phra winai nai prawattisat phutthasatsana therawat: Jak sangkhayana thi 1 thueng thammanantha samaneri [The importance of the *vinaya* in the history of Theravada Buddhism: From the first rehearsal to Sāmaṇerī Dhammanandā]." *Chulalongkorn University Journal of Buddhist Studies* 9 (2): 7–30.

———. 2547a. "Kanbuat phiksuni nai sangkhom thai [The ordination of *bhikkhunīs* in Thai Society]." *Chulalongkorn University Journal of Buddhist Studies* 11 (2): 81–96.

———. 2547b. "Kansangkhayana nai mummong mai: Honthang su kankae panha khong khana song thai patjuban [New perspectives on the rehearsals: Ways to solving problems of the contemporary Thai saṅgha]." In *Khwam riang mai ruesang pratya tawanok* [New essays on the reconstructing of eastern philosophy], edited by Suwanna Satha-anand, 1–78. Bangkok: Chulalongkorn University Press.

———. 2551. *Phra song Thai nai anakhot bot samruat bueang ton wa duai khwam plianplaeng* [The Thai saṅgha in the future: A preliminary survey on change]. Bangkok: Sirindhorn Anthropology Centre.

Chao Asok. 2529. *Kotrabiap khong chao asok* [Regulations of the Asok people]. Bangkok: Thammasanti Foundation.

Chiwit lae ngan Luang Ta Sawai Siwayano haeng Suan Mokphalaram [The life and work of Luang Ta Sawai Sivañāṇo of Suan Mokkh]. 2540. Bangkok: Khana Sityanusit Luang Ta Siva.

Damrong Rajanubhab, Krom Phraya. 2514. "Prachum phra niphon kiao kap tamnan phra Phutthasatsana" [Collected writings on Buddhist history]. Cremation volume on the occasion of the royally sponsored cremation of Phra Thepkhunathan (Phon Jinaputto). Phra Nakhon: Rungruean Tham.

Damrongthammasan, Khunying Yai. 2474. "*Aṭṭhadhammapañha*" [Essays on eight questions on the dhamma]. In cremation volume of Noi Paurohitya (1), 1–10.

———. 2559. *Damrongtham*. Edited by Martin Seeger and Naris Charaschanyawong. Bangkok: Thammasapa.

[Damrongthammasan, Khunying Yai]. 2475a. *Patipattiwiphak wa duai khamtham khamtop thammapatibat* [Paṭipattivibhāga on questions and answers about the practice of the dhamma]. Phra Nakhon: Rongphim Phra Jan.

———. 2475b. *Patipattinithet wa duai khwampatipatti thang phra phutthasatsana* [Paṭipattinidesa on the Buddhist practice]. Phra Nakhon: Rongphim Phra Jan.

———. 2476a. *Patipattiwiphang wa duai khwampatipatti thang phra phutthasatsana* [Paṭipattivibhaṅga on the Buddhist practice]. Phra Nakhon: Rongphim Phra Jan.

———. 2476b. *Nangsue patipatti putcha wisatchana* [Paṭipattipucchā-vissajjanā]. Phra Nakhon: Rongphim Sophonphiphanthanakon.

———. 2477. *Patipattiwiphat wa duai khwam patibat* [*Paṭipattivibhajana* on the Buddhist practice]. [Bangkok].

Dhammadāna Foundation. 2544. *Thammasom thammamata* [Thammamata dhamma hermitage]. Bangkok: Fa Aphai.

Dhammanandā. 2546. *Phiksuni . . . buat mai dai: Watthakam thi kamlang mokha* [Bhikkhunīs . . . can't be ordained: The discourse that is becoming void]. Bangkok: Sukhaphapjai.

Dhamma practice center [anon.]. n.d. "Khwam pen ma khong samaneri nai samnak patibat tham . . ." [History of the *sāmaṇerīs* of the dhamma practice center . . .]. Loose-leaf informational handouts.

Duai det phra metta [Through the power of loving-kindness]. n.d. Bangkok: Khana sattha lae sityanusit Mae Chi Kaew Sianglam.

Duan Kamdee. 2551. "Kan rue fuen phiksuni song khong fai therawat [The revival of the Theravada bhikkhunī-saṅgha]." *Chulalongkorn University Journal of Buddhist Studies* 15 (3): 5–79.

Dunlayaphaksuwaman, Phra. 2554. "Somdet upatcha" [Somdet: My preceptor]. In *Pramuan kiatikhun Somdet Phra Phutthakhosajan Jaroen Yanawaro* [In honor of Somdet Phra Buddhaghosacariya Jaroen Ñāṇavaro], edited by Thirachai Thongthammachat, 12–36. Chon Buri: Yuwaphutthikasamakhom Chon Buri.

Jak jai [From the heart]. [2555?]. Munlanithi Khun Mae Dr. Siri Krinchai.

Jaturon Chumchumpu. 2557. "Khwamsamphan thang sapsin rawang sami phanraya lae kantokthot sapsin khong phra phiksu" [The property relations between husband and wife and the inheritance of monks' property]. Master's thesis, National Institute of Development Administration.

Kaset Noithip. 2550. "Mahatsajan Jatukhamramathep: Super braen haeng sattha dan ut phra khrueang thalu 3 muen lan" [The miraculous Jatukhamramathep amulet: Super brand of faith pushes the amulet industry above 30 billion baht]. *Matichon Weekly*, May 4–10 (issue 1394), 26.

Khun Yai Chi Soda Sosut. 2552. Khon Kaen: Khana sityanusit Mae Chi Soda Sosut.

Kritsana Raksachom, Mae Chi, and Martin Seeger. 2556. "Mae chi kap saphap panha lae okat nai kan khau thueng udomsueksa thi jat doi khana song thai" [Mae chis' access to higher monastic education in Thailand]. *Chulalongkorn University Journal of Buddhist Studies* 20 (2): 59–89.

Kulavir Prapapornpipat. 2548. "Kan to su khong phiksuni song therawat: Jak Si Lanka su Thai" [The fight of the Theravada bhikkhunī-saṅgha: From Sri Lanka to Thailand]. *Chulalongkorn University Journal of Buddhist Studies* 12 (2): 28–41.

Laddawan Tamafu. 2548. "Mae chi: Lok khong phuying thi thuk luem" [Mae chi: The forgotten world of women]. MA thesis, Chiang Mai University.

———. 2549. "Mae chi: Lok khong phuying thi thuk luem" [Mae chi: The forgotten world of women]. *Chiang Mai University Journal of Social Sciences* 18 (1): 104–31.

Lok ni lok ha dai [This world is a world that can be found]. 2550. 6th imprint. Bangkok: Khana sityanusit Mae Chi Kaew Sianglam.

Luang Pu Fan Ācāro, Wat Pa Udomsomphon, Amphoe Phannanikhom, Jangwat Sakon Nakhon. n.d. Buraphajan Book Project 11. http://www.watmaheyong.net/_books/burapa-11.pdf

Mahahansa Dhammahāso, Phra. 2548. "Kharuehat kap kan banlu phra arahattaphon" [Laypeople and the attainment of arahantship]. Online publication. http://www.mcu.ac.th/site/articlecontent_desc.php?article_id=401&articlegroup_id=101.

Mahanirut, Phra (Ṭhitasaṁvaro). 2552. *Khumue samanasak phatyot: Chabap sombun* [Handbook of the ecclesiastical titles and Fans: Complete edition]. Bangkok: Thongtham.

Maharatchamangkhalajan, Phra. 2507. "Bunruean anuson" [In memory of Mae Bunruean]. In *Prawat thamma Khun Mae Bunruean Tongbuntoem* [The life and dhamma of Khun Mae Bunruean Tongbuntoem], edited by Sujarit Thawonsuk.

Mahawichian, Phra (Jinavaṁso), Nuansiri Woramethawiwat, and Panuttacha Bunnak. 2553. *Phawanatham* [Bhāvanā-dhamma]. 2nd imprint. Bangkok: Students of the Vipassanā-Kammaṭṭhāna Group of Samakkhi Mi Bun Building at Wat Samphanthawong.

Mali Phruekphongsawali. 2552. *Yon roi sitthi khwampenkhon khong phuying* [A historical study of human rights of women]. Bangkok: National Human Rights Commission of Thailand.

Manop Nakkanrian. 2545. *Phra phutthasatsana kap satri sueksa* [Buddhism and women's studies]. Bangkok: Mahachulalongkorn University.

Matichon Dictionary of the Thai Language. 2547. Bangkok: Matichon.

Monastic Community of Wat Samphanthawong. 2553. *Chalong ayu watthana mongkhon 93 pi Somdet Phra Mahawirawong* [Celebrating the auspicious 93th birthday of Somdet Phra Mahawirawong]. Bangkok: Tumdee Team.

Montri Suepduang. 2551. "Naew phinit satri niyom wa duai phuying kap phra Phutthasatsana nai prathet Thai / Feminist Perspectives on Women and Theravada Buddhism in Thailand." PhD diss., Mahachulalongkornrajavidyalaya University, Bangkok.

Nathathai Chattinawat, Mae Chi. 2552. "Sathanaphap mae chi: Korani sueksa mae chi Wat Pak Nam Phasi Jaroen Krungthep" [The status of mae chis: A case study of the mae chis at Wat Pak Nam Phasi Jaroen, Bangkok]. MA thesis, Thammasat University.

Narin Phasit. (2472) 2544. *Thalaengkan rueang samaneri* [Official statement on the *sāmaṇerī*]. Reprint of the first edition. Bangkok: Amarin Printing.

Narirat Whiphat. 2554. *Phiksuni—mae chi: Senthang banlu tham jak samai phutthakan thueng patjuban* [Bhikkhunī—mae chi: The way of achieving the supramundane from the time of the Buddha to the present]. Nonthaburi: Amarin.

Nattha Kamonrattanakun. 2554. *Luang Ta Mahabua Yanasampanno: Chabap katun* [Luang Ta Mahabua Ñāṇasampanno: Cartoon edition]. Bangkok: Action Frame.

Natthapat Janthawit. 2539. *Phra borommasaririkathat* [The relics of the Buddha]. Bangkok: Amarin.

Nidhi Eoseewong. 2545. *Wa duai phet: khwam khit tua ton lae akhati thang phet phuying ke phet sueksa lae kamarom* [On gender: Ideas, self, and prejudices about gender, women, gays, gender studies, and libido]. Bangkok: Matichon.

———. 2549. *Mahawitthayalai thiang khuen* [Midnight University]. Bangkok: Matichon.

———. 2560. "Watwithi nok rat" [Practices outside the state]. *Matichon Weekly*, March 10–16 (issue no. 1908), 30–31.

Niti Kasikoson. 2544. "Phra khrueang: khwamsattha nai sangkhom Thai" [Amulets: Beliefs in Thai society]. In *30 pi Thai khadi sueksa* [30 years Thai studies], 32–49. Bangkok: Thai Khadi Sueksa, Mahawitthayalai Thammasat.

Parinyayokhawibun, Luang. 2554. "Phap prathap jai" [An Impressive Image]. In *Pramuan kiatikhun Somdet Phra Phutthakhosajan Jaroen Yanawaro* [In honor of Somdet Phra Buddhaghosacariya Jaroen Ñāṇavaro], edited by Thirachai Thongthammachat. 56–59., Chon Buri: Yuwaphutthikasamakhom Chon Buri

Pathom Takhananan, 2551. *Khana song sang chat samai ratchakan thi 5* [The saṅgha and nation-building during the time of Rama V]. Bangkok: Matichon.

Payutto, Phra [Phra Dhammapiṭaka]. 2538a. *Photjananukrom phutthasat chabap pramuan sap* [Dictionary of Buddhism, lexicon edition]. 8th imprint. Bangkok: Mahawitthayalai Mahachulalongkornrajavidyalaya.

———. 2538b. *Photjananukrom phutthasat chabap pramuan tham / Dictionary of Buddhism*. 8th imprint. Bangkok: Mahawitthayalai Mahachulalongkorn-rajavidyalaya.

———. 2544. *Panha phiksuni: Bot thotsop sangkhom Thai* [The bhikkhunī problem: A test of Thai society]. 2nd imprint. Bangkok: Sukhaphapjai.

———. 2547. "Khwam hen to warasan Phutthasat sueksa" [Opinion about the Journal of Buddhist Studies]. *Chulalongkorn University Journal of Buddhist Studies* 11 (1): 63–88.

——— [Phra Brahmagunabhorn]. 2551. *Photjananukrom Phutthasat chabap pramuan sap* [Dictionary of Buddhology, lexicon edition]. 11th imprint. Bangkok: S. R. Printing.

———. 2552. *Khon Thai chai kop thao? Therawat vs. latthi ajan* [Are Thai people an elderly frog? Theravada versus the teaching of the masters]. Bangkok: Q Print Management.

———. 2554. *Top doktoe Matin: Phutthawinai thueng phiksuni* [Clarifying the questions of Dr. Martin Seeger: The Buddha's vinaya and the bhikkhunī]. 2nd imprint. Bangkok: Sahamit Print and Publishing.

———. 2555a. *Top doktoe Matin: Donthin ariyachon satri lutphon khuen nuea mahaphrom* [Clarifying the questions of Dr. Martin Seeger: Reaching the noble land, women, liberated, rise above mahabrahma]. Bangkok: Phlitham.

———. 2555b. *Phutthatham chabap prap khayai* [Buddhadhamma: Extended and amended edition]. 32nd imprint. Bangkok: Phalitham.

———. 2556. *Mueang Thai ja wikrit tha khon Thai mi sattha wiparit* [Thailand will face a crisis if Thai people have incorrect beliefs]. 14th imprint. Bangkok: Buddhadhamma Foundation.

Paisal Visalo, Phra. 2544. "Phiksuni song thanglueak thi liang mai dai [The bhikkhunī-saṅgha: The unavoidable alternative]." *Sekhiyatham*, July-September (49), 1–3.

———. 2546. *Phutthasatsana Thai nai anakhot: Naeo-nom lae thang ok jak wikrit* [Thai Buddhism in the future: Tendencies and ways out of the crisis]. Bangkok: Sitsi-Saritwong Foundation.

Phaiyon Kasi. n.d. *Photchangkhaparit phuttharit phichit rok* [Bojjhaṅga-Paritta: Buddha's Miraculous Powers Defeat Illnesses]. Bangkok: Liangchiang.

Phakdiphuri. 2554. "Khun Ya Chi Nari Karun: ariyasawika phu banlu arahan (thi thuk luem)" [Khun Ya Chi Nari Karun: The noble follower who achieved arahantship (but has been forgotten)]. *Lokthip*, December (501), 86–88.

———. 2555a. "Khun Ya Chi Nari Karun: Ariyasawika phu banlu arahan (thi thuk luem) [Khun Ya Chi Nari Karun: The noble follower who achieved arahantship (but has been forgotten)]." *Lokthip*, January (502), 51–53.

———. 2555b. "Khun Ya Chi Nari Karun: ariyasawika phu banlu arahan (thi thuk luem) [Khun Ya Chi Nari Karun: The Noble Follower who achieved arahantship (but has been forgotten)]." *Lokthip*, February (503), 38–39.

Phanom Phaetkhun. 2532. "Phra Phuttho Noi Khun Mae Bunruean Tongbuntoem." *Lan Pho*, issues 14,515–15,530.

Phanthakan Kimthong. n.d. *Phra arahan . . . mi jing: Sayam prathet mai wang jak phra arahan* [Arahants . . . exist indeed: Siam is not devoid of arahants]. Nakhon Ratchasima: Thanyaphat.

Phatharaphon Sirikanjana, 2540. "Samnak Santi Asok: Khwam pen ma lae botbat thang satsana nai sangkhom Thai" [Santi Asok: Its development and religious role in Thai society]. Research Report. Center of Buddhist Studies, Chulalongkorn University.

Phensi Makaranon. 2549. *Khun Mae Chi Kaew Sianglam: Khon khai rai sut thai* [Khun Mae Chi Kaew Sianglam: The last patient]. Bangkok: Prayunwong Printing.

Phikun Wiphatprathip, ed. 2547. *Khon* [People]. Bangkok: Plan Printing Ltd.

Phimpha Wongsa-udom. 2553. *Rueang khong Khun Mae Chi Phimpha Wongsa-udom* [The story of Khun Mae Chi Phimpha Wongsa-udom]. Reprinted as cremation volume with an additional foreword. Sri Chiang Mai: Wat Hinmakpeng.

Phisit Jansi. 2549. "Yisip pi haeng khwam sattha to Mae Bunruean Tongbuntoem" [Twenty years of belief in Khun Mae Bunruean Tongbuntoem]. *Khom Chat Luek* online, December 19. http://www.khomchadluek.net/2006/12/19/j001_75486.php?news_id=75488, accessed May 17, 2007.

Phra Ratchamethaphon khunanuson lae prawat Wat Thammikaramworawihan [In memory of Phra Ratchamethaphon and the history of Wat Thammikaramworawihan]. 2542. Khana song lae sityanusit.

Phu banlu chuai luea juea jun [The kindness of those who have attained]. 2552. Hagiography on Mae Chi Kaew Sianglam. Khon Kaen: Khana Sityanusit [of Phra Ajan Inthawai Santussako].

Pracha Pasannathammo, Phra. 2535. *Lao wai muea wai sonthaya attachiwaprawat khong Than Phutthathat* [Narrated in the twilight period of life: The autobiography of Buddhadāsa]. Bangkok: Komon Khimthong Foundation.

Prachumphon Jaksurak. n.d. *Patipatha khong Khun Yai* [The spiritual practice of Khun Yai]. Bangkok: Amon Products.

Pramuan Pengjan. 2544. "Phiksuni: Khati rue akhati" [Bhikkhunīs: Tradition or prejudices?]. Bhikkhunī: The Controversial Issue. Transcription of a joint lecture with Apinya Feungfusakul, February 7. Part 1 of 2. Midnight University's Buddhism Religion Issue. http://v1.midnightuniv.org/finearts2544/newpage1.html.

Prasok (Jamrat Duangthisan). 2554. "Phra sawok khong Phra Phutthajao" [A venerable disciple of the Buddha]. In *Pramuan kiatikhun Somdet Phra*

Phutthakhosajan Jaroen Yanawaro [In honor of Somdet Phra Buddhaghosacariya Jaroen Ñāṇavaro], edited by Thirachai Thongthammachat, 49–55. Chon Buri: Yuwaphutthikasamakhom Chon Buri.

Prasop Pasāro, Phra, and Khunying Yai Damrongthammasan. 2527. *Tat buang kam* [Cutting the kammic fetters]. Bangkok: Kanphim Phra Nakhon.

Prathum Choti-anan, Mae Chi. 2539. *Prawat chiwit khong khaphajao* [The history of my life]. Khana sit Mae Chi Prathum Choti Anan [Group of Students of Mae Chi Prathum Choti-anan].

Prawat kan sueksa khong song [Education history of the *saṅgha*]. 2527. Bangkok: Ministry of Education.

"Prawat lae ngan khong Khun Mae Bunruean Tongbuntoem 7." 2556. [The history and work of Khun Mae Bunruean Tongbuntoem, part 7]. *Pratu su tham* [Dharma gateway]. Compiled February 2556. http://www.dharma-gateway.com/ubasika/boonruen/ubasika-boonruen-08-07.htm.

Prawat Ubasika Kao Saetan [Biography of Upāsikā Kao Saetan]. 2511. Nakhon Pathom: Khana phiksu samanen lae ubasok ubasika Wat Saneha [Monastic and lay community of Wat Saneha].

Rabiebrat Pongpanith [Rabiaprat Pongpanit]. 2546. "Kanpathakan khong khwamru rawang pitathipatai kap naksatriniyom to kansathapana phiksuni nai prathet Thai / The Discursive Contestation of Knowledge Between Patriarchy and Feminism: A Study of the Bhikkhuni Debate in Thailand." MA thesis, Thammasat University.

Ratchabanditayasathan. 2546. *Photjananukrom chabap Ratchabandityasathan* [Royal Institute dictionary]. Bangkok: Nanmeebooks.

Ratchasitthimuni, Phra, comp. 2511. *Chiwaprawat khong Ubasika Nu-nueang Thapmeng* [The biography of Upāsikā Nu-nueang Thapmeng].

Rom thamma rom phrueksa haeng pa khao suan luang: Anuson bupphajan [In the shade of the dhamma and flowers of the forest of Khao Suan Luang: In remembrance of the great teachers]. 2547. Ratchaburi: Khao Suan Luang.

Saichol Satayanurak. 2546. *Somdet Kromphraya Damrong Rajanubhab: Kansang attalak "mueang Thai" lae "chan" khong chao Sayam* [Prince Damrong Rajanubhab: Identity building of "mueang Thai" and "class" in Siam]. Bangkok: Matichon.

Saipan Puriwanchana. 2555. "Itthi patihan kap kan sang rueang lau saksit: Khanop niyom lae phonlawat nai prawat Phra Keji Ajan nai sangkhom Thai phak klang / Miracles and the Making of Sacred Narratives: Convention and Dynamism in the Life History of Phra Kechi Achan in Central Thai Society." PhD diss., Chulalongkorn University.

Saithip. 2548a. "Prasopkan lilap: Khun Mae Bunruean Tongbuntoem ubasika phu mi phalang jit mahatsajan (1)" [Mysterious Experiences: Khun Mae Bunruean Tongbuntoem, the upāsikā who possesses miraculous mind powers (1)]. *Ying Thai*, May (710). http://www.yingthai-mag.com/detail.asp?ytcolumnid=2811&ytissueid=710&ytcolcatid=2&ytauthorid=46, accessed June 22, 2007.

Saithip. 2548b. "Prasopkan lilap: Khun Mae Bunruean Tongbuntoem ubasika phu mi phalang jit mahatsajan (jop)" [Mysterious experiences: Khun Mae Bunruean Tongbuntoem, the upāsikā who possesses miraculous mind powers (end)]. *Ying Thai*, May (711). http://www.yingthai-mag.com/detail.asp?ytcolumnid=2834&ytissueid=711&ytcolcatid=2&ytauthorid=46, accessed June 22, 2007.

Sakdina Chatrakun Na Ayutthaya. 2536. *Chiwit naeo-khit lae kan to su khong Narin Klueng rue Narin Phasit: Khon khwang lok* [Life, Ideas, and Struggles of Narin Klueng or Narin Phasit: Against the world]. Bangkok: Matichon.

Sam somdet [Three somdets]. 2523. Bangkok: Sathiankoset Nakhaprathip Foundation.

Sathuean Suphasophon. 2526. "Khun Mae Bunruean: Phu song aphinya [Khun Mae Bunruean: The person who possesses abhiññās]." *Phalang nuea lok: Nittayasan thammapatibat* [Transworldly powers: Magazine of Buddhist practice], June (year 11, issue no. 17), 12–19.

Seeger, Martin, and Naris Charaschanyawong. 2556a. "Tam rueangrao khong nak patibat tham ying dot den thi thuk luem: Khunying Yai Damrongthammasan (2429–87) lae panha wa duai khwam pen jao khong phon ngan praphan choeng phut an samkhan" [Researching the biography of a forgotten, outstanding female Buddhist practitioner: Khunying Yai Damrongthammasan (1886–1944) and the question of authorship of an important Buddhist treatise]. *Sinlapawatthanatham: Art & Culture Magazine*, April, 154–69.

———. 2556b. "Phutthamamika ek u haeng yuk 2475: Khunying Yai Damrongthammasan" [Buddhamamika ek-u during the time of the 1932 Siamese revolution: Khunying Yai Damrongthammasan]. *Sinlapawatthanatham: Art & Culture Magazine*, November, 136–45.

———. 2558. "'Sammajarini' khong Wat Thepsirintharawat samai Somdet Phra Phutthakhosajan (Jaroen Yanawaro): Khwamsamkhan khong mukhapatha lae khwamsongjam nai kan sueksa thamma" [The 'sammācāriṇī' of Wat Thepsirin during the time of Somdet Phra Buddhaghosacariya (Jaroen Ñāṇavaro): The significance of orality and memory for the study of the dhamma]. *Sinlapawatthanatham: Art & Culture Magazine*, April, 152–69.

———. 2559a. "Chiwaprawat kansueksa kanpatibattham Khunying Damrongthammasan" [The life, education and dhamma practice of Khunying Damrongthammasan]." In Damrongthammasan, *Damrongtham*, 327–424.

———. 2559b. "Nangsue 'damrongtham' doi Khunying Yai Damrongthammasan (Yai Wisetsiri, pho so 2425–87): Banthoeng tham nai wichakan sanjon" [The book "Damrongtham" by Khunying Damrongthammsan (Yai Wisetsiri, 1882–1944): Dhammic joy on a research journey]. *Sinlapawatthanatham: Art & Culture Magazine*, August, 160–69.

Singhon. 2546. *Bukkhon yuk ton witcha lem 3* [The persons of the beginning period of vijjā dhammakāya, volume 3]. Bangkok: Sukhumwith Kanphim.

Sipariyattimoli, Phra. 2544. *Satri nai phra phutthasatsana* [Women in Buddhism]. Bangkok: Sukhaphapjai.

Sisak Wanliphodom. 2546. *Khwammai phra borommathat nai arayatham Sayam prathet* [The meaning of relics in the civilization of Siam]. Bangkok: Mueang Boran.

Sittha Chetawan. n.d. *Prawat Khun Mae Bunruean Tongbuntoem Wat Awutwikasitaram Bang Phlat Krungthepmahanakhon* [The life of Khun Mae Bunruean Tongbuntoem, Wat Awutwikasitaram, Bang Phlat, Bangkok].

So. Chanasongkhram. 2544. "Jamloei thang sangkhom khong mae chi Thai" [Being a defendant of society: Thai mae chis]. *Sekhiyatham*, no. 47 (January–March 2544), 6–9.

Somchai Maitree, et al. 2546. *Rai ngan wijai chabap sombun rueang kan sueksa khwam pen pai dai khong kan buat phiksuni nai prathet Thai / A Study of Feasibility of Bhikkhuni Ordination in Thailand.* Bangkok: Buddhist Studies Institute, Mahawitthayalai Mahachulalongkornrajavidyalaya.

Somphong Suthinsak, comp. 2537. *Wat Thammikaram jangwat Prajuap Khiri Khan* [The history of Wat Thammikaram in Prachuap Khiri Khan province]. Bangkok: Liang Chiang.

Sopha Onophat and Aphichat Siwirot. 2546. "Mae chi: Withi phuying tai rom ngao Phutthasatsana" [Mae chis: The way of women in the shade of Buddhism]. Thailand Research Fund.

Sujarit Thawonsuk, ed. 2507. *Prawat thamma Khun Mae Bunruean Tongbuntoem* [The life and dhamma of Khun Mae Bunruean Tongbuntoem].

Sulak Sivaraksa. 2542. *Khwam khaojai nai rueang phra rattanatrai jak mum mong So Siwarak* [Understanding the three jewels from the perspective of S. Sivaraksa]. Bangkok: Religious Committee for Development.

———. 2550. *Phra phutthasatsana nai mueang Thai thi tem pai duai khwak nam* [Buddhism in Thailand which is full of obstacles]. Bangkok: Sueksitsayam.

Sunai Setbunsang. 2534. *Udomkan thang sangkhom nai phutthasatsana tam naeo-khit khong samnak Santi Asok* [The social ideals in Buddhism according to the ideas of the Santi Asok school]. Bangkok: Fa Aphai.

Suniwan Tangphaithunsakun. 2549. "Phu nam satri chao phut kap kan phoei phrae kan patibat kammathan sueksa korani chapho Khun Mae Chi Kaew Sianglam samnak chi Ban Huai Sai amphoe Kham Cha-i jangwat Mukdahan" [The leader of female Buddhists and the dissemination of kammaṭṭhāna practice: The case study of Khun Mae Chi Kaew Sianglam mae chi residence, Ban Huai Sai, amphoe Kham Cha-i, Mukdahan province]. MA thesis, Mahidol University.

Supreme Court of Thailand (*San dika*). 2480. Case number 384, 375–80.

Suthep Phongphianchop. 2554. *Rom pho sai: Luang Pho Sangwan Khemako Wat Thung Samakkhitham* [Our Protector: Luang Pho Sangwan Khemako of Wat Thung Samakkhitham]. Samchuk: Romphosai Group.

Sutthithamrangsikhamphiramethajan, Phra (Li Dhammadharo). 2552. *Naeo thang patibat wipatsana kammatthan* [The way to practice vipassanā-kammaṭṭhāna], Bangkok: Chomrom Kanlayanatham. [available as e-book; http.//www.watconcord.org/index.php?option=com_content&view=article&id=274:-1-&catid=6:2010-12-24-05-19-10&Itemid=25.

"Sutyot watthumongkhon khong Khun Mae Bunruean Tongbuntoem" [The supreme talisman of Khun Mae Bunruean Tongbuntoem]. 2549. *Khom Chat Luek*. Online. November 20. http://www.khomchadluek.net/2006/11/20/j001_66928.php?news_id=66928, accessed May 17, 2007.

Tavivat Puntarigvivat. 2543. "Phutthasatsana kap sitthi satri" [Buddhism and Women's Rights]. *Silpakorn University Journal* 19–20 (1): 101–32.

Thai Mae Chi Institute. 2547. *Rabiap patibat Sathaban Mae Chi Thai an pen fai thurakan* [The regulations of the administration department of the Thai Mae Chi Institute]. 9th imprint. Bangkok: Thai Mae Chi Institute Foundation.

Thai Post. 2545. "Maechi kho ok kotmai [Mae chis ask for legislation]." *Sekhiyatham*, October–December (54), 12–13.

Thaidam. 2527. "Khun Ya Chi Nari Karun ayu 97 pi: Sit ek Luang Pu Man Phurithatto fai ubasika" [Khun Ya Chi Nari Karun (97 years old): A major female disciple of Luang Pu Man Bhūridatto]. *Lokthip*, July (36), 84–105.

Thammathan bucha khun: 100 pi than Ko. Khao Suan Luang [A gift of the dhamma, showing respect to goodness: 100 years of Ko. Khao Suan Luang]. 2544. Ratchaburi: Khao Suan Luang.

Thepjetiyajan, Phra (Wiriyang, Sirindharo). 2551. *Prawat Phra Ajan Man Phurithatto chabap sombun lae tai saman samnuek* [The complete edition of the biography of Phra Ajan Man Bhūridatto and with common sense]. 2nd imprint. Bangkok: Luang Pho Wiriyang Sirindharo Foundation.

Thiaranan. 2550. *Winathi banlu tham lok mai wang jak phra arahan* [The moment of attainment: Arahants do really exist]. Vol. 2. Bangkok: Krin Panyayan.

Thirachai Thongthammachat, ed. 2554. *Pramuan kiatikhun Somdet Phra Phutthakhosajan Jaroen Yanawaro* [In honor of Somdet Phra Buddhaghosacariya Jaroen Ñāṇavaro]. 2nd imprint. Chon Buri: Yuwaphutthikasamakhom Chon Buri.

Thongkham Cāruṇṇo, Luang Ta. 2552. *Ramluek wan wan* [Remembering past days]. 2nd imprint. Bangkok: Kongthun Saengtawan Wat Pathumwanaram.

Thotsaphon Bunthewaphithak, Mae Chi. 2550. *Chiwit tit kam* [Life is interlaced with kamma]. Bangkok: Smart Intercommunications.

Thotsaphon Chaiprakhong, Mae Chi. n.d. "Koet tae kam pritsana haeng kam 1" [Caused by kamma: The riddle of kamma 1]. VCD. Bangkok: Media of Medias.

Tossapol Jangpanichkul. 2548. *Phra borommasaririkkathat: Phra arahanta that* [The Buddha's relics: Relics of arahants]. 2nd imprint. Bangkok: Khomma.

———. 2553. *Phrathat phra ariyasong sawakathat yuk kueng phutthakan* [Relics of noble disciples in the era during half of the Buddhist time]. Bangkok: Komma.

Vapi Busbakara, Princess. 2522. *Banthuek thet Somdet Phra Phutthakhosajan Yanathera Wat Thepsirintharawat* [Recordings of the the dhamma sermons of Somdet Phra Buddhaghosacariya Jaroen Ñāṇavaro, Wat Thepsirin]. Phra Nakhon: Mahawitthayalai Mahamakut Ratchawitthayalai.

Vāsana, Somdet Phra Buddhaghosacariya. 2554. "Saṅghasobhaṇagāthā". In *Pramuan kiatikhun Somdet Phra Phutthakhosajan Jaroen Yanawaro* [In honor of Somdet Phra Buddhaghosacariya Jaroen Ñāṇavaro], edited by Thirachai Thongthammachat, 101–17. Chon Buri: Yuwaphutthikasamakhom Chon Buri.

Veerachart Nimanong. 2545. "Sathanaphap mae chi Thai: Panha thi ro thang ok (1)" [The status of Thai mae chis: The problem that waits for a solution (1)]. *Buddhacakra* 56 (11): 24–30.

Wachirayan, Prince Patriarch (Somdet Phra Mahasamanajao). 2537. *Thammawiphak parichet thi 2* [Dhammavibhāga: Second text]. 38th imprint. Bangkok: Mahawitthayalai Mahamakut Ratchawitthayalai.

Wanjai Chukon, Ajan Mae Chi. 2549. *Attachiwaprawat lae phon ngan: 72 pi Ajan Mae Chi Wanjai Chukon* [Autobiography and work: 72 years of Ajan Mae Chi Wanjai Chukon]. Khana sit Mae Chi Wanjai Chukon [Group of students of Mae Chi Wanjai Chukon].

Wannaphon Bunyasathit. 2553. *Jomnang haeng Sayam nai samai ratchakan thi 4 thueng ratchakan thi 6 kap krasae watthanatham tawan tok* [Ladies of the inner court in Siam during the time period between the reigns of Rama IV and Rama VI and the western cultural influences]. 3rd imprint. Bangkok: Sangsan Books.

Wirasak Jansongsaeng. 2553. *Phra Ajan Man Phurithatto: Ariyasong haeng yuk samai* [Phra Ajan Man Bhūridatto: A noble one of our era]. Bangkok: Sarakhadi.

Wirat Thiraphanmethi and Thongbai Thirananthangkun. 2546. *Khumue phra sangkhathikan* [The handbook for saṅgha administrators]. Bangkok: Sahathammik.

Wiwitwanpricha, Prince. 2524. *Phet nai hin: Maruettayukatha rue morananuson wiwitthathammothai* [Diamonds inside the stone: Verses on death or the recollection of death, Wiwitthathammothai]. Bangkok: Mahawitthayalai Mahamakut Ratchawitthayalai.

Wuthinan Jiawitthayanan. 2553. *Rueang jing an saksit: Kvet nimit patihan* [True sacred occurrences: Miraculous visions]. Nonthaburi: Think Beyond.

Sources in Western Languages

Adiele, Faith. 2004. *Meeting Faith: The Forest Journals of a Black Buddhist Nun*. New York: Norton. Reprinted in 2005 with subtitle *An Inward Odyssey*.

An, Yang-Gyu. 2005. *The Buddha's Last Days: Buddhaghosa's Commentary on the Mahāparibbāna Sutta*. Oxford: Pali Text Society.

Anālayo. 2007. "Oral Dimensions of Pali Discourses: Pericopes, other Mnemonic Techniques and the Oral Performance Context." *Canadian Journal of Buddhist Studies* 6 (3): 5–33.

———. 2008a. "The Sixfold Purity of an Arahant according to the Chabbisodhana-sutta." *Journal of Buddhist Ethics* 15:241–77.

———. 2008b. "Uttarimanussadhamma." In *Encyclopaedia of Buddhism*, edited by W. G. Weeraratne, vol. 8, no. 2, pp. 462–65. Sri Lanka: Department of Buddhist Affairs.

———. 2011. *A Comparative Study of the Majjhima-nikāya*. Vol. 2, Studies of Discourses 91 to 152, Conclusion, Abbreviations, References, Appendix. Taipei: Dharma Drum.

———. 2012. "Dabba's Self-cremation in the Saṃyukta-āgama." *Buddhist Studies Review* 29 (2): 153–74.

———. 2013. "The Legality of Bhikkhunī Ordination." *Journal of Buddhist Ethics* 20:210–333.

———. 2014a. "Defying Māra: Bhikkhunīs in the Saṃyukta-āgama." In *Women in Early Indian Buddhism: Comparative Textual Studies*, edited by A. Collett, 116–39. New York: Oxford University Press.

———. 2014b. "Outstanding Bhikkhunīs in the Ekottarika-āgama." In *Women in Early Indian Buddhism: Comparative Textual Studies*, edited by A. Collett, 97–115. New York: Oxford University Press.

———. 2014c. "On the Bhikkhunī Ordination Controversy." *Sri Lanka International Journal of Buddhist Studies* 3:1–20.

———. 2014d. "Karma and Female Birth." *Journal of Buddhist Ethics* 21:107–51.

———. 2015. "Miracle-working Nuns in the Ekottarika-āgama." *Indian International Journal of Buddhist Studies* 16:1–27.

———. 2016a. "The Going Forth of Mahāpajāpatī Gotamī in T60." *Journal of Buddhist Ethics* 23:1–31.

———. 2016b. *The Foundation History of the Nuns' Order*. Hamburg Buddhist Studies 6. Bochum: Projektverlag.

———. 2017. *Vinaya Studies*. Dharma Drum Institute of Liberal Arts Research Series 7. Taipei: Dharma Drum.

Angenendt, Arnod. 2007. *Heilige und Reliquien: Die Geschichte ihres Kultes vom frühen Christentum bis zur Gegenwart*. 2nd edition. Hamburg: Nikol.

Appleton, Naomi. 2011. "In the Footsteps of the Buddha: Women and the Bodhisatta Path in Theravāda Buddhism." *Journal of Feminist Studies in Religion* 27 (1): 33–51.

Arai, Paula. 1999. "Japanese Buddhist Nuns: Innovators for the Sake of Tradition." In *Buddhist Women Across Cultures: Realizations*, edited by Karma Lekshe Tsomo, 105–22. New York: State University of New York Press.

Barmé, Scot. 2002. *Woman, Man, Bangkok: Love, Sex, and Popular Culture in Thailand*. Lanham, MD: Rowman and Littlefield.

Battaglia, Lisa J. 2007. "Women Who Have Gone Forth: Gender and Religious Identity among Buddhist Nuns in Thailand." PhD. diss., Vanderbilt University.

———. 2014. *Women Who Have Gone Forth: Thai Buddhist Nuns and the Debate over Women's Ordination*. Saarbrücken: Scholar's Press.

———. 2015. "Becoming Bhikkhunī? Mae Chis and the Global Women's Ordination Movement." *Journal of Buddhist Ethics* 22:25–62.

Bell, Sandra. 2000. "Being Creative with Tradition: Rooting Theravāda Buddhism in Britain." *Journal of Global Buddhism* 1:1–23.

Bessey, Allan. 1990. "Women and Buddhism in Thailand: A Changing Identity For Religious Women." In *Radical Conservatism: Buddhism in the Contemporary World: Articles in Honor of Bhikkhu Buddhadasa's 84th Birthday Anniversary*, 311–45. Bangkok: Thai Inter-Religious Commission for Development and International Network of Engaged Buddhists, Sathirakoses-Nagapradipa Foundation.

de Bernon, Olivier. 1996. "Chi (jī), un mot d'origine khmère en usage dans la langue thaïe, considéré à tort comme d'origine sanskrite." *Journal of the Siam Society* 84 (1): 87–90.

Bingenheimer, Marcus. 2006. "Roushen pusa and Corpus Integrum: Whole Body Relics in Buddhism and Christianity." In *The Contribution of Buddhism to World Culture*, edited by Kalpakam Sankarnarayan, 275–99 Mumbai: Somaiya.

Blackburn, Anne M. 2010. "Buddha-Relics in the Lives of Southern Asian Polities." *Numen* 57 (3/4): 317–40.

Blackstone, Kathryn R. 2000. *Women in the Footsteps of the Buddha: Struggle for Liberation in the Therīgathā*. Delhi: Motilal Banarsidass.

Bodhi, Bhikkhu, trans. 2000. *The Connected Discourses of the Buddha: A Translation of the Saṃyutta Nikāya*. Boston: Wisdom Publications.

———. 2012. *The Numerical Discourses of the Buddha: A Translation of the Aṅguttara Nikāya*. Bristol: Pali Text Society.

Bond, George D. 1984. "The Development and Elaboration of the Arahant Ideal in the Theravada Tradition." *Journal of the American Academy of Religion* 52, no. 2 (June): 227–42.

———. 1988. "The Arahant: Sainthood in Theravāda Buddhism." In *Sainthood: Its Manifestations in World Religions*, edited by R. Kieckhefer and G. D. Bond, 140–71. Berkeley: University of California Press.

Bowie, Katherine A. 2011. "Polluted Identities: Ethnic Diversity and the Constitution of Northern Thai Beliefs on Gender." In *Southeast Asian Historiography: Unravelling the Myths*, edited by Volker Grabowsky, 112–27. Bangkok: River Books.

———. 2014. "The Saint with Indra's Sword: Khruubaa Srivichai and Buddhist Millenarianism in Northern Thailand." *Comparative Studies in Society and History* 56 (3): 681–713.

Brown, Sid. 2001. *The Journey of One Buddhist Nun: Even Against the Wind.* Albany: State University of New York Press.

Buddhaghosa, Bhadantācariya. 1976. *The Path of Purification (Visuddhimagga).* Vol 1. Translated from the Pali by Bhikkhu Ñāṇamoli. Berkeley, CA: Shambhala.

Buddharakkhita, Acharya, trans. 1985. *The Dhammapada: The Buddha's Path of Wisdom.* Kandy: Buddhist Publication Society.

Bunnag, Jane. 1973. *Buddhist Monk, Buddhist Layman: A Study of Urban Monastic Organization in Central Thailand.* Cambridge: Cambridge University Press.

Burlingame, Eugene Watson, trans. 2005. *Buddhist Legends: Translated from the Original Pali Text of the Dhammapada Commentary.* Edited by Charles Rockwell Lanman. 3 vols. Harvard Oriental Series 28–30 (reprint). Delhi: Motilal Banarsidass.

Carrithers, Michael. 1983. *The Forest Monks of Sri Lanka: An Anthropological and Historical Study.* Delhi: Oxford University Press.

Chalong Soontravanich. 2013. "The Regionalization of Local Buddhist Saints: Amulets, Crime and Violence in Post-World War II Thai Society." *Sojourn* 28 (2): 179–215.

Chatsumarn Kabilsingh. 1991. *Thai Women in Buddhism.* Berkeley: Parallax Press.

Chetana Nagavajara. 1994. "Literature in Thai Life: Reflections of a Native." *South East Asia Research* 2 (1): 12–52.

Collett, Alice. 2016. *Lives of Early Buddhist Nuns: Biographies as History.* New Delhi: Oxford University Press.

Collins, Steven. 1990. *Selfless Persons: Imagery and Thought in Theravāda Buddhism.* Cambridge: Cambridge University Press.

———. 1992. "Notes on some Oral Aspects of Pali Literature." *Indo-Iranian Journal* 35:121–35.

———. 1998. *Nirvana and Other Buddhist Felicities: Utopias of the Pali Imaginaire.* Cambridge: Cambridge University Press.

———. 2011. *Civilisation et Femmes Célibataires dans le bouddhisme en Asie du Sud et du Sud-Est: Une «étude de genre»*. Paris: Cerf.

Collins, Steven, and Justin McDaniel. 2010. "Buddhist 'nuns' (*mae chi*) and the teaching of Pali in contemporary Thailand." *Modern Asian Studies* 44:1373–1408.

Cook, Joanna. "Hagiographic narrative and monastic practice: Buddhist morality and mastery amongst Thai Buddhist nuns." *Journal of the Royal Anthropological Institute* 15 (2): 349–64.

———. 2010. *Meditation in Modern Buddhism: Renunciation and Change in Thai Monastic Life*. Cambridge: Cambridge University Press.

Cook, Nerida. 1981. "The Position of Nuns in Thai Buddhism: The Parameters of Religious Recognition." MA thesis, Australian National University.

Cook, Nerida M., and Peter A. Jackson. 1999. "Introduction/Desiring Constructs: Transforming Sex/Gender Orders in Twentieth-Century Thailand." In *Genders & Sexualities in Modern Thailand*, edited by Peter A. Jackson and Nerida M. Cook, 1–27. Chiang Mai: Silkworm Books.

Costa, LeeRay. 1997. "Exploring the History of Women's Education and Activism in Thailand." *Explorations* in *Southeast Asian Studies: A Journal of the Southeast Asian Studies Student Association* 1 (2), http://hdl.handle.net/10125/2288.

Crosby, Kate. 2014. *Theravada Buddhism: Continuity, Diversity, and Identity*. West Sussex: Wiley-Blackwell.

Darunee Tantiwiramanond. 1997. "Changing Gender Relations in Thailand: A Historical and Cultural Analysis" *Indian Journal of Gender Studies* 4 (2): 167–98.

Delia, Nicola. 2014. "Mediating between Gendered Images of 'Defilement' and 'Purity': Continuity, Transition and Access to Spiritual Power in a Northern Thai Buddhist Monastic Community for Women." MA diss., University of Hamburg.

Fiordalis, David V. 2008. "Miracles and Superhuman Powers in South Asian Buddhist Literature." PhD diss., University of Michigan.

Gabaude, Louis. 1988. *Une herméneutique bouddhique contemporaine de Thaïlande: Buddhadasa Bhikkhu*. Paris: École française d'Extrême-Orient.

———. 1997. "Le renouveau bouddhiste en Thaïlande est-il possible? Le cas de l'ascétisme social." In *Renouveaux religieux en asie*, edited by Catherine Clémentin-Ojha, 155–75. Paris: École française d'Extrême-Orient.

———. 2003a. "Where ascetics get comfort and recluses go public: Museums for Buddhist saints in Thailand." In *Pilgrims, Patrons, and Place: Localizing*

Sanctity in Asian Religions, edited by Phyllis Granoff and Koichi Shinohara, 103–23. Vancouver: University of British Columbia Press.

———. 2003b. "A new phenomenon in Thai monasteries: The Stūpa-museum." In *The Buddhist Monastery: A Cross-Cultural Survey*, edited by Pierre Pichard and François Lagirarde, 169–86. Paris: École française d'Extrême-Orient.

Gethin, Rupert. 1992. "The Mātikās: Memorization, Mindfulness and the List." In *In the Mirror of Memory: Reflections on Mindfulness and Remembrance in Indian and Tibetan Buddhism*, edited by J. Gyatso, 149–72. Albany: State University of New York.

———. 2008. *Sayings of the Buddha: A Selection of Suttas from the Pali Nikāyas*. Oxford: Oxford University Press.

Gifford, Julie. 2003. "The insight guide to hell: Mahāmoggallāna and Theravāda Buddhist cosmology." In *Constituting Communities: Theravāda Buddhism and the Religious Cultures of South and Southeast Asia*, edited by John Clifford Holt et al., 71–84. Albany: State University of New York Press.

Giustarini, Giuliano. 2012. "The Role of Fear (Bhaya) in the Nikāyas and in the Abhidhamma." *Journal of Indian Philosophy* 40 (5): 511–31.

Gombrich, Richard F. 1971. *Precept and Practice: Traditional Buddhism in the Rural Highlands of Ceylon*. Oxford: Clarendon Press.

———. 2006. *Theravāda Buddhism: A Social History from Ancient Benares to Modern Colombo*. 2nd ed. Oxon: Routledge.

Gosling, David L. 1998. "The Changing Roles of Thailand's Lay Nuns (*Mae Chii*)." *Southeast Asian Journal of Social Science* 26 (1): 121–42.

Graham, William A. 1987. *Beyond the Written Word: Oral Aspects of Scripture in the History of Religion*. Cambridge: Cambridge University Press.

Griswold, A. B., and Prasert Na Nagara. 1969. "The Asokārāma Inscription of 1399 A.D.: Epigraphic and Historical Studies, No.2*." *Journal of the Siam Society* 57 (1): 29–56.

———. 1971. "Epigraphic and Historical Studies No. 9: The Inscription of Ramkhamhaeng of Sukhothai (1292 A.D.)." *Journal of the Siam Society* 59 (2): 179–228.

Gross, Rita M. 2013. "Buddhist Perspectives on Gender Issues." In *A Companion to Buddhist Philosophy*, edited by Steven M. Emmanuel, 663–74. Wiley-Blackwell.

Gyatso, Janet. 1998. *Apparitions of the Self: The Secret Autobiographies of a Tibetan Visionary*. Princeton: Princeton University Press.

Harvey, Peter. 2013. *An Introduction to Buddhism: Teachings, History and Practices.* 2nd ed. Cambridge: Cambridge University Press.

Heikkilä-Horn, Marja-Leena. 2000. "The Status and Values of the Santi Asoke Sikkhamat." In *Innovative Buddhist Women: Swimming Against the Stream,* edited by Karma Lekshe Tsomo, 72–83. Richmond: Curzon Press.

Heinze, Ruth-Inge. 1994. "Book Review of Forest Monks and the Nation State: An Anthropological and Historical Study in Northeastern Thailand. By J. L. Taylor." *Journal of Asian Studies* 53 (2): 661–62.

Holt, John C. 1995. *Discipline: The Canonical Buddhism of the Vinayapiṭaka.* 2nd ed. Delhi: Motilal Banarsidass.

Hüsken, Ute. 1997. *Die Vorschriften für die buddhistische Nonnengemeinde im Vinaya-Piṭaka der Theravādin.* Berlin: Reimer.

Ishii, Yoneo. 1986. *Sangha, State, and Society: Thai Buddhism in History.* Translated by Peter Hawkes. Honolulu: University of Hawai'i Press.

Ito, Tomomi. 1999. "Buddhist Women in Dhamma Practice in Contemporary Thailand: Movements Regarding Their Status as World Renunciates." *Journal of Sophia Asian Studies* 17:147–81.

———. 2007. "Dhammamātā: Buddhadāsa's Notion of Motherhood in Buddhist Women Practitioners." *Journal of Southeast Asian Studies* 38 (3): 409–32.

———. 2012a. "Questions of ordination legitimacy for newly ordained Theravāda *bhikkhunī* in Thailand." *Journal of Southeast Asian Studies,* Vol. 43, Issue 1, pp. 55-76.

———. 2012b. *Modern Thai Buddhism and Buddhadāsa Bhikkhu: A Social History.* Singapore: NUS Press.

Itoh, Ayako. 2013. "The Emergence of the bhikkhunī-saṅgha in Thailand: Contexts, Strategies and Challenges." PhD thesis, École pratique des hautes études (Paris).

Jackson, Peter. 1999b. "Royal spirits, Chinese gods and magic monks: Thailand's boom time religions of prosperity." *South East Asia Research* 7 (3): 245–320.

Jory, Patrick. 2008. "Luang Pu Thuat and the integration of Patani." In *Thai South and Malay North: Ethnic Interactions on a Plural Peninsula,* edited by Michael J. Montesano and Patrick Jory, 292–303. Singapore: National University of Singapore.

Juo-Hsüeh Shih, Bhikkhunī. 2000. *Controversies Over Buddhist Nuns.* Oxford: Pali Text Society.

Kamala Tiyavanich. 1997. *Forest Recollections: Wandering Monks in Twentieth-Century Thailand.* Chiang Mai: Silkworm Books.

Kameniar, Barbara. 2009. "Thai Buddhist Women, 'Bare Life' and Bravery." *Australian Religion Studies Review* 22 (3): 281–94.

Kawanami, Hiroko. 2009. "Charisma, Power(s), and the Arahant Ideal in Burmese-Myanmar Buddhism." *Asian Ethnology* 68 (2): 211–37.

Kepner, Susan Fulop, ed. and trans. 1996. *The Lioness in Bloom: Modern Thai Fiction about Women*. Berkeley: University of California Press.

Keyes, Charles F. 1982. "Death of Two Buddhist Saints in Thailand." In *Charisma and Sacred Biography*. Edited by Michael Williams. *Journal of American Academy of Religions, Thematic Studies* 48 (nos. 3 and 4): 149–80.

———. 1991 "The Proposed World of the School: Thai Villagers' Entry into Bureaucratic State System." In *Reshaping Local Words: Formal Education and Cultural Change in Rural Southeast Asia*, edited by Charles F. Keyes, 89–130. New Haven, CT: Yale University Southeast Asia Studies.

———. 1999. "Moral authority of the Sangha and modernity in Thailand: Sexual scandals, sectarian dissent, and political resistance." In *Socially Engaged Buddhism for the New Millennium: Essays in Honor of the Ven. Phra Dhammapitaka (Bhikkhu P. A. Payutto) on his 60th Birthday Anniversary*, 121–47. Bangkok: Sathirakoses-Nagapradipa Foundation & Foundation for Children.

———. 2014. *Finding their Voice: Northeastern Villagers and the Thai State*. Chiang Mai: Silkworm Books.

Kieffer-Pülz, Petra. 2005. "Ehejahre oder Lebensjahre? Die Altersangabe für eine 'verheiratete' Frau (gihigatā) in den Rechtstexten der Theravādin." *Zeitschrift der Deutschen Morgenländischen Gesellschaft* 155 (1): 199–238.

Kieschnick, John. 2003. *The Impact of Buddhism on Chinese Material Culture*. Princeton: Princeton University Press.

King, Sallie B. 1996. "Conclusion: Buddhist Social Activism." In *Engaged Buddhism: Buddhist Liberation Movements in Asia*, edited by Christopher S. Queen and Sallie B. King, 401–36. Albany: State University of New York Press.

Kirsch, A. Thomas. 1966. "Development and mobility among the Phu Thai of northeast Thailand." *Asian Survey* 6 (7): 370–78.

———. 1967. "Phu Thai religious syncretism: A case study of Thai religion and society." PhD thesis, Harvard University.

Kleine, Christoph. 1998. "Portraits of Pious Women in East Asian Buddhist Hagiography: A Study of Accounts of Women who Attained Birth in Amida's Pure Land." *Bulletin de l'École française d'Extrême-Orient* 85:325–61.'

Kornfield, Jack. 2007. *Modern Buddhist Masters*. Kandy: Buddhist Publication Society.

Krey, Gisela. 2010a. "On Women as Teachers in Early Buddhism: Dhammadinnā and Khemā." *Buddhist Studies Review* 27 (1): 17–40.

———. 2010b. "Some Remarks on the Status of Nuns and Laywomen in Early Buddhism." In *Dignity and Discipline: Reviving Full Ordination for Buddhist Nuns*, edited by Thea Mohr and Jampa Tsedroen. Boston: Wisdom Publications.

Lai, Suat Yan. 2011. "Engendering Buddhism: Female Ordination and Women's 'Voices' in Thailand." PhD diss., Claremont Graduate University.

Lindberg Falk, Monica. 2000a. "Women in between: Becoming religious persons in Thailand." In *Women's Buddhism, Buddhism's Women: Tradition, Revision, Renewal*, edited by Ellison Banks Findly, 37–57. Boston: Wisdom Publications.

———. 2000b. "Thammacarini Witthaya: The first Buddhist school for girls in Thailand." In *Innovative Buddhist Women: Swimming Against the Stream*, edited by Karma Lekshe Tsomo, 61–71. Richmond: Curzon Press.

———. 2002. "Making fields of merit: Buddhist nuns challenge gendered orders in Thailand." PhD diss., Göteburg University.

———. 2007. *Making Fields of Merit: Buddhist Female Ascetics and Gendered Orders in Thailand*. Copenhagen: NIAS Press.

———. "The Struggle for Recognition and Justice: Gender Equality and Socially Engaged Buddhism in Thailand." In *Gendered Inequalities in Asia: Configuring, Contesting and Recognizing Women and Men*, edited by Helle Rydstrøm, 149–69. Copenhagen: NIAS Press.

Loos, Tamara. 2006. *Subject Siam: Family, Law, and Colonial Modernity in Thailand*. Ithaca, NY: Cornell University Press.

Mackenzie, Roy. 2007. *New Buddhist Movements in Thailand: Towards an Understanding of Wat Phra Dhammakāya and Santi Asoke*. Oxon: Routledge.

Mahā Boowa Ñāṇsampanno, Ācariya. 2003. *Venerable Ācariya Mun Bhūridatta Thera: A Spiritual Biography*. Translated from the Thai by Bhikkhu Dick Sīlaratano. Baan Taad: Wat Pa Baan Taad.

Martin, Dan. 1994. "Pearls from Bones: Relics, Chortens, Tertons and the Signs of Saintly Death in Tibet." *Numen*. 41 (3): 273–324.

McDaniel, Justin Thomas. 2008. *Gathering Leaves and Lifting Words: Histories of Buddhist Monastic Education in Laos and Thailand*. Seattle: University of Washington Press.

———. 2011. *The Lovelorn Ghost and the Magical Monk: Practicing Buddhism in Modern Thailand*. New York: Columbia University Press.

Mellick Cutler, Sally. 1994. "The Pali Apadāna Collection." *Journal of the Pali Text Society* 20:1–42.

Mettiko, Bhikkhu, ed. and trans. 2014. *Muttodaya—Hommage an ein befreites Herz: Leben und Lehre von Than Phra Ācān Bhūridatto*. Stammbach: Muttodaya Dhamma.

Morgan, David. 2010. "Introduction: the Matter of Belief." In *Religion and Material Culture: The Matter of Belief*, edited by David Morgan, 1–19. Oxon: Routledge.

Mrozik, Susanne. 2007. *Virtuous Bodies. The Physical Dimensions of Morality in Buddhist Ethics*. Oxford: Oxford University Press.

Muecke, Marjorie. 2004. "Female Sexuality in Thai Discourses about *Maechii* (แม่ชี 'lay nuns')." *Culture, Health & Sexuality* 6, no. 3 (May–June): 221–38.

Murcott, Susan. 2006. *First Buddhist Women: Poems and Stories of Awakening*. Berkeley: Parallax Press.

Ñāṇamoli, Bhikkhu, and Bhikkhu Bodhi. 1995. *The Middle Length Discourses of the Buddha: A New Translation of the Majjhima Nikāya*. Boston: Wisdom Publications.

Narumon (Pook) Hinshiranan. 1993. "The Case of Buddhist Nuns in Thailand." *Sakyadhita Newsletter* 4 (1), http://www.sakyadhita.org/NewsLetters/4:1.htm#Thailand, accessed June 15, 2007.

Nattier, Jan. 1991. *Once Upon a Future Time: Studies in a Buddhist Prophecy of Decline*. Nanzan Studies in Asian Religions. Berkeley: Asian Humanities Press.

Nilsen, Marte. 2011. "The Spirit of a Heroine: Ya Mo—Spirit Reverence, Patriotism and Thai Buddhism." *Modern Asian Studies* 46 (6): 1599–1625.

Nyānatiloka. 1999. *Buddhistisches Wörterbuch*. Stammbach-Herrnschrot: Beyerlein and Steinschulte.

Olson, Grant Allan. 1989. "A Person-Centered Ethnography of Thai Buddhism: The Life of Phra Rajavaramuni (Prayudh Payutto)." PhD diss., Cornell University.

———. 1992. "Thai Cremation Volumes: A Brief History of a Unique Genre of Literature." *Asian Folklore Studies* 51 (2): 279–94.

O'Connor, Richard Allan. 1978. "Urbanism and Religion: Community, Hierarchy and Sanctity in Urban Thai Buddhist Temples." PhD diss., Cornell University.

Parichart Suwanbubbha. 2003. "Development and Buddhism Revisited: Arguing the Case for Thai Religious Nuns (Mae Chees)." *Development* 45 (4): 68–73.

Pattana Kitiarsa. 2005. "Beyond Syncretism: Hybridization of Popular Religion in Contemporary Thailand." *Journal of Southeast Asian Studies* 36 (3): 461–87.

Peach, Lucinda. 2009. "Sex or Sangha? Non-normative gender roles for women in Thai law and religion." In *Women in Asia*. Edited by Louise Edwards and Mina Roces. Vol. 1, *Women and Political Power*, 306–42. London: Routledge.

Pranke, Patrick. 2010. "On Saints and Wizards: Ideals of Human Perfection and Power in Contemporary Burmese Buddhism." *Journal of the International Association of Buddhist Studies* 33 (1–2): 453–88.

Ray, Reginald A. 1994. *Buddhist Saints in India: A Study in Buddhist Values and Orientations*. Oxford: Oxford University Press.

Reynolds, Craig James. 1973. *The Buddhist Monkhood in Nineteenth Century Thailand*. PhD diss., Cornell University.

Reynolds, Frank E., and Charles Hallisey. 1987. "Buddha." In *Encyclopedia of Religion*, edited by M. Eliade. New York: Macmillan.

Rozenberg, Guillaume. 2010. *Renunciation and Power: The Quest for Sainthood in Contemporary Burma*. Translated by Jessica Hackett. Yale Southeast Asia Studies, monograph 59. New Haven, CT: Yale University.

———. 2011. "The Saint Who Did Not Want to Die: The Multiple Deaths of an Immortal Burmese Holy Man." *Journal of Burma Studies* 15 (1): 69–119.

Samuels, Jeffrey. 2010. *Attracting the Heart: Social Relations and the Aesthetics of Emotion in Sri Lankan Monastic Culture*. Honolulu: University of Hawai'i Press.

Sanitsuda Ekachai. 1999. "What is the Status of Women in Buddhism?" In *Socially Engaged Buddhism for the New Millennium in Honor of the Ven. Phra Dhammapitaka (Bhikkhu P.A. Payutto) on his 60th Birthday Anniversary*, 227–34. Bangkok: Sathirakoses-Nagapradipa Foundation & Foundation for Children.

———. 2001. *Keeping the Faith: Thai Buddhism at the Crossroads*. Edited by Nick Wilgus. Bangkok: Post Books.

Schmithausen, Lambert. 1997. *Maitrī and Magic: Aspects of the Buddhist Attitude toward the Dangerous in Nature*. Vienna: Verlag der Österreichischen Akademie der Wissenschaften.

———. 2000. "Buddhism and the Ethics of Nature—Some Remarks." *The Eastern Buddhist* 32 (2): 26–78.

Scott, Rachelle M. 2009. *Nirvana for Sale? Buddhism, Wealth, and the Dhammakāya Temple in Contemporary Thailand*. Albany: State University of New York Press.

———. 2012. "Buddhism, Miraculous Powers, and Sacred Biographies: Re-thinking the Stories of Theravāda Nuns." *Journal of the International Association of Buddhist Studies* 33 (2) : 489–511.

Seeger, Martin. 2005. "Phra Dhammapiṭaka und die Pāli-Kanon-Debatte in Thailand: Ein Beitrag zur Untersuchung des modernen Buddhismus." PhD diss, Universität Hamburg. http://ediss.sub.uni-hamburg.de/volltexte/2005/2342/.

———. 2006 (2008). "The *bhikkhunī*-ordination controversy in Thailand." *Journal of the International Association of Buddhist Studies* 29 (1): 155–83.

———. 2009a. "The Changing Roles of Thai Buddhist Women: Obscuring Identities and Increasing Charisma." *Religion Compass* 3 (5): 806–22.

———. 2009b. "Phra Payutto and Debates on 'On the Very Idea of the Pali Canon' in Thai Buddhism." *Buddhist Studies Review* 26:1–31.

———. 2010a. "Theravāda Buddhism and Human Rights: Perspectives from Thai Buddhism." In *Buddhist Approaches to Human Rights: Dissonances and Resonances*, edited by Meinert, Carmen, and Hans-Bernd Zöllner, 63–92. Bielefeld: Transcript.

———. 2010b, "'Against the Stream': The Thai Female Buddhist Saint Mae Chi Kaew Sianglam (1901–1991)." *South East Asia Research* 18, no. 3 (September): 555–95.

———. 2012. Review of *Meditation in Modern Buddhism: Renunciation and Change in Thai Monastic Life*, by Joanna Cook. *South East Asia Research* 20, no. 1 (March): 151–56.

———. 2013. "Reversal of Female Power, Transcendentality, and Gender in Thai Buddhism: The Thai Buddhist Female Saint Khun Mae Bunruean Tongbuntoem (1895–1964)." *Modern Asian Studies* 47:1488–1519.

———. 2014a. "Orality, Memory, and Spiritual Practice: Outstanding Female Thai Buddhists in the Early 20th Century." *Journal of the Oxford Centre for Buddhist Studies* 7:153–90.

———. 2014b. "Ideas and Images of Nature in Thai Buddhism: Continuity and Change." In *Environmental and Climate Change in South and Southeast Asia. How are Local Cultures Coping?*, edited by Barbara Schuler, 43–74. Leiden: Brill.

———. 2015. "'The (Dis)appearance of an Author': Some Observations and Reflections on Authorship in Modern Thai Buddhism." *Journal of the International Association of Buddhist Studies* 36 (2013) and 37 (2014): 499–536.

———. 2016. "The Inspiring Life Story of a Twentieth-Century Thai Buddhist Woman: Khunying Yai Damrongthammasan (1882–1944)." Afterword to *Lives of Early Buddhist Nuns: Biographies as History*, by Alice Collett, 231–45. New Delhi: Oxford University Press.

Sharf, Robert H. 1995. "Buddhist Modernism and the Rhetoric of Meditative Experience." *Numen* 41:228–83.

———. 1999. "On the Allure of Buddhist Relics." *Representations* 66:75–99.

Sīlaratano, Bhikkhu. 2009. *Mae Chee Kaew: Her Journey to Spiritual Awakening and Enlightenment*. Udon Thani: Forest Dhamma Books.

Sirimane, Yuki. *Entering the Stream to Englightment: Experiences of the Stages of the Buddhist Path in Contemporary Sri Lanka*. Bristol, CT: Equinox.

Skilling, Peter. 1995. "Female Renunciants *(nang chi)* in Siam According to Early Travellers' Accounts." *Journal of the Siam Society* 83 (1–2): 55–61.

———. 2005. "Cutting across Categories: The Ideology of Relics in Buddhism." Annual Report of the International Research Institute for Advanced Buddhology at Soka University for the Academic Year 2004. Vol. 8 (March). 269–322.

Sponberg, Alan. 1992. "Attitudes toward Women and the Feminine in Early Buddhism." In *Buddhism, Sexuality, and Gender*, edited by José Ignacio Cabezón, 3–36. Albany: State University of New York Press.

Strong, John S. 1979. "The Legend of the Lion-roarer: A Study of the Buddhist Arhat Piṇḍola Bhāradvāja." *Numen* 26, no. 1 (June): 50–88.

Strong, John S. 2004. *Relics of the Buddha*. Princeton: Princeton University Press.

Sulak Sivaraksa. 1994. "Biography and Buddhism in Thailand (Presented at the University of Hawai'i, April 30, 1993)." *Biography* 17, no. 1. (Winter): 2–19.

Swearer, Donald, and Sommai Premchit. 1998. *The Legend of Queen Cāma: Bodhiraṃsi's Cāmadevīvaṃsa: A Translation and Commentary*. Albany: State University of New York Press.

Swearer, Donald. 2004. *Becoming the Buddha: The Ritual of Image Consecration in Thailand*. Princeton: Princeton University Press.

———. 2009. *The Buddhist World of Southeast Asia*. 2nd ed. Chiang Mai: Silkworm Books.

Tambiah, S[tanley]. J. 1970. *Buddhism and the Spirit Cults in North-East Thailand*. Cambridge: Cambridge University Press.

———. 1984. *The Buddhist Saints of the Forest and the Cult of Amulets: A Study in Charisma, Hagiography, Sectarianism, and Millennial Buddhism*. Cambridge: Cambridge University Press.

———. 1987. "The Buddhist arahant: Classical Paradigm and Modern Thai Manifestations." In *Saints and Virtues*, edited by John Stratton Hawley, 111–26. Berkeley: University of California Press.

Tannenbaum, Nicola. 1999. "Buddhism, Prostitution, and Sex: Limits on the Academic Discourse on Gender in Thailand." In *Genders and Sexualities in Modern Thailand*, edited by Peter A. Jackson and Nerida M. Cook, 243–260. Chiang Mai: Silkworm Books.

Tate, Venerable Ajahn. 1997. *The Autobiography of a Forest Monk*. Translated by Bhikkhu Ariyesako et al. 2nd ed. Nongkhai: Wat Hin Mark Peng.

Taylor, J[ames] L. 1993. *Forest Monks and the Nation-State: An Anthropological and Historical Study in Northeastern Thailand*. Singapore: Institute of Southeast Asian Studies.

———. 1997. "The Textualization of a Monastic Tradition: Forest Monks, Lineage, and the Biographical Process in Thailand." In *Sacred Biography in the Buddhist Traditions of South and Southeast Asia*, edited by Juliane Schober, 289–309. Honolulu: University of Hawai'i Press.

———. 2008. *Buddhism and Postmodern Imaginings in Thailand: The Religiosity of Urban Space*. Aldershot: Ashgate.

Terwiel, B[arend] J[an]. 1994. *Monks and Magic: An Analysis of Religious Ceremonies in Central Thailand*. 3rd ed. Bangkok: White Lotus.

———. 2007. "Some Problems in Establishing the Bhikkhunī-Sangha in Theravāda Thailand." Paper presented at the First International Congress on Buddhist Women's Role in the Sangha: Bhikshuni Vinaya and Ordination Lineages. University of Hamburg, July 18–20.

———. 2010. *The Ram Khamhaeng Inscription: The Fake That Did Not Come True*. Reihe Gelbe Erde 5. Gossenberg: Oastasien Verlag.

———. 2011. *Thailand's Political History: From the 13th Century to Recent Times*. Rev. ed. Bangkok: River Books.

———. 2012. *"Siam": Ten Ways to Look at Thailand's Past*. Reihe Gelbe Erde 9. Gossenberg: Ostasien Verlag.

Thanissaro Bhikkhu. 1995. "Upasika Ki Nanayon and the Social Dynamic of Theravadin Buddhist Practice." *Access to Insight (Legacy Edition)*. http://www.accesstoinsight.org/lib/thai/kee/dynamic.html.

———. 1999. "The Customs of the Noble Ones." *Access to Insight (Legacy Edition)*. http://www.accesstoinsight.org/lib/authors/thanissaro/customs.html.

———. 2005. "The Traditions of the Noble Ones: An Essay on the Thai Forest Tradition and its Relationship with the Dhammayut Hierarchy." Paper presented at the 9th International Conference on Thai Studies, Northern Illinois University, Dekalb, IL, April. https://www.dhammatalks.org/Archive/Writings/CrossIndexed/Uncollected/MiscEssays/The%20Traditions%20of%20the%20Noble%20Ones.pdf.

Tomalin, Emma. 2006. "The Thai *bhikkhunī* movement and women's empowerment." *Gender & Development* 14 (3): 385–97.

Tosa, Keiko. 2009. "The Cult of Thamanya Sayadaw: The Social Dynamism of a Formulating Pilgrimage Site." *Asian Ethnology* 68 (2): 239–64.

Trainor, Kevin. 1997. *Relics, Ritual, and Representation in Buddhism: Rematerializing the Sri Lanka Theravāda Tradition*. Cambridge: Cambridge University Press.

Van Esterik, John. 1996. "Women Meditation Teachers in Thailand." In *Women of Southeast Asia*, edited by Penny Van Esterik, 33–41. DeKalb, IL: Center for Southeast Asian Studies, Northern Illinois University.

Van Esterik, Penny. 2000. *Materializing Thailand*. Oxford: Berg.

Varaporn Chamsanit. 2006. "Reconnecting the Lost Lineage: Challenges to Institutional Denial of Buddhist Women's Monasticism in Thailand." PhD thesis, Australian National University.

Veidlinger, Daniel M. 2006. *Spreading the Dhamma: Writing, Orality, and Textual Transmission in Buddhist Northern Thailand*. Chiang Mai: Silkworm Books.

Walshe, Maurice, trans. 1987. *The Long Discourses of the Buddha: A Translation of the Dīgha Nikāya*. Boston: Wisdom Publications.

Walters, Jonathan S. 1995. "Gotamī's Story." In *Buddhism in Practice*, edited by Donald S. Lopez Jr., 113–38. Princeton: Princeton University Press.

———. 2013. "Apadāna: Therī-apadāna; Wives of the Saints: Marriage and Kamma in the Path to Arahantship." In *Women in Early Buddhism: Comparative Textual Studies*, edited by Alice Collett, 160–91. Oxford: Oxford University Press.

Williams, Paul. 2000. *Buddhist Thought: A Complete Introduction to the Indian Tradition*. With Anthony Tribe. London: Routledge.

Wilson, Liz. 1996. *Charming Cadavers: Horrific Figurations of the Feminine in Indian Buddhist Hagiographic Literature*. Chicago: University of Chicago Press.

Zivkovic, Tanya Maria. 2010. "The Biographical Process of a Tibetan Lama." *Ethnos* 75 (2): 171–89.

Index

Abhidhamma, 32, 91, 123, 186, 261n112, 268n127, 292n6
Abhidhammatthasaṅgaha, 186, 202, 283n20
abhiññās, 75, 121, 129, 274n82
Abhivaṇṇā, Mae Chi, 211–12
acalasaddhā, 108, 190
Adhimutta, 109
Adiele, Faith, 41
Amaradevo Bhikkhu, 140, *148*, 148–49
amulets, 22, 116, 139, 144, 170–76, 179–80, 251–52
  amulet cult, 117–18
  collectors of, 70–71, 172, 173
  consecration of, 8, 73, 153, 169–75, 180
  magazines for, 10, 71, *172*
  markets for, 172–73, 280n109
  medallion amulets, 5, *6*, *155*, 173–75, 220, 257n29
  powder amulets, 174
Anālayo, Bhikkhu, 21, 189, 272n61, 283n35
Ānanda, 96, 112–13, 139, 207, 270n2, 285n109
  relics of, 141
ānāpānasati, 200
Anāthapiṇḍika, 133
anattā, 58–59, 109, 157–58, 188
androcentrism, 26, 165, 216, 250
Aṅgulimāla, 77
antaradhāna, 112–16
Apadāna, 52, 60, 122, 264n50
Apinya Feungfusakul, 35–36
arahants, 75, 77, 107–11, 118–24, 277n43
  books on, 24–25, 50
  in current times, 25, 111–15, 127, 132
  in early Buddhism, 150, 275n107
  lay *arahants*, 132–33
  See also sainthood
Arai, Paula, 247
ariya, 42, 51, 77, 101, 120, 128, 151, 159–60, 226. See also *ariya-puggala*; noble path; and Noble Truths
ariya saṅgha, 151. See *ariya-puggala*; *ariyasong*
ariyapariyesanā, 200
ariya-puggala (noble person), 42, 77, 107–11,114–18, 122, 125, 134–35
  anāgāmī (nonreturner), 108, 113, 120, 129–31, 136, 189, 272n53
  sakadāgāmī (once-returner), 108, 113
  sotāpanna (stream-enterer), 43, 108, 113, 114, 123, 129, 168
  See also arahants; sainthood; *and entries for individual saints*
ariya-sāvaka, 188
ariya-sāvikā, 130
ariyasong, 25, 39, 50, 109, 122. See also *ariya-puggala*
āsava, 108–10, 127
Asoka, Emperor, 150, 151
athitthan, 6–7, 73, 76–78, 81, 84, 148, 168, 171
Aṭṭhadhammapañha, 67, 187, 190
aṭṭhi (*atthi*), 101, 149
autobiography
  in early Indian Buddhism, 51–60
  in modern Thai Buddhism, 47–48, 51–60, 263n28
avijjā, 108, 226
awakening, 115, 122, 130, 132, 249
  levels of, 2, 39, 67, 79, 107–11, 136 (see also *ariya-puggala*)
  women and awakening, 17, 20, 152, 159
  See also arahant; sainthood
āyatana, 283n21

Bāhiya, 132
bali sueksa, 222
Ban Chiwuek, 12–15

Ban Huai Sai, 83, 87–88, 156, 161, 178, 203
Ban Nong Phue, 177, 207
Battaglia, Lisa, 165, 217
Beatrice Bhadrayuvadi, Princess, 212, 264n29
Bessey, Allan, 39–40, 43, 261n128
Bhaddanta Āsabha, Phra, 235
bhikkhus, 18–19, 27, 36, 56, 256n3, 275n107
  monastic age of, 220–21, 287n19
  role models for, 291n109
Bhikkhunī Dhammanandā (Chatsumarn Kabilsingh), 26, 216
bhikkhunīs, 18–19, 26–27, 158–59, 164, 245, 275n107
  absence of, 29, 32, 56, 132, 151, 206, 222, 247–48
  bhikkhunī-saṅgha: alternative to, 29–32, 35–37, 132–35; foundation of, 112–13
  etadagga ("foremost"), 23
  ordination debate over, 26–28, 35, 39, 46, 256n5, 259n67
  revival of, 26–28, 212, 248, 251
Bimbisāra, King, 132
biographies, 47–62, 144, 157, 170, 177–80, 248–52
  of female practitioners, 2–15, 25, 45, 53–62
  of male practitioners, 45, 47–53, 55–56
  sacred. *See* hagiography
bodhisatta, 122, 292n4
Boy Thaphrajan, 172
brahmacariya, 56, 113, 127, 134, 239
Brown, Sid, 40–41
buat. See *nak buat*
Buddha, 36, 59, 107, 112–13, 121–22
  early Indian biographies of, 49, 249, 263n7
  images of, 22, 23, 70, 128, 163, 168, *169*
  relics of, 20, 141, 143–44, 146, 149–51, 163, 175–76
  unusual body of, 79, 146
Buddha Metteyya, 112
Buddhadāsa Bhikkhu, 30, 133, 193, 198, 288n26
Buddhadhamma (book by Phra Payutto), 218
Buddhaghosa, 84, 112, 146, 273n69
Buddhaghosacariya, Somdet Phra (ecclesiastical title), 288n26
Buddhaghosacariya, Somdet Phra (Jaroen Ñāṇavaro), *192*, 200, 208, 212, 271n44, 280n97
  on *ariya-puggala*, 116
  and Khunying Yai, 10, 64–65, 185, 191, 208, 232
  and orality and memory, 193–98, 284n60
Buddhaghosacariya (Phra Payutto), Somdet Phra, 288n26. *See also* Payutto, Phra
Buddhaghosacariya (Wat, Vāsano), Somdet Phra, 82
buddhavisaya, 149
Bunma Sianglam, 86–87
Bunmi Wetchasan, Mae Chi, 174, 235–36, 239–41
Bunnag, Jane, 114
Bunruean Tongbuntoem, (Khun) Mae, 5–7, 48, 74–83, 163, 245
  amulets of, 170–75, *171*, *172*, 176, 180
  cremation volume of, 53–54, 167
  documentary film on, 25
  on gender, 223–29
  hagiography of, *6*, 53–54, 56, 70–74, 129, 249–51, 265n72
  kammically inscribed body of, 79–81
  mango tree miracle of, 77–78
  memorial hall of, 167–70
  museum for veneration of, 167–70, *170*
  and orality and memory, 204–5
  popularity of, 75–79, 153–54
  relics of, 82, 151, 167–70, 176
  sainthood of, 121, 129–37
  shrine for, *73*, 73–74, 167–70

Cāmadevī, Queen, 23, 158, 159
Carrithers, Michael, 112
cetasika, 226, 292n6
cetiya, 20, 80, 92, 143, 158–63, 257n16, 279n81. See also *stūpas*
cetiya museums, 159–65
Chalong Soontravanich, 117–18
Chandra Khonnokyoong, Mae Chi, 34, 159, 167, 278n72, 280n101, 292n11
chanting, 74, 265n68, 266n75
  book for, 185, 193
  of Buddhist texts, 78, 87, 169, 189, 196, 202–4, 209
  daily, 183, 188, 193, 198
  for funerals, 91–92, 203
  of wishes, 73

charisma, 128, 137, 154, 176–79
charismatic teacher/monks, 8, 22, 43, 47, 50, 55, 153
cult of, 117
institutional, 32, 35–36, 244,
of Thai women, 35, 152, 157, 173, 211, 247
Chatsumarn Kabilsingh. *See* Bhikkhunī Dhammanandā
Chetana Nagavajara, 183–84
Chodok Ñāṇasiddhi, Phra, 200
Chonlathopamakhun (Phut Puṇṇakathera), Phra, 257n29
Citta, 133
Civil and Commercial Code, 290n69
Civil Court, 233
Collett, Alice, 21
Collins, Steven, 28, 40, 46, 189, 257n16, 262n136
colonization, 117
Cook, Joanna, 8, 41–42, 43, 52, 216–18
Cook, Nerida, 262n135
corpses, 70, 82, 276n13
contemplation of, 57, 85, 238
as relics, 142–43
cosmology, 225–26, 228, 230, 249. See also under *kamma*
Costa, LeeRay, 181–82, 206, 281n2
Court of Appeals, 233
cremation volumes, 9–10, *11*, 50–51, 53–54, 92, *99*, 255n9, 263n9

Dabba Mallaputta, 277n30
Damrong Rajanubhab, Prince, 183
Damrongthammasan (Yai Wisetsiri), Khunying. *See* Khunying Yai
Damrongthammasan (Sang Wisetsiri), Phraya, 63
Darunee Tantiwiramanond, 181–82, 206, 282n4
dasasilmātā, 30
Department for Tourism, 168
Department of Religious Affairs, 33, 256n5
devas, 47, 189
dhamma lists, 185, 187, 194–95, 201, 210
Dhammadinna, 273n69
Dhammakāya, 22, 60, 159, 278n72, 292n11
Dhammapada, 59, 65, 77–78, 121, 146–49, 181, 184–85, 289
Dhammatrailokajan, Chaokhun, 194
dhammavinaya, 33, 86, 113, 115, 204
Dhammayuttika-nikāya, 64, 156, 210, 265n57
dhātu, 141, 146–47, 149, 159, 163, 185, 279n81
dhutaṅga (*thudong*), 13, 86, 90, 201–2, 213, 237–40, 284n85
documentary film, 25, 51, 251
dukkha, 1, 20, 58, 91, 158, 210, 234, 237
Dun Atalo, Luang Pu, 85
Dunlayaphaksuwaman, Phra, 193–94

education, 28–29, 32, 37, 41, 217, 227–28
and access to Buddhist knowledge, 241–43 (*see also chapter 5*)
compulsory, 182–83, 206, 281n3, 282n5
formal, 152, 183, 202, 281n2
monastic, 28–29, 40, 182, 208, 221–23, 288n25
state-planned, 181
women's, 181–82, 208, 222–23, 244, 281n2, 282n4
ekaggatā, 228. See also *jhāna*
etadagga ("foremost"), 132
*bhikkhunī*s, 23, 245
laywomen, 23, 80–81, 190
monks, 79, 89–90, 121, 150

Fan Ācāro, Luang Pu, 88, 125–28
fan (*phat yot*), 221
fear, 97, 99–100, 109–11, 234, 237–41, 242–43
of death, 82, 127, 240
of ghosts, 240 (see also *phi*)
and mindfulness, 240
of rape and gender-based violence, 238–39, 291n90
of tigers, 291n95
female practitioners
academic study of, 1–15, 39–46, 53–62, 247–52
as role models, 25–26, 97, 100, 136, 226, 245–46, 291n105
forest, 1, 116–17, 177, 224, 237–38
Frauwallner, Erich, 263n7
funerals, 4, 9, 119, 144–45, 176, 249
chanting at, 91, 203–4

Gabaude, Louis, 120, 147, 219–21, 279n81
*garudhamma*s, 112–13, 164–65, 248, 258n66

gender, 7–9, 41–42, 139, 171–72, 182, 190
bias, 20
constraints due to, 203, 222–23, 224, 231–46
ephemerality of, 228–31
hierarchy of, 42, 56, 163–65, 176–78, 216–23, 247–48, 250
imbalances in, 18–27, 45–46, 47, 150–51, 281n2
insubstantiality of, 228–31
and *kamma*, 127, 228–31
relations, 3, 19, 48, 206–9, 216–19, 250
soteriological irrelevance of, 127, 223–25, 231, 245, 250
See also chapter 6
Gervaise, Nicolas, 206, 290n82
Gethin, Rupert, 189, 194
ghosts. See *phi*
Gombrich, Richard, 112, 116
Graham, William, 288n25
Grand Palace, 116, 158–59
Gross, Rita, 34
Giustarini, Giuliano, 243
Guṇūpamācariya (Siricando, Jan), Chaokhun, 53, 200
Gyatso, Janet, 59

hagiography
cartoon books as, 51, 263n15
in early Indian Buddhism, 49, 61, 248–49
of female practitioners, 4–5, 8–9, 47–62
of male practitioners, 8, 43–44, 47–53, 55
in modern Thai Buddhism, 4, 7, 47–62, 71, 248–49
objectives of, 60–61
Hallisey, Charles, 49
halos, 123
Heinze, Ruth-Inge, 34
hells, 88, 108, 126, 237
hierarchy, 218, 246
administrative, 220–23, 244, 288n26
of ecclesiastical ranks, 221–22, 244, 287n22, 288n24, 288n26
of educational achievement, 221–23, 244, 288n25
of gender, 3, 42, 56, 163–64, 178, 216–46
patriarchal, 231–37
popular, 220–21, 244, 287n19
hierarchy (*continued*)
religious, 114, 163–65, 216–23, 248
religio-political, 220
social, 227
vassa-age, 220–21, 287n19
vinaya, 220–21, 244, 287n19, 288n26
historiography, 247
Holy Men movements, 272n47
homiletic texts, 9, 51, 54, 60, 72, 100, 223
of Mae Bunruean, 5, 78, 223, 249

illiteracy. *See* literacy
institutional androcentrism, 26, 165, 216, 250
Inthawai Santussako, Phra Ajan, 274n76
and Mae Chi Kaew, 83, 92, 161, 163, 245
and Mae Chi Phimpha, 101
Ito, Tomomi, 262n139

Jaeo Sianglam, Khruba, 135, 267n104, 278n59
Jamroen, Mae Chi, 211
Jan Kaenkaew (mother of Luang Pu Man), 17, 120
Jan Thomanakon, Upāsikā, 211–12
Jandi Lohitdi, Khun Mae, 25
Jaran Ṭhitadhammo, Luang Pho, 57, 238
jhāna, 73, 75, 84, 129, 148, 271n37, 274n82
Jinakālamālī, 147
Jīvaka-Komārabhacca, 168, *169*
Joi Tongbuntoem, 74, 75, 76
Juan Kulajeṭṭho, Luang Pu, 102–3, 272n53

kae bon, 32
Kaew Sianglam, Mae Chi, 2, 3, 45, 48, 255n4, 262n144
amulets of, *155*, 155–56, 174
biography of, 57, 83–92, 166, 278n59
cremation of, 91–92, 156
English-language hagiography of, 45, 60–61, 251, 267n103
famousness of, 152–56
and gender, 228–30, 232, 234–35
hagiographies of, 54, 57, 60–61, 249, 250, 267n103
and Luang Pu Man, 85–86, 88, 292n5
and Luang Ta Mahabua, 88–90, 91–92
and orality and memory, 202–4, 210–11, 249
relics of, 92, 150–52, 154–58, 163–65, 174, 176–80

Kaew Sianglam (*continued*)
 sainthood of, 90, 128–37, 166, 249, 251
 *stūpa*s of, 83, 92, 159–65, *160*, 170, 174, 245, 249
 stūpa museum of, 162, 274n76
 veneration of, 35, 137, 176
Kamala Tiyavanich, 44–45, 292n3
kamma (karma), 65, 86, 168, 188, 226–28, 242, 289n45
 and biological sex, 126–27, 228–30
 and education, 241–42
 good *kamma, 219*
 kammic-cosmic view, 225–31, 236, 244–46, 248
 law of, 61, 80, 228, 230–31, 249
 negative *kamma*, 38–39, 126, 127, 223
 physical markers of, 79–81, 273n73
Kang Thephin, Mae Chi (Khun Yai), 47, 177–79, 207–8
Kasem Ācinṇasīlo, Phra, 273n69
Kasetraksa (Chuang), Phraya, 63
Keyes, Charles, 50, 118, 119–20, 282n3, 282n5
*khandha*s, 1, 58, 105, 134, 188, 194, 275n103
Khanong Dhammadhīro, Luang Pho, 55–56
Khao Anālayo, Luang Pu, 85, 115, 128, 163
Khao Chong Krachok hill, 63
Khao Suan Luang, 198
Khemā, 21, 132, 245, 274n95
Khim Wongsa-udom, 98–99, 234–35
khīṇāsava, 108, 109–10, 270n13
Khujjuttarā, 80–81, 189, 190, 245, 283n35
Khunying Kasetraksa, 63
Khunying Yai (Khunying Damrongthammasan [Yai Wisetsiri]), 48, *66*, *186*, 290n68
 as author of Buddhist texts, 10, 12, 67–69, 265n59, 265n63
 biography of, 57–58, 62–70, 190, 246, 250–52, 282n15, 290n69
 and Buddhist practice, 59, 64–67, 131, 187–93, 210
 cremation volume of, 9–10, *11*, *66*, 185
 funeral of, 70
 and gender, 68, 189–90, 225–29, 232–33
 and orality and memory, 65, 184–98, 208, 210–11, 292n6
Ki Nanayon, Upāsikā (Ko. Khao Suan Luang), 2, 43, 65, 128–29, 213
 corpse of, 276n13
 and orality and memory, 198–99
Kieschnick, John, 139
kilesa (mental defilements), 31, 81, 88–89, 103, 195–96, 224, 248
 and arahantship, 81, 109, 120, 133
 See also *vipassanūpakilesa*
Ko. Khao Suan Luang. *See* Ki Nanayon, Upāsikā
kodha, 226
Kongma Cirapuñño, Luang Pu, 88, 210
Kritsana Raksachom, Mae Chi, 19
Kukrit Pramoj, 272n64
Kulavir Prapapornpipat, 19–20

La (Khemapatto), Luang Pu, 53
la Loubère, Simon de, 290n82
Laws on Husbands and Wives, 233, 290n69, 290n71
laywomen, 34, 134
Li Dhammadharo, Luang Pu (also Luang Pho), 53, 120–21, 211–12
Lindberg Falk, Monica, 19, 25–26, 28, 40, 41–42, 290n61
literacy, 181–84, 203, 206–7, 210, 213, 241–42, 281n3, 282n5
lobha (greed), 37, 108, 226
Lokthip (*Divine world* magazine), 54–55, 56, 93
Lui Candasāro, Luang Pu (Ajan Lui Candasāro,), 85, 95, 96–97, 207, 230, 263n23

mae chis, 18–19, 26–46, 100, 154, 175, 203, 206
 in academic literature, 39–46
 and access to education, 28, 40, 41, 46, 222–23, 241–43
 age restrictions for ordination of, 235–37, 290n82
 and amulets, 174–75, 281n114
 and *bhikkhunī*s, 26–32, 35–37, 132–37, 151, 247–48
 college for, 37–38
 ecclesiastical vocabulary for, 33–34
 and the *garudhamma*s, 165, 248
 and hagiographical literature, 55–57, 59
 and hierarchy, 216–23, 231–35
 ID cards of, 33, 37
 Manual for Thai mae chis, 33, 37, 222

mae chis (*continued*)
number of, 18, 256n5
ordination of, 28, 32–34, 36–37, 132–37, 231–37
regional differences of, 261n117
samnak chi (nunneries), 28, 32, 37, 38, 41, 42
Thai Mae Chi Institute, 33, 34, 37–38, 40, 256n4, 260n105
vassa hierarchy among, 222
magga, 105, 119–20. *See also* noble path
Mahabua Ñāṇasampanno, Luang Ta, 25, 124, 165, 208–9, 273n67
author of biography of Luang Pu Man, 50, 124, 208
cartoon book on, 51, 263n15
cremation of, 144–46, 179
cremation volume of, 50–51
and Mae Chi Kaew, 83, 88–92, 128, 134–35, 207, 274n76
on relics, 178–79
relics of, *145*, 145–46
Mahāmoggallāna, 89–90, 96, 121
Mahānāga, 273n69
Mahāpajāpatī Gotamī, 112–13, 122
Maharatchamangkhalajan (Thet, Niddesako), Phra, 56, 72–73, 82, 204–5, 265n72
Mahathongsuk, Luang Pu, 98–99
Maliyadeva, 112
Mallikā, 190
Man Bhūridatto, Luang Pu, 22, 49, 82, 116, 119, 124, 280n97
authorship falsely ascribed to, 10, 12, 69, 265n63
documentary films on, 25
funeral of, 144, 265n63, 276n20
hagiographies of, 50, 115, 177, 249
and Mae Chi Kaew, 85–86, 88, 202–3, 207, 234, 262n144, 292n5
and Mae Chi Kang, 47, 177–79, 207–8
and Mae Chi Nari, 93–97, 230, 232
and Mae Chi Nu-nueang, 202
mother of, 17, 120
and orality and memory, 210
relics of, 147, 151, 155, 163, *178*, 276n20
Māra, 20–21, 126–27, 257n19, 257n21
married life, 74–75, 86–86, 98, 203, 232–35
material culture, 35. *See also* amulets; relics; *stūpas*; *and chapter 4*
Chinese, 139
Matichon, *145*, 145–46
Matichon Dictionary, 32
McDaniel, Justin, 28, 40, 46, 50, 139, 263n9
meditation, 20–21, 46, 87–89, 102–3, 123, 146–47, 157–58
in cemeteries, 57, 99, 200, 207, 238, 240
deconstructions of body in, 89–90
experiences during, 1, 47, 124–27, 131, 208, 235–36, 249
of female practitioners, 45, 46, 67, 244, 251–52
female teachers of, 40, 44, 255n3, 261n128
and former lives, 65, 80, 84–86, 125, 228–30
in the forest, 100, 237
gendered obstacles for, 44, 86–87, 203, 207, 224–25, 234, 237–39
meeting arahants in, 49, 96, 269n138
and recitation of Buddhist texts, 189, 195–96 (*see also* memory)
See also *ānāpānasati*; *jhāna*; *samādhi*; *vipassanā*; and *vipassanūpakilesa*
Mellick Cutler, Sally, 60
memory, 65, 241, 282n15, 284n60, 292n6. *See also chapter 5*
memorization of Buddhist texts, 183, 292n6. *See also* memory
menstrual blood, 20, 22, 41, 171
metta, 104, 125
Milindapañha, 133
mindfulness, 42, 189, 195–96, 209, 225, 285n109
of breathing (*ānāpānasati*), 200
and fear, 126–27, 240
Ministry of Interior, 33
Ministry of Transport and Communications, 33
miracles (*pāṭihāriya*, *patihan*), 76–78, 136, 220, 266n73
miraculous healings, 73
miraculous powers/abilities, 23, 50, 73, 121, 167
and relics, 141–44, 146, 169
See also powers
Mongkut, King. *See* Rama IV
Morgan, David, 180
mundane (worldly), 128. *See also* supramundane
Muttodaya, 209

Naeb Mahaniranon, Ajan, 2, 42–43, 123, 213, 286n136
Nai Chaemchoi, Mae Chi, 264n28
nak buat (ordained one), 13, 19, 32–33, 37–38, 134–35, 260n93
nak tham, 202, 221–22
Naresuan, King, 24
Nari Karun, Mae Chi, 232, 235
  amulets of, 174, *175*
  biography of, 92–97
  museum for, 92–93, 97, 179
  and recollection of former lives, 229–30
Narin Phasit, 212
Naris Charaschanyawong, 9–10, 69, 265n59, 282n15
National Office of Buddhism, 256n3, 256n5, 257n18
nibbāna (*nirvāṇa*), 20, 30, 51, 92, 115
  in biographies of female practitioners, 98, 200, 248–49
  in current times, 133–35, 147, 150, 161, 174, 177
  nibbāna element, 82
  in Pali texts, 18, 132, 146–47, 269n138
  as spiritual goal, 32, 88, 200, 224–25, 245, 278n78
nibbidā, 243, 266n82
Nidhi Eoseewong, 37, 183, 292n6
nimit, 73, 84–85, 94, 103, 235–36. *See also* visions
nirodha-samāpatti, 129–30
nīvaraṇa, 195–96
niyyānikadhamma, 210
No (Dhammavitakko), Chaokhun, 267n99, 271n44, 272n64
noble path, 105, 224
Noble Truths, 47, 185
Noi Paurohitya, 196–97
Nu-nueang Thapmeng, Mae Chi, 210, 237, 239, 241–42, 251–52, 263n28
  biography of, 200–202, 263n28, 284n80, 284n87, 285n88

obhāsa, 124–25, 235–36
Oep na Bangchang, 69
Olson, Grant, 9, 52, 255n11
orality, 48–50, 54, 63, 101, 125, 152, 229
  and its importance for research, 12–15, 57–58, 71
  and its importance in Buddhist practice, 241, 249 (*see also chapter 5*)
ordination hall (*uposathāgāra*), 20, 23, *64*, 65, 67, 70, 199

pabbajjā, 33, 36
pacceka-buddha, 80–81, 139, 141, 275n1
pacchimā vācā (last words), 91, 249
pācittiya, 124, 271n37
Paisal Visalo, Phra, 12, 28–29
Pali language, 33, 38, 65, 193, 202
  grammar books, 202
  language exams, 183, 221–23
  scholars of, 28, 31, 32, 40, 193–96, 243
Pali canon, 7–8, 29, 37, 48–49, 67, 79–80, 193–94
  on arahantship of laypersons, 132–33, 135
  canonical law, 26–27, 29, 112–13. See also *vinaya*
  commentary texts (*aṭṭhakathā*), 7, 80, 246, 248–49, 266n73
  multivocality on women, 20–21, 165, 250
  and Thai hagiographies, 48–49, 60, 107, 250
  See also chanting; *specific Pali canonical texts and persons*; *and under* sainthood
paññā (wisdom), 126, 188, 194, 224, 287n21
Paññāvaḍḍho, 150
pāpa (*bap*), 103, 134, 163, 201, 230, 239
pārājika, 35–36, 124, 126
paramattha-sacca (ultimate truth), 133, 165, 279n94
Pārāyana-vagga (*Soḷasapañha*), 185, 189–90, 283n30
parian tham, 221–23, 288n26
paritta, 77, 183
pariyatti, 65, 69, 188, 210, 213, 242
participant observation, 40, 42, 70, 71
Pasenadi, King, 146
Pathom *cetiya*, 143–44, 199
pāṭihāriya (*patihan*). *See* miracle
paṭikūlasaññā, 158
pāṭimokkha, 36, 222
  227 rules (for monks), 19, 39, 183, 210, 223, 287n19
  311 rules (for nuns), 19
  bhikkhunīpāṭimokkha, 31
paṭipatti, 58, 69, 188, 213, 270n12
paṭipattivibhāga, 187
paṭipattivibhajana, 191
paṭisambhidā, 113

pavāraṇā, 240
Payutto, Phra, 52, 261n118, 275n107, 287n20, 288n25, 288n26
  on "arahant," 120
  on gender, 230–31
  on hierarchy, 218
  on *mae chis*, 31, 32
peta, 126
Phakdiphuri (pen name), 93, 179, 269n131
Phensi Makaranon, 91
phet, 114, 127, 134, 237, 290n83
phi, 88, 93, 100, 240
Phimpha Wongsa-udom, Mae Chi, 1, 215, 223, 240–41, 291n96, 291n105
  and access to Buddhist knowledge, 242–43
  and autobiography 55, 59, 245, 264n28
  biography of, 97–101
  and fear, 291n95
  and Luang Pu Thet Desaraṅsī, 1, 55, 97, 100–101, 215, 242, 245
  and rape, 291n90
  on rebirth, 226–28
  and relics, 101, 151
  and renunciation, 233–35
Phothirak, Samana, 30, 273n67
Phra Khongkhwan, 281n114
Phra Khotsetthi (amulet), 175
phra that
  definition of, 140–43
  scientific study of, *148*, 148–49
  thep nimit, 142
  transformation into, 140–42, 144–58, 161, 167, 175–79, 277n37, 279n82 (*see also individual* mae chi*s*)
  See also relics
Phra That Phanom *stūpa*, 162, *164*, 279n85
Phring, Luang Ta, 74, 204
Phu Thai, 83, 84, 93, 102, 152, 268n106, 274n76
Phueng Chuenjit, 191
pilgrimage, 149, 158, 161, 162, 166, 180
piṇḍapāta, 28, 239
Piṇḍolabhāradvāja, 121, 272n61
power, 5
  apotropaic, 81
  of the Buddha, 239
  curative/healing, 73–74, 77, 130, 250
  polluting, 20, 22, 41, 171
  of precepts, 222
power (*continued*)
  protective, 7, 72–73, 76–77, 167–75, 220
  structures, 231–37, 243
  sacred, 140, 170
  See also supernatural powers
Prachumphon Jaksurak, Mae Chi, 57, 238–39
Pramote (Pāmojjo), Luang Pho, 245, 291n106
Prasop Wisetsiri, 63, 184, 232, 282n15
Prathum Choti-anan, Mae Chi, 17–18, 142–43, 175, 263n28
precepts, 187
  eight precepts, 30, 36, 134–36, 195–96: of mae chis, 13, 32, 38, 87, 256n4; of laypeople, 75, 190, 198, 201, 261n117
  five precepts, 135–36
  of laypeople, 48, 74, 78, 135, 144, 201, 239
  of *mae chis*, 125, 203, 222
  of monastics, 56
  ten precepts, 13, 32, 34, 36–37, 256n4
predicting one's death, 81–82, 267n99
puthujjana, 110–11, 123, 124, 270n12, 270n13, 273n69

Rabiap Sunthornlikhit, Khunying, 213
Rājagaha, 121
Ram Khamhaeng, King, 143
Rama I, King, 233
Rama III, King, 23, 24, 268n106
Rama IV (Mongkut), King, 67, 115, 143, 183, 201, 265n57, 284n87
Rama V, King, 115, 141, 143, 212, 264n29, 271n37, 285n87
Rama VI, King, 63, 64, 143
Rama VII, King, 193
Rama IX, King, 95–96, 128
rape, 126, 230, 238–39, 291n90
Ray, Reginald, 157, 292n5
rebirth, 67, 77, 82, 84, 90, 105, 115
  as an animal, 95, 225, 228–29
  as a human, 95, 215, 224–26, 229–32, 244
  as a man, 95, 224, 228–31
  as a woman, 20, 95, 224, 228–31, 244, 273n72
  into blissful existence (*sugati*), 225, 249
  cycle of (*saṃsāra*), 95, 105, 123, 125, 225–28, 236, 244
  in woeful existence (*duggati*), 225, 237, 249

recitation, 184, 195–207, 283n45
of Abhidhamma texts, 268n127
of Buddhist texts, 65, 67, 69–70, 185, 188–90, 234, 241
communal recitation, 193
for ordination, 33
of *pāṭimokkha*, 36
See also chanting; *suat mon*
recollection of former lives, 65, 75, 80, 84, 95, 125, 228–30. *See also* rebirth
relics, 5, 8, 20, 249, 279n81, 279n84
books on, 144, 151–52, 177, 178
of the Buddha, 20, 74, 141, 149, 163, 175–76, 279n81
in Burmese Buddhism, 175–76
exhibitions of, 149–51
multiplication of, 141, 144
museums for, 149–51, 156
posters of, 151, 177, 178
powder of, 174
of Thai monks, 51, 95, 141–46, 150–51, 158
of Thai women, 101, 150–51, 158–59, 175–80, 251–52
transformation of, 79, 82, 96–97, 141–42, 144, 146–49, 248
whole-body relics, 142
See also *phra that*; *see also chapter 4 and under entries for individual persons*
Reynolds, Frank, 49
robes, 90
of *mae chis*, 13, 36–37, 78, 87, 96, 126, 235
of monks, 20, 27, 35–37, 97, 114, 142, 160, 164
of non-Theravada ordained women, 31
of *sikkhamat*, 30–32
royal family, 35, 37, 63, 78, 128, 264n29
royal monastery, 23, 64, 128, 168
Rozenberg, Guillame, 111, 122, 175, 177, 281n118

sacca-kiriyā, 77
Sadap Ladavalya, Chao Chom Mom Rajawongse, 264n29
saddhā, 227, 284n60. See also *acalasaddhā*
saddhammo, 113, 289n39
sainthood
assertion of, 122–24: self-assertions, 124, 273n67
attribution of, 24–25
in Burmese Buddhism, 116–17, 176–77, 272n49, 272n56
conceptualization of, 118–22, 250
as edification for others, 60–61
female sainthood in modern Thai Buddhism, 1–2, 8, 54, 71, 244–45, 248–52 (*see also chapter 3*): contestations of, 4, 131–36; material expressions of, 258n32 (*see also chapter 4*)
in Indian Pali literature, 82, 89–90, 107–11, 292n4, 292n5 (*see also names of individual saints*)
male sainthood in modern Thai Buddhism, 2, 97 (*see also* names of individual saints)
mistaken belief in, 124–28, 235–36, 273n69
in modern times, 111–18, 292n3
physical manifestations of, 79–81
veneration of Thai saints, 8, 12, 22–26, 44, 219 (*see also* relics)
verification of, 109–11, 147–49
visible manifestations of, 79, 119–20 (*see also* relics)
See also arahants; *ariya*; *ariyasong*; *ariya-puggala*; *and under individual women*
Sala Santisuk, 167
Sali Thomanakon, Mae Chi, 211–12
samādhi, 188, 194, 209, 224
sāmaṇera, 18, 256n3
sāmaṇerī, 18, 26, 30, 32, 36–37, 233, 256n5
Samakkhiwisutthi, 78, 154
samanasak, 221–22, 244, 288n26
Sāmāvatī, Queen, 190
sammācāriṇī, 197
sammāsambuddha, 130, 275n1
sammati/sammuti, 58, 134, 165
sammati-sacca/sammuti-sacca (conventional truth), 133, 165, 279n94 (see also *sammati/sammuti*)
Samorn Thophaengjan, 93
saṃsāra. *See* rebirth
Samuels, Jeffrey, 3
saṃyojanas, 67, *108*, 125, 185, 224, 270n13
saṃvega, 76, 243

saṃvejanīyaṭṭhānas, 166
saṅgha, 30, 33, 130, 218, 221, 260n105
  bhikkhu-saṅgha, 27, 29, 32, 36, 89
  mae chi saṅgha, 38
  sammuti-saṅgha, 134
  Thai *saṅgha*, 26, 134, 137
  See also *ariya-saṅgha*; *bhikkhunīs*; *and* Triple Gem
Saṅgha Act, 38
Saṅgha Supreme Council (Mahatherasamakhom), 26, 78, 135, 256n5, 288n26
Saṅghamittā, 150, 151
saṅgha-rāja, 220. *See also* supreme patriarch
saṅgīti, 36
  Sangwan (Khemako), Luang Pu, 245
  Saṅkicca, 109
saññā, 188. See also *paṭikūlasaññā*; *saññāvipallāsa*
saññāvipallāsa, 127
Sanprasoet (Tri Nakhaprathip), Phra, 197
Sansanee Sthirasuta, Mae Chi, 24, 34, 255n3
Santati, 132, 146–47
Santi Asok, 30–32
Sao Kantasīlo, Luang Pu, 17, 22, 85, 116, 128, 151, 163
Sāriputta, 79, 110, 150, 287n21
Sāsanavaṃsa, 116
Sathuean Suphasophon, 54
sāvikā, 161
sensual craving, 108, 136, 270n1
sensual desires, 126, 270n1
sermons, 127–28, 134–35, 180, 182, 187, 193–94, 209, 288n25
  in biographies, 100
  of early Buddhism, 49, 166, 190, 195–96
  in hagiographies, 50–51
  listening to, 84, 206–7, 211–12
  about women, 10, 72, 83, 178–79: at their funerals, 82, 97, 101
  by women, 5, 10, 70, 72, 154, 198, 205: as a medium, 126
  See also homiletic texts
sex change, 229–31
Sharf, Robert, 157
sikkhamat, 30–32, 259n77
sīla, 78, 90, 134, 188, 194, 196, 224. *See also* precepts
Sīlaratano, Bhikkhu (Ajan Dick), 45, 60–61, 267n103
Singthong Dhammavaro, Phra Ajan, 160
Sirikit, Queen, 23, 95–96, 144
Sirimā, 80, 190
Sirindhorn, Princess, 96
Siwichai, Khruba, 122, 145, 249, 292n4
Skilling, Peter, 140, 262n142
Soda Sosut, Mae Chi,
  amulets of, 174
  biography of, 101–5
  cremation of, 104, 280n97
  phra that of, 104–5
  renunciation of, 235
  stūpa of, *104*, 105, 167
Soḷasapañha. See *Pārāyana-vagga*
Somdet To (Somdet Phra Phutthajan To Phrommarangsi), 22, 142, 266n91
Somparn Promta, 27–28
Soṇa, 150
Sot Candasaro, Luang Pho, 22, 60, 292n11
soteriological inclusiveness, 151, 165, 177–78, 216, 231, 250
Sponberg, Alan, 216, 250
Sri Mahāvīro, Luang Pu, 22–23
Ṣrī Sajjanālai, 143
Strong, John, 157, 272n61
stūpas, 20, 22–23, 139–42, 157, 176, 180, 280n101
  definition of, 257n16, 278n70
  miniature *stūpas*, 144, 150, 169, 177–78
  for the veneration of Thai women, 158–65, 249, 251, 278n71
  See also under individual mae chi*s*
Suan Mokkh, 20, 288n26
suat (*mon*), 73, 87, 91, 188, 234. *See also under* chanting; recitation
Suddhodana, 132
sukha, 58
Sukhothai, 22, 143, 147, 287n22
Sulak Sivaraksa, 60, 114
Sumaṅgalavilāsinī, 146
Suniwan Tangphaithunsakun, 255n4, 267n103
supernatural powers, 75, 129
  magazines on, 10, 54, 153
  magical powers, 22, 118, 171, 272n56 (*see also* amulets)
  of men, 50, 97
  mental powers, 5–7, 79, 82, 149, 171
  miraculous powers, 23, 50, 121, 167–68
  monastic rules on use of, 124, 223

supernatural powers (*continued*)
  to prolong one's life, 81–82, 109
  and relics, 20, 143–44
  superhuman powers, 21, 249
  and supramundane states of mind, 120–22, 127, 249, 273n69
  wholesome/beneficial powers, 20, 73–74, 170
  of women, 2, 5, 38–39, 53–54, 72–73, 97, 127 (*see also individual female practitioners*)
  See also *abhiññās*; *jhāna*; *and* power
Suphankanlaya, Princess, 24
supramundane attainments/knowledge/states of mind, 50, 96, 97, 117–18, 221, 225–26, 230
  of Thai women (assumed), 2–3, 54, 65, 101, 129–37, 167, 250–51
  understandings of supernatural powers and, 120–21, 127, 235–36, 272n56
  See also *ariya*; *ariya-puggala*; *ariyasong*; sainthood; *and individual saints*
Supreme Court of Thailand, 32, 63, 233
Supreme Patriarch, 37, 82, 287n22
  Chinawornsiriwat, Krommaluang, 26
  Ñāṇasaṁvara, Somdet Phra, 92, 128, 155, 163, 288n26
Suriyothai, Queen, 158, 159
suttas, 187, 188, 204, 209, 261n112
  Abhiṇhapaccavekkhitabbaṭhāna-sutta, 289n45
  Acinteyya-sutta, 277n40
  Bākula-sutta, 146
  Bhaddekaratta-sutta, 289n40
  Bhayabherava-sutta, 291n95
  Brahmāyu-sutta, 267n93
  Chabbisodhana-sutta, 110
  Cūḷakammavibhaṅga-sutta, 227, 228
  Dhammacakkappavattana-sutta, 183, 196, 197, 209
  Dutiyakaṇhasappa-sutta, 21
  Gotamī-sutta, 270n24
  Lakkhaṇa-sutta, 79
  Mahācundattherabojjhaṅgasutta, 266n84
  Mahākassapattherabojjhaṅga-sutta, 266n84
  Mahāmoggallānattherabojjhaṅga-sutta, 266n84
  Mahāparinibbāna-sutta, 81, 139, 146, 166, 207, 277n43
suttas (*continued*)
  Mahāsamaya-sutta, 183, 209
  Mahāsatipaṭṭhāna-sutta, 65, 185, 196–97, 202
  Mettānisaṁsa-sutta, 196
  Nandamātā-sutta, 189
  Paṭhamakaṇhasappa-sutta, 21
  Uposatha-sutta, 195
Suwanna Satha-anand, 28
Suwat (Suvaco), Luang Pu, 125

Taksin, King, 114
Talap, Mae Chi, 201–2, 251, 284n87, 285n88
Tambiah, Stanley, 44, 50, 60, 114–15, 144–45, 292n3
taṇhā, 111, 226, 257n19
Tat, Mae Chi, 124–28, 229–30, 273n73
Tat Janthawongsa, Mae Chi, 281n122
Tavivat Puntarigvivat, 27
Taylor, James, 44, 115, 255n4, 262n144
Terwiel, Barend Jan, 84–85, 143, 171, 282n5
Thai massage, 74, 76–77
Thai nation, 117, 150, 227
thamma sueksa, 222
Thang Kotchasut, Khunnai, 65–67
Ṭhānissaro Bhikkhu, 27, 43, 115, 198, 217, 271n37
Thao Suranari, 24
Thepsumethi (Yuak Cattamalo), Phra, 64, 65, 184–85, 190, 228
Theragāthā, 52
Therāpadāna, 52
Therīgāthā, 52
Therī-apadāna, 122
Thet Desaraṅsī, Luang Pu, 79, 85, 115
  and autobiography, 52–53, 55
  and Mae Chi Phimpha Wongsa-udom, 1, 55, 97, 100–101, 215, 242, 245
Thongkham Cāruvaṇṇo, Luang Ta, 115
Thongsuk Samdaengpan, Mae Chi, 292n11
Thotsaphon (Bunthewaphithak), Mae Chi, 24, 34, 38–39, 223, 255n3, 261n125
Three Seals Law, 233
Thuam (Phra Khrubaidikaphayakon, Vesārajjo), Luang Pho, 236
Thuat, Luang Pu, 22, 142, 171
thudong. See *dhutaṅga*
thūpārahapuggala, 161
Thūpavaṃsa, 147

Tipiṭaka. *See* Pali canon
tiracchāna, 84, 225
Tossapol Jangpanichkul, 140–41, 146, 277n37
Transworldly powers: Magazine of Buddhist practice, 54
Triple Gem, 92, 163, 188, 223–24
Tusita, 112
TV, 25, 136, 251

Udāyī, 96
Udom Ciradhammo, Phra, 102
Uggasena, 133
Upagupta, 276n9
Upāli Guṇūpamācariya (Siricando, Jan), Chaokhun, 53, 200
upasampadā (higher ordination), 220–21, 275n107
Upasena, 82, 109
upāsikā (*ubasika*), 23, 34, 197, 201–2, 206, 213, 251. *See also* laywomen
Uppalavaṇṇā, 141, 245
urgency in spiritual practice, 59, 166, 226–28, 232, 236, 248
Uttara, 150
Uttarā, 80, 190

V. Vajiramedhi, Phra, 31
Vajirañana, Prince. *See* Wachirayan, Prince Patriarch
Van Esterik, John, 42–43, 261n128
Van Esterik, Penny, 20
Vapi Busbakara, Princess, 212, 286n132
Vasabha, King, 111, 270n14
VCDs, 25, 51
Veerachart Nimanong, 256n5
Veḷukaṇṭakī Nandamātā, 189, 245
Vessavaṇa (deva king), 189
vimutti, 166
vinaya (monastic discipline), 7, 52, 124, 165, 193, 195, 219
  and female ordination, 30, 112–13
  and longevity of Buddhism, 30, 36, 244, 261n112
  and spiritual practice of Thai women, 38, 79, 136–37, 208, 222–23, 237
  and supernatural powers, 124, 272n61
  See also *dhammavinaya*; *pāṭimokkha*; and *vinaya* hierarchy
vinayapiṭaka, 30
Vinayamukha, 271n37
vipassanā, 42, 116–17, 224–25, 252, 255n3, 273n70
  Burmese-style, 200, 235
  See also *vipassanūpakilesa*
vipassanūpakilesa, 127, 273n70
Visākhā, 133
visions, 84, 85–86, 88–89, 94–96, 140. See also *nimit*
Visuddhimagga, 84, 112, 202, 273n69
viveka (seclusion), 224–25

Wachirayan, Prince Patriarch (Prince Vajirañana), 115, 194–95, 271n37
Waen Suciṇṇo, Luang Pu, 142, 162
Wan, Mae Chi, 12–15
wan phra, 98, 102
Wanarat (Thap, Buddhasiri), Somdet Phra, 64, 115, 190, 201, 285n88
Wanjai Chukon, Mae Chi, 60
Wat Awutwikasitaram, 70, 73, 83, 167–72, 265n68, 266n74, 266n75
Wat Bangpakok, 74, 204
Wat Chiwuek, 12–15
Wat Doi Mae Pang, 142, 162
Wat Hinmakpeng, 100
Wat Jedi Luang, 156
Wat Khao Bang Sai, 10, *192*, 257n29, 280n97
Wat Kukut (also known as Wat Cāmadevī), 158
Wat Pa Ban Nong Phue, 95, 177–78, 280n97
Wat Pa Ban Tat, 51, 90, 144–45, 149–51, 178
Wat Pa Kaew Chumphon, 156, *160*
Wat Pa Na Kham Noi, 156
Wat Pa Samyaek, 273n69
Wat Pa Wiwekwatthanaram, 141, 276n9
Wat Pak Nam, 262n135, 281n114
Wat Phichaiyat, 211
Wat Phra Chetuphon (Wat Pho), 23, 211
Wat Phra Pathom Jedi, 199
Wat Phra Sai (Wat Phochai), 266n86
Wat Phra Thammakai, 159
Wat Phuthok, 102–3
Wat Prok, 213
Wat Saensukwisutthiwararam, 236
Wat Saket, 141
Wat Samphanthawong, 74–76, 167, 168–70, *170*, 235, 265n68
Wat Saneha, 199–200, 202, 213
Wat Sangkhathan, 167, 265n68
Wat Santitham, 156

Wat Saranat, 167
Wat Sattanatpariwat, 64, 65–66, 68, 70, 213
Wat Somanat Wihan, 64, 115, 190, 213
Wat Suan Luang Sop Sawan, 158
Wat Sutthawat, 95–96, 99
Wat Thammikaram, 9, *64*, 64-65, 67, 70, 185, *186*, 191, 213
Wat That Thong, 82
Wat Thepsirin, 65, 70, 197, 208, 213, 271n44
Wat Yanasangwon, 128
Watchara Ngamchitcharoen, 133
Williams, Paul, 61
Winai-sangwon, Phra Khru, 202, 285n95
Wiriyang (Sirindharo), Luang Pho, 53, 209
Wiwitwanpricha, Prince, 67, 115–16
World War II, 10, 62, 70, 117–18
worship of ancestor spirits, 93
Wuek, Mae Chi, 12–15, *14*
Wuthinan Jiawitthayanan, 151–52

Yantra Amaro, Phra, 55
Yasa, 133, 266n82
YouTube, 25, 51, 71, 251

Zen, 75